Women and Moral Theory

Women and Moral Theory

Edited by

EVA FEDER KITTAY

and

DIANA T. MEYERS

ROWMAN & LITTLEFIELD
PUBLISHERS, INC.

ROWMAN & LITTLEFIELD PUBLISHERS, INC.

Published in the United States of America in 1987
by Rowman & Littlefield, Publishers
(a division of Littlefield, Adams & Company)

Library of Congress Cataloging-in-Publication Data

Women and moral theory.

"Largely created for or inspired by the conference on
women and moral theory, held at the State University of
New York, Stony Brook, in March 1985"—Introd.
Includes index.
1. Ethics—Congresses. 2. Women—Psychology—
Congresses. 3. Sex differences (Psychology)—
Congresses. 4. Moral development—Congresses.
I. Kittay, Eva Feder. II. Meyers, Diana T.
BJ19.W65 1987 170'.88042 86–11828
ISBN 0–8476–7381–2
ISBN 0–8476–7382–0 (pbk.)

Printed in the United States of America
Reprinted in 1989 by Rowman & Littlefield Publishers, Inc.

To Jeffrey
and
to Lewis

Contents

PART IV
Beyond Moral Theory: Political and Legal Implications of Difference

Acknowledgments

Many people have helped us produce this book. Above all, we are grateful to Sharon Meagher for her indispensible assistance in organizing the Conference on Women and Moral Theory that provided the basis for this study. We also want to thank her for her editorial assistance in preparing the manuscript, and especially for her contribution to the chapter summaries. (The initials S.M. indicate that Sharon Meagher wrote the summary.) Ms. Meagher assumed her tasks with an independence, an intelligence, and an unflagging energy that was invaluable.

In addition, we want to thank Mary Bruno and Virginia Massaro for their help in managing the details of the Conference. We appreciate the efforts of the many graduate students at State University of New York (SUNY), Stony Brook who helped with conference arrangements and offered their comments on the Conference papers. The commentators, chairpersons, and conference participants were immensely important in the development of this volume. We must thank Lewis, Jeffrey, Leo, and Sesha for their forebearance during the preparation of this collection. Lewis deserves special mention for his meticulous editorial comments on the Introduction, and Jeffrey for the splendid meals he prepared during our work.

The Conference on Women and Moral Theory and the preparation of this manuscript were funded by the Exxon Educational Foundation. Additional funding has been provided by the Dean for Humanities and Fine Arts, SUNY, Stony Brook; the Department of Philosophy, SUNY, Stony Brook; and the New York Society for Philosophy and Public Affairs. Without their financial support, this volume would not have been possible.

Women and Moral Theory

Introduction

DIANA T. MEYERS AND EVA FEDER KITTAY

In recent years, we have seen major advances in moral and political philosophy. John Rawls published his comprehensive, seminal work, *A Theory of Justice*, and numerous thinkers have grappled with urgent social issues. Coinciding with this renaissance has been another important development in the treatment of social and ethical issues—the growth of feminist theory. Feminist research has posed a challenge to both traditional and contemporary assumptions underlying moral theory. In particular, Carol Gilligan's psychological work on moral development purports to offer empirical evidence that undercuts standard assumptions about moral autonomy, moral principles, and the universality of moral doctrines. The essays in this book explore the potential of this recent feminist research to redirect and enhance moral theory.

These articles were largely created for or inspired by the conference on Women and Moral Theory, held at The State University of New York, Stony Brook, in March 1985. In formulating the issue to be addressed at the conference, we relied on Carol Gilligan's thesis that women undergo a moral development distinct from but parallel to that of men. In her articles and in her book, *In a Different Voice*, Gilligan has distinguished a morality of rights and formal reasoning, which she now labels the "justice perspective," from a morality of care and responsibility, the "care perspective." The morality of rights and formal reasoning is the one familiar to us from the liberal tradition of Locke, Kant, and, most recently, Rawls. It posits an autonomous moral agent who discovers and applies a set of fundamental rules through the use of universal and abstract reason. The morality of care and responsibility is an alternate set of moral concerns that Gilligan believes she has encountered in her investigation of women's moral decision-making. Here, the central preoccupation is a responsiveness to others that dictates providing care, preventing harm, and maintaining relationships. Gilligan believes that what we have here are two distinct domains of moral concern empirically linked to a gender difference. She suggests that the former moral system typically dominates the moral development of men, which Lawrence Kohlberg has outlined, whereas the latter is found predominantly in the moral development of women, which she describes. In privileging the justice perspective, Kohlberg's approach to moral development comports with recent moral and political philosophy in which the moral domain uncovered by Gilligan's research on women has largely been eclipsed. The fact that research on women has highlighted the care perspective suggests that attention to women's experience could have significant implications for moral theory. This book provides a forum for examining the philosophical problem of women and morality.

To call to mind the topic of women and morality may be to suggest the various problems with which women contend—abortion, sexual harassment, pornography—and those that women share with other subordinate groups—discrimination, affirmative action, and reverse discrimination. Much has been written on these issues of applied ethics. In this book, we deal instead with more fundamental theoretical problems—the source and content of moral principles, the process of moral deliberation, and the concept of moral agency. Furthermore, a number of works have addressed the exclusion, misapprehension, or distortion of women's relation to morality throughout the history of philosophy.[1] These examinations of the historical record regularly conclude with a call for reconceiving the status of women and their contribution to moral and political life. Whereas these works tend to emphasize a critical approach to past thought, the essays in this book build on these criticisms and begin the project of theory construction to which they give rise.

We have divided this volume into four parts. In the first, Carol Gilligan presents the thesis of women's moral difference. In the second, several authors trace some traditional roots of an Ethics of Care. The third section comprises an assortment of issues in moral theory. While some authors explore the theoretical implications of women's concrete experience and of the care perspective, others debate the significance of gender-differentiated morality. In the fourth, an interdisciplinary group of writers assesses the relevance of gender difference to political and legal issues.

1. The Justice Tradition

The most prominent representatives of the justice tradition, John Locke, Immanuel Kant, and, recently, John Rawls, share two core views. Substantively, each of these theories is committed to personal liberty, and, methodologically, each of them relies on a social contract model. Together, these elements form the basis for the ideal of individual autonomy that distinguishes the justice tradition.

In the justice tradition, individual autonomy has two main dimensions: moral autonomy and personal autonomy. People gain moral autonomy when they use reason to discern which principles ought to be followed; personal autonomy is their entitlement to pursue their own visions of the good in their own way. These aspects of autonomy stem from the themes of social contractarianism and personal liberty, respectively.

Social contract theories use as a model a group of people consenting to a set of mutually acceptable principles to justify a social order. The idea is that rational individuals who have both common and opposing interests can agree to rules to facilitate their cooperation and to resolve their disputes. Though some social contract theorists have seemed to suggest that an actual agreement must be reached to found a society, this literal interpretation is widely rejected today. Instead, the social contract is considered a hypothetical agreement—an agreement that reasonable people, charged with the responsibility for deciding upon moral and political principles, would conclude under fair bargaining conditions.

Construed as a hypothetical contract, the social contract provides a framework that any individual can use to reflect on moral and political principles. The idea of a social contract is invoked to ensure the rationality and impartiality of the principles people elect. While rational individuals would not agree to principles injurious to their own interests, neither could these individuals expect others to agree to principles deleterious to theirs. According to the justice tradition, people ought to comply with principles that would be accepted by individuals who do not want to sacrifice their own interests but who are willing to compromise in order to obtain a mutually beneficial agreement. Moreover, when these principles conflict, the moral agent can again resort to the social contract model to rank them.

The social contract model, developed in the seventeenth century, was an important advance because it liberated the individual moral agent from thralldom to external religious and political authorities. By establishing criteria for acceptable ethical reasoning that any rational being could apply, the social contract model at once certified conscientious individuals as moral authorities and obliged them to assume full responsibility for their moral beliefs, as well as for the actions issuing from them. In the justice tradition, the individual is self-governing; that is, each person is the source of the moral and political principles that person obeys. Thus, people are subject to regulations, and yet remain free. This ideal of moral autonomy, in turn, forms the basis for the justice tradition's stress on the dignity of the individual person.

The justice tradition's doctrine of human dignity finds its primary, normative expression in the idea of personal liberty, and, more specifically, in the idea of human rights. Because people are capable of moral autonomy, they are morally entitled and ought to be legally entitled to conduct their lives as they see fit. Their rights protect them from others' aggression and free them to do what they want, provided that they do not violate others' rights. Locke's list of natural rights—the rights to life, liberty, and property—was seminal. Though variously interpreted and supplemented in subsequent theories, this set of rights captures a constant of the justice tradition. People are surely entitled to noninterference; they may not be entitled to aid. Though it is morally commendable to help the needy, and though justice may require helping the needy, it is disputable whether anyone has a *right* to such positive benefits as medical care, decent housing, or education. In this respect, the justice tradition is individualistic. The rights it recognizes morally equip people to take care of themselves while morally shielding them both from the demands of others and from the invasiveness of the state.

The protections these rights afford are designed to grant people the possibility of personal autonomy. According to the justice tradition, there is no conception of the good life suitable for everyone, since each person is unique. Thus, the good is a personal matter, and all people should be free to envisage and pursue their own plans of life embodying their own conceptions of the good. No one knows better than individuals themselves what their needs and aspirations are, and no one ought to be empowered to dictate to individuals how they should live their lives. Rights secure for the individual an arena of discretionary activity—that is, an arena of personal liberty.

In marking out the justice tradition, we have identified it with Locke, Kant, and Rawls. However, closely connected with this view is John Stuart Mill's Utilitarianism. The justice tradition is a branch of the broader liberal tradition of which Mill is an exemplar. Though Mill eschews the social contract model of moral reasoning and embraces the Principle of Utility, which requires us to promote the greatest happiness of the greatest number, he shares with the justice tradition an abiding concern with personal liberty. Though scholars dispute whether Mill's utilitarian doctrine can accommodate rights, it is undeniable that Mill sought to incorporate rights into his theory.

Mill's link to the justice tradition is germane to our inquiry because he and Mary Wollstonecraft, whose views belong more squarely in the justice tradition, were among the earliest champions of women's equality. Unlike Locke and Kant, Mill and Wollstonecraft explicitly argued that women should be accorded the same rights as men and should be expected to have the same strength of moral character.

Reversing this line of thought, Lawrence Kohlberg, a prominent researcher in the field of moral development, has called into question the maturity of women's moral judgment. Though he does not suggest that women should not have the same rights as men, and though the evidence that women do not perform as well as men on Kohlberg's tests of moral reasoning is disputed, Kohlberg's studies do not clearly confirm that women are capable of the same degree of moral autonomy as men.

Kohlberg maintains that moral development involves a six-stage process divided into three two-stage levels.[2] Initially, people are at a preconventional level—at first, simply deferring to authority (Stage 1) but, eventually, learning to satisfy their own needs and even to consider the needs of others somewhat (Stage 2). From the preconventional level, people move on to the conventional level. At this point, they seek others' approval by conforming to stereotypical roles (Stage 3). This conformity is later augmented by a sense of the value of maintaining the social order and of the contribution of dutiful conduct to that order (Stage 4). Finally, individuals attain the postconventional level. Here they associate morality with rights and standards endorsed by society as a whole (Stage 5). But ultimately, they go on to think in terms of self-chosen, yet universal principles of justice (Stage 6).

Plainly, Kohlberg's theory identifies moral progress with ever closer approximations to the justice tradition's ideal of the person. (See the following Section 2 for Kohlberg's qualification of this position.) Moral maturity is the fulfillment of that ideal. Taking issue with this single-track conception of moral development, Gilligan argues that the care perspective provides an alternative course of development leading to equally adequate moral reflection. If women do not advance as far as men on Kohlberg's developmental scale, Gilligan urges, it is because many women follow this second track.

2. The Care Perspective

In her book, *In A Different Voice,* Gilligan sets forth empirical data, gathered in three studies, concerning the moral decision-making strategies of women. Her results lead her to conclude that the justice perspective fails to capture the import of the concerns expressed by the women, the decision-making strategies employed by the women, and the course of women's distinctive moral development. Gilligan's research includes a study of college students enrolled in a course on political and moral choice: an abortion-decision study interviewing women from diverse ethnic and social backgrounds, and ranging in age from fifteen to thirty-three referred by a pregnancy counselling service; and a rights and responsibility study involving males and females, matched along a number of parameters including education and social class from the ages of six through sixty. Gilligan's paper for this volume, brings her research up to date.

In place of the hierarchical ordering of values characteristic of the justice perspective, Gilligan's female respondents describe "a network of connection, a web of relationships that is sustained by a process of communication." (Gilligan 1982, 33) For these women, moral problems do not result from a conflict of rights to be adjudicated by ranking values. Rather, moral problems are embedded in a contextual frame that eludes abstract, deductive reasoning. For many of the women studied, making moral decisions required not a deductive employment of general principles, but a strategy that aimed to maintain ties where possible without sacrificing the integrity of the self.

The traditional perspective Kohlberg adopts portrays the responses of women as deficiencies in moral capacities. Against this view, Gilligan argues that the moral trajectories of many women are distinct from those of most men but, nevertheless, are of commensurate moral worth. The process of moral development Gilligan has discovered comprises a six-stage series marked by three levels of development. At the preconventional level, the orientation is toward individual survival. The first stage is marked by a focus on caring for the self in order to ensure survival. In the transitional second stage, the concern of the first stage is judged to be selfish. The move from the first to the second stage facilitates the transition from selfishness to responsibility. At the conventional level, the focus is on care and conformity, and there is a concomitant desire to please others. What is good is caring for others, and goodness is frequently equated with self-sacrifice (Stage 3). This sacrifice of self causes a disequilibrium that initiates the transition from the concern with "goodness" to the concern with "truth." The illogic of the inequality between self and other becomes evident in Stage 4. At the postconventional level, which Gilligan characterizes as a morality of nonviolence, Stage 5 is dominated by a dynamics of relationships that leads to a dissipation of the tension between self and other in Stage 6. Relations now are understood to require the participation and interaction of integral selves rather than the sacrifice of the self which marks Stage 3. In Stage 6, care becomes a self-chosen principle, one which recognizes the interdependence of self and other and is accompanied by a universal condemnation of exploitation and hurt. Progress from stage to stage is motivated, in part, by the individual's increasing understanding of human relationships and, in part, by the attempt to maintain one's own integrity and care for one's self without neglecting others. Throughout this process, women regard their selves as selves-in-relation.

Gilligan claims that this developmental trajectory is as morally adequate as Kohlberg's. For Kohlberg, however, the end point of moral development is given within the framework of the justice tradition. Because Gilligan questions this framework, it is less clear what criterion of adequacy she employs in tracing moral development. Gilligan shows that the maturational account of the care perspective follows the same sequence of preconventional, conventional, and postconventional morality exhibited by Kohlberg. Insofar as she succeeds in establishing this point, she succeeds in demonstrating that, while the moral content within each of these levels is distinguishable from its analogue in the justice perspective, the sequence exhibits the same progress toward an increasingly mature stance. Furthermore, in the essay included in this volume, Gilligan recounts that subjects who spontaneously adopt the justice perspective often agree that the solution suggested by exponents of the care perspective is the *better* solution.

While the justice perspective is backed up by a solid and well known canon of ethical doctrine, the care perspective emerges as a vantage point revealed in a sensitive detailing of empirical data. There are, nevertheless, some theoretical precedents for the care perspective. The interest in alternatives to a deductive, calculative approach to moral decision-making, with its strong emphasis on individual autonomy, may be traced back to Aristotle and Hume and finds expression in a number of contemporary moral philosophers who stress the importance of virtue, rather than justice, in moral life. For Aristotle, moral deliberation must determine the right thing to do, at the right time, in the right place, to the right person, in the right way. Such deliberation requires the cultivation of moral character and is set within a given political and social organization. For Aristotle, moral judgment springs from a moral character attuned to circumstantial and contextual features. It is not the product of an abstract concept of the Good. Moreover, Aristotle stresses the social embeddedness of the human being, a political animal by nature. In a related vein, Hume's ethics are grounded in emotion and personal concern. Hume argued that reason itself could not move us to act morally, but that our ethical life is guided by moral sentiments. Again, attention to relationships is prominent in this view. Alistair McIntyre and Bernard Williams are among the contemporary moral philosophers who call for a return to the notions of virtue, of moral character, and of a personal point of view to counteract the excessive formalism, the calculative ratiocination, and the impersonal perspective of the dominant moral traditions of Kant, on the one hand, and utilitarianism, on the other.

Gilligan's reconceptualization of women's moral perspective is part of an ongoing feminist critique of women's place within the philosophical and psychological tradition that has made the experience of men the measure of human experience, but has claimed universality for its positions. Some early articles, exploring women and moral thought, saw a trap in the assignment of distinct and positive virtues to women: the altruism considered more characteristic of women conflicted with the possibility of autonomy. Such an elevated notion of woman's morality is indeed insidious.[3] But Carol McMillan, in *Women, Reason, and Nature,*[4] argues that it is their failure to accept the human condition that moves feminists to want to suppress sex difference, and that women have distinct virtues that are not self-victimizing and do not destroy agency.

Gilligan's affirmation of a gender-difference in moral thought follows the work of a group of feminist authors, who, while recognizing that gender-specificity arises out of the different experiences of men and women, value these differences positively. Nancy Chodorow, in *The Reproduction of Mothering,* asserts that because early child care is universally provided by women, girls and boys grow up with gender-differentiated personalities. Women's capacity for nurturance is enhanced; men's capacity for relatedness and nurturance is repressed in favor of a continual development toward autonomy. Chodorow overturns the usual valuation of autonomy and dependency, stressing instead women's positive relational capabilities. Jean Baker Miller, in a less psychoanalytic work, *Toward a New Psychology of Women,* examines those psychological features that characteristically emerge from women's role as caretakers. She argues that, as women emerge from their subordinate role, these traditional feminine characteristics, often viewed as weaknesses to be overcome, can be reevaluated as strengths to build on. The writer and poet, Adrienne Rich, in both her poetry and in prose works such as *Of Woman Born,* has been important in calling attention to the silencing of women, and has encouraged women to think of their different characteristics as productive of new social visions. These books have helped to create an intellectual climate congenial to the philosophical investigation we propose to make.[5]

In a number of collections of feminist philosophy, the authors attempt to broach the connections between feminist insight and morality. The view that a morality of rights is insufficient to moral issues that concern women, particularly those of pregnancy and abortion, has been anticipated by a number of feminist philosophers who presage Gilligan's use of an abortion study to illuminate the stages of a morality of care.[6] The idea of women's distinctive and positively valued morality appears in the work of Sara Ruddick[7], and in the recent book by Nel Noddings, *Caring.*[8] Noddings argues that the mother's experience of caring and everyone's remembrance of being cared for constitute the basis of ethics.

With the emergence of Gilligan's work, the problem of women and morality has acquired a focus, along with a more clearly defined set of questions than was previously available. Several major journals have already begun to address these questions.[9] In the journal, *Ethics,* Owen Flanagan appeals to Carol Gilligan's work to show how philosophically weak is Kohlberg's defense of his conception of moral maturity; Flanagan goes on to suggest a more context-sensitive approach to moral commitment. In his response to Flanagan's essay, Lawrence Kohlberg states that he tentatively accepts Gilligan's hypothesis. Although he claims that it is not clear that women score less well than men on his scale of moral competence, he acknowledges that women may arrive at their moral decisions through different paths of deliberation and that his exclusive preoccupation with the justice tradition may have been too narrow to account fully for moral development. The Autumn 1983 issue of *Social Research*[10] is specifically devoted to women and morality. The essays included in this issue acknowledge Gilligan's work as a stimulus to thought; however, they are largely conceived as critiques. While valuable, the collection does not draw upon the more suggestive aspects of Gilligan's work to advance moral theory.

This literature is a beginning, but it is only that. It remains for others to map out the conceptual territory Gilligan's work has opened up. That is the project of this book. *Women and Moral Theory* examines the challenges that attention to women's experience pose to traditional moral theory, and indicates possibilities for the development of novel and more adequate moral systems.

3. Themes

While divided into parts based on distinct problems, this volume is unified by a set of themes addressed throughout the collection. In this section, we shall consider a number of these.

SELF AND AUTONOMY

A morality of rights and abstract reason begins with a moral agent who is separate from others, and who independently elects moral principles to obey. In contrast, a morality of responsibility and care begins with a self who is enmeshed in a network of relations to others, and whose moral deliberation aims to maintain these relations.

Using a Humean perspective, Annette Baier criticizes Rousseau and Kant for establishing autonomy as the core of moral theory. But Thomas E. Hill, Jr. reminds us of several traditional senses of moral autonomy—impartiality, noninterference and self-fulfillment—that we may want to uphold, even as we affirm the importance of interdependence and dependency in the moral sphere.

The nature of the moral actor and moral autonomy is a specific focus of the essays by Kathryn Addelson, Jonathan Adler, Seyla Benhabib, and Diana T. Meyers. Both Addelson and Benhabib, though coming out of the divergent traditions of Social Interactionism and Critical Theory, stress that the moral agent is enmeshed in a network of social and institutional relations. In his study of moral reasoning, Adler maintains that the role of a moral agent should be likened to a judge working within a system of established precedents rather than a lone legislator creating laws anew. Meyers argues that self-governance and therefore autonomy can be understood in terms of responsibility reasoning as opposed to abstract rationality.

The contrast between a separate self and self-in-relation throws new light on the egoism-altruism controversy. If the boundaries of the self extend to others, the boundaries between self-interest and altruism blur. Virginia Held, in exploring the possibilities of a feminist morality, suggests that this debate is defused once the self is no longer conceived as an atomic entity.

PRINCIPLES IN ETHICS

The morality of rights and abstract reason has been formulated in terms of universal, general principles, whereas the morality of care and responsibility has been voiced through narratives that specify fitting responses to proximate situations. There are several ways to conceive of the difference between the role of principles in the care perspective and in the justice perspective.

In view of the fact that adherents of the care perspective relate their moral insights through narrative, the question arises whether principles play as significant a role in the care perspective as they do in the justice perspective. Some authors claim that a distinctive feature of a care morality is a contextual and narrative method rather than a deductive application of general principles. For example, Addelson's treatment of unwed mothers depicts the stories through which these individuals resolve their moral predicaments. She calls this process a "moral passage" and rejects the idea of moral standards existing independently of actual social experience. Working with the notion of moral competency, Meyers denies that competent moral deliberation and judgment necessarily involves an explicit appeal to rules.

Some authors maintain that both perspectives require principles, but that the source, content, and implementation of the principles differ. In the justice tradition, the basic injunctions are noninterference, defined as respect for others' rights; and self-determination, defined as the pursuit of one's own good in one's own way. In the care perspective, the basic injunctions are to give care appropriate to the individual, to avoid harm by considering what is harmful to each distinctive individual, and to maintain ties while maintaining one's integrity. Virginia Held and Sara Ruddick hold that the principles of the care perspective derive from the distinctive experiences of women. Both agree that the experience of mothering is one such source; Held adds that women's ability to give birth and the experience some women have of giving birth may influence women's moral view. Although Held maintains a "moral division of labor" in which different principles pertain to different domains of activity, she nevertheless argues that no one type of principle should hold exclusive sway in any domain. Likewise, Ruddick attempts to apply what she has characterized as "maternal thinking" to the problem of international affairs, particularly peacemaking; and Katzenstein and Laitin defend the viability of a progressive, egalitarian politics rooted in the principles of a care perspective. In contrast, Hasse is skeptical about integrating such principles into the American legal domain.

George Sher takes such skepticism farther. He argues that morality cannot do without principles and that it is possible to derive all principles, including those governing close personal relationships, from the original position of the hypothetical contract model. Moreover, Sher maintains not only that no conflict exists between general moral principles and sensitivity to context, but also that general moral principles cannot be applied without a subtle understanding of context. In this respect, the care perspective does not differ from other moral theories.

Against this view, Friedman argues that the exigencies of personal relationships can override considerations of justice, that the moral force of personal relationships cannot be captured in universalizable principles, and that context can alter our conception of justice. Though Stocker maintains that friendship must be guided by principles, he denies that friendship can simply be assimilated to justice. In addition, Adler claims that foregrounding context reduces the scope of the applicability of general principles and that good moral deliberation is not necessarily as general as possible.

In a somewhat different spirit, Baier argues that the principles of impartial reason fail to capture the emotionally imbued morality of friendship and family. Along with Hume, Baier insists that emotion is pertinent to forming moral principles. Christina Hoff Sommers agrees that emotional ties are integral to morality, but she holds that our duties are shaped by institutional as well as emotional ties. For example, the expectations arising from the institution of the family give rise to filial obligations.

However we explain the source and content of moral principles, we may want to argue that different moral perspectives require different modes of implementing these principles. And, in fact, corresponding to the two perspectives are two strategies for moral deliberation. Within the justice perspective and its overarching injunctions, more specific principles can be identified. These are the rights and duties familiar from the liberal tradition—the right to life, the right to personal liberty, the duty to keep promises. These principles are easily articulated as formulae in which the recipients of the conduct are represented as variables. Any person can instantiate these variables. What results when the principles are applied and the variables are instantiated is an imperative for the moral agent. The overarching injunctions of the care perspective may not allow for such a deductive application of general principles to particular situations. The injunction to give care remains empty without first considering the different sorts of situations in which we can give care. In this regard it does not differ from the precept of noninterference, for we need to consider types of situations to determine what rights and duties people have. However, giving care further requires attuning oneself to the needs and desires that the recipients of the caring conduct have in a given situation. At this level, individuals must always be considered distinctive rather than typical, and decisions must be made responsively rather than deductively. Benhabib criticizes the contractarian tradition for its neglect of the particularities that constitute moral predicaments. Adler points out that the best moral solutions may be found by a process of compromise and accommodation that is sensitive to the needs and interests of the people involved and that acknowledges that values may be incommensurable. Sommers develops the notion of "differential pull" to incorporate the insights of the care perspective. Against the model of impartiality, in which all potential recipients of moral concern exert an equal pull on all moral agents, the principle of differential pull allows for the differential consideration of persons who stand in certain relations to the moral agent.

THE CLAIM TO UNIVERSALITY IN ETHICS

In the past, moral systems generally have laid claim to universality. That is, they have claimed to hold true for all persons, at all times, in all places. Gilligan's empirical data, revealing a gender difference in morality, have led her to contend that there are two independent, equally adequate moral systems that cannot be synthesized. The systems bear the relation to one another that we find in ambiguous figures, such as the drawing that may be seen as a duck or as a rabbit. Just as we cannot simultaneously see the duck and the rabbit, so we cannot simultaneously understand a situation from the perspective of care and from the perspective of justice. Moreover, Gilligan reports that people often prefer solutions stemming from the care perspective, which suggests that this morality is at least as good as the justice morality. But if morality can be gender-based, might moral systems not also be subject to other constraints—cultural, historical, economic—that undercut the claim to universality?

Sandra Harding challenges the universality of Western moral thought by directing our attention to the African world view. She notes a number of significant parallels between the feminine and African outlook, and traces these parallels to a common source—oppression. From this vantage point, the justice perspective appears as the ideology of a dominant class rather than as a universal truth.

Though Michael Stocker affirms the importance of the care perspective, he maintains that a unitary morality is necessary. Using friendship as a test case, he seeks to demonstrate that the concerns of care and duty are inextricable from one another. In other words, care cannot be understood without duty, and duty cannot be understood without care. If Stocker is correct, then it may be possible to save the universality of some sufficiently comprehensive moral system.

THE NEED FOR A FEMINIST MORAL THEORY

Whether morality is universal or not, and whether the two perspectives can be consolidated or not, Gilligan's work implies the need to take women's experience seriously and to build feminist moral theory. The task of feminist moral theory, then, is either to integrate the insights of women into a comprehensive theory, or to establish an independent theory that makes women's ethical concerns its core.

It is arguable that the care perspective arises from the experience of women in the private sphere of the household and in their experience as mothers (Cf. Held and Ruddick). Similarly, it is arguable that traditional moral theory is based on the experience of men in the public sphere—the economic and the political realms. Such a position constitutes part of the critique of the categories of traditional moral theory supplied by Benhabib. Theories that give priority to the public domain have privileged the standpoint of the "Generalized Other"—the other conceived as self abstracted from the particularities that form an individual's identity. In contrast, Benhabib develops the notion of the "Concrete Other"—the other understood within the individual's concrete personal and cultural history. Gilligan's findings concerning women's moral thinking direct us to a consideration of the importance of a concept of the "Concrete Other" in moral theory.

Addelson attends both to a problem that confronts women exclusively and to the details of the process by which women solve this problem. She argues that the meaning of women's actions is not properly understood when it is cast in the traditional moral categories of autonomy and objectivity. On the contrary, she urges that the situations she has studied call for an appreciation of the women's subjective perspective and the institutional context imposed upon them. Held points out that women have different capacities and have been assigned different social roles. She then asks if these capacities and roles have ethical significance and suggests that only feminist moral theory can discover the import of women's difference. Friedman uses the strategy of gender reversal in standard moral dilemmas to test whether our intuitions about moral solutions are gender-sensitive. She implies that gender is a salient contextual factor. Katzenstein and Laitin as well as Ruddick take feminist moral theory to be a necessary basis for a more satisfactory politics.

WOMEN AND POLITICS

A final consideration is the practical political implications of distinguishing gender-correlated moral approaches. In the past, women's moral sense was either denigrated or elevated in one of four ways. Woman was seen as the source or instigation of sin, the figure of Eve. Alternatively, she was judged against as ostensibly universal standard and found deficient:

> The weakness of their [women's] reasoning faculty also explains why it is that women show more sympathy for the unfortunate than men do, and so treat them with more kindness and interest; and why it is that, on the contrary, they are inferior to men in point of justice, and less honourable and conscientious. For it is just because their reasoning power is weak that present circumstances have such a hold over them, and those concrete things which lie directly before their eyes exercise a power which is seldom counteracted to any extent by abstract principles of thought, by fixed rules of conduct, firm resolutions, or, in general, by consideration for the past and the future, or in regard of what is absent or remote. [Arthur Schopenhauer, "On Women," p. 146 in Mahowald]

Aristotle was an early representative of a variant conception of women's moral failings, later exemplified by Kant and Rousseau, that woman should be accorded a distinct moral virtue, which is complementary but inferior: "The temperance of a man and of a woman, or courage and justice of a man and of a woman, are not, as Socrates maintained, the same; the courage of a man is shown in commanding, of a woman in obeying. And this holds of all other virtures." (*Politics*, Book 13). Finally, women's distinct virtue may be so exalted that femininity represents an unrealizable ideal. The excessively sentimental verses that follow exemplify this idealization/idolization:

> No angel, but dearer, all dipt
> In angel instincts, breathing Paradise,
> Interpreter between the gods and men . . .,
>
> ["The Princess" by Alfred Lord Tennyson
> quoted in Jesse Barnard, *The Future of Motherhood* p. 4]

> Don't poets know it
> Better than others?
> God can't be always everywhere: And , so,
> Invented Mothers.
>
> ["Mothers" by Sir Edwin Arnold
> quoted in Jesse Barnard, *The Future of Motherhood* p. 3]

Despite their differences, each of the four characterizations we have sketched serves to bar women from the realm of public action and power.

Supposing that Gilligan has correctly identified a gender divide in moral thought, how can we articulate this difference without reinforcing the stereotypes exemplified above and the subordinate status attaching to them? Katzenstein and Laitin argue that there is both progressive and regressive potential in political arguments relying on claims of moral difference. Harding, however, questions whether the women who are having a positive political impact on the status of women subscribe to a feminine morality. Sara Ruddick attempts to celebrate, without exaggerating, maternal virtues and to derive from them models for peace politics. She thereby affirms that the morality conceived in the private sphere traditionally occupied by women is applicable to the public domain hitherto controlled by men. Hasse points out that, since the American legal system is predicated on a rights perspective, it blocks the introduction of other moral viewpoints.

Conclusion

Analyzing the broad problem of women and moral theory, the essays referred to above open a new area of inquiry; they focus sharply on concerns that are only beginning to be articulated. It is well that they are. For it is our conviction that the liberation of women cannot proceed unless people come to grips with the moral position of women. Similarly, the completeness and integrity of the Western intellectual tradition depend on thinkers confronting this problem. For these reasons, the significance of the recent movement away from sex-segregated social and economic roles must be brought to bear on and must direct the future development of the intellectual corpus.

Notes

1. For representative passages from Aristotle, Aquinas, Rousseau, Hume, Nietzsche, and Freud see *Philosophy of Woman,* edited by Mary Briody Mahowald Indianapolis: Hackett Publishing Co., 1978); *Woman in Western Thought,* edited by Martha Lee Osborne (New York: Random House, 1979); *Philosophy and Women,* edited by Sharon Bishop and Marjorie Weinzweig (Belmont, California: Wadsworth Publishing Co., 1979). Articles discussing the moral standing these traditional thinkers assigned to women include Christine Garside Allen's "Can a Woman be Good in the Same Way as a Man?" and Kathryn Pyne Parson's "Nietzsche and Moral Change" (both in the Osborne volume); Elizabeth Rapaport's "On the Future of Love: Rousseau and The Radical Feminists," and Caroline Whitbeck's "Theories of Sex Difference" (both in *The Philosophical Forum: Special Issue: Women and Philosophy,* vol. V, nos. 1–2, 1973–1974). See also Susan Moller Okin's *Women in Western Political Thought* (Princeton: Princeton University Press, 1979); Jean Bethke Elshtain's *Public Man, Private Woman,* (Princeton: Princeton University Press, 1981); and Zillah Eisenstein's *The Radical Future of Liberal Feminism* (New York: Longman, 1981).

2. Lawrence Kohlberg, *Essays on Moral Development,* vol. 1, pp. 409–12 (San Francisco: Harper and Row, Publishers, 1981).

3. See, for example, "Altruism and Women's Oppression" by Blum, Homiak, Housman, and Scheman (in *The Philosophical Forum: [special issue] Women and Philosophy);* "The Compassion Trap" by Margaret Adams in *Women in Sexist Society,* edited by Gornick and Morgan (New York: New American Library, 1972); and "Women and Voluntarism" by Doris Gold (also in *Women in Sexist Society).*

4. Carol McMillan, *Women, Reason, and Nature* (Princeton: Princeton University Press, 1982).

5. Nancy Chodorow's *The Reproduction of Mothering* (Berkeley: University of California Press, 1978); Jean Baker Miller's *Toward a New Psychology of Women* (Boston: Beacon Press, 1976); and Adrienne Rich's *Of Woman Born* (New York: Bantam Books, 1976).

6. See for example, Caroline Whitbeck, "The Moral Implications of Regarding Women as People: New Perspectives on Pregnancy and Personhood," in *Abortion and the Status of the Fetus,* edited by W. B. Bondesman, H. T. Engelhardt, Jr., S. F. Spicker, and D. Winship (Dordrecht: Reidel Publishing Co.); Jane Farrell Smith, "Rights-Conflict, Pregnancy and Abortion," in Carol C. Gould, ed., *Beyond Domination* (Totowa, N.J.: Rowman and Allanheld, 1984).

7. Sara Ruddick, "Maternal Thinking" and "Preservative Peace and Military Destruction: Some Reflections on Mothering and Peace" in *Mothering: Essays in Feminist Theory,* edited by Joyce Treblicot (Totowa, N.J.: Rowman and Allanheld, 1983).

8. Nel Noddings, *Caring* (Berkeley: University of California Press, 1984).

9. *Ethics* (vol. 92, no. 3, April 1982).

10. *Social Research* (vol. 50, no. 3, Autumn 1983).

PART I

Gender Difference and Morality: The Empirical Base

1

Moral Orientation and Moral Development

CAROL GILLIGAN

Summary

In her book, *In a Different Voice,* Carol Gilligan cited empirical studies of moral development and identified a moral perspective focused on care. This perspective differed from the orientation toward justice that represents a dominant tradition in moral theory and that frames the choice of all-male samples in the developmental studies of Jean Piaget and Lawrence Kohlberg. The care perspective, voiced by the women Gilligan studied, has largely been obscured in both philosophical and psychological studies of moral judgment. In this article, Gilligan addresses the question of the relationship between the two moral orientations. She draws an analogy to the ambiguous figure of Gestalt psychology to illuminate her position. Like the figure that may be seen as a vase or as two female profiles, or the drawing that may be seen as a duck or as a rabbit, a situation of moral consequence may be framed in terms of justice or in terms of care. The care and justice perspectives, claims Gilligan, cannot simply be integrated, nor are they polar opposites. But as in the case of the ambiguous figure, so we can see the same situation only from one perspective at a time. We can shift our view, but we cannot see both images or moral frames simultaneously. Updating the research begun in her book, Gilligan uses later studies to elucidate why the care perspective has not been recognized and to clarify the relation of gender and moral perspective. She examines the roots of the two moral orientations and tentatively explores the significance of a moral viewpoint articulated by women.

E.F.K.

When one looks at an ambiguous figure like the drawing that can be seen as a young or old woman, or the image of the vase and the faces, one initially sees it in only one way. Yet even after seeing it in both ways, one way often seems more compelling. This phenomenon reflects the laws of perceptual organization that favor certain modes of visual grouping. But it also suggests a tendency to view reality as unequivocal and thus to argue that there is one right or better way of seeing.

The experiments of the Gestalt psychologists on perceptual organization provide a series of demonstrations that the same proximal pattern can be organized in different ways so that, for example, the same figure can be seen as a square or a diamond, depending on its orientation in relation to a surrounding frame. Subsequent studies show that the context influencing which of two possible organizations will be chosen may depend not only on the features of the array presented but also on the perceiver's past experience or expectation. Thus, a bird-watcher and a rabbit-keeper are likely to see the duck-rabbit figure in different ways; yet this difference does not imply that one way is better or a higher form of perceptual organization. It does, however, call attention to the fact that the rabbit-keeper, perceiving the rabbit, may not see the ambiguity of the figure until someone points out that it can also be seen as a duck.

This paper presents a similar phenomenon with respect to moral judgment, describing two moral perspectives that organize thinking in different ways. The analogy to ambiguous figure perception arises from the observation that although people are aware of both perspectives, they tend to adopt one or the other in defining and resolving moral conflict. Since moral judgments organize thinking about choice in difficult situations, the adoption of a single perspective may facilitate clarity of decision. But the wish for clarity may also imply a compelling human need for resolution or closure, especially in the face of decisions that give rise to discomfort or unease. Thus, the search for clarity in seeing may blend with a search for justification, encouraging the position that there is one right or better way to think about moral problems. This question, which has been the subject of intense theological and philosophical debate, becomes of interest to the psychologist not only because of its psychological dimensions—the tendency to focus on one perspective and the wish for justification—but also because one moral perspective currently dominates psychological thinking and is embedded in the most widely used measure for assessing the maturity of moral reasoning.

In describing an alternative standpoint, I will reconstruct the account of moral development around two moral perspectives, grounded in different dimensions of relationship that give rise to moral concern. The justice perspective, often equated with moral reasoning, is recast as one way of seeing moral problems and a care perspective is brought forward as an alternate vision or frame. The distinction between justice and care as alternative perspectives or moral orientations is based empirically on the observation that a shift in the focus of attention from concerns about justice to concerns about care changes the definition of what constitutes a moral problem, and leads the same situation to be seen in different ways. Theoretically, the distinction between justice and care cuts across the familiar divisions between thinking and feeling, egoism and altruism, theoretical and practical reasoning. It calls attention to the fact that all human relationships, public and private, can be characterized *both* in terms of equality and in terms of attachment, and that both inequality and detachment constitute grounds for moral concern. Since everyone is vulnerable both to oppression and to abandonment, two moral visions—one of justice and one of care—recur in human experience. The moral injunctions, not to act unfairly toward others, and not to turn away from someone in need, capture these different concerns.

The conception of the moral domain as comprised of at least two moral orientations raises new questions about observed differences in moral judgment and the disagreements to which they give rise. Key to this revision is the distinction between differences in developmental stage (more or less adequate positions within a single orientation) and differences in orientation (alternative perspectives or frameworks). The findings reported in this paper of an association between moral orientation and gender speak directly to the continuing controversy over sex differences in moral reasoning. In doing so, however, they also offer an empirical explanation for why previous thinking about moral development has been organized largely within the justice framework.

My research on moral orientation derives from an observation made in the course of studying the relationship between moral judgment and action. Two studies, one of college students describing their experiences of moral conflict and choice, and one of pregnant women who were considering abortion, shifted the focus of attention from the ways people reason about hypothetical dilemmas to the ways people construct moral conflicts and choices in their lives. This change in approach made it possible to see what experiences people define in moral terms, and to explore the relationship between the understanding of moral problems and the reasoning strategies used and the actions taken in attempting to resolve them. In this context, I observed that women, especially when speaking about their own experiences of moral conflict and choice, often define moral problems in a way that eludes the categories of moral theory and is at odds with the assumptions that shape psychological thinking about morality and about the self.[1] This discovery, that a different voice often guides the moral judgments and the actions of women, called attention to a major design problem in previous moral judgment research: namely, the use of all-male samples as the empirical basis for theory construction.

The selection of an all-male sample as the basis for generalizations that are applied to both males and females is logically inconsistent. As a research strategy, the decision to begin with a single-sex sample is inherently problematic, since the categories of analysis will tend to be defined on the basis of the initial data gathered and subsequent studies will tend to be restricted to these categories. Piaget's work on the moral judgment of the child illustrates these problems since he defined the evolution of children's consciousness and practice of rules on the basis of his study of boys playing marbles, and then undertook a study of girls to assess the generality of his findings. Observing a series of differences both in the structure of girls' games and "in the actual mentality of little girls," he deemed these differences not of interest because "it was not this contrast which we proposed to study." Girls, Piaget found, "rather complicated our interrogatory in relation to what we know about boys," since the changes in their conception of rules, although following the same sequence observed in boys, did not stand in the same relation to social experience. Nevertheless, he concluded that "in spite of these differences in the structure of the game and apparently in the players' mentality, we find the same process at work as in the evolution of the game of marbles."[2]

Thus, girls were of interest insofar as they were similar to boys and confirmed the generality of Piaget's findings. The differences noted, which included a greater tolerance, a greater tendency toward innovation in solving conflicts, a greater willingness to make exceptions to rules, and a lesser concern with legal elaboration, were not seen as germane to "the psychology of rules," and therefore were regarded as insignificant for the study of children's moral judgment. Given the confusion that currently surrounds the discussion of sex differences in moral judgment, it is important to emphasize that the differences observed by Piaget did not pertain to girls' understanding of rules *per se* or to the development of the idea of justice in their thinking, but rather to the way girls structured their games and their approach to conflict resolution—that is, to their use rather than their understanding of the logic of rules and justice.

Kohlberg, in his research on moral development, did not encounter these problems since he equated moral development with the development of justice reasoning and initially used an all-male sample as the basis for theory and test construction. In response to his critics, Kohlberg has recently modified his claims, renaming his test a measure of "justice reasoning" rather than of "moral maturity" and acknowledging the presence of a care perspective in people's moral thinking.[3] But the widespread use of Kohlberg's measure as a measure of moral development together with his own continuing tendency to equate justice reasoning with moral judgment leaves the problem of orientation differences unsolved. More specifically, Kohlberg's efforts to assimilate thinking about care to the six-stage developmental sequence he derived and refined by analyzing changes in justice reasoning (relying centrally on his all-male longitudinal sample), underscores the continuing importance of the points raised in this paper concerning (1) the distinction between differences in developmental stage within a single orientation and differences in orientation, and (2) the fact that the moral thinking of girls and women was not examined in establishing either the meaning or the measurement of moral judgment within contemporary psychology.

An analysis of the language and logic of men's and women's moral reasoning about a range of hypothetical and real dilemmas underlies the distinction elaborated in this paper between a justice and a care perspective. The empirical association of care reasoning with women suggests that discrepancies observed between moral theory and the moral judgments of girls and women may reflect a shift in perspective, a change in moral orientation. Like the figure-ground shift in ambiguous figure perception, justice and care as moral perspectives are not opposites or mirror-images of one another, with justice uncaring and care unjust. Instead, these perspectives denote different ways of organizing the basic elements of moral judgment: self, others, and the relationship between them. With the shift in perspective from justice to care, the organizing dimension of relationship changes from inequality/equality to attachment/detachment, reorganizing thoughts, feelings, and language so that words connoting relationship like "dependence" or "responsibility" or even moral terms such as "fairness" and "care" take on different meanings. To organize relationships in terms of attachment rather than in terms of equality changes the way human connection is imagined, so that the images or metaphors of relationship shift from hierarchy or balance to network or web. In addition, each organizing framework leads to a different way of imagining the self as a moral agent.

From a justice perspective, the self as moral agent stands as the figure against a ground of social relationships, judging the conflicting claims of self and others against a standard of equality or equal respect (the Categorical Imperative, the Golden Rule). From a care perspective, the relationship becomes the figure, defining self and others. Within the context of relationship, the self as a moral agent perceives and responds to the perception of need. The shift in moral perspective is manifest by a change in the moral question from "What is just?" to "How to respond?"

For example, adolescents asked to describe a moral dilemma often speak about peer or family pressure in which case the moral question becomes how to maintain moral principles or standards and resist the influence of one's parents or friends. "I have a right to my religious opinions," one teenager explains, referring to a religious difference with his parents. Yet, he adds, "I respect their views." The same dilemma, however, is also construed by adolescents as a problem of attachment, in which case the moral question becomes: how to respond both to oneself and to one's friends or one's parents, how to maintain or strengthen connection in the face of differences in belief. "I understand their fear of my new religious ideas," one teenager explains, referring to her religious disagreement with her parents, "but they really ought to listen to me and try to understand my beliefs."

One can see these two statements as two versions of essentially the same thing. Both teenagers present self-justifying arguments about religious disagreement; both address the claims of self and of others in a way that honors both. Yet each frames the problem in different terms, and the use of moral language points to different concerns. The first speaker casts the problem in terms of individual rights that must be respected within the relationship. In other words, the figure of the considering is the self looking on the disagreeing selves in relationship, and the aim is to get the other selves to acknowledge the right to disagree. In the case of the second speaker, figure and ground shift. The relationship becomes the figure of the considering, and relationships are seen to require listening and efforts at understanding differences in belief. Rather than the right to disagree, the speaker focuses on caring to hear and to be heard. Attention shifts from the grounds for agreement (rights and respect) to the grounds for understanding (listening and speaking, hearing and being heard). This shift is marked by a change in moral language from the stating of separate claims to rights and respect ("I have a right . . . I respect their views.") to the activities of relationship—the injunction to listen and try to understand ("I understand . . . they ought to listen . . . and try to understand."). The metaphor of moral voice itself carries the terms of the care perspective and reveals how the language chosen for moral theory is not orientation neutral.

The language of the public abortion debate, for example, reveals a justice perspective. Whether the abortion dilemma is cast as a conflict of rights or in terms of respect for human life, the claims of the fetus and of the pregnant woman are balanced or placed in opposition. The morality of abortion decisions thus construed hinges on the scholastic or metaphysical question as to whether the fetus is a life or a person, and whether its claims take precedence over those of the pregnant woman. Framed as a problem of care, the dilemma posed by abortion shifts. The connection between the fetus and the pregnant woman becomes the focus of attention and the question becomes whether it is responsible or irresponsible, caring or careless, to extend or to end this connection. In this construction, the abortion dilemma arises because there is no way not to act, and no way of acting that does not alter the connection between self and others. To ask what actions constitute care or are more caring directs attention to the parameters of connection and the costs of detachment, which become subjects of moral concern.

Finally, two medical students, each reporting a decision not to turn in someone who has violated the school rules against drinking, cast their decision in different terms. One student constructs the decision as an act of mercy, a decision to override justice in light of the fact that the violator has shown "the proper degrees of contrition." In addition, this student raises the question as to whether or not the alcohol policy is just, i.e., whether the school has the right to prohibit drinking. The other student explains the decision not to turn in a proctor who was drinking on the basis that turning him in is not a good way to respond to this problem, since it would dissolve the relationship between them and thus cut off an avenue for help. In addition, this student raises the question as to whether the proctor sees his drinking as a problem.

This example points to an important distinction, between care as understood or construed within a justice framework and care as a framework or a perspective on moral decision. Within a justice construction, care becomes the mercy that tempers justice; or connotes the special obligations or supererogatory duties that arise in personal relationships; or signifies altruism freely chosen—a decision to modulate the strict demands of justice by considering equity or showing forgiveness; or characterizes a choice to sacrifice the claims of the self. All of these interpretations of care leave the basic assumptions of a justice framework intact: the division between the self and others, the logic of reciprocity or equal respect.

As a moral perspective, care is less well elaborated, and there is no ready vocabulary in moral theory to describe its terms. As a framework for moral decision, care is grounded in the assumption that self and other are interdependent, an assumption reflected in a view of action as responsive and, therefore, as arising in relationship rather than the view of action as emanating from within the self and, therefore, "self governed." Seen as responsive, the self is by definition connected to others, responding to perceptions, interpreting events, and governed by the organizing tendencies of human interaction and human language. Within this framework, detachment, whether from self or from others, is morally problematic, since it breeds moral blindness or indifference—a failure to discern or respond to need. The question of what responses constitute care and what responses lead to hurt draws attention to the fact that one's own terms may differ from those of others. Justice in this context becomes understood as respect for people in their own terms.

The medical student's decision not to turn in the proctor for drinking reflects a judgment that turning him in is not the best way to respond to the drinking problem, itself seen as a sign of detachment or lack of concern. Caring for the proctor thus raises the question of what actions are most likely to ameliorate this problem, a decision that leads to the question of what are the proctor's terms.

The shift in organizing perspective here is marked by the fact that the first student does not consider the terms of the other as potentially different but instead assumes one set of terms. Thus the student alone becomes the arbiter of what is *the* proper degree of contrition. The second student, in turn, does not attend to the question of whether the alcohol policy itself is just or fair. Thus each student discusses an aspect of the problem that the other does not mention.

These examples are intended to illustrate two cross-cutting perspectives that do not negate one another but focus attention on different dimensions of the situation, creating a sense of ambiguity around the question of what is the problem to be solved. Systematic research on moral orientation as a dimension of moral judgment and action initially addressed three questions: (1) Do people articulate concerns about justice and concerns about care in discussing a moral dilemma? (2) Do people tend to focus their attention on one set of concerns and minimally represent the other? and (3) Is there an association between moral orientation and gender? Evidence from studies that included a common set of questions about actual experiences of moral conflict and matched samples of males and females provides affirmative answers to all three questions.

When asked to describe a moral conflict they had faced, 55 out of 80 (69 percent) educationally advantaged North American adolescents and adults raised considerations of both justice and care. Two-thirds (54 out of 80) however, focused their attention on one set of concerns, with focus defined as 75 percent or more of the considerations raised pertaining either to justice or to care. Thus the person who presented, say, two care considerations in discussing a moral conflict was more likely to give a third, fourth, and fifth than to balance care and justice concerns—a finding consonant with the assumption that justice and care constitute organizing frameworks for moral decision. The men and the women involved in this study (high school students, college students, medical students, and adult professionals) were equally likely to demonstrate the focus phenomenon (two-thirds of both sexes fell into the outlying focus categories). There were, however, sex differences in the direction of focus. With one exception, all of the men who focused, focused on justice. The women divided, with roughly one third focusing on justice and one third on care.[4]

These findings clarify the different voice phenomenon and its implications for moral theory and for women. First, it is notable that if women were eliminated from the research sample, care focus in moral reasoning would virtually disappear. Although care focus was by no means characteristic of all women, it was almost exclusively a female phenomenon in this sample of educationally advantaged North Americans. Second, the fact that the women were advantaged means that the focus on care cannot readily be attributed to educational deficit or occupational disadvantage—the explanation Kohlberg and others have given for findings of lower levels of justice reasoning in women.[5] Instead, the focus on care in women's moral reasoning draws attention to the limitations of a justice-focused moral theory and highlights the presence of care concerns in the moral thinking of both women and men. In this light, the Care/Justice group composed of one third of the women and one third of the men becomes of particular interest, pointing to the need for further research that attends to the way people organize justice and care in relation to one another—whether, for example, people alternate perspectives, like seeing the rabbit and the duck in the rabbit-duck figure, or integrate the two perspectives in a way that resolves or sustains ambiguity.

Third, if the moral domain is comprised of at least two moral orientations, the focus phenomenon suggests that people have a tendency to lose sight of one moral perspective in arriving at moral decision—a liability equally shared by both sexes. The present findings further suggest that men and women tend to lose sight of different perspectives. The most striking result is the virtual absence of care-focus reasoning among the men. Since the men raised concerns about care in discussing moral conflicts and thus presented care concerns as morally relevant, a question is why they did not elaborate these concerns to a greater extent.

In summary, it becomes clear why attention to women's moral thinking led to the identification of a different voice and raised questions about the place of justice and care within a comprehensive moral theory. It also is clear how the selection of an all-male sample for research on moral judgment fosters an equation of morality with justice, providing little data discrepant with this view. In the present study, data discrepant with a justice-focused moral theory comes from a third of the women. Previously, such women were seen as having a problem understanding "morality." Yet these women may also be seen as exposing the problem in a justice-focused moral theory. This may explain the decision of researchers to exclude girls and women at the initial stage of moral judgment research. If one begins with the premise that "all morality consists in respect for rules,"[6] or "virtue is one and its name is justice,"[7] then women are likely to appear problematic within moral theory. If one begins with women's moral judgments, the problem becomes how to construct a theory that encompasses care as a focus of moral attention rather than as a subsidiary moral concern.

The implications of moral orientation for moral theory and for research on moral development are extended by a study designed and conducted by Kay Johnston.[8] Johnston set out to explore the relationship between moral orientation and problem-solving strategies, creating a standard method using fables for assessing spontaneous moral orientation and orientation preference.* She asked 60 eleven- and fifteen-year-olds to state and to solve the moral problem posed by the fable. Then she asked: "Is there another way to solve this problem?" Most of the children initially constructed the fable

Editor's note: For an example of one of the fables used in the study, see Diana T. Meyers' chapter, this volume, p. 141.

problems either in terms of justice or in terms of care; either they stood back from the situation and appealed to a rule or principle for adjudicating the conflicting claims or they entered the situation in an effort to discover or create a way of responding to all of the needs. About half of the children, slightly more fifteen- than eleven-year-olds, spontaneously switched moral orientation when asked whether there was another way to solve the problem. Others did so following an interviewer's cue as to the form such a switch might take. Finally, the children were asked which of the solutions they described was the best solution. Most of the children answered the question and explained why one way was preferable.

Johnston found gender differences parallel to those previously reported, with boys more often spontaneously using and preferring justice solutions and girls more often spontaneously using and preferring care solutions. In addition, she found differences between the two fables she used, confirming Langdale's finding that moral orientation is associated both with the gender of the reasoner and with the dilemma considered.[9] Finally, the fact that children, at least by the age of eleven, are able to shift moral orientation and can explain the logic of two moral perspectives, each associated with a different problem-solving strategy, heightens the analogy to ambiguous figure perception and further supports the conception of justice and care as organizing frameworks for moral decision.

The demonstration that children know both orientations and can frame and solve moral problems in at least two different ways means that the choice of moral standpoint is an element of moral decision. The role of the self in moral judgment thus includes the choice of moral standpoint, and this decision, whether implicit or explicit, may become linked with self-respect and self-definition. Especially in adolescence when choice becomes more self-conscious and self-reflective, moral standpoint may become entwined with identity and self-esteem. Johnston's finding that spontaneous moral orientation and preferred orientation are not always the same raises a number of questions as to why and under what conditions a person may adopt a problem-solving strategy that he or she sees as not the best way to solve the problem.

The way people chose to frame or solve a moral problem is clearly not the only way in which they can think about the problem, and is not necessarily the way they deem preferable. Moral judgments thus do not reveal *the* structure of moral thinking, since there are at least two ways in which people can structure moral problems. Johnston's demonstration of orientation-switch poses a serious challenge to the methods that have been used in moral judgment and moral development research, introducing a major interpretive caution. The fact that boys and girls at eleven and fifteen understand and distinguish the logics of justice and care reasoning directs attention to the origins and the development of both ways of thinking. In addition, the tendency for boys and girls to use and prefer different orientations when solving the same problem raises a number of questions about the relationship between these orientations and the factors influencing their representation. The different patterns of orientation use and preference, as well as the different conceptions of justice and of care implied or elaborated in the fable judgments, suggest that moral development cannot be mapped along a single linear stage sequence.

One way of explaining these findings, suggested by Johnston, joins Vygotsky's theory of cognitive development with Chodorow's analysis of sex differences in early childhood experiences of relationship.[10] Vygotsky posits that all of the higher cognitive functions originate as actual relations between individuals. Justice and care as moral ideas and as reasoning strategies thus would originate as relationships with others—an idea consonant with the derivation of justice and care reasoning from experiences of inequality and attachment in early childhood. All children are born into a situation of inequality in that they are less capable than the adults and older children around them and, in this sense, more helpless and less powerful. In addition, no child survives in the absence of some kind of adult attachment—or care, and through this experience of relationship children discover the responsiveness of human connection including their ability to move and affect one another.

Through the experience of inequality, of being in the less powerful position, children learn what it means to depend on the authority and the good will of others. As a result, they tend to strive for equality of greater power, and for freedom. Through the experience of attachment, children discover the ways in which people are able to care for and to hurt one another. The child's vulnerability to oppression and to abandonment thus can be seen to lay the groundwork for the moral visions of justice and care, conceived as ideals of human relationship and defining the ways in which people "should" act toward one another.

Chodorow's work then provides a way of explaining why care concerns tend to be minimally represented by men and why such concerns are less frequently elaborated in moral theory. Chodorow joins the dynamics of gender identity formation (the identification of oneself as male or female) to an analysis of early childhood relationships and examines the effects of maternal child care on the inner structuring of self in relation to others. Further, she differentiates a positional sense of self from a personal sense of self, contrasting a self defined in terms of role or position from a self known through the experience of connection. Her point is that maternal child care fosters the continuation of a relational sense of self in girls, since female gender identity is consonant with feeling connected with one's mother. For boys, gender identity is in tension with mother-child connection, unless that connection is structured in terms of sexual opposition (e.g., as an Oedipal drama). Thus, although boys experience responsiveness or care in relationships, knowledge of care or the need for care, when associated with mothers, poses a threat to masculine identity.[11]

Chodorow's work is limited by her reliance on object relations theory and problematic on that count. Object relations theory ties the formation of the self to the experience of separation, joining separation with individuation and thus counterposing the experience of self to the experience of connection with others. This is the line that Chodorow traces in explicating male development. Within this framework, girls' connections with their mothers can only be seen as problematic. Connection with others or the capacity to feel and think *with* others is, by definition, in tension with self-development when self-development or individuation is linked to separation. Thus, object-relations theory sustains a series of oppositions that have been central in Western thought and moral theory, including the opposition between thought and feelings, self and relationship, reason and compassion, justice and love. Object relations theory also continues the conventional division of psychological labor between women and men. Since the idea of a self, experienced in the context of attachment with others, is theoretically impossible, mothers, described as objects, are viewed as selfless, without a self. This view is essentially problematic for women, divorcing the activity of mothering from desire, knowledge, and agency, and implying that insofar as a mother experiences herself as a subject rather than as an object (a mirror reflecting her child), she is "selfish" and not a good mother. Winnicott's phrase "good-enough mother" represents an effort to temper this judgment.

Thus, psychologists and philosophers, aligning the self and morality with separation and autonomy—the ability to be self-governing—have associated care with self-sacrifice, or with feelings—a view at odds with the current position that care represents a way of knowing and a coherent moral perspective. This position, however, is well represented in literature written by women. For example the short story "A Jury of Her Peers," written by Susan Glaspell in 1917, a time when women ordinarily did not serve on juries, contrasts two ways of knowing that underlie two ways of interpreting and solving a crime.[12] The story centers on a murder; Minnie Foster is suspected of killing her husband.

A neighbor woman and the sheriff's wife accompany the sheriff and the prosecutor to the house of the accused woman. The men, representing the law, seek evidence that will convince a jury to convict the suspect. The women, collecting things to bring Minnie Foster in jail, enter in this way into the lives lived in the house. Taking in rather than taking apart, they begin to assemble observations and impressions, connecting them to past experience and observations until suddenly they compose a familiar pattern, like the log-cabin pattern they recognize in the quilt Minnie Foster was making. "Why do we *know*—what we know this minute?" one woman asks the other, but she also offers the following explanation:

> We live close together, and we live far apart. We all go through the same things—it's all just a different kind of the same thing! If it weren't—why do you and I *understand*.[13]

The activity of quilt-making—collecting odd scraps and piecing them together until they form a pattern—becomes the metaphor for this way of knowing. Discovering a strangled canary buried under pieces of quilting, the women make a series of connections that lead them to understand what happened.

The logic that says you don't kill a man because he has killed a bird, the judgment that finds these acts wildly incommensurate, is counterposed to the logic that sees both events as part of a larger pattern—a pattern of detachment and abandonment that led finally to the strangling. "I *wish* I'd come over here once in a while," Mrs. Hale, the neighbor, exclaims. "That was a crime! Who's going to punish that?" Mrs. Peters, the sheriff's wife, recalls that when she was a girl and a boy killed her cat, "If they hadn't held me back I would have—" and realizes that there had been no one to restrain Minnie Foster. John Foster was known as "a good man . . . He didn't drink, and he kept his word as well as most, I guess, and paid his debts." But he also was "a hard man," Mrs. Hale explains, "like a raw wind that gets to the bone."

Seeing detachment as the crime with murder as its ultimate extension, implicating themselves and also seeing the connection between their own and Minnie Foster's actions, the women solve the crime by attachment—by joining together, like the "knotting" that joins pieces of a quilt. In the decision to remove rather than to reveal the evidence, they separate themselves from a legal system in which they have no voice but also no way of voicing what they have come to understand. In choosing to connect themselves with one another and with Minnie, they separate themselves from the law that would use their understanding and their knowledge as grounds for further separation and killing.

In a law school class where a film-version of this story was shown, the students were divided in their assessment of the moral problem and in their evaluation of the various characters and actions. Some focused on the murder, the strangling of the husband. Some focused on the evidence of abandonment or indifference to others. Responses to a questionnaire showed a bi-modal distribution, indicating two ways of viewing the film. These different perspectives led to different ways of evaluating both the act of murder and the women's decision to remove the evidence. Responses to the film were not aligned with the sex of the viewer in an absolute way, thus dispelling any implication of biological determinism or of a stark division between the way women and men know or judge events. The knowledge gained inductively by the women in the film, however, was also gained more readily by women watching the film, who came in this way to see a logic in the women's actions and to articulate a rationale for their silence.

The analogy to ambiguous figure perception is useful here in several ways. First, it suggests that people can see a situation in more than one way, and even alternate ways of seeing, combining them without reducing them—like designating the rabbit-duck figure both duck and rabbit. Second, the analogy argues against the tendency to construe justice and care as opposites or mirror-images and also against the implication that these two perspectives are readily integrated or fused. The ambiguous figure directs attention to the way in which a change in perspective can reorganize perception and change understanding, without implying an underlying reality or pure form. What makes seeing both moral perspectives so difficult is precisely that the orientations are not opposites nor mirror images or better and worse representations of a single moral truth. The terms of one perspective do not contain the terms of the other. Instead, a shift in orientation denotes a restructuring of moral perception, changing the meaning of moral language and thus the definition of moral conflict and moral action. For example, detachment is considered the hallmark of mature moral thinking within a justice perspective, signifying the ability to judge dispassionately, to weigh evidence in an even-handed manner, balancing the claims of others and self. From a care perspective, detachment is *the* moral problem.

> "I could've come," retorted Mrs. Hale . . . "I wish I had come over to see Minnie Foster sometimes. I can see now . . . If there had been years and years of—nothing, then a bird to sing to you, it would be awful—still—after the bird was still. . . . I know what stillness is."

The difference between agreement and understanding captures the different logics of justice and care reasoning, one seeking grounds for agreement, one seeking grounds for understanding, one assuming separation and thus the need for some external structure of connection, one assuming connection and thus the potential for understanding. These assumptions run deep, generating and reflecting different views of human nature and the human condition. They also point to different vulnerabilities and different sources of error. The potential error in justice reasoning lies in its latent egocentrism, the tendency to confuse one's perspective with an objective standpoint or truth, the temptation to define others in one's own terms by putting oneself in their place. The potential error in care reasoning lies in the tendency to forget that one has terms, creating a tendency to enter into another's perspective and to see oneself as "selfless" by defining oneself in other's terms. These two types of error underlie two common equations that signify distortions or deformations of justice and care: the equation of human with male, unjust in its omission of women; and the equation of care with self-sacrifice, uncaring in its failure to represent the activity and the agency of care.

The equation of human with male was assumed in the Platonic and in the Enlightenment tradition as well as by psychologists who saw all-male samples as "representative" of human experience. The equation of care with self-sacrifice is in some ways more complex. The premise of self-interest assumes a conflict of interest between self and other manifest in the opposition of egoism and altruism. Together, the equations of male with human and of care with self-sacrifice form a circle that has had a powerful hold on moral philosophy and psychology. The conjunction of women and moral theory thus challenges the traditional definition of human and calls for a reconsideration of what is meant by both justice and care.

To trace moral development along two distinct although intersecting dimensions of relationship suggests the possibility of different permutations of justice and care reasoning, different ways these two moral perspectives can be understood and represented in relation to one another. For example, one perspective may overshadow or eclipse the other, so that one is brightly illuminated while the other is dimly remembered, familiar but for the most part forgotten. The way in which one story about relationship obscures another was evident in high-school girls' definitions of dependence. These definitions highlighted two meanings—one arising from the opposition between dependence and independence, and one from the opposition of dependence to isolation ("No woman," one student observed, "is an island.") As the word "dependence" connotes the experience of relationship, this shift in the implied opposite of dependence indicates how the valence of relationship changes, when connection with others is experienced as an impediment to autonomy or independence, and when it is experienced as a source of comfort and pleasure, and a protection against isolation. This essential ambivalence of human connection provides a powerful emotional grounding for two moral perspectives, and also may indicate what is at stake in the effort to reduce morality to a single perspective.

It is easy to understand the ascendance of justice reasoning and of justice-focused moral theories in a society where care is associated with personal vulnerability in the form of economic disadvantage. But another way of thinking about the ascendance of justice reasoning and also about sex differences in moral development is suggested in the novel *Masks,* written by Fumiko Enchi, a Japanese woman.[14] The subject is spirit possession, and the novel dramatizes what it means to be possessed by the spirits of others. Writing about the Rokujo lady in the *Tales of Genji,* Enchi's central character notes that:

> Her soul alternates uncertainly between lyricism and spirit possession, making no philosophical distinction between the self alone and in relation to others, and is unable to achieve the solace of a religious indifference.[15]

The option of transcendance, of a religious indifference or a philosophical detachment, may be less available to women because women are more likely to be possessed by the spirits and the stories of others. The strength of women's moral perceptions lies in the refusal of detachment and depersonalization, and insistence on making connections that can lead to seeing the person killed in war or living in poverty as someone's son or father or brother or sister, or mother, or daughter, or friend. But the liability of women's development is also underscored by Enchi's novel in that women, possessed by the spirits of others, also are more likely to be caught in a chain of false attachments. If women are at the present time the custodians of a story about human attachment and interdependence, not only within the family but also in the world at large, then questions arise as to how this story can be kept alive and how moral theory can sustain this story. In this sense, the relationship between women and moral theory itself becomes one of interdependence.

By rendering a care perspective more coherent and making its terms explicit, moral theory may facilitate women's ability to speak about their experiences and perceptions and may foster the ability of others to listen and to understand. At the same time, the evidence of care focus in women's moral thinking suggests that the study of women's development may provide a natural history of moral development in which care is ascendant, revealing the ways in which creating and sustaining responsive connection with others becomes or remains a central moral concern. The promise in joining women and moral theory lies in the fact that human survival, in the late twentieth century, may depend less on formal agreement than on human connection.

Notes

1. Gilligan, C. (1977). "In a Different Voice: Women's Conceptions of Self and of Morality." *Harvard Educational Review* 47 (1982):481–517; *In a Different Voice: Psychological Theory and Women's Development*. Cambridge, Mass.: Harvard University Press.
2. Piaget, J. (1965). *The Moral Judgment of the Child*. New York, N.Y.: The Free Press Paperback Edition, pp. 76–84.
3. Kohlberg, L. (1984). *The Psychology of Moral Development*. San Francisco, Calif.: Harper & Row, Publishers, Inc.
4. Gilligan, C. and J. Attanucci. (1986). *Two Moral Orientations*. Harvard University, unpublished manuscript.
5. See Kohlberg, L. *op. cit.*, also Walker, L. (1984). "Sex Differences in the Development of Moral Reasoning: A Critical Review of the Literature." *Child Development* 55 (3):677–91.
6. Piaget, R., *op. cit.*
7. Kohlberg, L., *op. cit.*
8. Johnston, K. (1985). *Two Moral Orientations—Two Problem-solving Strategies: Adolescents Solutions to Dilemmas in Fables*. Harvard University, unpublished doctoral dissertation.
9. Langdale, C. (1983). *Moral Orientation and Moral Development: The Analysis of Care and Justice Reasoning Across Different Dilemmas in Females and Males from Childhood through Adulthood*. Harvard University, unpublished doctoral dissertation.
10. Johnston, K., *op. cit.;* Vygotsky, L. (1978). *Mind in Society*. Cambridge, Mass.: Harvard University Press; Chodorow, N. (1974). "Family Structure and Feminine Personality" in *Women, Culture and Society*, L. M. Rosaldo and L. Lamphere, eds., Stanford, Calif.: Stanford University Press; see also Chodorow, N. (1978). *The Reproduction of Mothering: Psychoanalysis and the Sociology of Gender*, Berkeley, Calif.: University of California Press.
11. Chodorow, N., *op. cit.*
12. Glaspell, S. (1927). *A Jury of Her Peers*, London: E. Benn.
13. *Ibid.*
14. Fumiko, E. (1983). *Masks*. New York: Random House.
15. *Ibid.* p. 54.

PART II

The Traditional Roots of an Ethics of Responsibility

Hume, the Women's Moral Theorist?

ANNETTE C. BAIER

Summary

In her analysis, Annette C. Baier first outlines Hume's moral theory by contrasting it with Kant's theory and by showing its congenialty to Gilligan's findings. According to Hume, moral theory is not a matter of obedience to universal law, but of cultivating proper character traits. The traits, or virtues, that are most important are those concerning relations with others. It is proper, then, to emphasize the importance of sentiment rather than universal reason, and of sympathetic sharing of sentiment. Moral development occurs through the correction of the sentiments, which happens only through actual activity. Thus, for Hume, as for the women in Kohlberg's and Gilligan's studies, the attempt to draw upon relevant principles with only limited information about a fictitious problem is an improper model for moral judgment.

In many ways, Hume does seem to be the women's moral theorist. But Hume also made many comments about women's weakness in his writings for which we must also account. Baier argues that, for the most part, Hume's comments can be read as descriptions of his society in which women were powerless. These reports of female weakness are neither descriptive of all conditions, nor do they describe any weakness in women's *moral* capabilities. In the moral domain and in the family, sentiment, sympathy, and the recognition of others are important, and these features are characteristic of women's lives, even when they are powerless. S.M.

In his brief autobiography, David Hume tells us that "as I took particular pleasure in the company of modest women, I had no reason to be displeased with the reception I met with from them." This double-edged remark is typical of Hume's references to women. Suggesting as it does that what pleased Hume was the women's pleasure in his pleasure in *their* company, it both diminishes the significance of their welcome to him, since "whoever can find the means either by his services, his beauty or his flattery to render himself useful or agreeable to us is sure of our affections" (Hume 1978, p.

388) and makes us wonder about the sources of his particular pleasure in their company. Pleasure in the ample returns he got for a little flattery? Yet his flattery of women, in his writings, is itself double-edged, as much insult as appreciation. Their "insinuation, charm and address" he tells us, in the section on justice in his *Enquiry Concerning the Principles of Morals,* will enable them to break up any incipient male conspiracy against them. His archness of tone in "Of love and Marriage," the patronizing encouragement to the greater intellectual effort of reading history instead of romances in "Of the Study of History," were reason enough for him to suppress those two essays (as he did, but for unclear reasons, and along with the more interesting and more radical "Of Moral Prejudices" where he describes a man who is totally dependent, emotionally, on his wife and daughter, and a woman who makes herself minimally dependent on the chosen father of her child).[1] It is not surprising that despite his popularity with the women, modest and less modest, who knew him, his writings have not met with a very positive reception from contemporary feminists. They fix on his references to the "fair" and the "weak and pious" sex, on his defense in the essay on "The Rise of the Arts and Sciences" of the claim that male gallantry is as natural a virtue as respect for one's elders, both being ways of generously allaying others' well founded sense of inferiority or infirmity: "As nature has given *man* the strength above *women,* by endowing him with greater strength both of mind and body, it is his part to alleviate that superiority, as much as possible, by a studied deference and complaisance for all her inclinations and opinions." Hume's "polite" displays of concern for the sex that he saw to be weaker in mind and body are not likely to encourage feminists to turn to him for moral inspiration any more than Kant's exclusion, in the *Metaphysical Elements of Justice,* §46, of all women from the class of those with "civil personality," fit to vote, will encourage them to look to him.

Our main concern here is not with feminism, but rather with the implications, for ethics and ethical theory, of Carol Gilligan's findings about differences between males and females both in moral development and in mature versions of morality. Whether those differences reflect women's weakness, their typical natural inferiority to men in mind and body, or their social inferiority, or their superiority, is not our central concern. Our central concern is with the concept of morality many women have, and the sort of experience, growth, and reflection on it, which lead them to have it. Our interest in a moral theory like Hume's in this context then, should primarily be with the extent to which the version of morality he works out squares or does not square with women's moral wisdom. Should the main lines of his account prove to be true to morality as women conceive of it, then it will be an ironic historical detail if he showed less respect than we would have liked for those of his fellow persons who were most likely to find his moral theory in line with their own insights. And whatever the root causes of women's moral outlook, of the tendency of the care perspective to dominate over the justice perspective in their moral deliberations, be it difference in childhood situation, or natural "inferiority" of mind and body, natural superiority of mind and heart, or just difference in mind, heart, and body, now that we have, more or less, social equality with men, women's moral sense should be made as explicit as men's moral sense, and as influential in structuring our practices and institutions. One way, not of course the only or the best way, to help make it explicit is to measure the influential men's moral theories against it. That is what I propose to do with Hume's theory. This can be seen as a prolegomenon to making wise women's theories influential. Then, once I have examined Hume's theory and its fit or misfit with women's moral wisdom, I shall briefly return to the question of how his own attitude to women relates to his moral theory.

As every student of the history of philosophy knows, Hume was the philosopher Kant set out to "answer," and both Kant's theory of knowledge and his ethics stand in significant contrast to Hume's. And Kant's views, through their influence on Jean Piaget and John Rawls, are the views which are expressed in Kohlberg's version of moral maturity and the development leading to it, the version which Gilligan found not to apply to girls and women as well as it did to boys and men. So anyone at all familiar with the history of ethics will wonder whether other non-Kantian strands in Western ethics, as developed in the philosophical tradition, might prove less difficult to get into reflective equilibrium with women's (not specifically philosophical) moral wisdom than the Kantian strand. For there certainly is no agreement that Kant and his followers represent the culmination of all the moral wisdom of our philosophical tradition. Alasdair MacIntyre's recent attacks on the Kantian tradition, and all the controversy caused by attempts to implement in high schools the Kohlberg views about moral education shows that not all men, let alone all women, are in agreement with the Kantians. Since the philosopher Kant was most notoriously in disagreement with Hume, it is natural to ask, after Gilligan's work, whether Hume is more of a women's moral theorist than is Kant. We might do the same with Aristotle, Hegel, Marx, Mill, MacIntyre, with all those theorists who have important disagreements with Kant, but a start can be made with Hume.

He is inviting, for this purpose, in part because he did try to attend, for better or worse, to male-female differences, and in his life, did, it seems, listen to women; and also because he is close enough in time, culture, and in some presuppositions to Kant, for the comparison between their moral theories to hold out the same hope of reconciliation that Gilligan wants or in her book wanted to get, between men's and women's moral insights. There are important areas of agreement, as well as of disagreement, or at least of difference of emphasis. And I should also add two more personal reasons for selecting Hume—I find his moral theory wise and profound, and I once, some years ago, in an introductory ethics course where we had read a little Aristotle, Aquinas, Hume, Kant, Mill, then Rawls and Kohlberg, had my students try to work out what each of our great moral theorists would have said about whether Heinz should steal the drug,[2] and why, so to measure *their* stage of moral develoment by the Kohlberg method.[3] Hume seemed to check out at as merely second level, stage three, with some stage four features, just as did most of Gilligan's mature women. So I have, since then, thought of Hume as a second "conventional" level challenger of Kohlberg's claims about the superiority of the third post-conventional level over the second, or as an exemplar of a fourth level, gathering up and reconciling what was valuable and worth preserving in both the conventional and the post conventional Kohlberg levels—a fourth level which we could call "civilized," a favourite Humean term of approbation. For this reason, when I read Gilligan's findings that mature, apparently intelligent and reflective women appeared to "revert" to Kohlberg's stage three (lower stage of level two, the conventional level) my immediate thought was "perhaps we women tend to be Humeans rather than Kantians." That is the thought I want to explore here.

I shall list some striking differences between Kant's and Hume's moral theories, as I understand them, then relate these to the differences Gilligan found between men's and women's conceptions of morality.

Hume's ethics, unlike Kant's, make morality a matter not of obedience to universal law, but of cultivating the character traits which give a person "inward peace of mind, consciousness of integrity," (Hume 1975, p. 283) and at the same time make that person good company to other persons, in a variety of senses of "company," ranging from the relatively impersonal and "remote" togetherness of fellow citizens, to the more selective but still fairly remote relations of parties to a contract, to the closer ties between friends, family, lovers. To become a good fellow-person one doesn't consult some book of rules, but cultivates one's capacity for sympathy, or fellow feeling, as well as for that judgment needed when conflicts arise between the different demands on us such sympathy may lead us to feel. Hume's ethics requires us to be able to be rule-followers, in some contexts, but do not reduce morality to rule-following. Corrected (sometimes rule-corrected) sympathy, not law-discerning reason, is the fundamental moral capacity.

Secondly, there is Hume's difference from Kant about the source of what general rules he does recognize as morally binding, namely the rules of justice. Where Kant sees human reason as the sole author of these moral rules, and sees them as universal, Hume sees them as authored by self-interest, instrumental reason, and rationally "frivolous" factors such as historical chance, human fancy and what it selects as salient, and by custom and tradition. He does not see these rules, such as property rules, as universal, but as varying from community to community and changeable by human will, as conditions or needs, wishes, or human fancy change. His theory of social "artifice," and his account of justice as obedience to the rules of these social artifices, formed by "convention," and subject to historical variation and change, stands in stark opposition to rationalist accounts, like Aquinas's and Kant's, of justice as obedience to laws of pure practical reason, valid for all people at all times and places. Hume has a historicist and conventionalist account of the moral rules which we find ourselves expected to obey, and which, on reflection, we usually see it to be sensible for us to obey, despite their elements of arbitrariness and despite the inequalities their working usually produces. He believes it is sensible for us to conform to the rules of our group, those rules which specify obligations and rights, as long as these do redirect the dangerous destructive workings of self-interest into more mutually advantageous channels, thereby giving all the "infinite advantages" of increased force, ability, and security (compared with what we would have in the absence of any such rules), although some may receive *more* benefits of a given sort, say wealth or authority, than others, under the scheme we find ourselves in. So Hume's ethics seems to lack any appeal to the universal principles of Kohlberg's fifth and sixth stages. The moral and critical stance Hume encourages us to adopt to, say, the property rules of our society, before seeing the rights they recognize as *moral* rights, comes not from our ability to test them by higher more general rules, but from our capacity for sympathy, from our ability to recognize and sympathetically share the reactions of others to that system of rights, to communicate feelings and understand what our fellows are feeling, so realize what resentments and satisfactions the present social scheme generates. Self-interest, and the capacity to sympathize with the self-interested reactions of others, plus the rational, imaginative, and inventive ability to think about the likely human consequences of any change in the scheme, rather than an acquaintance with a higher law, are what a Humean appeals to at the post-conventional stage.

This difference from Kantian views about the role of general principles in grounding moral obligations goes along in Hume with a downplaying of the role of reason, and a playing up of the role of feeling in moral judgment. Agreeing with the rationalists that when we use our reason we all appeal to universal rules (the rules of arithmetic, or of logic, or of causal inference) and failing to find any such universal rules of morality, as well as failing to see how, even if we found them, they should be able, alone, to *motivate* us to act as they tell us to act, he claims that morality rests ultimately on sentiment, on a special motivating feeling we come to have once we have exercised our capacity for sympathy with others' feelings, and also learned to overcome the emotional conflicts which arise in a sympathetic person when the wants of different fellow-persons clash, or when one's own wants clash with those of one's fellows. Morality, on Hume's account, is the outcome of a search for ways of eliminating contradictions in the "passions" of sympathetic persons who are aware both of their own and their fellows' desires and needs, including emotional needs. Any moral progress or development a person undergoes will be, for Hume, a matter of "the correction of sentiment," where what corrects it will be contrary sentiments, plus the cognitive-cum-passionate drive to minimize conflict both between and within persons. Reason and logic are indispensable "slaves" to the passions in this achievement, since reason enables us to think clearly about consequences or likely consequences of alternative actions, to foresee outcomes and avoid self-defeating policies. But "the ultimate ends of human actions can never, in any case, be accounted for by *reason,* but recommend themselves entirely to the sentiments and affections of mankind, without any dependence upon intellectual faculties" (Hume 1975, p. 293). A lover of conflict will have no reason, since he will have no motive, to cultivate the moral sentiment, and nor will that man of "cold insensibility" who is "unaffected with the images of human happiness or misery" (Hume 1975, p. 225). A human heart, as well as human reason, is needed for the understanding of morality, and the heart's responses are to particular persons, not to universal principles of abstract justice. Such immediate responses may be corrected by general rules (as they will be when justice demands that the good poor man's debt to the less good miser be paid) and by more reflective feeling responses, such as dismay and foreboding at unwisely given love and trust, or disapproval of excessive parental indulgence, but what controls and regulates feeling will be a wider web of feelings, which reason helps us apprehend and understand, not any reason holding authority over all feelings.

The next point to note is that Hume's version of what a typical human heart desires is significantly different from that both of egoists and of individualists. "The interested passion," or self-interest, plays an important role, but so does sympathy, and concern for others. Even where self-interest is of most importance in his theory, namely in his account of justice, it is the self-interest of those with fairly fluid ego boundaries, namely of family members, concerned with "acquiring goods and possessions for ourselves and our nearest friends", (Hume 1978, pp. 491–2). This is the troublesome passion that needs to be redirected by agreed rules, whereby it can control itself so as to avoid socially destructive conflict over scarce goods. Its self-control, in a society-wide cooperative scheme, which establishes property rights, is possible because the persons involved in it have already learned, in the family, the advantages that can come both from self-control and from cooperation (Hume 1978, p. 486). Had the rough corners of "untoward" and uncontrolled passions, selfish or unselfish, not been already rubbed off by growing up under some parental discipline, and were there no minimally sociable human passions such as love between man and woman, love of parents for their children, love of friends, sisters and brothers, the Humean artifice of justice could not be constructed. Its very possibility as an artificial virtue depends upon human nature containing the natural passions, which make family life natural for human beings, which make parental solicitude, grateful response to that, and the restricted cooperation thereby resulting, phenomena that do not need to be contrived by artifice. At the very heart of Hume's moral theory lies his celebration of family life and of parental love. Justice, the chief artificial virtue, is the offspring of family cooperativeness and inventive self-interested reason, which sees how such a mutually beneficial cooperative scheme might be extended. And when Hume lists the natural moral virtues, those not consisting in obedience to agreed rules, and having point even if not generally possessed, his favourite example is parental love and solicitude. The good person, the possessor of the natural virtues, is the one who is "a safe companion, an easy friend, a gentle master, an agreeable husband, an indulgent father" (Hume 1978, p. 606). We may deplore that patriarchal combination of roles—master, husband, father, but we should also note the virtues these men are to display—gentleness, agreeability, indulgence. These were more traditionally expected from mistresses, wives, and mothers than from masters, husbands, and fathers. Of course, they are not the only virtues Human good characters show, there is also due pride, or self-esteem, and the proper ambition and courage that that may involve, as well as generosity, liberality, zeal, gratitude, compassion, patience, industry, perseverance, activity, vigilance, application, integrity, constancy, temperance, frugality, economy, resolution, good temper, charity, clemency, equity, honesty, truthfulness, fidelity, discretion, caution, presence of mind, "and a thousand more of the same kind" (Hume 1975, p. 243).

In Hume's frequent lists of virtues, some are conspicuous by their absence, or by the qualifications accompanying them, namely the martial "virtues" and the monastic or puritan "virtues." Martial bravery and military glory can threaten "the sentiment of humanity" and lead to "infinite confusions and disorders . . . the devastation of provinces, the sack of cities" (Hume 1978, p. 601), so cool refletion leads the Humean moral judge to hesitate to approve of these traditionally masculine traits. The monastic virtues receive more forthright treatment. They, namely celibacy, fasting, penance, mortification, self-denial, humility, silence, solitude "are everywhere rejected by men of sense, because they serve no manner of purpose. We observe, on the contrary, that they cross all these desirable ends, stupify the understanding and harden the heart, obscure the fancy and sour the temper" (Hume 1975, p. 270). Here speaks Hume the good companion, the one who enjoyed cooking for supper parties for his Edinburgh friends, the darling, or perhaps the intellectual mascot, of the pleasure-loving Parisian salons. Calvinist upbringing and the brief taste he had in youth of the military life seem to have left him convinced of the undesirability of such styles of life; and his study of history convinced him of the dangers for society both of religious dedication, "sacred zeal and rancor," and of military zeal and rancor. So his list of virtues is a remarkably unaggressive, uncompetitive, one might almost say, womanly list.

Although many of the virtues on his list are character traits that would show in a great range of contexts, most of those contexts are social contexts, involving relations to others, and many of them involve particular relationships such as parent-child, friend to friend, colleagues to each other, fellow conversationalists. Even when he tries to list virtues that are valued because they are useful and agreeable to their possessor, rather than valued primarily for their contribution to the quality of life of the virtuous person's fellows, the qualities he lists are ones involving relations to others—the ability to get and keep the trust of others, sexual self-command and modesty, (as well as sexual promise, that is the capacity to derive "so capital a pleasure in life" and to "communicate it" to another (Hume 1975, p. 245), temperance, patience, and sobriety, are virtues useful (long term) to their possessor; while among those he lists as immediately agreeable to their possessor are contagious serenity and cheerfulness, "a proper sense of what is due to oneself in society and the common intercourse of life" (Hume 1975, p. 253), friendliness and an avoidance of "perpetual wrangling, and scolding and mutual reproaches" (Hume 1975, p. 257), amorous adventurousness, at least in the young, liveliness of emotional response and expressive powers—all agreeable traits which presuppose that their possessor is in company with others, reacting to them and the object of their reactions. There may be problems in seeing how a person is to combine the various Humean virtues—to be frugal yet liberal, to be sufficiently chaste yet show amorous enterprise, to have a proper sense of what is due one yet avoid wrangling and reproaches. Hume may, indeed, be depending on a certain sexual division of moral labor, allocating chastity to the women and amorous initiative to the men, more self-assertion to the men and more avoidance of wrangling to the women, but we should not exaggerate the extent to which he did this.

The title page of Book Three of the *Treatise* invokes Lucan's words referring to the lover of difficult virtue, and Humean virtues may be difficult to unify. Only in some social structures, indeed, may they turn out to be a mutually compatible set. Some investigation not only into what virtue is and what the true virtues are, but into the social precondition of their joint exemplification, may be needed in the lover of difficult virtue. Indeed everything Hume says suggests that these are not independent enterprises, since what counts as useful and agreeable virtues will depend in part on the social and economic conditions in which their possessors live, just as the acceptability of those social and economic conditions depends on what sort of virtues can flourish there, and how they are distributed within the population. Hume points out that the usefulness of a trait like good memory will be more important in Cicero's society than in his own, given the lesser importance in the latter of making well turned speeches without notes, and given the general encouraged reliance there on written records in most spheres of life. The availability, accessibility, and portability of memory substitutes will vary with the customs and technological development of a society, and Hume is aware that such facts are relevant to the recognition of character traits as functional virtues. The ease of simulation or perversion of such traits will also affect virtue-recognition—in an age when private ambition is easily masked as public spirit, or tax exemption as benevolence, the credit given to such easily pretended virtues may also understandably sink. The status of a character trait as a virtue need not be a fixed matter, but a matter complexly interrelated with the sort of society in which it appears. This makes good sense, if moral virtues are the qualities that enable one to play an acceptable part in an acceptable network of social roles, to relate to people in the variety of ways that a decent society will require, facilitate, encourage, or merely permit.

The next point I want to stress in Hume's moral theory is that in his attention to various interpersonal relations, in which our Humean virtues of vices show, he does not give any special centrality to relationships between equals, let alone autonomous equals. Since his analysis of social cooperation starts from cooperation within the family, relations between those who are necessarily unequals, namely parents and children, is at the center of the picture. He starts from a bond which he considers "the strongest and most indissoluble bond in nature" (Hume 1975, p. 240), "the strongest tie the mind is capable of" (Hume 1978, p. 352), namely the love of parents for children, and in his moral theory he works out, as it were, from there. This relationship, and the obligations and virtues it involves, lack three central features of relations between moral agents as understood by Kantians and contractarians—it is intimate, it is unchosen, and is between unequals. Of course, the intimacy need not be "indissoluble," the inequality may be temporary, or later reversed, and the extent to which the initial relationship is unchosen will vary from that of unplanned or contrary-to-plan parenthood, to intentional parenthood (although not intentional parenting of a given particular child) to that highest degree of voluntariness present when, faced with an actual newborn child, a decision is taken not to let it be adopted by others, or, when a contrary decision is taken by the biological parent or parents, by the decision of adoptive parents to adopt such an already encountered child. Such fully chosen parenthood is rare, and the norm is for parents to *find themselves* with a given child, perhaps with any child at all, and for parental affection to attach itself fairly indiscriminately to its unselected objects. The contractarian model of morality as a matter of living up to self-chosen commitments gets into obvious trouble both with duties of young children to their unchosen parents, to whom no binding commitments have been made, and of initially involuntary parents to their children. Hume has no problem with such unchosen moral ties, since he takes them as the paradigm moral ties, one's giving rise to moral obligations more self-evident than any obligation to keep contracts.

The last respect in which I wish to contrast Hume's moral philosophy with its more Kantian alternative is in his version of what problem morality is supposed to solve, what its point is. For Kantians and contractarians, the point is freedom, the main problem how to achieve it given that other freedom-aspirants exist and that conflict between them is likely. The Rousseau-Kant solution is obedience to collectively agreed-to general law, where each freedom-seeker can console himself with the thought that the legislative will he must obey is as much his own as it is anyone else's. For Hume, that problem, of the coexistence of would-be unrestrained self-assertors, is solved by the invention of social artifices and the recognition of the virtue of justice, namely of conformity to the rules of such mutually advantageous artifices. But the problem morality solves is deeper; it is as much intrapersonal as interpersonal. It is the problem of contradiction, conflict, and instability in any one person's desires, over time, as well as conflict between persons. Morality, in theory, saves us from internally self-defeating drives as well as from self-defeating interpersonal conflict. Nor is it just an added extra to Hume's theory that the moral point of view overcomes contradictions in our individual sentiments over time. ("Our situation, with regard to both persons and things, is in continual fluctuation; and a man that lies at a distance from us, may, in a little time, become a familiar acquaintance." (Hume 1978, p. 581). His whole account of our sentiments has made them intrinsically reactive to other persons' sentiments. Internal conflict in a sympathetic and reassurance-needing person will not be independent of conflicts between the various persons in his or her emotional world. "We can form no wish, which has not a reference to society. A perfect solitude is, perhaps, the greatest punishment we can suffer. Every pleasure languishes when enjoy'd apart from company, and every pain more cruel and intolerable. Whatever other passions we may be actuated by, pride, ambition, avarice, revenge, or lust; the soul or animating principle of them all is sympathy; nor would they have any force were we to abstract entirely from the thoughts and sentiments of others" (Hume 1978, p. 363).

I have drawn attention ot the limited place of conformity to general rules in Hume's version of morality, to the historicist conventionalist account he gives of such rules, to his thesis that morality depends upon self-corrected sentiments, or passions, as much or more than it depends upon the reason that concurs with and serves those passions; to the nonindividualist, nonegoistic version of human passions he advances, to the essentially interpersonal or social nature of those passions which are approved as virtues, the central role of the family, at least at its best, as an exemplar of the cooperation and interdependency morality preserves and extends, the fact that moral cooperation, for him, includes cooperation in unchosen schemes, with unchosen partners, with unequal partners, in close initmate relations as well as distanced and more formal ones. And finally, I emphasized that the need for morality arises for Hume from conflicts within each person, as well as from interpersonal conflict. It is a fairly straightforward matter to relate these points to at least some of the respects in which Gilligan found girls' and women's versions of morality to differ from men's. Hume turns out to be uncannily womanly in his moral wisdom. "Since the reality of interconnexion is experienced by women as given rather than freely contracted, they arrive at an understanding of life that reflects the limits of autonomy and control" (Gilligan 1982, p. 172). Hume lived before autonomy became an obsession with moral and social philosophers, or rather lived while Rousseau was making it their obsession, but his attack on contractarian doctrines of political obligation, and his clear perception of the given-ness of interconnetion, in the family and beyond, his emphasis on our capacity to make others' joys and sorrows our own, on our need for a "seconding" of sentiments, and the inescapable mutual vulnerability and mutual enrichment that the human psychology and the human condition, when thus understood, entail, make autonomy not even an ideal, for Hume. A certain sort of freedom is an ideal, namely freedom of thought and expression, but to "live one's own life in one's own way" is not likely to be among the aims of persons whose every pleasure languishes when not shared and seconded by some other person or persons. "The concept of identity expands to include the experience of interconnexion" (Gilligan 1982, p. 173).

The women Gilligan studied saw morality as primarily a matter of responsibilities arising out of their attachment to others, often stemming from originally given rather than chosen relations. The men spoke more of their rights than of their responsibilities, and saw those rights as arising out of a freely accepted quasi-agreement between self-interested equals. Hume does in his account of justice have a place for quasi-agreement-based rights serving the long run interests of those respecting them, but he also makes room for a host of responsibilities which presuppose no prior agreement or quasi-agreement to shoulder them. The responsibilities of parents are the paramount case of such duties of care, but he also includes cases of mutual care, and duties of gratitude where "I do services to such persons as I love, and am particularly acquainted with, without any prospect of advantage; and they may make me a return in the same manner" (Hume 1978, p. 521). Here there is no right to a return, merely the reasonable but unsecured trust that it will be forthcoming. (There may even be something of an either/or, duck-rabbit effect, between his "artificial virtues," including justice, and his "natural virtues," including mercy and equity, in all those contexts where both seem to come in to play.)

Hume's conventionalism about the general rules we may have to obey, to avoid injustice to one another, has already been mentioned as dooming his theory of justice to mere stage four moral marks, if to get any critical appraisal of customary rules one must have moved on to social contracts or universal principles. Hume is a realist about the historical given-ness and inevitable arbitrariness of most of the general rules there is any chance of our all observing. Like Carol Gilligan's girls and women, he takes moral problems in concrete historical settings, where the past history as well as the realistic future prospects for a given group are seen as relevant to their moral predicaments, and their solutions. Even the fairly abstract and ahistorical social artifices of the *Treatise* are given a quasi-historical setting, and give way in the *Essays* and *History of England* to detailed looks at actual concrete social and moral predicaments, in full narrative depth.

The distrust of abstract ahistorical principles, the girls' need to fill out Kohlberg's puzzle questions with a story, before answering them, led to the suspicion that this poor performance on the application of universal principles to sketchily indicated particular cases, shorn of full narrative context, showed that their "reason" was less well developed than the boys' (Gilligan 1982, p. 28). It might rather have been, as it was in Hume's case, a conviction that this was a false model of how moral judgments are made. He endorses the emotional response to a fully realized situation as moral reflection at its best, not as one of its underdeveloped stages, and he mocks those rationalists who think abstract universal rules will ever show why, say, killing a parent is wrong for human beings but not for oak trees (Hume 1978, pp. 466–7).

At this point it may be asked whether Hume's account allows for any version of stages of moral development, whether it is not one of those "bag of virtues" accounts Kohlberg derides. Can one who thinks morality is a matter of the passions find room for any notion of individual moral progress or development? The answer is yes. Although he does not give us such a theory for the individual, Hume does speak of a "correction of sentiment" and of a "progress of sentiments," especially where "artificial" virtues are concerned. Since morality depends for him on a *reflective* sentiment, and on self-corrected self-interest and corrected sympathy, it is plain that more experience and more reflection could lead an individual through various "levels" of moral response. The interesting questions are those of what the outlines of such an alternative developmental pattern might be. Clearly this is not a matter that can be settled from a philosopher's armchair, and psychological research of the sort Gilligan is doing would be needed to find out how human passions do develop, and which developments are seen as moral progress by those in whom they occur, and by others. Some features of women's development are indicated in the latter chapters of Gilligan, features which would not necessarily show up on the Kohlberg tests. In "Concepts of Self and Others" (Gilligan 1982), she describes transitions from self-centered thinking (which presumably is likely in women reacting to let-down by the fathers of the fetuses the women who were interviewed were considering aborting, rather than a natural starting point for a girl or woman) to a condemnation of such "selfishness" (or an alternation between "selfish" and "unselfish" impulses) on to what is seen as a clearer perception of the "truth" concerning the human relations in which they are involved, leading perhaps to a cool or even ruthless determination to protect themselves from further hurt and exploitation, then later to a revised version of what counts as their own interests, to a realization that those interests require attachment to and concern for others (see especially Gilligan 1982, p. 74).

If alternatives to Kohlberg's rationalist scenario are to be worked out in detail, probably some guiding moral as well as psychological theory will be needed, as well as empirical tests. There will be a need for something to play a role like that which Rawls' and Kant's moral theory played in getting Kohlberg to look for certain particular moral achievements, and to expect some to presuppose other earlier ones. It might even be that, once we had a nonrationalist yet dynamic moral theory, and an expected developmental pattern going with it, empirical tests would show it to be true not merely of women but of men. The gender difference may not be in the actual pattern of development of passions, or in our reasoning and reflection about the satisfaction of our passions, but merely in our intellectual opinions, as voiced in interviews, as to whether this is or is not *moral* development. For both Gilligan's and Kohlberg's tests have so far looked at verbally offered versions of morality, at intellectual reflection on morality, not at moral development itself, at motivational changes and changed emotional reactions to one's own and other's actions, reactions and emotions. As I understand it, only in Gilligan's abortion study were people interviewed while actually in the process of making a moral decision—and those women may not have been a representative sample of women decision-makers, since they were selected for their apparent indecisiveness, for what was judged their need to think and talk more about their decision. The clear-headed or at least the decisive women simply did not get into this study (Gilligan 1982, p. 3).

We should not equate a person's moral stance with her intellectual version of it, nor suppose that a person necessarily knows the relative strength of her own motives and emotions. To test people's emotional and motivational growth, we would need emotion and motive experiments, not thought experiments, and they can be tricky to design safely. Hume said "When I am at a loss to know the effects of one body on another in any situation, I need only put them in that situation and observe what results from it. But should I endeavour to clear up after the same manner any doubt in moral philosophy by placing myself in the same case with that which I consider, 'tis evident that this reflection and premeditation would so disturb the operation of my natural principles as must render it impossible to form any just conclusion from the phaenomenon" (Hume 1978, xxiii). By moral philosphy, here, he means simply the investigation of human nature, in both its unreflective and its more reflective operations. Moral psychology, as he understands it, is indeed a matter of letting reflection and premeditation make a difference to the operation of natural motives and passions, so moral experiments, in the narrow sense of moral, would not necessarily be contaminated by the reflection or self-consciousness that the self-experimentation would involve. Knowing that when we react in a given situation, what we are doing is being treated as a display of moral character, as a test of moral progress, might merely encourage that progress, not lead to its misrepresentation. But such "experiments" as Hume is thinking of are real life ones, not either our own, after-the-fact, versions of them, nor our responses, intellectual or emotional, to merely imagined situations, in which one knows one is not really involved. Not merely are these too thin and sketchy, as Amy clearly felt in the story of Heinz[3] and the expensive medicine, but even if a fully worked out fictional narrative were given—a whole novel, let us say, there is still no reason to think that one's response to a fictional situation is a good indicator of what one's own response would be, were one actually in a predicament like that of a novelist's character. Reading good novels and attending or acting in good plays may be the most harmless way to prepare oneself for real life moral possibilities, but this isn't moral "practise." There is no harmless practising of moral responses, no trial runs or dress rehearsals. Children's play, the theater, novels, knowledge about and sympathy with friends' problems, may all play a useful role in alerting us to the complexities of moral situations, but one's performance there is no reliable predictor of what one's response to one's own real life problems will be. As Aristotle said, the only way to learn to be morally virtuous is to perform virtuous actions—real ones, not fantasy ones. And only from one's moral practice, not from one's fantasy moral practice, or rationalized versions of past moral practice, can we learn the stage of moral development a person actually exhibits. As Hume said, it seems that only a cautious observation of human life, of "experiments" gleaned as they occur in the "common course of the world" in people's "behaviour in company, in affairs, and in their pleasure" (ibid.) can found any empirical science of moral development.

Let me repeat that I am not saying that knowledge that one is being observed is what would spoil the results of contrived moral "tests;" rather that what would spoil them would be the knowledge that the tests are fantasy ones, not real world ones. I do not want to deny that what one takes to be one's sincere beliefs about what morality demands, as they might be expressed in an interview with a psychologist, or in a reaction to a fictional situation, have some connection with one's actual moral choices. But I agree with Carol Gilligan in wondering how close the connection is, especially for reactions to sketched fictional situations. The old question "How can I know what I think until I see what I write?" can be adapted for moral convictions: "How can I know what I judge right until I see what decisions I make and how I then live with them?" But even that may be too optimistic about our ability to size up how we are living with our past decisions—we naturally tend either to avoid recognizing bad conscience or to exaggerating and self-dramatizing it, in our own follow-up reactions to a moral decision. We tend to interpret our own pasts deceptively, as possibly displaying tragedy or demonic wickedness, but not moral error, stupidity, or ordinary vice. We glaze our own pasts over with the pale cast of self-excusing, or in some cases self-accusing, self-denigrating, self-dramatizing thought. So I see no non-suspect way, by interviewing people about other people's actual or hypothetical decisions or even about their own past actual ones, to gauge what are or were their *effective* moral beliefs.

That was a sceptical, epistemological interruption in my exploration of what sort of pattern of development one might expect as experience of the common course of the world changes our passions as well as the thoughts that guide them when they motivate our actions. One thing that several of the Gilligan women *say* happened to them is that they developed both a sense of their own competence to control their lives and affairs, and that their attitudes to selfishness and unselfishness underwent change. Clearly both these dimensions, of general competence at and confidence in responsible decision-making, and of understanding the relations between self-concerned and other-concerned passions, are ones along which one would expect change and variation, as experience deepens and opportunity widens. A child's opportunity for responsible decision-making is small, and yet the child's experience of having to live with others' decisions, reactions to inconsiderate decisions, willingness to discern, protest, understand, or forgive decisions by superiors which affect her badly, is a vital preparation for later responsible decision-making. The person who has forgotten what it was like to be the relatively powerless one, the decided-for not the decision-maker, is not going to be able even to anticipate the protests or grievances their own decisions produce, let alone be a wise or compassionate decision-maker. So development along what we could call the sympathy and memory dimensions—development and enrichment of the ability to understand others' reactions, will be something one hopes will occur in normal development.

Recent studies by Judith A. Hall and Robert Rosenthal and their associates, have shown, interestingly enough, that women typically are better readers of other people's *nonverbal* communications of feelings (in facial expression, "body language," and tone of voice) than are men, and women also are more easily read. It seems to make good evolutionary sense to suppose that there is an innate basis for such superiority, since women have been the ones who had both to communicate with infants and to interpret their communications, before the child has learned a natural language. Not only may women's moral voice be different from men's, and often unheard by men, but women's *tone* of voice, and nonverbal expression, may be subtler, more expressive, and understood more easily by other women than by men. Both in the Humean virtue of "ease of expression" and in facility in recognizing expressed feelings, women seem to outperform men.

The second dimension of expected change and development concerns the weight a person gives to the understood preferences of the various others involved in her decision, when she decides. How one sees their interests in relation to one's own will also change as experience grows. Even if infant egoism is where we all start, it seems to be infant egoism combined with infant trust in parents, and with faith in the ease of communication of feelings. In parent-child relations, Hume says, the other "communicates to us all the actions of his mind, and lets us see, in the very instant of their production, all the emotions, which are caus'd by any object" (Hume, 1978, p. 353). Where we start, in infancy, seems to be in optimism about ease of mutual understanding, even without language, and about harmony in wills. What we may have to learn, by experience, is that conflict of wills is likely, that concealing one's feelings can be prudent, and that misunderstanding is frequent. Hume's own versions of childhood attitudes in, e.g., the *Treatise*,

Bk. II, section "Of the Love of Relations," show an incredibly strong and dominant memory or fantasy of such parent-child trusting harmonious intimacy. Parents and children are seen to take pride in one another's achievements and successes, not to compete with one another for eminence, "Nothing causes greater vanity than any shining quality in our relations" (Hume 1978, p. 338). But this idyll of shared interests, concerted wills, and shared pride or self assertion, must soon be interrupted by experience of what Hume calls "contrariety," and of that "comparison" of competition which interferes with sympathy and cooperation. A most important dimension of the moral development one would look for on a Humean moral theory would be this one, of the interplay of what he calls the opposed principles of sympathy and comparison. Although on his account sympathy is what morality chiefly depends upon, the opposed principle of comparison, a due sense of when our interests are or would be in conflict with those of others, and of what is then our due, also plays a not unimportant role in the generation of a sense of the virtue of justice, as he describes it. But the interpersonal problem to which various versions of morality give better or worse solutions, on Hume's account, is the problem of how to *minimize* opposition of interests, how to arrange life so that sympathy, not hostile comparison, will be the principle relating our desires to those of our fellows. Where, on the more contractarian model, morality regulates and arbitrates where interests are opposed, on a Humean view, as on Amy's, morality's main task is to rearrange situations so that interests are no longer so opposed.

There is, for Hume, an intimate interplay between the operation of sympathy and the sense of what are one's own interests. On the one hand it may seem that only relative to some already fixed sense of which desires are and are not my own desires could I recognize any reaction of my own as sympathy with another's desires. But in fact, as Hume describes the workings of sympathy, they serve as much to determine, by outward expansion as well as by reinforcement of the inner core, what counts as "my interests." Since he believes that every human desire languishes unless it receives sympathetic reverberation from another, (Hume 1978, p. 363) then unless someone sympathizes with my "selfish" pleasures they will not persist. But the fact that another does so sympathize both makes that pleasure less purely selfish, more "fertile" for others, and also evokes in me a sympathy with the other's sympathy for me—a "double reverberation," and a grateful willingness to sympathize with that one's pleasures, as long as sympathy is not drowned by comparison of our respective social statuses. Hence Hume can say that "it seems a happiness in the present theory that it enters not into that vulgar dispute concerning the degrees of benevolence or self love which prevail in human nature" (Hume 1975, p. 271).

Hume has a famously fluid concept of the self, and the fluid ego boundaries that allows work interestingly in his moral psychology. One could say that, on a Humean version of moral development, the main task is to work to a version of oneself and one's own interests which both maximizes the richness of one's potential satisfactions and minimizes the likely opposition one will encounter between one's own and others' partially overlapping interests. This is both an individual and a social task—a matter of the social "artifices" which divide work so as to increase not decrease the real ability of all workers, which conjoin forces so that not just the collective power but each person's power is augmented, and which arrange that "by mutual succor we are less expos'd to fortune and accidents" (Hume 1978, p. 485). The additional force, ability, and security which acceptable social institutions provide, he later says, must be a "system of actions concurr'd in by the whole society, . . . infinitely advantageous to the whole and to every part" (Hume 1978, p. 498). This may seem an absurdly high demand to make, one which no set of social institutions has yet met. But if we remember those endless added satisfactions which sypathetic enlargement of self-interest can bring to Humean persons, then we can see that a set of institutions that really did prevent oppositions of interest might indeed bring "infinite" or at least indeterminately great increase of power of enjoyment (such as that he described at T.365). Whether these increased satisfactions in fact come about will depend not just on the nature of the institutions, but on the individuals whose lives are structured by them—"a creature absolutely malicious and spiteful," or even "a man or cold insensibility or narrow selfishness" (Hume 1975, pp. 225–6) will not receive infinite advantages from even the best institutions. Hume, perhaps overoptimistically, thinks that given halfway decent institutions and customs of upbringing, these will be "fancied monsters," (Hume 1975, p. 235) not real possibilities, (he excuses Nero's actions by citing his grounds for fear, Timon's by his "affected spleen").

One dimension of moral development, then, for a Humean version of morality, will be change in the concept of one's own interest. "I esteem the man whose self-love, by whatever means, is so directed as to give him a concern for others, and to render him serviceable to society" (Hume 1975, p. 297). But equally important, and perhaps slower to develop in women in our society, is a realistic sense of whether or not one's agreeable moral virtues are being exploited by others, whether or not there is any "confederacy" of the more narrowly selfish, and of the sensible knaves, free-riding on the apron strings of those whose generous virtues they praise and encourage but do not envy or emulate. Due pride is a Humean virtue, and one cannot be proud of tolerating exploitation. Still, a realistic appraisal of the relative costs and benefits of cooperative schemes to their various participants, and an unwillingness to tolerate second class status, requires a realistic estimate of just how much real gain the "narrowly selfish" get from their exploitation of others' more generous other-including self-love. By Hume's accounting, the sensible knaves and the narrowly selfish don't do better than their victims—they are "the greatest dupes." The very worst thing the exploited can do, to improve their situation, is to try to imitate the psychology of their exploiters. The hard art is to monitor the justice of social schemes, to keep an eye on one's rights and one's group's rights, without thereby contracting one's proper self love into narrow selfishness in its "moralized" version—into insistence on one's rights, even when one gains nothing, and others lose, by one's getting them. A sense of what is due one can easily degenerate into that *amour propre* which is the enemy of the sort of extended sociable and friendly amour-de-soi which Hume, like Rousseau, sees as the moral ideal for human beings.

Will there by anything like Kohlberg's level-difference, in the moral development of Humean passions, if we see this as a change in concepts of self in relation to others, in our capacity to understand facts about likely and actual conflicts, and in our capacity to sympathize with others' reactions, developed through experience and maturation? For Hume a defining feature of a moral response is that it be a response to a response—that it be a matter of a "reflexion," that it be a sentiment directed on sentiments. One can postulate a fairly clear difference between levels of "reflection," parallel to Kohlberg's jumps in critical ability if one distinguishes the mere ability to sympathize (and to react negatively to others' feelings) which young children show, a sort of proto-moral response, from that more legitimized version of it which comes when we sympathize with others as right-holders in some conventional scheme, and sypathize with their resentments at insult or injury (a level two response) a sort of officially "seconded" sympathy, comparison, sense of self, and recognition of recognized conflicts of interest; and yet reserve the title of really moral response to the reflexive turning of these capacities for sympathy, for self-definition and for conflict recognition on themselves, leading to sympathetic comparative evaluation of different styles of self-definition, styles of watching for and managing conflicts, of inhibiting or cultivating sympathy. The Humean concept of "reflexion" performs the same sort of job as Kantian reason—it separates the mature and morally critical from the mere conformers. A moral theory which developed Gilligan's women's moral strengths could make good use of Hume's concept of reflection.

I end with a brief return to the question of how this wise moral theory of Hume's could allow its author to make the apparently sexist remarks he did. Now, I think, we are in a position to see how harmless they might be, a display of his social realism, his unwillingness to idealize the actual. Women in his society *were* inferior in bodily strength and in intellectual achievement. Neither of these, however, for someone who believes that reason should be the slave of reflective and moralized passions, are the capacities that matter most. What matters most, for judging moral wisdom, are corrected sentiments, imagination, and cooperative genius. There Hume never judges women inferior. He does call them the "timorous and pious" sex, and that is for him a criticism, but since he ties both of these characteristics with powerlessness, his diagnoses here are of a piece with his more direct discussions of how much power women have. In those discussions he is at pains to try to point out not just the subordination of their interests to those of men in the existing institutions (marriage in particular) but also to show women where their power lies, should they want to change the situation.

As he points out, a concern for "the propagation of our kind" is a normal concern of men and women, but each of us needs the cooperation of a member of the other sex to further this concern, and "a trivial and anatomical observation" (Hume 1978, p. 571) shows us that no man can know that his kind has been propagated unless he can trust some woman either to be sexually "faithful" to him, or to keep track of and tell him the truth about the paternity of any child she bears. This gives women great, perhaps dangerously great, threat advantage in any contest with men, a power very different from any accompanying the "insinuation, charm and address" (Hume 1975, p. 191) that Hume had invoked as sufficient to break any male confederacy against them. The non self-sufficiency of persons in reproductive respects that he goes on in the next paragraphs to emphasize, and the need of the male for a trustworthy female, in order to satisfy his postulated desire for offspring he can recognize as his (a desire Hume had emphasized in the *Treatise* section "Of Chastity and Modesty,") put some needed iron into the gloved hands of the fair and charming sex. Hume gives many descriptions in his *History* and *Essays* of strong independent women, and he dwells on the question of whether the cost of their iron wills and their independence is a loss of the very moral virtues he admires in anyone but finds more often in women than in men—the "soft" nonmartial compassionate virtues. Need women, in ceasing to be timorous and servile, cease also to be experts at care and mutual care? His moral tale of a liberated woman who chooses to be a single mother, (in "Of Moral Prejudices") suggests not—that avoidance of servile dependence on men can be combined with the virtues of the caring and bearing responsibility, that pride and at least some forms of love can be combined.

Notes

1. The three essays referred to in this section were published by Hume in the first edition of *Essays Moral and Political* 1741–2, but removed by him in subsequent editions. They can be found in Hume, ed. Miller, 1985, in an appendix "Essays Withdrawn and Unpublished."
2. See Kohlberg, 1981, p. 12.
3. See Introduction to this volume.
4. See Gilligan, 1982, pp. 25ff.

References

Gilligan, Carol. 1982. *In a Different Voice: Psychological Theory and Women's Development*. Cambridge, Mass., London: Harvard University Press.

Hall, Judith A. 1984. *Non Verbal Sex Differences*. Baltimore: The Johns Hopkins University Press.

Hume, David. 1975. *Enquiries*. L. A. Selby-Bigge and P. H. Nidditch, eds. Oxford: Clarendon Press.

———. 1978. *A Treatise of Human Nature*. L. A. Selby-Bigge and P. H. Nidditch, eds. Oxford: Clarendon Press.

———. 1985. *Essays Moral, Political and Literary*. Ed. Eugene F. Millar. Indianapolis: Liberty Classics.

———. *History of England*. any edition.

Kant, Immanuel. 1965. *The Metaphysical Elements of Justice*. John Ladd, trans., Indianapolis, New York, Kansas City: Bobbs-Merrill.

Kohlberg, Lawrence. 1971. *Collected Papers on Moral Development and Moral Education*. Harvard University: Moral Education Research Foundation.

———. 1981. *The Philosophy of Moral Development*. San Francisco, Calif.: Harper & Row.

Rosenthal, Robert, J. A. Hall, M. R. DiMatteo, P. L. Rogers, and D. Archer. 1979. *Sensitivity to Nonverbal Communication: The PONS Test*. Baltimore: The Johns Hopkins University Press.

Duty and Friendship

Toward a Synthesis of Gilligan's Contrastive Moral Concepts

MICHAEL STOCKER

Summary

While Michael Stocker is sympathetic to Gilligan's research and finds it suggestive, he is also critical of her work. Stocker claims that Gilligan's characterization of the postconventional stage by means of a contrastive schema, the dichotomy between an ethics of care and responsibility and a rights-based morality, is problematic, for it conceals the possibility of a synthesis of these two views. Each view derives from a different model of moral theory. The care perspective utilizes the model of the family, while the rights perspective draws on the model of the contract. Stocker contends that the categories at the center of these two paradigms are more closely related than is usually thought, and he hopes to reveal this interconnection through an inquiry into the relationship between friendship and duty—two important moral categories, one from each of these models. Importantly, Stocker anticipates and confronts one possible objection to his argument: that friendship and duty are wholly distinct concepts because friendship is a natural category, while duty is a moral one. By means of an analysis of the distinction between generative and constitutive naturalism, Stocker overcomes this division.

According to Stocker, friendship and duty are internally connected ideas, and can be fully understood only in relation to one another. This suggests that although the male rights-based morality is *different* from the female care morality, the two are not *completely distinct,* and that each might fruitfully inform the other. S.M.

It is abundantly clear that those women with the moral and psychological makeup described by Carol Gilligan are mature and admirable people. It is also clear that they do not satisfy some of the strictures of various moral theories, including those of Kohlberg. It is further clear that this tells against those strictures, not against those women. What may not be clear is how we are to understand the morality of Gilligan's women, nor how we are to understand the differences between the theories which are inadequate to these women and those that are adequate.

I disagree with Gilligan about the way to understand these differences. Where she seems to find formal or categorial differences, I find other sorts of differences. To clarify our differences, I will start with some points of agreement.

First, I too hold that to understand a particular doctrine about virtue or a list of virtues, it is important to understand the psychological make-up of those who do, or who are to, embody those virtues. For, among other things, virtues deal with what is natural, dangerous, or problematic for those concerned—and here people do, or are thought to, differ. Aristotle and Nietzsche make this point convincingly. So, I see every reason to believe that if people differ, e.g., in ego boundaries, they will have and need different, even if related, virtues.

Second, I agree that to understand a person's or a group's ethical views, we need to investigate not only the categories they invoke but also the order in which they find and develop the categories. So, a person who starts from a stage of rights and only later moves to rights plus responsibilities can be expected to have a different understanding of both rights and responsibilities than a person who moves from responsibilities to rights or to both at the same time.

Third, I agree that the ethical views Gilligan finds in her women are at least as attractive and morally enlightened as those she finds in her men. Moreover, any adequate ethical theory must give important weight to the views expressed by these women.

These points are important for understanding Gilligan. They allow for a useful, rather than a carping and profession-chauvinistic, way to acknowledge that the terms she uses in talking about ethical matters may well not be employed in just the ways they would be used by ethicists. Take for example the distinction she makes between rights and responsibilities and the weight she places on this distinction. We are now in a position to allow for this distinction and its importance for Gilligan, while also acknowledging that there is a great variety of rights or claimed rights. One person can claim a right to freedom or autonomy, another can claim a right to a caring community. Similarly for responsibilities. One person can see the world in terms of family or interpersonal responsibilities, another can see the world in terms of business or financial responsibilities. So, it might well seem that the categories of rights and responsibilities do not, as such, help us make much progress.[1]

Returning to my opening points, however, it should be noted first, that it seems significant that Gillian's women do not claim their world as a world that is theirs *by right*—even if philosophical usage would allow them to do so. Second, the relative order of these moral elements, be they called rights or responsibilities, is different in her men and her women. Third, even if women used the same categories as men, the material and concrete content of the claimed rights would, for all that, still be different.

Two other areas of agreement between the sort of ethics Gilligan and I are interested in are these: We agree about, first, the importance of exemplars, of role models, or ideal people and ideal lives, and second, the importance of basic ethical models or pictures. We both guide and understand ourselves in terms of these role models and ethical models. Some would see these points as indicating that it is no accident that the Hobbesian social contract is seen as so true and explanatory of our society and thus so appealing or appalling.

Were we, however, to join Gilligan's women—and, as Baier shows us, Hume—in taking the family, and people as family members, as our source of role models and our basic ethical model, then our ethics will undoubtedly be importantly different from that of Hobbes. But, it is important to note, these differences will involve, even if they also transcend, the material and concrete ways we understand both models—the contract and the parties making the contract, on the one hand, and the family and family members, on the other. For, it may well be possible to replicate the same goods and lives claimed by adherents of one model in terms of the other model. My point here is a simple one: how we understand the family and its members or the contract and its parties is also important, perhaps as important as whether we think in terms of the category of family or of contract.

For example, to understand a contract theory, it is of the utmost importance to understand the sorts of people taking part in it. This requires understanding the nature of the people entering it and of those living under it, and the relations between these. The need for this is shown by the fact that contract theories differ importantly on whether the contract leaves people essentially as they were, with, e.g., the same needs, and interests, and also understandings, and simply secures surer or better satisfaction of these, as Hobbes holds, or whether, as Rousseau holds, the contract creates a new person with new needs, interests, and understandings irreducible to the precontract ones.[2]

What is important, then, is the sort, not merely the fact or category of, family and family member. And not merely the sort, but also the situation of the family. After all, we can all recognize that it can be—and both historically and personally it is—liberating to destroy or simply escape from certain sorts of families, family-understood ties, or certain political ideologies depending on particular understandings of the family writ large or small. This is no news, and in making this point I do not in any way mean to suggest that Gilligan is glorifying the family, or that she is suggesting that it somehow provides a fully adequate model for adequate, even good, lives. She does give great importance to the family and family-modeled life, especially for women's ethical thought. But, she is suggesting something else, at once subtle and important, when she talks about the differences between seeing morality in terms of rights and seeing it in terms of responsibilities.

As noted, I do not wish to argue whether these are different ways of having and seeing morality. Rather, I wish to show that the categories at the center of these different models are more closely related than is thought. But to show this would require far more than one chapter. What I will do toward this end is to show that friendship and duty—two important moral categories, one from each of these models—are far more closely related than is thought. I will do this by showing that an adequate understanding of duty and friendship involves situating it within the other model. I will further restrict my focus by concentrating on showing that an adequate account of duty requires room left for friendship: a theory of duty that leaves no room for friendship is an inadequate theory of duty.

To be sure, friendship and duty are not Gilligan's central contrastive categories. But, first, they are important in her work. Second, friendship has its natural home in that part of ethics understood in terms of family, intimacy, and affection, and thus, if Gilligan is right, in women's morality. Duty, on the other hand, has its natural home in that part of ethics understood as focusing on rights. And certainly, duty, at least as much as rights, has been an important element in recent ethical works.

I have several goals here. First, I want to show that duty and friendship need not be seen as antagonistic. They are intimately related. Indeed, neither can be understood adequately without the other. This, I think, goes against at least some suggestions in Gilligan. It definitely goes against many claims in recent duty-centered ethics. As this last is meant to suggest, I am not concerned to show that friendship poses no problems for contemporary accounts of duty and duty-centered ethics. On the contrary, it offers a corrective for them. But what this corrective generates is a synthesis of both duty and friendship. Second—now in agreement, I think, with Gilligan—I want to show that what has been seen as the superior or more mature ethics must be modified to take account of the supposedly inferior and less mature ethics.

I do not know whether the men or the women in Gilligan's studies would find their views or lives reflected in these syntheses. My concern, however, will be to argue that these syntheses are needed for morally correct or even morally plausible accounts of friendship and duty—and thus for morally correct or even plausible morality or moralities.

In a way I hope will become clear, these comments lead to my second goal: for I want to present one objection to trying to understand the issues in terms of dichotomous categories as Gilligan did in *In a Different Voice* or as she did in her conference paper in terms of alternating field and ground.

Let us start with hierarchies. Gilligan and others claim that only men's morality involves hierarchies. Perhaps this is so for certain sorts of hierarchies. But friendship, and to that extent women's morality, also involves certain hierarchies. Some friendships may involve no hierarchies. But equally clearly, some friendships do involve hierarchies. Some friends are better friends; some friends come and should come before other friends. This can involve a ranking of, e.g., responsibilities toward different friends. Were this not so, many clashes concerning friends could not be resolved.

Despite the fact that there are hierarchies of friends, there are also possibilities of problématic resolutions of conflicts, perhaps even dilemmas within friendships. There may be, that is, no completely successful or satisfactory resolution of these problems. At a level of low theoretical interest, there can be problems created by one person's improper involvement with different friends. So a person with a commitment to one friend can improperly make a clashing commitment with another. At a level of far more interest, there is the possibility that through no one's fault, a friend will have incompatible commitments to friends. These can range from the rather minor problems of scheduling time to the far more serious problems of choosing which friend or love gets preference.

In regard to friendship, the correct course of action and of feeling may not be a wholly good one, nor even one which allows one to escape guilt, shame, and the like, or to escape wronging, not merely harming, others. These are complex matters, but an example should help illustrate some of what I mean: as our interests or values change, we may find some of our old friends no pleasure to be with, or tiresome, or a hindrance to the sort of life we now think we should be leading. Terminating the friendship may be no easy matter—it may involve hurting the legitimate feelings of the old friend. Yet, continuing the friendship may be far worse. In such a situation, even if it is clear that one ought to break off the friendship, there will be a real moral and personal cost for both the friend and oneself. The realm of friendships, then, may preclude acting or feeling in completely whole and blameless ways.

But this lack of resolubility is not a feature that divides friendship from duty when the latter is properly understood. For as is now being widely argued and coming to be accepted, the realm of ethics, including that of duties, admits of irresoluble conflicts—of dirty hands, unavoidable compunction, guilt or shame, and dilemmas. Some see these features as natural, even if not strictly necessary, consequences of allowing that there are mutually irreducible values, e.g., duties and other ethical considerations.

Further, perhaps as a natural consequence of allowing for a plurality of duties, duties cannot be understood as involving clearly defined, easily, or mechanically applied categories. To operate well in regard to duties, one must be morally sensitive, and one must sensitively appreciate a wealth of details and contexts. Moral education and sensitivity, and what some see as contextualism, are as needed for duty as for friendship.

So far, then, I have noted two ways, often related, that friendships and duties have some of the same structural features: hierarchies and conflicts. But, as important as these shared features are, we here need a more detailed investigation of duty and friendship to see if, as I claim, they do involve each other.

To this end, let us turn to some other issues about friendship and duty. One view that must be exposed—and then rejected—is that friendship and duty *cannot* be interrelated because friendship is *natural* and duty is *moral*. (The similarity between this view and others that have been used to denigrate women and women's concerns is no accident.) As some put it, friendship and what is valuable about it are premoral or extramoral, i.e., natural. In one sense of the terms, friendship is a natural good and not a moral good. Both the attraction and value of friendship are held to be independent of moral and perhaps other conceptual views. In ways explained further on, the claimed independence is constitutive, not—or not only—generative.

The question of whether friendship's *attraction* is natural or moral is importantly similar to the question, now receiving some attention, of whether natural desires, as opposed to moral or other sorts of reasons, are needed to explain actions. Considered as *generative* claims, in both cases it is held that all attractions and desires either are or are causally explained by—i.e., are generated from—attractions and desires that do not involve moral or evaluational views, but that are inborn, arise through processes of biological maturation, or through other natural, nonreason-based processes.

This generative claim is not that all desires and attractions are natural, but that all are either natural or develop from natural ones. So the claim can hold that a newborn's desire for milk is inborn, that some sexual desires arise through wholly biological processes, but that a desire for a full-bodied, well balanced wine only develops out of a natural desire, e.g., for pleasant tastes.

Allowing that not all desires and attractions are natural, but only develop out of what are natural, makes room for the fact that our developed desires and attractions do make use of reason and indeed of moral views. It is entirely consistent with the claims of a generative naturalism that desires and attractions develop or change in various ways. The change can be one from an end to a means—e.g., a desire to sit at the dinner table in order to satisfy a desire for food.

But the change can be more than this. Through a psychological process such as association, it can involve the creation of what is—but only after the change—attractive in its own right. So, my desire to fulfill moral duties might arise from my natural, childhood desire not to suffer pain and my childhood belief that I would suffer unless I fulfilled my duties. In the beginning, I would not have had the desire about the duties unless I had the desire about pain and that belief. But now, that desire may well be conceptually split off from its origins and may be a final desire in its own right. I can have that desire even though I no longer believe there is such a connection between failing one's duty and pain.

A *constitutive* naturalism is concerned with the nature, not the origin, of desires and attractions. It holds that whatever is desired or attractive in its own right is natural. It holds that whatever is desired or attractive is so either in its own right or because it is thought to conduce to what is so in its own right. The "because" in the last clause is a constitutive one: that, as is thought, it conduces to what is desired or attractive in its own right is what is desired or attractive about these things.

This view can allow that I now have the desire not to violate any moral duties. But it requires, for example, that what I there desire is avoiding pain, which I believe is likely to result from violating duties. Here the relation between the ultimate and intermediate desires is a causal, means-end one. (Although most constitutive naturalisms see the relation between the desires this way, other relations, such as exemplification, would also satisfy those views.)

Borrowing from the talk about naturalism in regard to desire and attraction, naturalism about *value* can be put quickly. Here too, there is the distinction between generative and constitutive naturalisms. Generative naturalisms about value hold that our values either are natural or develop from what is naturally valued and valuable. Constitutive naturalisms hold that whatever is valued or valuable in itself is natural and that everything that is valued or valuable is so either in itself or because it is thought to conduce to what is.[3]

Perhaps there are some desires, attractions, and values that are in the requisite sense constitutively natural. Some bodily pleasures and some aspects of health might be like this. And perhaps there are some desires, attractions, and values that, constitutively, are in no way natural, but depend simply on moral and other conceptual views. Here we might think of some desires that are had by adherents of abstract aesthetic or political doctrines.

For some purposes, it is important to know whether there are any wholly natural or wholly moral items. But for our purposes, what is important is that at least many of our attractions, desires, and values are, constitutively, neither wholly natural nor wholly moral, but are at once natural and moral.

This may best be seen developmentally, in a way that allows for and even trades on generative naturalism. So, it seems reasonable to hold that to the extent that valuing involves a cognitive appreciation, infants' goals will involve only desires and not values. We might also think of young children's goals as going beyond mere desire and attraction but only by involving judgments of how to satisfy those desires and attractions. So taken, these children's goals would involve desire, attraction, and reason, but not value.

But adults' goals—or at least many of them—constitutively involve desire, attraction, reason, *and value*. These goals are not means to the end of satisfying, or other forms of mere specifications of, such natural desires as those for natural pleasure. Rather, they involve objects of desire and attraction which we have only because of both generative and constitutive evaluative considerations.

For example, acquiring the goal of *being a philosopher* typically involves being subjected to the standards of philosophy—being judged and guided by these standards. This involves the use of philosophy's values and other values as well, such as wanting to be well thought of by one's teachers, a desire for doing well at whatever one is doing, and the like. This is to speak generatively.

Constitutively, to have being a philosopher as a goal involves valuing, and being moved by, philosophy's standards themselves. Of course, one may still have as a goal being well thought of. But now one wants to be well thought of for one's philosophy. So too, one may still have as a goal doing well at whatever one does. But one now also wants to do well at philosophy. Before, one may have seen that philosophy is a good, but not as one now does—viz., as one's own good and as something it would be a loss to give up.

This combined generative and constitutive account is, of course, drawn from Aristotle, especially his discussion of habituation—understood as involving training, education, and moral criticism, and not mere rote copying.[4] But, parallels should be found in most any acceptable moral psychology, especially one that deals with developmental issues.

We have already seen one example of a constitutively mixed goal: doing philosophy and being a philosopher. For other examples of constitutively mixed goals, we can profitably examine the goals of the various moral virtues discussed by Aristotle, such as courage, temperance, truthfulness, cheerfulness, sociality, and liberality. But of course, what is of most importance for us is that we can here examine friendship, which, we might note, Aristotle says is or involves a virtue (Nicomachean Ethics, VIII, 1).

It is pointless, and almost certainly impossible, to divide the elements of these mixed goals into those that are wholly natural and those that are wholly moral. We should rather understand those goals as having both natural and moral elements or aspects, which form and inform each other. In both generative and constitutive ways, each has developed by changing and being changed by the other.

The naturalness of adult friendship is shown in any number of ways, including its similarities with the affection of infants. Its moral nature is shown by the constitutive fact that friends care for and are concerned with the well-being of friends. Care, concern, and well-being are clearly evaluative and also clearly serve as sources of motivation in a friendship.

There is a closely related point about friendship that has already been touched on but that should be taken up again here: although it might be agreed that friendship constitutively involves moral categories and understandings, it might be suggested that, nonetheless, it has only (what some call) natural goodness, as opposed to moral goodness. This charge is of particular importance for understanding the propriety of discussing Gilligan's theses by means of discussing friendship. For exactly the same charge can be levelled against her basic claim that women have a different morality from men. The charge would not be that men and women understand the world in the same categories, nor that those peculiar to women are not important. Rather, the charge is that the women's categories are only naturally, not morally, important.

This, as should be clear, raises immensely difficult questions about the nature of morality. But even these brief remarks may be of use: there is a sense of the moral such that if one is deficient in regard to morality so understood, then one deserves censure, blame, perhaps even punishment. In what follows, I will suggest that friendship falls, to some extent, under this understanding of the moral, even if it also falls largely outside of it. The responsibilities Gilligan's women see as so important in their lives may also be importantly outside of the moral so understood. After all, it does seem that a person—even, as many think, a woman—has the moral right not to enter into activities and relations which call for or even allow for those responsibilities.

But there is another, albeit importantly related, sense of the moral that concerns such issues as what sort of lives people must lead if they are not to be deficient, even defective. It also concerns character traits, forms of appreciation, areas of interest and concern. Here, too, even if we think there are many good combinations, we also think that there are many that can be realized only in a poor life, a life that is not truly human.

Put very briefly, the first sense of morality concerns duty, especially as discussed by Kant or his followers, and the second concerns what is good for people, what is truly human, as discussed by Plato, Aristotle, Hume, and their followers. Even if friendship and Gilligan's responsibilities fall more in the second than the first, this is no bar to their being through and through moral. For it is clear that they are essential to a good, human life. They are, indeed, the very stuff of a good, human life.

So far, I have shown that duty and friendship share some structural features and that, so far as the naturalness of friendship is concerned, there is no bar to duty and friendship being interrelated. We can now sketch some ways they are interrelated by thinking explicitly in terms of *prima facie* considerations, including *prima face duties*. I here draw from W. D. Ross, in his *The Right and the Good* and *Foundations of Ethics*. But I do not accept his list or account of such duties. Indeed, much of what I say below is contrary to his understanding of duty. As noted earlier, accounts of duty need correcting—and this can, in part, be done by taking account of friendship.

A complete discussion of Ross would be out of place here. For our purposes the following should suffice. We recognize, Ross held, that some acts are our *overall* or *actual* duty, because they are acts of promise-keeping; so too, for acts of beneficence, acting justly, telling the truth, making reparations, showing gratitude, and so on. This is to say that in some case the *ultimate* reason why an act is a duty is that it has one of those features. That it is an act of promise-keeping is why it is our actual duty. But we cannot hold that whenever an act has one of those features—is an act of promise-keeping, for example—it is right to do, much less is our duty to do. First, doing it might involve not doing an act with another such right-making or duty-making feature. Thus, one would be involved in practical contradictions if one held that whatever act had such a feature was one's real duty.

Second, the moral importance of these features differs: e.g., some promises are more important than others, some cases of justice more pressing. This is to say that each sort of consideration can differ in importance. Third, no one of these features is always more important than another. This is to say that they are not lexically ordered. So for example, in one situation, keeping a particular promise is more important than making reparations; in another case, the reverse.

Ross held that two hallmarks of prima facie duties are that a person may be unable to fulfill all of them—e.g., both keep a promise and show gratitude—and that it may be permissible to do one rather than the other. This allows that it may be completely right to do one prima facie duty while not doing another, provided that the one that is done is at least as strong as the one not done.

There are, I now want to suggest, acts other than prima facie duties that can conflict with prima facie duties and that a person can, with complete moral correctness, do instead of any duty. This is to say that doing an act that is not a prima facie duty can make it permissible not to do what is one's strongest prima facie duty.

Cases of self-regard and supererogation bear this out by creating *moral options*. It is, obviously, not my duty to act supererogatorily. But I may do so. If the supererogatory act includes the duty—as in going the second mile—I have an option either simply to do my duty or to do it and also the supererogatory (part of the) act. I shall call this a *simple* option to contrast it with a *contrary-to-duty* option—a moral option not to do one's duty.

Some supererogatory acts create contrary-to-duty options: my running into a burning building to rescue someone can be supererogatory even if it makes me unable to do what is my duty, e.g., keeping an appointment. (The issue of whether "is my duty" should be "otherwise would be my duty" is taken up below.)

We also have moral options generated by some *self-regarding* acts. For example, there are simple options where I would not violate a duty by allowing someone to take my share of some goods, but where I could nonetheless act with complete justification in taking my share. There are also contrary-to-duty self-regarding options. In certain cases at least, I am entitled to save myself from being harmed even if in so doing I will violate my duty not to cause or allow harm to another.[5]

Some acts of friendship also introduce simple options. I may well not violate a duty either by seeing or not seeing a friend. Some of these options are contrary-to-duty options. This, I further suggest, is not simply because of their self-regarding or supererogatory aspects.[6] Consider a case where an old friend is passing through town, for what looks like the last time. It may well be that it is not my overall duty to visit with the friend—perhaps speaking on the phone would be sufficient (to put it coolly). Or if I really should visit with the friend, I may do nothing wrong if I stay for only a short while. Nonetheless, I do not think it morally lax to hold that it can be all right to stay the entire afternoon, even if this involves not doing my duty, e.g., keeping an appointment.

Friendship and duty are also related in the ways prima facie duties are. For, friendship gives rise to special duties of friendship. I speak here of dut*ies* of friendship, not *the duty* of friendship. The latter suggests a duty to seek, have, or maintain friendship. Perhaps we have such a duty. But I am here interested in the duties we have in, and as a result of, friendship.

Even if we, or our most prominent academic moral theories, do not talk about duties of *friendship,* reflection on how we think friends should or must treat each other will dispel doubts about the propriety or importance of such talk. We do, or can easily enough, recognize that friends owe friends certain special forms of care, consideration, and the like. These duties go beyond, and are in other ways different from, what is owed nonfriends. Duties of friendship are at once constitutive of, and grounded by, the friendship. It is more than a merely definitional matter that I am not your friend if, often enough, I pay no special attention to you and your particular needs, interests, desires, and even whims. Indeed, I can violate a special duty of friendship by not according a friend such special care and attention.

Some might worry here that I have at least set the stage for having duties of affection—of having and showing affection. One important reason for this worry is the thought that we cannot summon up affection at will and that since "ought" implies "can", we therefore cannot have duties of affection. My reply here will have to be exceedingly brief: first, we are far more in control of our emotions than philosophers at least commonly think—as Iris Murdoch and others have argued so cogently.

Second, we have duties to do many things we cannot do at will. So, a person may have a duty to support children or learn a foreign language.

What here seems important is whether, through various means, one can do the duty. And affections are not so recalcitrant to attention and development that we cannot develop them.

Third, we do criticize ourselves and others for not having or showing proper affection. For example, parents are criticizable if they do not have and express love for their children. And friends and lovers are criticizable if they do not, e.g., take the time and make room for affection.

According special care and attention can be a duty of friendship and can also be one's overall duty. Since duties of friendship are not lexically weaker than other prima facie duties, this overall duty can involve not doing what otherwise would be the strongest prima facie duty. But since duties of friendship are not lexically stronger than other prima facie duties, one need not, and indeed one must not, favor a friend in every circumstance, come what may and to just any and every extent.

No general, and certainly no precise, answer can be given to the question of the relative weights of the duties of friendship and other duties. This is one source of the need for the sensitivity and judgment I earlier said duty requires. Further, it is clear enough that we cannot give any general or precise answer about the extent to which one may justifiably favor a friend over many, perhaps even any number of, others. Nonetheless, it is clear that to treat a friend as just one person among all people may, as such, be to wrong the friend—e.g., to violate the friend's rights. Here, as in many other cases, the impartial point of view is incorrect and immoral.[7]

That there are prima facie duties of friendship forces a redescription of at least some of the cases used to show that friendship can require immorality—e.g., Forster's hope that he would have the courage to betray his country to save a friend. If there is a prima facie duty to help friends even in such situations, then even where helping a friend would be immoral, this immorality need not involve letting features irrelevant to duty override features that are relevant. Rather, it might involve an importantly different sort of immorality—viz, giving undue weight to one prima facie duty over others.

I have suggested that friendship must be thought of as involving duty, especially once we correct the notion of duty to include duties of friendship. But of course, much that is of evaluative importance about friendship is outside duty, even after duty is expanded to include duties of friendship. Friendship shows—as is shown in other ways by distinctions between self and other, and in still other ways by supererogation—that an adequate ethics extends far beyond duty, and of course rights.

So, it is clear that a good person who is, in all senses, a good friend will take care not to violate any duties of friendship. But it is equally clear that much of what is constitutive of, and importantly valuable about, acts of friendship is not a duty, not even a duty of friendship. On the contrary. Indeed, if for too long a period, people fulfill only their duties of friendship when they could easily do otherwise, they are not very much of a friend, if a friend at all.

The relations between friendship and the duties of friendship are important enough to indicate some of their other complexities. First, failure to fulfill these duties may end—perhaps justify or require ending—the friendship. Second, acts of friendship and the duties of friendship include doing what friends do—e.g., spend time together—and also doing these out of friendship. To some extent, but only to some extent, one can fulfill one's duties of friendship—and do some of what is involved in friendship in addition to duty—without acting from friendship. A full appreciation of this involves understanding the moral status of expressing, maintaining, or developing attitudes, emotions, and the like.

Many relations between friendship and duty have yet to be discussed. For example, we have not even touched on the difficult issue of how relating to people as friends differs from relating to them on principle, from duty. I think there is something very important in the thought that when we relate to people in a way proper to and expressive of friendship we relate to them personally, as individuals; but that when we relate to people in a way proper to and expressive of at least the traditional duties, we relate to them impersonally, that we there consider them only as place holders in moral principles. As this, and much else in my paper, is intended to show, even if I am right that there are important connections between duty and friendship, there are important differences, too.

Even with these lacks, I trust enough has been shown to show that the relations between duty and friendship are complex and in need of detailed investigation. It is still unclear how, or even to what extent, friendship and duty stand in friendly relations with each other. But it is clear that unless they are understood together, neither will be understood. This should at least suggest that rights and responsibilities, and perhaps other contrastive moral categories advanced by Gilligan, are internally interconnected.

Notes

1. This seems the gravamen of George Sher's argument.

2. Seyla Benhabib did not, I think, pay sufficient attention to this diachronic or developmental issue.

3. Some find constitutive naturalisms about attraction, desire, and value in Hume, e.g., as exemplified in his claim that reason is and should be the slave of the passions. And some find them in such utilitarians as J. S. Mill, because of his use of pleasure. I mention these historical claims to identify naturalism, not to endorse them. For, as I understand Hume and Mill, they were only generative naturalists, holding a mixed constitutive view of the sort sketched below.

4. For a good discussion of Aristotle, see Myles Burnyeat, "Aristotle on Learning to Be Good," in Amelie O. Rorty (ed.), *Essays on Aristotle's Ethics* (Berkeley: University of California Press, 1980).

5. On some aspects of the optionality of self-regarding and supererogatory acts, see my "Agent and Other: Against Ethical Universalism," *The Australasian Journal of Philosophy*, vol. 74, 1976, pp. 206–20. Michael Slote argues similarly about self- and other–regarding harms—"Morality and Self-Other Asymmetry," *The Journal of Philosophy*, vol. 81, 1984, pp. 179–92. For an argument that there can be contrary-to-duty supererogatory acts, see my *Supererogation* (doctoral dissertation, Harvard University, 1966), especially chap. 6, "Duty Precluding Supererogatory Acts," and

Frances Myrna Kamm, "Supererogation and Obligation," *The Journal of Philosophy*, vol. 82, 1985, pp. 118–38.

6. Some acts of friendship are morally good and in other ways, too, they are good but not obligatory. Some conclude from this that they are supererogatory. See, e.g., Neera K. Badhwar. "Friendship, Justice, and Supererogation," *American Philosophical Quarterly*, vol. 22, 1985, pp. 121–31, also Thomas Hill, Jr., "Kant on Imperfect Duty and Supererogation," *Kant Studien*, vol. 62, 1971, pp. 55–77. A better conclusion is that those features are not sufficient for supererogation. I would suggest that in addition to those, moral heroism or saintliness or lesser forms of them are also needed for supererogation.

7. See e.g., John Cottingham, "Ethics and Impartiality," *Philosophical Studies*, vol. 43, 1983, pp. 83–99.

Filial Morality

CHRISTINA HOFF SOMMERS

Summary

Christina Hoff Sommers takes up the question concerning the obligation of adult children to their parents. Kantians and utilitarians subscribe to a model of impartiality in which all moral patients exert equal pull (EP) on all moral agents. Therefore, no special consideration can be granted to family members. "Sentimentalists," in contrast, criticize formalist EP theories and attend to the morality of special relations from a "care perspective." The weakness of this solution to the problem of filial morality is that it neglects the impersonal institutional or social context that situates and qualifies all special relations.

Given the inadequacy of both the EP and the sentimentalist approaches to dilemmas concerning filial morality, Sommers suggests another approach—a "differential pull" morality. DP allows for greater consideration of special cases, yet stands on a minimal deontological principle of noninterference. Using a DP theory of morality, we can better understand the nature of filial obligation: failure to act on these duties causes unwarranted interference with the rights of the moral patient, since neglected parents experience humiliation and loss of dignity. The particular cases of filial morality that Sommers discusses are used to show "that DP offers moral philosophers an approach that is socially responsible and personally sensitive." S. M.

> We not only find it hard to say exactly how much a son owes his parents, but we are even reluctant to investigate this.
>
> Henry Sidgwick[1]

What rights do parents have to the special attentions of their adult children? Prior to this century, there was no question that a filial relationship defined

Reprinted from *The Journal of Philosophy*, vol. 83, no. 8 (August 1986), pp. 439–456, by permission of the author and publisher.

This paper has benefitted from lengthy discussion with Fred Sommers, and from critical comments by A. I. Melden, Diana Meyers, Marcia Baron, David Wong, Michael Lockwood, Jonathan Adler, and Patrick Derr.

a natural obligation; philosophers might argue about the nature of filial obligation, but not about its reality. Today, not a few moralists dismiss it as an illusion, or give it secondary derivative status. A. John Simmons[2] expresses "doubts . . . concerning the existence of 'filial debts' " and Michael Slote[3] seeks to show that the idea of filial obedience is an illusion whose source is the false idea that one owes obedience to a divine being. Jeffrey Blustein[4] argues that parents who have done no more than their duty may be owed nothing, and Jane English[5] denies outright that there are any filial obligations not grounded in mutual friendship.

The current tendency to deny or reconstrue filial obligation is related to the more general difficulty that contemporary philosophers have when dealing with the special duties. An account of the special obligations to one's kin, friends, community, or country puts considerable strain on moral theories such as Kantianism and utilitariansism, theories that seem better designed for telling us what we should be doing for everyone impartially than for explaining something like filial obligation. The moral philosopher of a utilitarian or Kantian persuasion who is concerned to show that it is permissible to give some biased vent to family feeling *may* go on to become concerned with the more serious question of accounting for what appears to be a special obligation to care for and respect one's parents—but only as an afterthought. On the whole, the question of special agent-relative duties has not seemed pressing. In what follows, I shall be arguing for a strong notion of filial obligation, and more generally, I shall be making a case for the special moral relations. I first present some anecdotal materials that illustrate the thesis that a filial duty to respect one's parents is not an illusion.

I. The Concrete Dilemmas

I shall be concerned with the filial duties of adult children and, more particularly, with the duty to honor and respect. I have chosen almost randomly three situations, each illustrating what seems to be censurable failure on the part of adult children to respect their parents or nurturers. It would not be hard to add to these cases, and real life is continually adding to them.

1. An elderly man was interviewed on National Public Radio for a program on old age. This is what he said about his daughter.

> "I live in a rooming house. I lost my wife about two years ago and I miss her very much. . . . My little pleasure was to go to my daughter's house in Anaheim and have a Friday night meal. . . . She would make a meal that I would enjoy. . . . So my son-in-law got angry at me one time for a little nothing and ordered me out of the house. That was about eight months ago. . . . I was back once during the day when he was working. That was about two and a half or three months ago. I stayed for about two hours and left before he came home from work. But I did not enjoy the visit very much. That was the last time I was there to see my daughter.

2. An eighty-two year old woman (call her Miss Tate) spent thirty years working as a live-in housekeeper and baby-sitter for a judge's family in

Massachusetts. The judge and his wife left her a small pension which inflation rendered inadequate. After her employers died, she lost contact with the children whom she had virtually brought up. One day Miss Tate arranged for a friend of hers to write to the children (by then middle-aged) telling them that she was sick and would like to see them. They never got around to visiting her or helping her in any way. She died last year without having heard from them.

3. The anthropologist Barbara Meyerhoff did a study of an elderly community in Venice, California.[6] She tells about the disappointment of a group of elders whose children failed to show up at their graduation from an adult education program.

> The graduates, 26 in all, were arranged in rows flanking the head table. They wore their finest clothing bearing blue and white satin ribbons that crossed the breast from shoulder to waist. Most were solemn and flushed with excitement. . . . No one talked openly about the conspicuous absence of the elders' children [Meyerhoff, 187, 104].

I believe it may be granted that the father who had dined once a week with his daughter has a legitimate complaint. And although Miss Tate was duly salaried throughout her long service with the judge's family, it seems clear that the children of that family owe her some special attention and regard for having brought them up. The graduation ceremony is yet another example of wrongful disregard and neglect. Some recent criticisms of traditional conceptions of filial duty (e.g., by Jane English and John Simmons) make much of examples involving unworthy parents. One may agree that exceptional parents can forfeit their moral claims on their children. (What, given his behavior, remains of Fyodor Karamozov's right to filial regard?) But I am here concerned with what is owed to the average parent who is neglected or whose wishes are disregarded when they could at some reasonable cost be respected. I assume that such filial disregard is wrong. Although the assumption is dogmatic, it can be defended—though not by any quick maneuver. Filial morality is but one topic in the morality of special relations. The attempt to understand filial morality will lead us to a synoptic look at the moral community as a whole and to an examination of the nature of the rights and obligations that bind its members.

II. Shifting Conceptions

Jeffrey Blustein's *Parents and Children* (loc. cit.) contains an excellent historical survey of the moral issues in the child-parent relationship. For Aristotle, the obligation to serve and obey one's parents is like an obligation to repay a debt. Aquinas too explains the commandment to honor one's parents as "making a return for benefits received."[7] Both Aristotle and Aquinas count life itself as the first and most important gift that the child is given.

With Locke, the topic of filial morality changes: the discussion shifts from a concern with the authority and power of the parent to concern with the less formal, less enforceable, right to respect.[8] Hume was emphatic on the subject of filial ingratitude saying, "Of all the crimes that human creatures are capable, the most horrid and unnatural is ingratitude, especially when it is committed against parents.[9] By Sidgwick's time the special duties are beginning to be seen as problematic: "The question is on what principles . . . we are to determine the nature and extent of the special claims of affection and kind services which arise out of . . . particular relations of human beings [Sidgwick 242]. Nevertheless, Sidgwick is still traditional in maintaining that "all are agreed that there are such duties, the nonperformance of which is ground for censure," and he is himself concerned to show how "our common notion of Justice [is] applicable to these no less than to other duties" (Sidwick 243).

If we look at the writings of a contemporary utilitarian such as Peter Singer,[10] we find no talk of justice or duty or rights, and *a fortiori,* no talk of special duties or parental rights. Consider how Singer, applying a version of R. M. Hare's utilitarianism, approaches a case involving filial respect. He imagines himself about to dine with three friends when his father calls saying he is ill and asking him to visit. What shall he do?

> To decide impartially I must sum up the preferences for and against going to dinner with my friends, and those for and against visiting my father. Whatever action satisfies more preferences, adjusted according to the strength of preferences, that is the action I ought to take (Singer 101).

Note that the idea of a special obligation does not enter here. Nor is any weight given to the history of the filial relationship that typically includes some two decades of parental care and nurture. According to Singer, "adding and subtracting preferences in this manner" is the only rational way of reaching ethical judgment.

Utilitarian theory is not very accommodating to the special relations. And it would appear that Bernard Williams is right in finding the same true of Kantianism. According to Williams, Kant's "moral point of view is specially characterized by its impartiality and its indifference to any particular relations to particular persons."[11] In my opinion giving no special consideration to one's kin commits what might be called the Jellyby fallacy. Mrs. Jellyby, a character in Charles Dickens's *Bleak House,*[12] devotes all of her considerable energies to the foreign poor to the complete neglect of her family. She is described as a "pretty, diminutive woman with handsome eyes, though they had a curious habit of seeming to look a long way off. As if they could see nothing nearer than Africa." Dickens clearly intends her as someone whose moral priorities are ludicrously disordered. Yet by some modern lights, Mrs. Jellyby could be viewed as a paragon of impartial rectitude. In the next two sections, I will try to show what is wrong with an impartialist point of view and suggest a way to repair it.

III. The Moral Domain

By a moral domain I mean a domain consisting of what G. J. Warnock[13] calls "moral patients." Equivalently, it consists of beings that have what Robert

Nozick calls "ethical pull."[14] A being has ethical pull if it is ethically "considerable;" minimally, it is a being that should not be ill treated by a moral agent and whose ill treatment directly wrongs it. The extent of the moral domain is one area of contention (Mill includes animals, Kant does not). The nature of the moral domain is another. But here we find more uniformity. Utilitarians and deontologists are in agreement in conceiving of the moral domain as constituted by beings whose ethical pull is equal on all moral agents. To simplify matters, let us consider a domain consisting only of moral patients that are also moral agents. (For Kant, this is no special stipulation.) Then it is as if we have a gravitational field in which the force of gravitation is not affected by distance and all pairs of objects have the same attraction to one another. Or, if this sort of gravitational field is odd, consider a mutual admiration society no member of which is, intrinsically, more attractive than any other member. In this group, the pull of all is the same. Suppose that Buridan's ass was not standing in the exact middle of the bridge but was closer to one of the bags of feed at either end. We should still say that he was equally attracted to both bags but that he naturally would choose the closer one. So too does the utilitarian or Kantian say that the ethical pull of a needy East African and that of a needy relative are the same but we can more easily act to help the relative. This theory of equal pull but unequal response saves the appearances for impartiality while acknowledging that, in practice, charity often begins and sometimes ends at home.

This is how the principle of impartiality appears in the moral theories of Kant and Mill. Of course their conceptions of ethical pull differ. For the Kantian, any being in the kingdom of ends is an embodiment of moral law whose force is uniform and unconditional. For the utilitarian, any being's desires are morally considerable, exerting equal attraction on all moral agents. Thus Kant and Mill, in their different ways, have a common view of the moral domain as a domain of moral patients exerting uniform pull on all moral agents. I shall refer to this as the *equal-pull (EP) thesis*. It is worth commenting on the underlying assumptions that led Kant and Mill to adopt this view of the moral domain.

It is a commonplace that Kant was concerned to free moral agency from its psychological or "anthropological" determinations. In doing so, he offered us a conception of moral agents as rational beings that abstracts considerably from human and animal nature. It is less of a commonplace that utilitarian theory, in its modern development, tends also to be antithetical to important empirical aspects of human nature. For the Kantian, the empirical demon to be combatted and exorcized lies within the individual. For the utilitarian it is located within society and its customs, including practices that are the sociobiological inheritance of the species. According to an act utilitarian like Singer, reason frees ethical thought from the earlier moralities of kin and reciprocal altruism and opens it to the wider morality of disinterestedness and universal concern: "The principle of impartial consideration of interests . . . alone remains a rational basis for ethics" (Singer 109). The equal pull thesis is thus seen to be entailed by a principle of impartiality, common to Kantian and utilitarian ethics, which is seen as liberating us from the biased dictates of our psychological, biological, and socially conventional natures.[15]

IV. Differential Pull

The doctrine of equal ethical pull is a modern development in the history of ethics. It is certainly not attributable to Aristotle or Aquinas, nor, arguably, to Locke. Kant's authority gave it common currency and made it, so to speak, foundational. It is, therefore, important to state that EP is a dogma. Why should it be assumed that ethical pull is constant regardless of circumstance, familiarity, kinship and other special relations? The accepted answer is that EP makes sense of impartiality. The proponent of the special duties must accept this as a challenge: alternative suggestions for moral ontology must show how impartiality can be consistent with differential ethical forces.

I will refer to the rival thesis as the *thesis of differential pull (DP)*. According to the DP thesis, the ethical pull of a moral patient will always partly depend on how the moral patient is related to the moral agent on whom the pull is exerted. Moreover, the "how" of relatedness will be determined in part by the social practices and institutions in which the agent and patient play their roles. This does not mean that every moral agent will be differently affected, since it may be that different moral agents stand in the same relation to different moral patients. But where the relations differ in certain relevant ways, there the pull will differ. The relevant factors that determine ethical pull are in a broad sense circumstantial, including the particular social arrangements that determine what is expected from the moral agent. How particular circumstances and conventions shape the special duties is a complex question to which we cannot here do justice. We shall, however, approach it from a foundational standpoint that rejects EP and recognizes the crucial role of conventional practice, relationships, and roles in determining the nature and force of moral obligation. The gravitational metaphor may again be suggestive. In DP morality, the community of agents and patients is analogous to a gravitational field where distance counts and forces vary in accordance with local conditions.

V. Filial Duty

Filial duty, unlike the duty to keep a promise, is not self-imposed. But keeping the particular promise one has made is also a special duty, and the interplay of impartiality and specific obligation is more clearly seen in the case of a promise. We do well, therefore, to look at the way special circumstances shape obligations by examining more carefully the case of promise making.

A. I. Melden has gone into the morality of promise keeping rather thoroughly, and I believe that some features of his analysis apply to the more general description of the way particular circumstances determine the degree of ethical pull on a moral agent.[16] Following Locke, Melden assumes the natural right of noninterference with one's liberty to pursue one's interests (including one's interest in the well-being of others) where such pursuit does not interfere with a like liberty for others. Let an interest be called *invasive* if it is an interest in interfering with the pursuit of someone else's interests. Then the right that every moral patient possesses is the right not to be interfered with in the pursuit of his or her noninvasive interests. (In what follows, "interest" will mean noninvasive interest.)

According to Melden, a promiser "gives the promisee the action as his own." The promise-breaking failure to perform is then "tantamount to interfering with or subverting endeavours he [the promisee] has a right to pursue" [Melden 47]. The promisee is "as entitled to [the action] as he is, as a responsible moral agent, entitled to conduct his own affairs." What is special about this analysis is the formal grounding of the special positive duty of promise keeping in the minimalist negative obligation of noninterference. The negative, general, and indiscriminate obligation not to interfere is determined by the practice of promise making as a positive, specific, and discriminate obligation to act. Note how context here shapes and directs the initial obligation of noninterference and enhances its force. Given the conventions of the practice of promise making, the moral patient has novel and legitimate expectations of performances caused by the explicit assurances given by the promiser who, in effect, has made over these performances to the promisee. And given these legitimate expectations, the agent's nonperformance of the promised act is invasive and tantamount to active interference with the patient's rights to its performance.

It is in the spirit of this approach to make the attempt to analyze other special obligations in the same manner. We assume a DP framework and a minimal universal deontological principle (the duty to refrain from interfering in the lives of others). This negative duty is refracted by the parochial situation as a special duty that may be positive in character, calling on the moral agent to act or refrain from acting in specific ways toward specific moral patients. This view of the special obligations needs to be justified. But for the present I merely seek to state it more fully.

The presumption of a special positive obligation arises for a moral agent when two conditions obtain: (1) In a given social arrangement (or practice), there is a specific interaction or transaction between moral agent and patient such as promising and being promised, nurturing and being nurtured, befriending and being befriended. (2) The interaction in that context gives rise to certain conventional expectations (e.g., that a promise will be kept, that a marital partner will be faithful, that a child will respect the parent). In promising, the content of the obligation is verbally explicit. But this feature is not essential to the formation of other specific duties. In the filial situation, the basic relationship is that of nurtured to nurturer, a type of relationship that is very concrete, intimate, and long lasting, and is considered to be more morally determining than any other in shaping a variety of rights and obligations.

Here is one of Alasdair MacIntyre's descriptions of the denizens of the moral domain:

> I am brother, cousin, and grandson, member of this household, that village, this tribe. These are not characteristics that belong to human beings accidentally, to be stripped away in order to discover "the real me."

They are part of my substance, defining partially at least and sometimes wholly my obligations and my duties [McIntyre 32].

MacIntyre's description takes Aristotle's dictum that man is a social animal in a sociological direction. A social animal has a specific social role whose prerogatives and obligations characterize a particular kind of person. Being a father or mother is socially as well as biologically descriptive; it not only defines what one is, it also defines who one is and what one owes.

Because it does violence to a social role, a filial breach is more serious than a breach of promise. In the promise, the performance is legitimately expected, being, as it were, explicitly made over to the promisee as "his." In the filial situation, the expected behavior is implicit and the failure to perform affects the parent in a direct and personal way. To lose one's entitlements diminishes one as a person. Literature abounds with examples of such diminishment; King Lear is perhaps the paradigm. When Lear first becomes aware of Goneril's defection, he asks his companion: "Who am I?" to which the reply is "A shadow." Causing humiliation is a prime reason why filial neglect is tantamount to active interference. One's sense of dignity varies with temperament. But dignity itself—in the context of an institution like the family—is objective, being inseparable from one's status and role in that context.

The filial duties of adult children include such things as being grateful, loyal, attentive, respectful, and deferential to parents (more so than to strangers). Many adult children, of course, are respectful and attentive to their parents out of love, not duty. But, as Melden says: "The fact that normally, there is love and affection that unites the members of the family . . . in no way undercuts the fact that there is a characteristic distribution of rights and obligations within the family circle" [Melden 67].

The mutual understanding created by a promise is simplicity itself when compared with the range of expected behavior that filial respect comprises. What is expected in the case of a promise is clearly specified by the moral agent but with respect to most other special duties there is little that is verbally explicit. Filial obligation is thus essentially underdetermined although there are clear cases of what counts as disrespect—as we have seen in our three cases. The complexity and inspecificity of expected behavior that is written into the domestic arrangements do not affect what the promissory and the filial situation have in common: both may be viewed as particular contexts in which the moral agent must refrain from behavior that interferes with the normal prerogatives of the moral patient.[17]

By taking promising as a starting point in a discussion of special duties, one runs the risk of giving the impression that DP is generally to be understood as a form of social contract theory. But a more balanced perspective considers the acts required by any of the special duties as naturally and implicitly "made over" within the practices and institutions that define the moral agent in his particular role as a "social animal." Within this perspective, promising and other forms of contracting are themselves special cases and not paradigmatic. Indeed, the binding force of the obligation to fulfill an explicit contract is itself to be explained by the general account to be given of special duties in a DP theory.

VI. Grateful Duty

One group of contemporary moral philosophers, whom I shall tendentiously dub *sentimentalists,* has been vocal in pointing out the shortcomings of the mainstream theories in accounting for the morality of the special relations. But they would find my formal and traditional approach equally inadequate. The sentimentalists oppose deontological approaches to the morality of the parent-child relationship, arguing that *duties* of gratitude are paradoxical, that the "owing idiom" distorts the moral ideal of the parent-child relationship that should be characterized by love and mutual respect. For them, each family relationship is unique, its moral character determined by the idiosyncratic ties of its members. Carol Gilligan has recently distinguished between an "ethic of care" and an "ethic of rights."[18] The philosophers I have in mind are objecting to the aridity of the "rights perspective" and are urging moral philosophers to attend to the morality of special relations from a "care perspective." The distinction is suggestive, but the two perspectives are not necessarily exclusive. One may recognize one's duty in what one does spontaneously and generously. And just as a Kantian caricature holds one in greater esteem when one does what is right against one's inclination, so the idea of care, responsibility, and personal commitment, without formal obligation, is an equally dangerous caricature.

Approaches that oppose care and friendship to rights and obligations can be shown to be sadly inadequate when applied to real life cases. The following situation described in this letter to Ann Landers is not atypical:

> Dear Ann Landers:
> We have five children, all overachievers who have studied hard and done well. Two are medical doctors and one is a banker. . . . We are broke from paying off debts for their wedding and their education. . . . We rarely hear from our children. . . . Last week my husband asked our eldest son for some financial help. He was told 'File bankruptcy and move into a small apartment.' Ann, personal feelings are no longer a factor: it is a matter of survival. Is there any law that says our children must help out?[19]

There are laws in some states that would require that these children provide some minimal support for their indigent parents. But not a few contemporary philosophers could be aptly cited by those who would advocate their repeal. A. John Simmons, Jeffrey Blustein, and Michael Slote, for example, doubt that filial duty is to be understood in terms of special moral debts *owed* to parents. Simmons offers "reasons to believe that [the] particular duty meeting conduct [of parents to children] does not generate an obligation of gratitude on the child" [Simmons 182]. And Blustein opposes what he and Jane English call the "owing idiom" for services parents were obligated to perform. "If parents have any right to repayment from their children, it can only be for that which was either above and beyond the call of parental duty, or not required by parental duty at all."[20] (The "overachievers" could not agree more.) Slote finds it "difficult to believe that one has a *duty* to show gratitude for benefits one has not requested" (Slote 320). Jane English characterizes filial duty in terms of the duties one good friend owes another. "After a friendship ends, the duties of friendship end" [English 354, 356].

Taking a sentimentalist view of gratitude, these philosophers are concerned to remove the taint of onerous duty from what should be a spontaneous and free desire to be considerate of one's parents. One may agree with the sentimentalists that there is something morally unsatisfactory in being considerate of one's parents *merely* out of duty. The mistake lies in thinking that duty and inclination are necessarily at odds. Moreover, the *having* of certain feelings and attitudes may be necessary for carrying out one's duty. Persons who lack feeling for their parents may be morally culpable for that very lack. The sentimentalist objection that this amounts to a paradoxical duty to *feel* (grateful, loyal, etc.) ignores the extent to which people are responsible for their characters; to have failed to develop in oneself the capacity to be considerate of others is to have failed morally, if only because many duties simply cannot be carried out by a cold and unfeeling moral agent.[21] Kant himself speaks of "the universal duty which devolves upon man of so ordering his life as to be fit for the performance of all moral duties."[22] And MacIntyre, who is no Kantian, makes the same point when he says, "moral education is an 'education sentimentale' " [MacIntyre 151].

Sentimentalism is not harmlessly false. Its moral perspective on family relationships as spontaneous, voluntary, and duty-free is simply unrealistic. Anthropological observations provide a sounder perspective on filial obligation. Thus Corinne Nydegger warns of the dangers of weakening the formal constraints that ensure obligations are met. "No society, including our own, relies solely on . . . affection, good will and enlightened self-interest."[23] She notes that the aged, in particular, "have a vested interest in the social control of obligations."

It should be noted that the sentimentalist is arguing for a morality that is sensitive to special relations and personal commitment; this is in its own way a critique of EP morality. But sentimentalism ignores the extent to which the "care perspective" is itself dependent on a formal sense of what is fitting and morally proper. The ideal relationship cannot be "duty-free" if only because sentimental ties may come unravelled, often leaving one of the parties at a material disadvantage. Sentimentalism then places in a precarious position those who are not (or no longer) the fortunate beneficiaries of sincere personal commitment. If the EP moralist tends to be implausibly abstract and therefore inattentive to the morality of the special relations, the sentimentalist tends to err on the side of excessive narrowness by neglecting the impersonal "institutional" expectations and norms that qualify all special relations.

VII. DP Morality: Some Qualifications

It might be thought that the difference between EP and DP tends to disappear when either theory is applied to concrete cases, since one must in any case look at the circumstances to determine the practical response. But this is to underestimate how what one *initially* takes to be the responsibility of moral agents to patients affects the procedure one uses in making practical decisions in particular circumstances. Recall again how Peter Singer's EP procedure pits the preferences of the three friends against the preferences of the father and contrast this with a differential pull approach that assumes discriminate and focused obligations to the father. Similarly, the adult children of the graduating elders and the children raised by Miss Tate gave no special weight to filial obligation in planning their day's activities.

There are, then, significant practical differences between a DP and an EP approach to concrete cases. The EP moralist is a respecter of the person whom he sees as an autonomous individual but no respecter of the person as a social animal within its parochial preserve. Moreover, a DP theory that grounds duty in the minimal principle of noninterference is sensitive to the distinction between strict duty and benevolence. Behaving as one is duty-bound to behave is not the whole of moral life. But duty (in the narrow sense) and benevolence are not commensurate. If I am right, the Anaheim woman is culpably disrespectful. But it would be absurd if (in the manner of Mrs. Jellyby) she were to try to compensate for excluding her father by inviting several indigent gentlemen to dine in his stead.

I am arguing for a DP approach to the morality of the special relations. Williams, Nozick, MacIntyre, and others criticize utilitarianism and Kantianism for implausible consequences in this area. I believe that their objections to much of contemporary ethics to be symptomatic of a growing discontent with the EP character of the current theories. It may be possible to revise the theories to avoid some of the implausible consequences. Rule utilitarianism seems to be a move in this direction. But, as they stand, their EP character leaves them open to criticism. EP is a dogma. But so is DP. My contention is that DP moral theories more plausibly account for our preanalytic moral judgments concerning what is right and wrong in a wide variety of real cases. Having said this, I will acknowledge that the proper antidote to the malaise Williams and others are pointing to will not be effectively available until DP moral theories are given a theoretical foundation as well worked out as those of the mainstream theories. Alsadair MacIntyre is a contemporary DP moralist who has perhaps gone farthest in this direction. Nozick and Williams are at least cognizant that a "particularistic" approach is needed.[24]

The DP moral theory is in any case better able to account for the discriminate duties that correspond to specific social roles and expectations. But of course not all duties are discriminate: there are requirements that devolve on everyone. This not only includes the negative requirement to refrain from harming one's fellowman, but also, in certain circumstances, to help him when one is singularly situated to do so. I am, for example, expected to help a lost child find its parent or to feed a starving stranger at my doorstep. Failure to do so violates an understanding that characterizes the loosest social ties binding us as fellow human beings. The "solitariness" that Hobbes speaks of is a myth; we are never in a totally unrelated "state of nature." The DP moralist recognizes degrees of relatedness and graded expectations. The most general types of positive behavior expected of anyone as a moral agent obey some minimal principle of Good Samaritanism applicable to "the stranger in thy midst."

Perhaps the most serious difficulty facing the DP approach is that it appears to leave the door widely open to ethical relativism. We turn now to this problem.

VIII. DP and Ethical Relativism

A theory is nonrelativistic if it has the resources to pass moral judgments on whole societies. My version of DP moral theory avoids ethical relativism by adopting a deontological principle (noninterference) that may be deployed in assessing and criticizing the moral legitimacy of the traditional arrangements within which purportedly moral interactions take place. We distinguish between unjust and merely imperfect arrangements. Arrangements that are essentially invasive are unjust and do not confer moral legitimacy on what is expected of those who are party to them. To correct the abuses of an unjust institution like slavery or a practice like suttee is to destroy the institution or practice. By contrast, an institution like marriage or the family will often contain some unjust features, but these are usually corrigible, and the institution itself is legitimate and morally determining in a straightforward sense.

In any case the DP moralist is in a position to hold that not all social arrangements impose moral imperatives. It is not clear to me that DP can avoid relativism without *some* deontological minimal ground. But conceivably a principle other than noninterference might better serve as universal ground of the special duties. What is essential to any deontologically grounded DP morality is the recognition that the universal deontological principle is differentiated and specified by local arrangements that determine what is legitimately expected of the moral agent.

It may now be clear in what sense I believe DP theories to be plausible. A moral theory is plausible to the extent that it accounts for our pretheoretical moral judgments. Such intuitive judgments are admittedly idiosyncratic and prejudicial, being conditioned by our upbringing and the traditions we live by. The EP moralist nobly courts implausibility by jettisoning prejudice and confronting moral decisions anew. By contrast, the DP moralist jettisons only those prejudices that are exposed as rooted in and conditioned by an unjust social arrangement. But for those institutions that are not unjust, our commonsense judgments of "what is expected" (from parents, from citizens, from adult children) are generally held to be reliable guides to the moral facts of life.

The version of DP that I favor accepts the Enlightenment doctrine of natural rights in the minimal form of a universal right to noninterference and the correlative duty of moral agents to respect that right. MacIntyre's version of DP is hostile to Enlightenment "modernism," abjuring all talk of universal rights or deontic principles of a universal character. It is in this sense more classical. An adequate version of DP must nevertheless avoid the kind of ethical relativism that affords the moral philosopher no way to reject some social arrangements as immoral. MacIntyre appears to suggest that this can be achieved by accepting certain teleological constraints on good societies. Pending more detail, I am not convinced that a teleological approach can, by itself, do the critical job that needs to be done if we are to avoid an unacceptable ethical relativism. But other nondeontic approaches are possible. David Wong has argued for a Confucian condition of adequacy that grades societies as better or worse depending on how well they foster human flourishing.[25] My own deontic approach is not opposed to teleological or Confucianist ways of judging the acceptability of social arrangements. If a given arrangement is degenerate, then that is in itself a good reason to discount its norms as morally binding. But conceivably even a flourishing society could be unjust; nevertheless its civic norms should count as morally vacuous and illegitimate. It seems to me, therefore, that MacIntyre's version of DP morality probably goes too far in its rejection of all liberal deontic principles.

I have argued that DP best explains what we intuitively accept as our moral obligations to parents and other persons that stand to us in special relations. And though my version of DP allows for criticizing unjust social arrangements, it may still seem unacceptably relativistic. For does it not allow that what is right for a daughter or son in one society is wrong for them in another? And does this not run afoul of the condition that what is right and wrong must be so universally? It should, I think, be ackowledged that the conservatism that is a feature of the doctrine of differential pull is somewhat hospitable to ethical relativism. Put another way: differential pull makes sense of ethical relativism's large grain of truth, but it does so without losing claim to its ability to evaluate morally the norms of different societies and institutions. Institutions that allow or encourage interference with noninvasive interests are unjust, and we have noted that the adherent of differential pull is in as good a position to apply a universal principle in evaluating an institution as anyone of an EP persuasion. But application of DP will rule out some institutions while allowing *diverse* others to count as legitimate and just. Only a just institution can assign and shape a moral obligation for those who play their roles within it. However, there are many varieties of just institutions, and so, in particular, are there many ways in which filial obligations are determined within different social and cultural contexts. What counts as filial respect in one context may not count as filial respect in another context. It is a virtue of our account that it not only tolerates but shows the way to justify different moral norms.

IX. Common Sense

The sociologist Edward Shils warns about the consequences of the modern hostility to tradition in ways reminiscent of ecologists warning us about tampering with delicate natural systems that have taken millenia to evolve.[26] The EP character of much of modern philosophy encourages a hasty style of playing fast and loose with practices and institutions that define the traditional ties binding the members of a family or community. And a duty-free sentimentalism is no kinder to traditional mores.

The appeal to common sense is often a way of paying proper attention to the way that particular circumstance and social practice enter into the shaping of obligations. This, to my mind, is Sidgwick's peculiar and saving grace. But many a moral philosopher lacks Sidgwick's firm appreciation of the role of accepted practice or common sense. I shall illustrate this by way of a final example.

Richard Wasserstrom, in "Is Adultery Immoral?,"[27] raises the question of whether the (alleged) obligation not to commit adultery might be explained by reasons that would apply to any two persons generally. It is, for example, wrong for any person to deceive another. And he discusses the destructive effects adultery has on the love that the marital partners bear to one another. What is missing from Wasserstrom's account is any hint that the obligations of marriage are shaped by the institution as it exists and that being "faithful" is a legitimate institutional expectation informing the way the partners may treat each other. Wasserstrom does say that "we ought to have reasons for believing that marriage is a morally desirable and just social institution" (300). But what follows if it is? Wasserstrom does not say. What we want here is an account of how and why a married person who commits adultery may be wronging the partner. How, in particular, might an act of adultery be construed as unwarranted interference? The shift from the examination of an obligation that has its locus and form within a given institution to evaluating the institution itself is legitimate; but it is all too often a way of avoiding the more concrete and immediate investigation that is the bread and butter of normative ethics.

EP is ethics without ethos. So too is sentimentalism. Both have a disintegrative effect on tradition. Where EP and sentimentalism sit in judgment on ethos, DP respects it and seeks to rationalize it. The EP moralist is reformist in spirit, tending to look upon traditional arrangements as obstacles to social justice. John Rawls, for example, is led to wonder whether the family is ethically justifiable.

> It seems that even when fair opportunity (as it has been defined) is satisfied, the family will lead to unequal chances between individuals. Is the family to be abolished then? Taken by itself and given a certain primacy, the idea of equal opportunity inclines in this direction. But within the context of the theory of justice as a whole, there is less urgency to take this course.[28]

Not urgent perhaps, but not unreasonable either. A defender of filial morality cannot with equanimity entertain the idea of abolishing the family. Here Sidgwick is the welcome antidote. For him the suggestion that ethical principles might require the elimination of something so central to "established morality" betrays a misconception of the job of ethics. Instead, Sidgwick demands of philosophers that they "repudiate altogether that temper of rebellion . . . into which the reflective mind is always apt to fall when it is first convinced that the established rules are not intrinsically reasonable."[29]

Reporting on how he arrived at his way of doing moral philosophy, Sidgwick tells of his rereading of Aristotle:

> [A] light seemed to dawn upon me as to the meaning and drift of [Aristotle's] procedure. . . . What he gave us there was the common sense morality of Greece, reduced to consistency by careful comparison: given not as something external to him but as what "we"—he and others—think, ascertained by reflection . . . might I not imitate this: do the same for *our* morality here and now, in the same manner of impartial reflection on current opinion? [Sidgwick XX]

Notes

1. Henry Sidgwick, *The Method of Ethics* (New York: Dover Publications, 1966), p. 243.
2. A. John Simmons, *Moral Principles and Political Obligations* (Princeton: Princeton University Press, 1979), p. 162.
3. Michael Slote, "Obedience and Illusion," in *Having Children*, eds. Onora O'Neill and William Ruddick (New York: Oxford University Press, 1979), pp. 319–25.
4. Jeffrey Blustein, *Parents and Children: The Ethics of the Family* (Oxford: Oxford University Press, 1982).
5. Jane English, "What Do Grown Children Owe Their Parents?," in *Having Children*, eds. Onora O'Neill and William Ruddick (New York: Oxford University Press, 1979), pp. 351–56.
6. Barbara Meyerhoff, *Number Our Days* (New York: Simon and Schuster, 1978), pp. 87, 104.
7. Aquinas, *Summa Theologiae*, Vol. 34, trans. R. J. Batten, O.P. (New York: Blackfriars, 1975), 2a2ae.
8. John Locke, *Two Treatises of Government*, ed. P. Laslett (New York: New American Library, 1965), Treatise 1, sec. 100.
9. David Hume, A *Treatise on Human Nature*, Bk. 111, p. 1, Sec. 1.
10. Peter Singer, *The Expanding Circle: Ethics and Sociobiology* (New York: Farrar, Straus and Giroux, 1981), p. 101.
11. Bernard Williams, "Persons, Character and Morality," in *Moral Luck* (Cambridge: Harvard University), p. 2.
12. New York: New American Library, 1964, p. 52.
13. G. J. Warnock, *The Object of Morality* (London: Methuen and Company, 1971), p. 152.
14. Robert Nozick, *Philosophical Explanations* (Cambridge: Harvard University Press, 1981), p. 451.
15. See Alasdair MacIntyre, *After Virtue* (Notre Dame: University of Notre Dame Press, 1981). When one contrasts this modern approach to morality with classical approaches that give full play to the social and biological natures of moral agents in determining the range of moral behavior, one may come to see the history of ethics in terms of a MacIntyrean Fall; MacIntyre speaks of the "crucial moral opposition between liberal individualism in some version or other and the Aristotelian tradition in some version or other" (p. 241). For MacIntyre, the Enlightenment is a new Dark Age both because of its abstract conception of the autonomous individual and because of the neglect of parochial contexts in determining the special obligations that were once naturally understood in terms of social roles.

16. A. I. Melden, *Rights and Persons* (Los Angeles: University of California Press, 1977).

17. Our account of the special moral relations is concentrating on the way the universal duty to refrain from invasive interference is refracted through circumstance into a variety of positive and discriminate duties. But a particular arrangement may produce the opposite effect: it may quality the universal obligation to refrain from invasive interference by allowing the moral agent liberties normally forbidden. A fair amount of invasive behavior is the norm in certain private and voluntary arrangements where there is an understanding that exceptional demands may be made. My particular concern with the positive (filial) obligations has led me to confine discussion to the way context obligates moral agents to perform and not with how or to what extent it may license them.

18. Carol Gilligan, *In a Different Voice* (Cambridge: Harvard University Press, 1983).

19. *The Boston Globe*, Thursday, March 21, 1985.

20. Blustein, p. 182. According to Blustein, parents who are financially able are *obligated* to provide educational opportunities for children who are able to benefit from them.

21. See Marcia Baron, "The Alleged Moral Repugnance of Acting from Duty," *The Journal of Philosophy*, Vol. 81, 4 (April, 1984), especially pp. 204–5. She speaks of "the importance of the attitudes and dispositions one has when one performs certain acts, especially those which are intended to express affection or concern" and suggests that these attitudes constitute "certain parameters within which satisfactory ways of acting from duty must be located."

22. Immanuel Kant, "Proper Self-Respect," from *Lectures on Ethics*, trans. Louis Enfield (New York: Harper & Row, 1963).

23. Corinne Nydegger, "Family Ties of the Aged in Cross-Cultural Perspective," *The Gerontologist*, vol. 23, no. 1, 1983.

24. Unfortunately, Nozick's particularlism is "sentimentalist": "Some [philosophers] countenance particularism on one level by deriving it from 'universalistic' principles that hold at some deeper level. This misconstrues the moral weight of particularistic ties it seems to me; it is a worthwhile task, one I cannot undertake explicitly here, to investigate the nature of a more consistently particularistic theory—particularistic all the way down the line." From *Philosophical Explanations* (Cambridge University Press, 1981), pp. 456–57. The particularistic ties Nozick has in mind are not objectively institutional but subjectively interpersonal ("valuing the particularity of the other").

25. David Wong, *Moral Relativity* (Berkeley: University of California Press, 1984).

26. Edward Shils, *Tradition* (Chicago: University of Chicago Press, 1981).

27. Richard Wasserstrom, "Is Adultery Immoral?" in *Today's Moral Problems*, ed. Richard Wasserstrom, pp. 288–300. Michael Tooley's arguments for the moral legitimacy of infanticide provide another example of the consequences of uninhibited EP zeal. See his book *Abortion and Infanticide*, (New York: Oxford University Press, 1984), and my critical review "Tooley's Immodest Proposal," *Hastings Center Report*, vol. 15, no. 5, 1985.

28. John Rawls, A *Theory of Justice*, (Cambridge: Harvard University Press) p. 511.

29. Sidgwick, p. 475. C. D. Broad especially cautions utilitarian readers of Sidgwick to take this side of him seriously. "When all relevant facts are taken into consideration it will scarcely ever be right for the utilitarian to break the rules of morality commonly accepted in his society." See C. D. Broad, *Five Types of Ethical Theory*, (New York: Humanities Press, 1951), p. 157.

PART III

Aspects of Moral Deliberation

A. *Taking Women's Experience Seriously*

Moral Passages

KATHRYN PYNE ADDELSON

Summary

Kathryn Pyne Addelson argues that Gilligan's approach to the problem of women and morality faces a difficulty also common to most philosophical models of moral theory—it fails to take account of the process by which moral explanations come to be made. Moral explanations are socially constructed, created through our interactions with others. This claim is illustrated by an analysis of sociological studies of unwed mothers in three different institutional settings: traditional maternity homes populated by middle-class white girls who were keeping their "mistake" a secret; a private institution in which middle-class white girls were offered a more psychotherapeutic setting; and an inner-city center for black, unwed mothers. In each of these settings, the girls' self-perceptions and moral explanations of their behavior changed over time. These explanations were influenced by their gender, class, and race, and by their interactions with the authority figures from their communities and the institution.

Given the complexity of the process of the construction of moral explanations, it seems inadequate simply to approach the problem of women and morality using either classical or revisionist philosophical theories. Instead, Addelson offers an account that draws upon the sociological discipline of symbolic interactionism and its concept of a "career." This allows for an understanding of moral decision-making as a moral passage, in which our own moral passages are but a few within a greater network of passages. S.M.

If we want to know about women and moral theory, in a way that isn't simply concerned with technical academic constructions, we have to be concerned with the question, "What is morality?" One of the deans of philosophical ethics in the United States, William Frankena, once said that answering that question was the philosopher's work in ethics.

> Contemporary moral philosophy may . . . be represented as primarily an attempt to understand what morality is, meaning by "morality" not the quality of conduct which is opposed to immorality but what Butler so nicely refers to as "the moral institution of life." The current endeavor is not to promote certain moral goals or principles, or to clarify only such words as "right" and "ought," but rather to grasp the nature of morality itself, as compared with law, religion or science. In this endeavor both Continental and English-speaking philosophers are engaged, though to different degrees, in different ways, and with different equipment. [Frankena 1963:1–2)

There is a certain ambiguity to the phrase, "the moral institution of life." There are, on the one hand, the philosophers' definitions and analyses of the moral institution. There is, on the other hand, the living human life that constitutes "the moral institution." Frankena, and other philosophers, write as if separating morality from law, religion, or science were a conceptual, not a political and social (and perhaps even moral) matter. As if one could understand the moral institution of life without being thoroughly enmeshed in helping to create or legitimate that institution. As if one had no need to see whether one's analysis respected the living human life.

In this chapter, I offer a different approach to understanding the moral institution of life by asking how morality itself emerges out of people's interactions. My approach is based on work in the sociological tradition called symbolic interactionism that allows us to find out about the place of authorities, like Frankena, in legitimating certain definitions of morality. In the end, it allows us to question fundamental models of moral explanation and action that have been widely assumed by traditional analysts as well as many of their feminist critics. Under these models, the analyst "grasps the nature of morality itself" by defining or uncovering categories of moral explanation—whether that explanation is in terms of principles justifying acts, or of characters or responsibility, or of some end like happiness or the good life. The analysts then assume that these general moral categories are (or ought to be) used by individuals in making their moral choices or in explaining their own and others' moral activities and lives. Sometimes the analysts offer the categories as ones to be autonomously chosen, sometimes they claim to be describing the categories people in fact use. The approach I take indicates that moral explanation (and the categories of explanation) are constructed in social interactions, and that when we examine those interactions, we find that systematic social and political relations are created and maintained in the process of the construction. The consequence is that we cannot properly understand problems of women and moral theory if we use the usual approaches. I'll begin making my case by taking up the moral problem of abortion.

The "classical" philosophical analysis of the moral problem of abortion is to treat it as a conflict of rights: the fetal right to life in conflict with the woman's right to decide what happens in and to her own body. (See, for example, articles in Pearsall 1986). If one decides that fetuses are not persons, morally speaking, then abortion becomes a practical decision, not a moral one. (See Smetana 1983; Sumner 1981.)

The "classical" analysis distinguishes two contexts in which the moral problem of abortion may arise: the primary context is the "personal" one in which people make their choices and justify actual abortions of fetuses. The secondary context is that of justifying public policy on abortion, understood as policy for regulating activities in the primary context. (Sumner 1981)

Although there are still many philosophers who take a conflict of rights approach, changes and challenges in philosophical ethics itself—as well as the politics of abortion—have brought criticisms. (Hauerwas 1983, Pearsall 1986) Two of the most interesting criticisms have been raised by Stanley Hauerwas and Beverly Harrison.

Hauerwas has argued strongly that "Christians" opposing abortion cannot properly represent *their* positions in the terms in which philosophers have set the moral problem of abortion. He says,

> When the issue is limited to the determination of when human life does nor does not begin, we cannot prevail, given the moral presuppositions of our culture. Put more forcefully, where the debate is limited to the issue of when human life begins, it has already been uncritically shaped by the political considerations of our culture. The "moral" has already been determined by the "political"—something we fail to notice in the measure that we simply presume the moral presuppositions of our culture to be valid. [Hauerwas 1980:327]

Hauerwas insists that Christian respect for life is a statement not about life but about God. Life is not ours to take. Furthermore, our place here on earth is to take part in the unfolding of the great Christian drama. Having children is one of the important ways we take part in God's great adventure. (Hauerwas 1980, 1983)

The "classic" philosophical analysis separates theories of the good (which concern morally good lives, among other things) from theories about obligation, rights, and what is morally right or wrong. Hauerwas's argument is that the "classic" analysis of abortion as a conflict of rights in fact *presupposes* a definition of the good life, one that is at odds with the Christian one he accepts. Hauerwas himself offers a very interesting alternative moral theory in terms of narratives; but what is important for my purposes here is that there is a difference not only in ideas of what constitutes a good life but also over what constitutes a moral problem. Taking part in the unfolding of the great Christian drama means (among other things) that sex and marriage and the *having* of children are moral matters that cannot be separated from the moral problem of abortion. The conflict of rights analysis rules them out, sometimes implicitly, sometimes explicitly.

Beverly Harrison takes a feminist standpoint. She says that the conflict of rights analysis does not take women seriously as moral agents. (Harrison

1984) One major reason is that the "classic" philosophical approach takes abortion as a "discrete deed" to be decided on in abstraction from the circumstances in which women make their procreative choices. In doing this, the analysis presupposes the existing social order—something Hauerwas describes as a "conservative thrust." (Hauerwas 1977, p. 19) Harrison insists that women must work to change the circumstances in which they make reproductive choices so that all children may be cared for. Women must make social changes so that they will be able to choose to have children, not merely not to have them. On the one hand, Harrison is taking seriously the situations in which individual women make their procreative choices. She is saying that procreation must be considered as part of the good life of women, children, and the community as a whole. On the other hand, she is saying that the moral problem of abortion cannot be gerrymandered out of the larger question of procreation. Women do not simply decide to abort or not to abort. Harrison is saying that we should see women's moral choice as making, at every moment, the choice to go on with the pregnancy, and after it, at every moment to rear the child. That is what procreative choice is about.[2]

Harrison is not the only feminist who has said that the standard analysis in terms of a conflict of rights will not do for women. Philosopher Caroline Whitbeck argued for a new moral theory on those grounds. (Whitbeck 1982)

One of the striking things about the philosophical debate on the ethics of abortion is how few women enter it. I believe that the relatively small number of women who enter the discussion is a result, as well as a cause, of the way in which the subject is demarcated, and the way in which it is conceptualized. Given the way in which the issue is presently framed, it is difficult for many women to find any position for which they wish to argue. I shall argue, first, that abortion is actually a fragment of several other moral issues surrounding pregnancy and childbirth so that the moral situation can be adequately understood only if this larger context is considered, and second, that the choice of the terms in which the analysis is generally carried out is mistaken. In particular, I shall argue that neglect of matters that cannot be adequately expressed in terms of "rights" and the employment of an atomistic model of people (a model that represents moral relationships as incidental to being a person) confuses many moral issues, but especially those concerning pregnancy, childbirth, and infant care. (Whitbeck, 1982, p. 247) Whitbeck argues that philosophers and other experts have neglected interpretations of the human condition from women's perspective.

Whitbeck explicitly offers an alternative ethics of responsibility. Harrison's discussion also seems to point toward an ethics of responsibility—one in which women take responsibility for the circumstances within which they make procreative choices. Both accept a rights analysis, but modified, and put in its proper place. This is also Carol Gilligan's strategy, although she bases her position on claims that she has empirically uncovered the new moral voice of responsibility and care.

Gilligan's work took off from anomalies she discerned in Lawrence Kohlberg's widely used theory of moral development. Kohlberg incorporated a technical, philosophical ethics (of the rights and obligations sort) into a basically Piagetian model of moral development.

Carol Gilligan was concerned that the style of moral explanation Kohlberg favored and the scoring method he used did not do justice (so to speak) to the moral thinking of women students and women subjects. In her now well-known abortion study (Gilligan 1977), she dropped the hypothetical dilemma approach and interviewed women about their own abortion experiences, recorded their explanations, then developed both moral categories and a scoring manual out of the interview material. She claims that her subjects think in terms of care and responsibility rather than justice and obligation, and a "psychologic logic of relationships" rather than the abstract logic suited to deriving decisions from principles or to solving hypothetical dilemmas.[3] Both women and men use the care-responsibility orientation, but women tend to use it more. Both men and women use the justice-obligation orientation, but men tend to use it more. In this volume, she speaks of a gestalt switch—the same relationships seen from two different orientations.

Although Gilligan's analysis doesn't accommodate Hauerwas's objections, it does seem to give an empirical grounding to the feminist approaches offered by Harrison and Whitbeck. It does, that is, if we suppose that accommodating moral explanations reported by individual women can alter accounts of the moral institution of life so that gender bias is overcome and women are taken seriously. But to suppose that is to give the game away. The reason isn't that women might be forgetful or self-deceptive in their reports, or that there is a white, middle-class bias, and that other women might explain things differently (though both of those factors are present). The reason is that the women's very explanations have been constructed as a part of a process of interaction which itself brings into existence gender, age, class, and race relations. The explanations which Gilligan uncovers cannot give us a fair and nonsexist account of the moral institution of life because those explanations themselves are products of processes by which gender, age, class, race, and other systematic, social-political relations are created and maintained. It is that process that must be examined if we are even to begin to understand the moral institution of life. As C. Wright Mills once said, the explanations people offer are themselves in need of explanation. (Mills 1963)

I shall argue these claims on the basis of sociological field studies. But serious objections can also be made (in a negative way) in terms of shortcomings of the general models which are presupposed. Two main objections are to the accounts of individual decision, choice, or action and to the accounts of how individual moral explanation is social.

So far as the individual goes, both the classic analysis and many of the revisionist ones are voluntaristic, in the sense that the person comes to the situation with a grasp of moral explanations and uses them as "guides" to action. In the paradigm case of explicit moral reasoning, one weighs principles then makes the moral decision. Or one ponders responsibilities and relationships, then chooses. In "nonparadigm cases" the thinking need not be explicit, and on other voluntarist accounts, one merely reads the situation and acts out of virtue or habit. There would not be a major objection to such voluntarism if we had some explanation of how it works, materially, in the moral institution of life. As I'll say in the conclusion to this chapter, we have none.[4]

Nearly all of the accounts, from "classical" to feminist, also presuppose that moral explanation by individuals is social in this sense: there are categories, principles, narratives, paradigm cases, language games, or other devices that are (or ought to be) shared among some group of people (or all humanity); individual members explain their moral activities in those group terms. In this light, Gilligan corrected Kohlberg's overgeneralization of the rights-obligations ethics by showing that there are two different kinds of moral explanations used by members of humanity. But this is a sociologically mistaken view of the relationship of individual to "group culture." It is a mistaken view of the relationship of individual to the moral institution of life. Let me begin by offering a more appropriate sociological account.

The sociological tradition I shall rely upon is called symbolic interactionism. The tradition began its development early in the century, at the University of Chicago; its practitioners now are widely dispersed. My own work has been with Howard Becker, and theoretically, I rely particularly on writings by his teachers, Herbert Blumer and Everett Hughes.[5] The tradition is marked by using methods of participant observation to do small group studies.

One basic premiss, which Blumer articulates well, is that any human social world consists of the actions and experiences of the people who make it up. Furthermore, the nature of both the social and the natural environment, and the objects composing them, is set by the meanings they have for those people. (Blumer 1969, pp. 11, 35) This sort of claim has become common enough in recent years, but it would be a mistake to make a leap to saying that the meanings are given in terms of the group rules or language games (as Winch and other Wittgensteinians do), or that they are given in terms of institutionalized norms that are interiorized through socialization (as even social constructionalists like Berger and Luckmann do). (Winch 1958; Berger 1966) The interactionist approach is to study actual processes of interaction by which the meanings are constructed: it is the social process in group life that creates and upholds the rules, not the rules that create and uphold group life. (Blumer 1969, p. 19). These social processes are studied by participant observation of small groups. They include processes that will aid in understanding the moral institution of life.

To investigate the processes involved in moral explanation, we need a perspicuous working notion. I shall use the notion of a moral passage. As I use it, it is derivative on the notion of a career, which is widely used in interactionist studies.[6]

A career covers both an individual's movement through an activity (in biographical terms) and the general pattern followed by any person going through "that sort of thing." The pattern is displayed in the movements from one *step* to another—so that a career is a pattern of steps. Howard Becker explains the steps in terms of career contingencies—continuing in the career is contingent on moving to the next in the series of steps. (Becker 1973, p. 24). The steps are uncovered by field investigation and they need not match the steps subjects take to be definitive. Nor do they explain psychological or moral differences among the people who finish the career and those who do not. The steps are contingencies in the sense that what people who make the passage have in common is that they pass through those steps.

To study abortion, we might begin by doing field studies of some women's passages through abortion—as Mary K. Zimmerman did (Zimmerman 1977). However, to make proper sense of Harrison's, Whitbeck's, and Hauwerwas's observations, those abortion passages would have to be placed in a larger network of passages suitable for field studies. That large network would accommodate Harrisons wide-ranging "procreative choice" and Whitbeck's "larger context," as well as Hauerwas's concern with sex, marriage, and the *having* of children. What we need is a schema that can serve as an hypothesis or theoretical guide for other, related field studies, or a schema that would (when empirically filled out) give us a pattern of social options that exist or that can be created, of which the passage through abortion is one. But how is such a schema to be constructed?

In this chapter, I shall use work by sociologist Prudence Rains to shed light on the moral institution of life. Rains herself did several field studies in the late 1960s, which she reported and discussed in her book, *Becoming an Unwed Mother.* They included studies of mainly white and middle-class young women at a home for unwed mothers and of black, mainly poor teenagers at a day school for unwed mothers. Rains opens the book with this statement.

> Becoming an unwed mother is the outcome of a particular sequence of events that begins with forays into intimacy and sexuality, results in pregnancy, and terminates in the birth of an illegitimate child. Many girls do not have sexual relations before marriage. Many who do, do not get pregnant. And most girls who get pregnant while unmarried do not end up as unwed mothers. Girls who become unwed mothers, in this sense, share a common career that consists of the steps by which they came to be unwed mothers rather than brides, the clients of abortionists, contraceptively prepared lovers, or virtuous young ladies. [Rains 1971, p. 1]

Rains studied one line of passage in this network of passages in the seas of young womanhood: becoming an unwed mother. Fieldworkers must limit themselves. But her understanding of the place of unwed motherhood in a larger network of passages gives us a way to make a schema of social options.

Figure 5.1 represents Rains's remarks. Rains herself names the common starting point, "the situation of moral jeopardy." The starting point is important and problematic. (See Addelson, n.d.)

The schema in figure 5.1 represents patterns of moral passages in the late 1960s, when Rains did her studies. There are branching paths to abortion

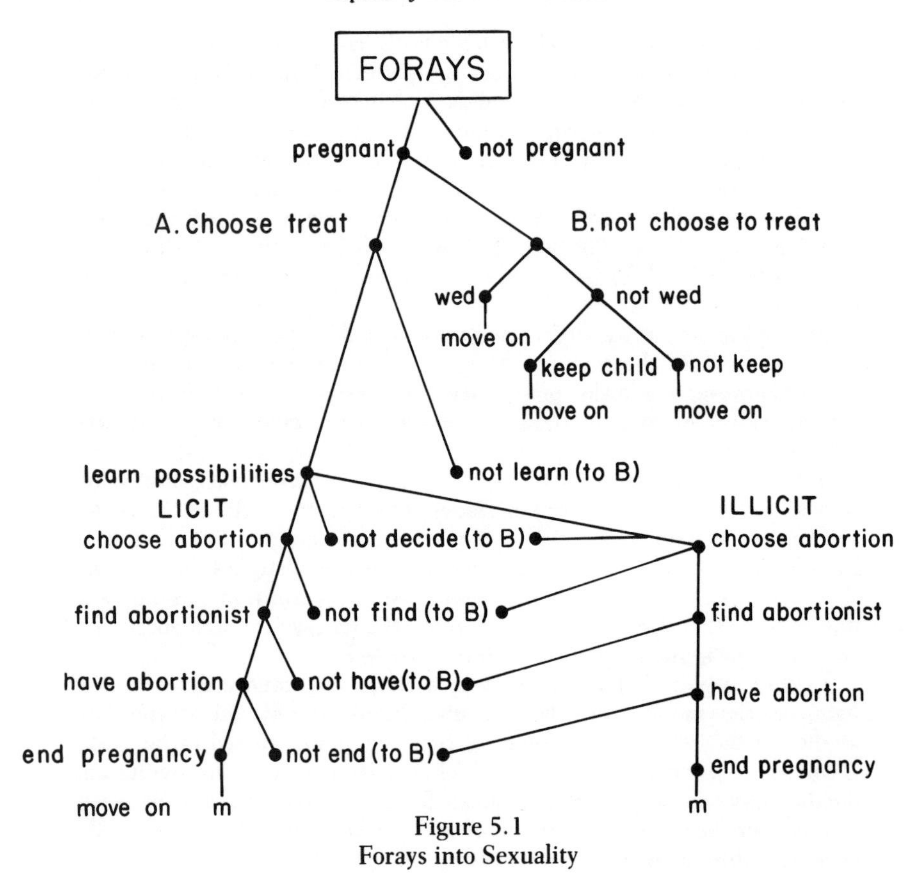

Figure 5.1
Forays into Sexuality

because restrictive abortion laws made abortion illicit in all but a few circumstances (or places). The figure operates as a guide to further empirical study. It is not a decision-making tree, nor does it define social options. But it does offer a theoretical aid to Harrison's and Whitbeck's discussions. Both women insist that we take women's circumstances seriously. Figure 5.1, as a guide to empirical study, offers a systematic way to discover what "women's circumstances" amount to in given times and places. In analogous ways, I believe, this sort of schema offers a necessary aid to any responsibility ethics, and to Hauerwas's account of "God's great adventure" as well.

The figure allows me to make a methodological distinction that is important. The terms "pregnant," "abortion," and "unwed motherhood," and others appear on the chart. Now Rains's subjects were involved in pregnancy, and some thought about abortion and other possible passages. The young women (and those around them) used the words "pregnancy" and "abortion" as *folk terms*. Folk terms are used by people in organizing their social interactions, and they carry with them assumptions about what activities are involved, what cast of characters is important, what courses might be followed. They offer guides as to what to expect.

The notion of a moral passage is a construct to be used by the scholarly investigator, not the "folk" who are being studied. The scholarly investigators use what Herbert Blumer calls *sensitizing concepts*. Blumer contrasts sensitizing concepts with definitive concepts—the sort philosophers usually concern themselves with. Definitive concepts refer to a class of objects, and they carry with them criteria or "benchmarks" by which one can tell whether something belongs to the class or not. Sensitizing concepts are not designed to offer such criteria but to offer guidance in approaching empirical instances.

Blumer goes on to say that even if definitive concepts were possible to construct in sociology, they would not be proper for sociologists to use in describing the human social world. Definitive concepts give what is common to the instances. With sensitizing concepts, "we seem forced to reach what is common by accepting and using what is distinctive to the given empirical instance." (Blumer, 1969, p. 152) This, he says, is due not to the immaturity of the discipline of sociology but to the nature of the empirical world that is its object of study.

In a certain way, Blumer takes meaning to be use—not use by the subject population but use by the sensitized researcher. He says that by taking concepts as sensitizing, his line of approach

> seeks to improve concepts by naturalistic research, that is, by direct study of our natural social world wherein empirical instances are accepted in their concrete and distinctive form. It depends on faithful reportorial depiction of the instances and on analytical probing into their character. As such its procedure is markedly different from that employed in the effort to develop definitive concepts. Its success depends on patient, careful and imaginative life study, not on quick shortcuts or technical instruments. While its progress may be slow and tedious, it has the virtue of remaining in close and continuing relations with the natural social world. [Blumer 1969, p. 152]

This is a statement of sociological theory as well as of sociological field method.

In my theoretical reconstruction of Rains' work, I would say that as a field researcher, she herself uses "unwed mother," and "pregnant" as sensitizing concepts—though she does not speak in these terms, nor does she distinguish her use from her subjects' use of those terms. However her studies show how the meanings of "pregnant" and "unwed mother" come to be constructed as folk terms among her subjects, and so it is theoretically necessary to take her to be using sensitizing concepts. In this light, I should remind readers that *who* gets pregnant is more a social than a biological question. (See Luker 1977; Harrison 1984.)

To write *Becoming an Unwed Mother*, Prudence Rains did three field studies. Two were the extended studies that form the core of the book. These are the study at "Hawthorne House," the home run by social workers for mostly white, middle-class young women; and the study at "The Project," a day school for pregnant, black, young women. In addition to these two, Rains briefly studied a traditional maternity home, which she called "Kelman Place." The restrictions on her data gathering there were severe because of secrecy requirements at the home, and she ultimately used the study only to contrast traditional homes with the situations at Hawthorn House and the Project.[7]

Rains's view is that illicit pregnancy is "the incidental product of the way sexual activity is *normally* organized among unmarried girls in this society. (Rains 1971, p. 4) She names the common situation out of which unwed mothers begin their careers, "The Situation of Moral Jeopardy." (See Figure 5.1) Somehow, in passing from childhood to womanhood, a girl must learn how to become the kind of woman she would be.[8] The learning takes place on many fronts, but girls (and boys) must come to change their early, childish ways to ways suitable to the adult world—and given our society, that means finding a place in a heterosexual world, though not necessarily as a heterosexual. In the process, the girl begins (with others) to construct her place as a woman in the adult world—a construction that includes her understanding of both self and world, as well as other people's understanding of her. These things are not simple opinions or beliefs for they exist in interactions, in the activities and doings that make up her life. Rains says that a central moral experience for the young women she studied is the ambivalence they feel when they find themselves acting in ways they only recently, as children, disapproved.

Rains says, "The central feature of these girls' moral careers as unwed mothers is the experience of coming to realign themselves with the conventional, respectable world; the central theme of this book has to do with the ways in which the maternity homes sponsor and organize this experience of moral realignment." (Rains 19781, p. 34)

Becoming pregnant was a blatant way of going public about things customarily hidden in the journey from childhood to adulthood (and hidden in adulthood as well). For the young men involved, it was usually relatively easy to restrict the range of the publicity. For a young woman, it required major, institutionalized methods to deal with the publicity. And it had to be dealt with because of what would be jeopardized by going public in an unrestricted way. The passages of Rains's unwed mothers show how managing the publicity was essential not only to the girls' futures but to the social organization of morality as well.

KELMAN PLACE

Rains quotes a remark by a spokesperson for a Florence Crittenden home that indicates the policy of traditional homes like Kelman Place. "These are your loving, trusting girls in here. Your other girl who is probably doing the same thing doesn't get caught because she is too smart. . . . What is needed is more understanding on the part of the parents and the general public. I don't mean condoning. I mean understanding . . . that this kind of thing can happen and these girls do need help." (Quoted in the St. Petersburg, Fla. *Times,* May 17, 1968; Rains 1971, p. 48) This "philosophy" was shared by staff at Kelman place. One staff member put it this way. "I talk a lot with the girls. In general, with the whole group, I would say they know what they have done is not condoned by society and never will be—never. I do not condemn a girl for making one mistake. I just hope they learn a lesson." (Rains 1971, p. 49) These remarks capture the major features of a classic sort of moral explanation. We do not condemn a person of good character who has made a mistake, who will learn from the mistake, and who is determined not to make the mistake again.

In the context, the explanation carries on old-fashioned image of a nice girl led astray, whose mistake is punishment enough in itself. This sort of explanation presupposes that reputation, self-respect, and respectability are risked by getting pregnant out of wedlock. It is not the simple getting pregnant that is the problem. It is the woman herself—her character or the motive one derives from traits of her character. Illicit pregnancy is a visible mark of character that somehow must be dealt with.

At both Kelman Place and Hawthorne House, the young women's explanations of their own pregnancies came to be in harmony with this venerable story. Rains quotes her field notes from Hawthorne House. "Louise asked during group meeting, 'Can you remember what you thought of unwed mothers in places like this before? I mean, think of what we thought, before we came here, about unwed mothers and maternity homes.' " Peg said, "That's right. Whenever I thought of places like this, I always thought, 'Well, I'm not that type of girl.' Everyone looked agreeing to this." (Rains 1971, pp. 43–44) Rains says, "Girls enter maternity homes expecting to confront the concrete proof of what they have become and encounter instead a reminder of what they "really" are, what they presumably have been all along." (Rains 1971, p. 54)

There is, however, a certain ominous tone in the staff member's remark, "I do not condemn a girl for making one mistake. I just hope they learn a lesson." The remark raises the awful spector that the event may happen again if the girl doesn't learn from it. This spector was raised at each of the three locations Rains studied, but it was dealt with differently at each of them. But interestingly enough, the young women at each of the locations begin with the same explanation: there were two kinds of girls—respectable and "that kind." (See figure 5.2) They then modified the explanation so that the "nice girl" category might contain a loop covering the passage through unwed motherhood, after which the girl returns to respectability if she learns her lesson. It was a loop they believed could only be taken once, otherwise the chart would have been the passage of "that type of girl." (See figure 5.3.)

At Kelman Place, the young women's self-respect and reputation were rescued by this explanation. I do not mean that the verbal explanation rescued them by magically changing people's opinions. Kelman Place had the material wherewithal to let the young women "move on" back to their

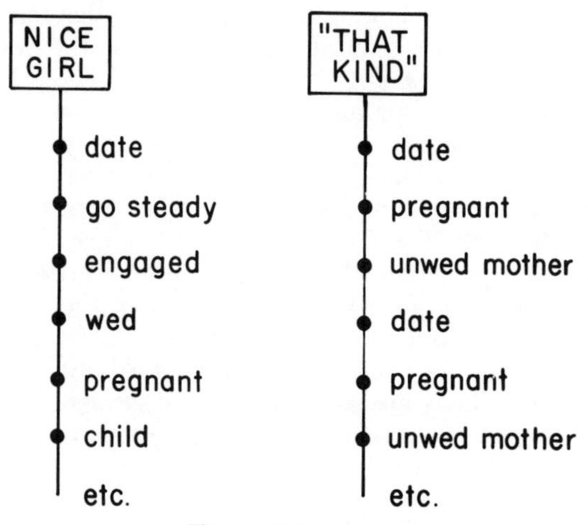

Figure 5.2

normal lives with their reputations saved by concealing their mistakes—and in fact, Kelman Place was part of the *institutionalized* means in the society for that kind of moral rescue.

An important part of the Kelman Place rescue turned on the ways in which a young woman's public interaction was altered. During her stay at a traditional home, secrecy was preserved as much as possible, so that the young woman might reenter respectable society without her mistake "ruining" her. Her passage was hidden by her physically leaving her usual public locations of home, school, and so on. It was also hidden by cover stories.[9]

Which authorities had to be dealt with varied with the young woman's previous life. For women in school they included principals and counselors, truant officers, and police; for women in college, they included the deans,

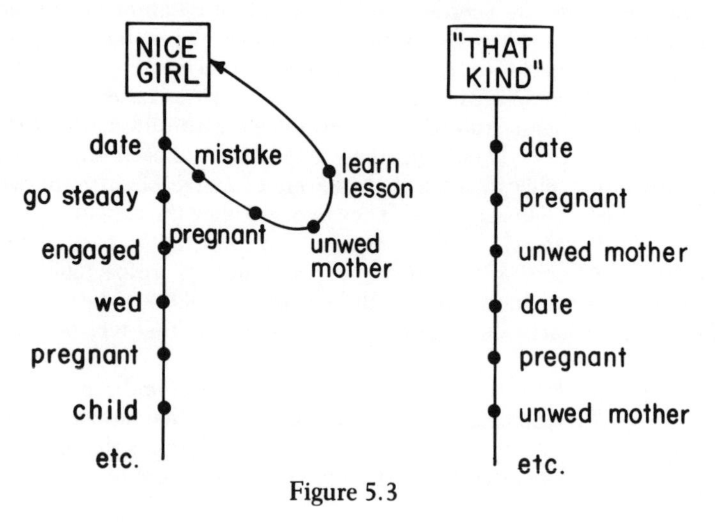

Figure 5.3

teachers, and registrars. For all of the young women, they included physicians, lawyers, adoption agency and birth registry officials, as well as the maternity home staff, whose stance was one of stern but benign rescue. Because of the way the rescue was institutionalized, the outside authorities involved were either kept in ignorance or were parties to the conspiracy. This was part of the standard operating procedure of maternity homes. The Kelman Place staff's judgment on character was accepted, and the category of "nice girl who made a mistake" was socially real, not a matter of opinion. The young women could accept authorities at face value because they could simply and unconsciously count on their protection in this hidden salvage operation. The institutional salvage included dealing with the public remainder of the "mistake"—the child—for nearly all of the girls gave their babies up for adoption. The entire operation confirmed the fact that the girl's past was really that of a nice girl who had make a mistake, by creating the possibility for her to be a respectable young woman in the future.

HAWTHORNE HOUSE

In entering Hawthorne House, the young women changed their public interactions in the same way the Kelman Place women did, for both homes had the same institutional status and connections. Hawthorne House staff dealt with authorities such as judges, lawyers, hospital personnel, and adoption agency staff generally by the same institutional means used at the traditional homes. However, Hawthorne House was operated by professional social workers whose disciplinary training was aimed at bringing people to face emotional and psychological realities and the truth about their motives.

The social workers regarded becoming an unwed mother as having its cause in a prior, unhealthy psychological state. Their task was to help the young women uncover and correct that state so that it would not continue to operate in the future, with the risk of repeated illicit pregnancy. When one father expressed reservations about "the girls" returning to dating, a staff member said, "We expect girls will resume their heterosexual relationships in the manner of dating, but we feel that if they have learned something during their stay here, they can communicate better with their parents and they don't need to act out in inappropriate ways." (Rains 1971, p. 98)

Rains says that the social workers were concerned that the young women accept responsibility for their behavior, as well as acknowledge the seriousness of the consequences. For the girls to accept the traditional explanation that they were trusting young woman who had made a mistake counted as denial. Understanding the emotional roots of their actions was necessary to avoid another illicit pregnancy. This amounts to a straightforward criticism of the traditional maternity homes. The criticism shows that the responsibility the social workers wanted was not responsibility for being a respectable woman in the traditional sense—and this marks a deep difference from the Kelman Place approach.

In criticizing traditional maternity home practices of extreme secrecy and protection, one staff member said,

> "After all, girls come here because they acted irresponsibly to start with, particularly now that ways to prevent getting pregnant are so common. And I don't think we should encourage that kind of thing. A lot of what we try to do is based on this philosophy that girls should be encouraged to accept responsibility for themselves, and to take responsibility." [Rains 1917, p. 63]

This is not the traditional moral view that having sex in itself is either irresponsible or promiscuous. In fact, it appears to be a liberated view that takes young women seriously as moral agents who autonomously choose their moral principles and who make their own lives.

From Rains's report, all the Hawthorne House women seem to accept the benign, helpful posture of the social workers, and they accepted the intrusion of these authorities into areas that are customarily hidden and private. This does not mean that they all accepted the psychotherapeutic explanation. One young woman said,

> "My social worker is always trying to convince me. . . . I keep telling her that it doesn't seem to me to be true, and she'll agree, but there's always the implied idea that there was an emotional reason. It's insinuated all the time, in every question. I just keep wondering where the explanation came from to begin with. I mean I wonder what girl they knew well enough to arrive at this idea, this explanation." [Rains 1971, p. 92]

But another girl responded,

> "I know I felt that way when I came, but I feel now that if you don't know why you're here, you'll end up here again." (Rains 1971, p. 92)

The first girl questions the social worker's redefinition of the past, and the second accepts it. On the social worker picture, the first girl will return to the fog of denial. (See figure 5.4.)

The adequacy of psychotherapeutic explanation does not turn on there *always* being a hidden explanation for illicit pregnancy, of course, for there may be many classes of exceptions. However what *is* essential to the viewpoint is the contrast between the inner truth and ordinary, everyday ways of explaining things. The professional social worker's job is to unveil the truth that is hidden under the illusions of "nice girl" and "that kind of girl." The body of knowledge that the professional learns through her training penetrates to the underlying realities. Everyone *can* come to know those kinds of truths, but with the expert's help. This is different from the Kelman Place staff's reliance on "what everyone knows," but like the Kelman Place explanation, it overlooks the effect of the arrangements for maintaining secrecy about the young woman's future.

THE PROJECT

The black teenagers of the Project dealt with the public reality in ways quite different from those used by the mainly white, middle-class women of the maternity homes—due in part to differences in their options and in their relationships with authorities. The Project teenagers' passages were public

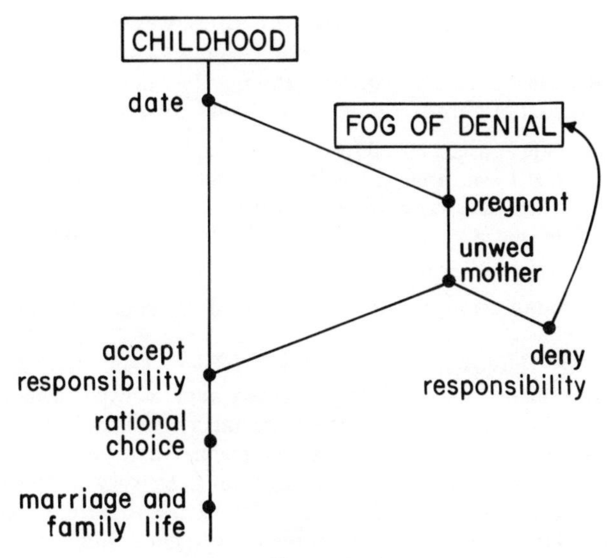

Figure 5.4

in two ways that those of the maternity home women were not. They were public in the sense that the teenagers continued to live at home, so the pregnancy was widely known and questions of respectability and responsibility had to be handled in school, on the street, and in the kitchen. They were also public in the sense that public officials and public records defined an *official* reputation for the young women.

At the time Rains did her study, "The Project" was funded as a pilot school for pregnant teens, located in a Black ghetto of a large Midwestern city—handling a maximum of about thirty-five teenagers (roughly fourteen-year-olds) at a time.[10] The Project staff included two teachers (one black, one white), a white psychiatric nurse, and a black social worker.

The social worker had standard, professional views on how group discussions should be handled, what sorts of problems should be discussed, and what the discussion should accomplish—views much like those of the social workers at Hawthorne House. She tried to encourage the girls to express themselves, and she hoped to help the girls develop abstract skills to help them take responsibility for the course of their lives. Accordingly, her style in running the meetings was one of "moral neutrality," encouraging the girls to speak of their feelings. Rains says that the style "was simultaneously unbelievable, unbelieved, misunderstood, and unacceptable to the Project girls." (Rains 1971, p. 132) Rains quotes one of the young women. "Dorene said, 'I mean why do social workers want to ask you all kinds of personal questions, but you can never ask them back?' " (Rains 1971, p. 133) They saw asking questions as implying a right to know—and they believed the social worker had no right to know some of the things she asked. This seemed to be both because she was an adult and because she was in a position of official authority.

The Project clients' experience with authorities, was quite different from that of the young women at the maternity homes. They had developed a warranted disbelief in moral neutrality and questions asked "for their own good." Here is part of a transcript of one of Rains' interviews.

> "The truant officer asked me all sorts of questions—had I been picked up for curfew, had I ever been in jail, the boy's name, where I lived, did I work after school. He say he didn't know if they would let me stay in school or throw me out." (How did you feel?) "He just be screaming at you like you was some slut dog." (Rains 1971, p. 134)

One of the young women said about official questioners, "They keep records."

The records the truant and probation officers kept were accessible records. They made up a public reputation that allowed authorities to meddle in the girl's future life. Was she an incorrigible and fit for reform school? Was she a fit mother? Were her claims that she was raped or assaulted to be given credence? Was an employer to be wary of offering her a job? Even social worker kept records, and the privacy that the middle-class people believed in was much less plausible in an agency which, for all of its humanitarian concerns, was part of a public effort to deal with the social problems of being poor and black, young and pregnant. In the mid 1960s, neither being middle-class and white, nor being an illicitly pregnant refined girl constituted a social problem.

In the Project girls' circumstances, there was no chance of rescue by redefining the past psychotherapeutically. The teenagers *did* consider themselves girls who had made a mistake, however.

Salvaging one's reputation did not have the same meaning for the black teenagers of the Project because reputation in the black community did not offer the same protection that it did for the middle-class women. Since the pregnancies of black women were not kept secret, the "mistake" view didn't function to preserve future options by salvaging their past reputations, but it did serve to say that they were not condemned to carry out the common fate they saw around them, of women on welfare, struggling to support their children, with or without a husband. Rains said, "An illegitimate pregnancy jeopardized more than moral respectability for these girls; it lessened their chances for continuing in school and possibly attaining a better way of life. Marriage was seen by many Project girls and their parents as more of an obstacle than a solution to this other sort of respectability. As one girl put it:

> Some of these girls just don't think ahead. They think they'll get married and leave school and they don't think that maybe their husband won't stay around and then where will they be when they can't do anything. Some of them don't even graduate from grammar school. What kind of mother could you be not even out of grammar school? If your kid has work from school, you can't even help him, maybe can't even read. At least that's one thing I've learned. When I got pregnant, my mother talked to me. She told me that everybody's ship is going to come in sometime, but that you had to be there when it came 'cause you can only get it once. She said I was only part way up the gangplank. I think it is foolish to get married with so much ahead of you. [Rains 1971, p. 39–40]

Going to the Project school was not simply an illusion of this other sort of respectability. It was *in fact* continuing on the path to respectable adult life by continuing in *school*. At fourteen, school was a major step toward a respectable life.

Nearly all of the black young women kept their babies. The social workers regarded it as their responsibility to point out the possibility of adoption or foster home placement. But often, girls and their mothers regarded the suggestion as a moral affront. Here are May's remarks. "She talked to my mother first—asked her did she want me to give the baby up for adoption. My mother say, 'No, May be a nice mother. Yes, she love that child and she feel about it like it was hers. She was mad about it at first.' " These feelings show in differences in the ways children were raised.

For most of the middle-class young women, "moving on" was publicly moving back to the original position of "respectable young woman." The passage was a loop. For the young black women of the project, moving on was moving from "pregnant girl" to "girl with a baby." It was this transformation that, in the end, stifled public comment. From Rains quotes, it appears that the Project girls gained strength from their *own* love and pride in the baby ("I love my baby enough that I don't care what they say." Rains, p. 169) But also, they gained from other people's love of babies—their interest focused on baby rather than girl. ("They just like babies".) Rains describes the situation:

> The Project girls shared a way of life in which motherly responsibilities were usually diffused among a number of persons. The Project girls themselves had been involved in caring for their younger brothers and sisters and were themselves cared for by a variety of aunts, stepfathers and stepmothers, mothers—persons who for reasons of blood relationship or sense of kinship took interest in them. The Project girls' babies thus did not so much enter the world to an exclusive relation to a single mother, as to a web of persons with a variety of interests and concerns in their welfare. (Rains 1971, p. 171)

There is much to be learned from Rains's cases. I'll begin with some further explanation as to why relying on women's own accounts, as Gilligan does, is not sufficient for understanding the moral institution of life, or for correcting bias in analysis. I'll go on to insist that academics ask serious questions about their authority and responsibility, and conclude with a mention of some positive contributions from my own approach.

We should note that the young women of Kelman Place and Hawthorne House certainly regarded getting pregnant as a moral matter that required explanation. But their explanations changed over time, through the process of the young woman's interactions with others—her intimates, neighbors, the other pregnant young women she met, and particularly, through her interaction with authorities. The young women reported the explanations and changes as belonging to themselves and to their own perceptions. (See remarks quoted above in the sections on Kelman Place and Hawthorne House). Yet these explanations were socially constructed, with the help of upstanding members of the general community at Kelman Place, and with the guidance of social workers at Hawthorne House. They were constructed differently in different social locations—differently in the maternity homes than at the Project, and with different effect. Let me discuss the social workers, because their model is in many ways the philosopher's model in ethics.

The authority which the social workers exercised was a professional authority that had been politically won during the 1920s, in the course of the struggle to have the occupation designated a profession. Theirs was a chapter in the great movement of professionalization that began in the United States after the Civil War, a movement that transformed our democracy. Professionalization produced new and powerful authorities who worked at defining health and disease, law and justice, nature and the good life—authorities that came to include not only doctors and lawyers but physicists, botanists, psychologists, and, of course, philosophers. (See Addelson 1983, 1985). The professional authorities eventually replaced the clergymen and the "educated laymen of good character" as advisors to the nation. The social workers' debunking of the "nice girl" explanation has a place in the secularization of "the moral institution of life" that was concurrent with the professionalization process in the United States. (Boller 1981; Haskell 1977) Nonetheless, they retained the basic religious model of explaining human activity: explanation in terms of preconditions of the activity, preconditions that exist somehow within the individual. They differed in the classifications of preconditions, using technical categories or their profession: preconditions may be irrational, as when a person is acting out, but with the social workers' help, the emotional preconditions may be dealt with and then the young woman may make free and reasonable choices. That is where the philosophers come in.

I am not here disputing the truth of psychotherapeutic explanations. Rather I am saying that truth does not come in a bottle with a lablel on it that says, TRUTH. What we call "truth" is based on the authority of someone or other. Some truths are based on "what everyone knows" ("everyone" here referring to some particular selection of people). Some truths may be based on first-hand experience. But in professionalized fields, the confirmation or falsification of truths is handled by professionals. What is relevant here is the authority the social workers had in constructing the explanations of the young women's pasts—explanations accepted by the young women at Hawthorne House and rejected by the young women at the Project (though despite this rejection, the social worker's explanation carried the day in the official records).

The rational action the social workers postulated as the fruit of overcoming denial is, in fact, the model of moral activity that many philosophers presuppose as the way that moral reasoning or moral explanation relates to moral activity. Preconditions exist in the explicit reasoning process that the agent goes through, although people also act out of preconditions of habit, unexpressed motive, good character, and so on. Even unarticulated preconditions can be retroactively captured in explanations. This is quite a realist view, for it presupposes that the preconditions of the act are objectively there to be uncovered later, by the person herself or by an outside judge. It requires, for the paradigm cases at least, that one's moral reasoning actually be applied in a situation so as to bring about one's action.

Unfortunately, there exists no adequate explanation of how moral reasoning is applied by a rational agent in an actual situation. Philosophers don't usually raise the question. Psychologists have not even hypothesized such a model, much less discovered the actual mechanisms. (See note 4.) But even if there *were* such a model hypothesized, we would have to ask, "On whose authority do we use this model in explaining our activities?" By what social means is that authority exercised? And what consequences does its use have?" All of these questions have answers in Rains's studies, and we see that consequences differ by class and race. These questions have answers, even when Rains's subjects come to report the explanations as their own.

Gilligan doesn't obviously use the "precondition" model. Her interest lies more in tracing the women's changing explanations and their relationship to changing conceptions of self. Her approach may be analogous to that of multitudes of social scientists who investigate folk explanations while remaining agnostic as to whether they pick out existing objects or acts—phlogiston and witches are time-worn examples. It is a peculiar sort of bracketing (to use the phenomenologist's term). Gilligan herself developed the "responsibilities-care" orientation by seeing that the Kohlberg scheme imposed gender dominance. She saw that moral reasoning was being socially constructed in the Kohlberg "laboratory" and classroom. But in developing her new "orientation," she did not relinguish the supposition that group members individually apply the concepts she defines in understanding their own moral activities (or in understanding what other group members do). In assuming this, she removes the moral institution of life from the social and political institutions of life. She ignores the processes by which explanations come to be socially constructed. It is within those processes that systematic relations of gender, age, class, and race come into existence and come to be preserved.

With their analyses of the moral institution of life, philosophers contribute to the processes and the preservation of systematic gender, age, class, and race divisions. Their authority to publish and teach their opinions is a professional authority, and it was politically won and it is politically maintained. (See (Boller 1981, Haskell 1977) Philosophers cannot simply assume that "academic freedom" allows them to teach and publish whatever definitions of the moral institution their graduate schools supported. Academic freedom is a political instrument, and it should not be used unless academics make explicit their moral, social, and political responsibilities. At a minimum, that requires knowing the implications of our work, and it requires asking by what authority we define the moral institution of life.

The dominant philosophic definitions of the moral institution analyze abortion as a conflict of rights. Academic feminists (including Gilligan) rightly complain that this silences women. Other academics complain that it silences Christians. By the results of Kohlberg's tests, it silences nonwhites, members of lower classes, and citizens of Third World nations—to say nothing of the clients of our prisons, mental institutions, and elementary schools. Some citizens complain about secular humanism, values clarification courses, and about the ethics hidden in sex education courses and family planning services. The ethical theories that support the definition of abortion as a conflict of rights are implicated in all these things. It is within these sorts of contexts that philosophers must ask about their own authority and responsibility. Members of all professions must do so, and the questions cannot be answered in narrow professional terms.[11] Feminist academics must ask as well, and their questions of authority and responsibility are as tangled as those of mainstream academics.

I believe that the first implication of being responsible in analyzing "the moral institution of life" is that philosophers must vacate their armchairs and developmental psychologists must vacate their "laboratories." Those who cannot give up the falsified models and abstract, elitist thinking should face the fact that the cloak of professional authority has come to resemble the emperor's new clothes. They might act honestly by quitting academia and earning their pay as workers for interest group organizations or industry (which would offer interesting market tests for theory validity). Those who elect to remain academics would have to vacate their armchairs and develop proper empirical and political sensitivities and go humbly to look the moral institution of life in the eyes. Humbly and naked, without the academic robes that have hidden our parts in the construction of moral explanations—hidden them from ourselves if from no others.

But I want to end this paper on a joyous note about what we begin to see if we pay heed to what is hidden and the means by which it is hidden. My discussion of Rains' cases makes it evident that the moral institution of life cannot be understood by looking at moral explanations and ignoring silences and secrets. (See Rich 1979.) The moral superiority of the respectable higher classes owes less to money than to the wealth of secrecy they control and use to cover their moral mistakes. The secrecy required is an official one, as well as a private, family one. The advantage of this wealth is evident when we see the consequences of lacking it—for example, in the publicity the young Project women faced, both in their neighborhoods and in the official records. Their experiences went on record, not in their own terms, but in the terms of the professionals.

These things we can learn from Rains's studies. But the general approach that I am suggesting offers us systematic ways of understanding many things feminists and others have pointed out. For example, when we take "abortion" as a folk term, we can trace its construction with Ruth Hubbard, Barbara Ehrenreich, and Dierdre English, and many others who have spoken of physicians' authority in medicalizing the definitions of our life experiences.

By taking the passage through abortion as one among a network of passages, we begin to have a way of representing some of the most fruitful criticisms of the standard analysis of the moral problem of abortion as a conflict of rights. The network of passages gives us a way to represent Hauerwas's Christian concerns. It gives us a way to represent Harrison's and Whitbeck's feminist concerns, and it shows that they are right in saying that the conflict of rights' analysis tears abortion out of the context of women's lives. In fact, the moral passages approach shows how the conflict or rights' analysis tears abortion out of the context of women's, children's, and men's lives. For although we may not make our passages as equals, we do make them together.

Notes

I am grateful for suggestions given by my commentators, the editors of this volume, and students at SUNY Stony Brook. I owe particular thanks to Howard Becker, Merideth Michaels, and Phil Temko. Prudence Rains was kind enough to read the original version of the paper. I am grateful to Libby Potter and Caroline Whitbeck for intellectual aid and comfort.

1. For the most part, questions of sex have been ignored by secular, academic moral theorists. Susan Teft Nicholson did raise the issue of sex—though only to dismiss it—in her book, *Abortion and the Roman Catholic Church* (Knoxville: Religious Ethics, Inc. 1978). She found a two-fold basis of Roman Catholic opposition: abortion as a sin of sex, and abortion as a sin of killing. Kurt Baier says in his introduction to the book, that Nicholson "doesn't probe" the argument on sex "because it rests on a moral premise, the tying of sexual activity to reproduction, which is not now . . . an element in the common moral convictions of our society." (p. xvii) But this is a curious remark, because we could just as well say that Nicholson *divides* sex and procreation, and then sees the religious ethic as joining them out of a "conviction" that is prohibited in a "secular society." Baier's appeal to "common moral convictions" is, in fact, an attempt to justify a particular "secular" authoritative definition of abortion. The moral problem of abortion becomes a question of fetal life.

2. Many thanks to Merideth Michaels for helping me to state Harrison's position in this perspicuous way.

3. Later work by Gilligan and others shows the care orientation also exists in presentation of dilemmas. (See Gilligan 1984.)

4. For a psychologist's case that we have none, see Blasi, 1980. See also papers in *Ethics* vol. 92, no. 3 (April 1982) I give a sociologist's case here, and more fully in my book in progress. Mills 1963, and Aubert 1965 are provocative, but Blumer (1969) offers my theoretical basis. Hauerwas's analysis in terms of narratives is an attempt to overcome what I would call a "free will" analysis of the moral institution. I am not saying we do not have free will. (Nor is Hauerwas.) I'm saying there is no psychological or sociological model for either free or unfree will, i.e., that the notion should be jettisoned and our decisions and choices must be otherwise analyzed. That would require jettisonning most of philosophical ethics.

5. I also owe more than I can say to Arlene Kaplan Daniels.

6. The concept of a career came initially from the sociology of occupations, particularly as it was developed by Everett Hughes and his students. It very quickly came to have a broader use, referring to patterns of changes over time, which were common to members of a variety of social categories, not merely occupational ones. For example, Howard Becker described the career of a marijuana user; Prudence Rains described the career of an unwed mother; Erving Goffman described the career of a mental patient.

Goffman takes a different emphasis from Becker, though the notion of a career is in many ways similar. In his paper, "The Moral Career of the Mental Patient," Erving Goffman puts forth reasons why the notion is valuable. "One value of the concept of career is its two-sidedness. One side is linked to internal matters held dearly and closely, such as the image of self and felt identity; the other side concerns official position, jural relations, and style of life, and is part of a publicly accessible institutional complex. The concept of career, then, allows one to move back and forth between the personal and the public, between the self and its significant society, without having to rely overly for data upon what the person says he thinks he imagines himself to be." (Goffman 1961, p. 127) Goffman calls his paper, "an exercise in the institutional approach to the self."

7. A fourth source of information was a small pilot study of contraceptive use among sexually experienced college women, which Rains used to supplement the published literature in giving the setting, or the origin point, from which unwed mothers begin their careers.

8. This "situation must be placed within systematic social themes. Rains does not do so. In the larger work from which this paper is drawn, I use the sensitizing concept of procreative responsibility to place it.

9. Cover stories were used to explain a young woman's absence from home ground and to explain her pregnancy in the new public life—for example, wearing a wedding ring and calling herself "Mrs." saved embarrassment at temporary jobs, or while out shopping. Within the maternity home, secrecy was maintained by not using last names, by using letter drops, and by various other means.

10. It was jointly sponsored by the city's boards of mental health and education. The services offered under the Project included a day school for the girls, prenatal care (at public clinics), and counseling. Initially, the school was limited to black girls in elementary school. The girls were from low-income backgrounds and many had records of truancy. When Rains did the major part of her study, most of them were about fourteen—many of them old for their grade because they had been "held back."

11. John Ladd has done very interesting work on professional responsibility, and philosophers would benefit from taking some of the advice he offers to engineers. See, for example, his "Philosophical Remarks on Professional Responsibility in Organizations," (*Applied Philosophy* vol. I, no. 2 (Fall, 1982). I discuss questions of research professionals' responsibility in (Addelson, n.d.). Both Ladd and Caroline Whitbeck are offering *moralities,* and at the moment, I find some version of their responsibility ethics to be useful to me as a member of a profession speaking to members of my own and other professions, i.e., as a folk morality in which my own place is clearly one of the folk. I don't mean that I can ever cease being one of the folk—that is the myth of disinterest and objectivity that shrouds professional authority. There is a difference in authority, social position, and political meaning when I talk as a worker to workers about our common moral concerns and when I speak as a professional out of the social location of academia. I have very serious reservations about taking my academic task to be to formulate an ethics or a metaethics. My discussion of moral passages is meant to be an aid to uncovering the moral institution of life, not a definition of it.

References

Addelson, Kathryn Pyne. 1983. "The Man of Professional Wisdom." *Discovering Reality.* S. Harding and M. Hintekka (eds.). Indrecht: D. Reidel. 1985. "Doing Science." *Proceedings of the Philosophy of Science Association* (Summer 1985).

———. 1986. "Moral Revolution." In Pearsall 1986.

———. n.d. *Moral Passages: Abortion and the Social Organization of Morality.* Book length manuscript in progress.

Aubert, Vilhelm. 1965. *The Hidden Society*. New Jersey: Bedminster Press.

Becker, Howard. 1970. *Sociological Work: Method and Substance*. Chicago: Aldine Publishing Co.

Berger, Peter and Thomas Luckmann. 1967. *The Social Construction of Reality*. London: Penguin.

Blasi, Augusto. 1980. "Bridging Moral Cognition and Moral Action: A Critical Review of the Literature." *Psychological Bulletin* (July 1980) 88, no. 1.

Blumer, Herbert. 1969. *Symbolic Interactionism: Perspective and Method*. Englewood Cliffs, N.J.: Prentice-Hall.

Boller, Paul F. 1981. *American Thought in Transition*. Washington, D.C.: University Press of America.

Ehrenreich, Barbara and Deirdre English. 1979. *For Her Own Good: 150 Years of Experts' Advice to Women*. Garden City, N.Y.: Anchor Press, Doubleday Publishing Co.

Feinberg, Joel. 1973. *The Problem of Abortion*. Belmont, Calif.: Wadsworth Publishing Co.

Freidson, Eliot. 1970. *Professional Dominance: The Social Structure of Medical Care*. Chicago: Aldine Publishing Co.

Gilligan, Carol. 1982. *A Different Voice: Psychological Theory and Women's Development*. Cambridge: Harvard University Press.

———. 1977. "In a Different Voice: Women's Conceptions of Self and of Morality." *Harvard Educational Review* 47 (4): 481–517.

———. 1984. "Remapping Development: The Power of Divergent Data." in L. Cirillo and S. Wapner, eds. *Value Presuppositions in Theories of Human Development*. Hillside, N.J.: Erlbaum Assoc.

Goffman, Erving. 1961. "The Moral Career of the Mental Patient," *Asylums*. Garden City, N.Y.; Doubleday.

Harrison, Beverly Wildung. 1984. *Our Right to Choose: Toward a New Ethic of Abortion*. Boston: Beacon Press.

Haskell, Thomas L. 1977. *The Emergence of Professional Social Science*. Urbana: University of Illinois Press.

Hauerwas, Stanley. 1977. *Truthfulness and Tragedy*. Notre Dame: Notre Dame University Press.

———. 1980. "Abortion: Why the Arguments Fail." in J. Burtchaell, ed., *Abortion Parlay*. New York: Andrews and McMeel. (reprinted in Hauerwas 1981).

———. 1981. *A Community of Character*. Notre Dame: University of Notre Dame Press.

Hauerwas, Stanley and Alasdair MacIntyre. 1983. *Revisions*. Notre Dame: University of Notre Dame Press.

Hubbard Ruth, M. S. Henifin, and B. Fried. 1982. *Biological Woman—The Convenient Myth*. Cambridge: Schenkman.

Hughes, Everett C. *The Sociological Eye*. 1984. New Brunswick: Transaction Books.

Kohlberg, Lawrence. 1971. "From Is to Ought" in Theodore Mischel, ed., *Cognitive Development and Epsitemology*. New York: Academic Press, pp. 151–232.

Luker, Kristin. 1975, *Taking Chances: Abortion and the Decision Not to Contracept*. Berkeley: University of California Press.

Mills, C. Wright. 1963. *Power Politics and People, The Collected Essays of C. Wright Mills, Edited and with an Introduction by Irving Louis Horowitz*, Ballantine Books: New York.

Nicholson, Susan Teft. 1978. *Abortion and the Roman Catholic Church*. Tennessee: Religious Ethics, Inc.

Pearsall, Marilyn. 1986. *Women and Value*. San Diego: Wadsworth.

Petchesky, Rosalind Pollack. 1984. *Abortion and Woman's Choice: The State, Sexuality, and Reproductive Freedom*. New York: Longman.
Rains, Prudence Mors. 1971. *Becoming an Unwed Mother*. Chicago: Aldine.
Rich, Adrienne. 1979. *On Lies, Secrets, and Silence: Selected Prose, 1966–1978*. New York: Norton.
Smetana, Judith. 1983. *Abortion*. New York: Praeger Special Studies.
Sumner, L. W. 1981. *Abortion and Moral Theory*. Princeton: Princeton University Press.
Sterba, James. 1984. *Morality in Practice*. Belmont: Wadsworth Publishing Co.
Whitbeck, Caroline. 1982. "The Moral Implications of Regarding Women as People: New Perspectives on Pregnancy and Personhood." In *The Concept of Person and Its Implications for the Use of the Fetus in Biomedicine*. Dordrecht: D. Reidel.
Winch, Peter. 1958. *The Idea of a Social Science*. London: Routledge and Kegan Paul.
———. 1964. "Understanding a Primitive Society." *American Philosophical Quarterly* 1: 307–24.
Zimmerman, Mary K. 1977. *Passage Through Abortion: The Personal and the Social Reality of Women's Experiences*. New York: Praeger.

⑥

Feminism and Moral Theory

VIRGINIA HELD

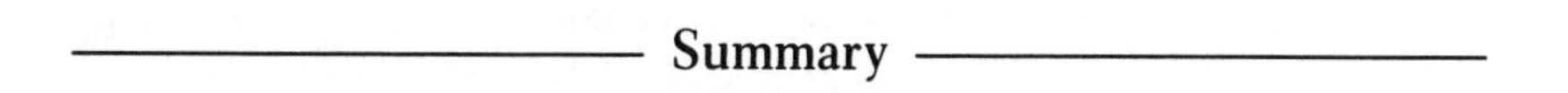

Summary

Moral theory generally has been drawn from predominantly "male" experience, often using the model of the economic exchange between buyer and seller as the paradigmatic human relationship. In this paper, Virginia Held urges that if we consider the mother-child relationship as paradigmatic, we can account for a domain frequently neglected in moral theory, the realm of particular others.

This reorientation helps us to understand better the motivation for ethical thinking and action, namely, caring about and valuing another, since the caring about and valuing of a child is central to the mother-child relationship. But Held also cautions feminists who want to disregard completely all principled moral thinking: such disregard could lead to abuse of power and could subvert women's claims to moral equality with men. Using the concept of "a division of moral labor," we could insist that different moral approaches apply to different domains of human activity. At a minimum, feminist moral theory calls for an approach to ethics in which women's experience must be taken as seriously as men's, and the morality of care given significant standing. This may lead to ethical pluralism. Or it might be found that a morality drawn from women's experience is superior to traditional moral theory, not only in domains traditionally occupied by women, but also in domains previously dominated by men. S. M.

I am especially grateful to my daughter Julia Held for the suggestions she made concerning a draft of this paper and for the many insights she provided; she had given birth to Alexander Held White shortly before I began the paper. I am also grateful to many others who have expressed their thoughts about the issues involved. I especially thank Annette Baier, Brian Barry, Sandra Bartky, Larry Blum, Nancy Fraser, Marilyn Friedman, Ann Garry, Carol Gilligan, Jeffrie Murphy, Lucius Outlaw, and Carole Pateman for their early comments, and Marcia Baron, Louise De Salvo, Dorothy Helly, Nancy Holmstrom, Amélie Rorty, Sara Ruddick, Christina Hoff Sommers, Joan Tronto, and the editors of this volume for additional later comments.

For financial support, I am grateful to the Center for Advanced Study in the Behavioral Sciences at Stanford, where I was a Fellow while writing the paper, to the Andrew Mellon Foundation, and to Hunter College of the City University of New York.

The tasks of moral inquiry and moral practice are such that different moral approaches may be appropriate for different domains of human activity. I have argued in a recent book that we need a division of moral labor.[1] In *Rights and Goods,* I suggest that we ought to try to develop moral inquiries that will be as satisfactory as possible for the actual contexts in which we live and in which our experience is located. Such a division of moral labor can be expected to yield different moral theories for different contexts of human activity, at least for the foreseeable future. In my view, the moral approaches most suitable for the courtroom are not those most suitable for political bargaining; the moral approaches suitable for economic activity are not those suitable for relations within the family, and so on. The task of achieving a unified moral field theory covering all domains is one we may do well to postpone, while we do our best to devise and to "test" various moral theories in actual contexts and in light of our actual moral experience.

What are the implications of such a view for women? Traditionally, the experience of women has been located to a large extent in the context of the family. In recent centuries, the family has been thought of as a "private" domain distinct not only from that of the "public" domain of the polis, but also from the domain of production and of the marketplace. Women (and men) certainly need to develop moral inquiries appropriate to the context of mothering and of family relations, rather than accepting the application to this context of theories developed for the marketplace or the polis. We can certainly show that the moral guidelines appropriate to mothering are different from those that now seem suitable for various other domains of activity as presently constituted. But we need to do more as well: we need to consider whether distinctively feminist moral theories, suitable for the contexts in which the experience of women has or will continue to be located, are better moral theories than those already available, and better for other domains as well.

The Experience of Women

We need a theory about how to count the experience of women. It is not obvious that it should count equally in the construction or validation of moral theory. To merely survey the moral views of women will not necessarily lead to better moral theories. In the Greek thought that developed into the Western philosophical tradition,[2] reason was associated with the public domain from which women were largely excluded. If the development of adequate moral theory is best based on experience in the public domain, the experience of women so far is less relevant. But that the public domain is the appropriate locus for the development of moral theory is among the tacit assumptions of existing moral theory being effectively challenged by feminist scholars. We cannot escape the need for theory in confronting these issues.

We need to take a stand on what moral experience is. As I see it, moral experience is "the experience of consciously choosing, of voluntarily accepting or rejecting, of willingly approving or disapproving, of living with these choices, and above all of acting and of living with these actions and their outcomes. . . . Action is as much a part of experience as is perception."[3] Then we need to take a stand on whether the moral experience of women is as valid a source or test of moral theory as is the experience of men, or on whether it is more valid.

Certainly, engaging in the process of moral inquiry is as open to women as it is to men, although the domains in which the process has occurred has been open to men and women in different ways. Women have had fewer occasions to experience for themselves the moral problems of governing, leading, exercising power over others (except children), and engaging in physically violent conflict. Men, on the other hand, have had fewer occasions to experience the moral problems of family life and the relations between adults and children. Although vast amounts of moral experience are open to all human beings who make the effort to become conscientious moral inquirers, the contexts in which experience is obtained may make a difference. It is essential that we avoid taking a given moral theory, such as a Kantian one, and deciding that those who fail to develop toward it are deficient, for this procedure imposes a theory on experience, rather than letting experience determine the fate of theories, moral and otherwise.

We can assert that as long as women and men experience different problems, moral theory ought to reflect the experience of women as fully as it reflects the experience of men. The insights and judgments and decisions of women as they engage in the process of moral inquiry should be presumed to be as valid as those of men. In the development of moral theory, men ought to have no privileged position to have their experience count for more. If anything, their privileged position in society should make their experience more suspect rather than more worthy of being counted, for they have good reasons to rationalize their privileged positions by moral arguments that will obscure or purport to justify these privileges.[4]

If the differences between men and women in confronting moral problems are due to biological factors that will continue to provide women and men with different experiences, the experience of women should still count for at least as much as the experience of men. There is no justification for discounting the experience of women as deficient or underdeveloped on biological grounds. Biological "moral inferiority" makes no sense.

The empirical question of whether and to what extent women think differently from men about moral problems is being investigated.[5] If, in fact, women approach moral problems in characteristic ways, these approaches should be reflected in moral theories as fully as are those of men. If the differing approaches to morality that seem to be displayed by women and by men are the result of historical conditions and not biological ones, we could assume that in nonsexist societies, the differences would disappear, and the experience of either gender might adequately substitute for the experience of the other.[6] Then feminist moral theory might be the same as moral theory of any kind. But since we can hardly imagine what a nonsexist society would be like, and surely should not wait for one before evaluating the experience of women, we can say that we need feminist moral theory to deal with the differences of which we are now aware and to contribute to the development of the nonsexist society that might make the need for a distinctively feminist moral theory obsolete. Specifically, we need feminist moral theory to deal with the regions of experience that have been central to women's experience and neglected by traditional moral theory. If the resulting moral theory would be suitable for all humans in all contexts, and thus could be thought of as a human moral theory or a universal moral theory, it would be a feminist moral theory as well if it adequately reflected the experience and standpoint of women.

That the available empirical evidence for differences between men and women with respect to morality is tentative and often based on reportage and interpretation, rather than on something more "scientific,"[7] is no problem at all for the claim that we need feminist moral theory. If such differences turn out to be further substantiated, we will need theory to evaluate their implications, and we should be prepared now for this possibility (or, as many think, probability). If the differences turn out to be insignificant, we still need feminist moral theory to make the moral claim that the experience of women is of equal worth to the experience of men, and even more important, that women themselves are of equal worth as human beings. If it is true that the only differences between women and men are anatomical, it still does not follow that women are the moral equals of men. Moral equality has to be based on moral claims. Since the devaluation of women is a constant in human society as so far developed, and has been accepted by those holding a wide variety of traditional moral theories, it is apparent that feminist moral theory is needed to provide the basis for women's claims to equality.

We should never forget the horrors that have resulted from acceptance of the idea that women think differently from men, or that men are rational beings, women emotional ones. We should be constantly on guard for misuses of such ideas, as in social roles that determine that women belong in the home or in educational programs that discourage women from becoming, for example, mathematicians. Yet, excessive fear of such misuses should not stifle exploration of the ways in which such claims may, in some measure, be true. As philosophers, we can be careful not to conclude that whatever tendencies exist ought to be reinforced. And if we succeed in making social scientists more alert to the naturalistic fallacy than they would otherwise be, that would be a side benefit to the development of feminist moral theory.

Mothering and Markets

When we bring women's experience fully into the domain of moral consciousness, we can see how questionable it is to imagine contractual relationships as central or fundamental to society and morality. They seem, instead, the relationships of only very particular regions of human activity.[8]

The most central and fundamental social relationship seems to be that between mother or mothering person and child. It is this relationship that creates and recreates society. It is the activity of mothering which transforms biological entities into human social beings. Mothers and mothering persons produce children and empower them with language and symbolic representations. Mothers and mothering persons thus produce and create human culture.

Despite its implausibility, the assumption is often made that human mothering is like the mothering of other animals rather than being distinctively human. In accordance with the traditional distinction between the family and the polis, and the assumption that what occurs in the public sphere of the polis is distinctively human, it is assumed that what human mothers do within the family belongs to the "natural" rather than to the "distinctively human" domain. Or, if it is recognized that the activities of human mothers do not resemble the activities of the mothers of other mammals, it is assumed that, at least, the difference is far narrower than the difference between what animals do and what humans who take part in government and industry and art do. But, in fact, mothering is among the most human of human activities.

Consider the reality. A human birth is thoroughly different from the birth of other animals, because a human mother can choose not to give birth. However extreme the alternative, even when abortion is not a possibility, a woman can choose suicide early enough in her pregnancy to consciously prevent the birth. A human mother comprehends that she brings about the birth of another human being. A human mother is then responsible, at least in an existentialist sense, for the creation of a new human life. The event is essentially different from what is possible for other animals.

Human mothering is utterly different from the mothering of animals without language. The human mother or nurturing person constructs with and for the child a human social reality. The child's understanding of language and of symbols, and of all that they create and make real, occurs in interactions between child and caretakers. Nothing seems more distinctively human than this. In comparison, government can be thought to resemble the governing of ant colonies, industrial production to be similar to the building of beaver dams, a market exchange to be like the relation between a large fish that protects and a small fish that grooms, and the conquest by force of arms that characterizes so much of human history to be like the aggression of packs of animals. But the imparting of language and the creation within and for each individual of a human social reality, and often a new human social reality, seems utterly human.

An argument is often made that art and industry and government create new human reality, while mothering merely "reproduces" human beings, their cultures, and social structures. But consider a more accurate view: in bringing up children, those who mother create new human *persons*. They change persons, the culture, and the social structures that depend on them, by creating the kinds of persons who can continue to transform themselves and their surroundings. Creating new and better persons is surely as "creative" as creating new and better objects or institutions. It is not only bodies that do not spring into being unaided and fully formed; neither do imaginations, personalities, and minds.

Perhaps morality should make room first for the human experience reflected in the social bond between mothering person and child, and for the human projects of nurturing and of growth apparent for both persons in the relationship. In comparison, the transactions of the marketplace seem peripheral; the authority of weapons and the laws they uphold, beside the point.

The relation between buyer and seller has often been taken as the model of all human interactions.[9] Most of the social contract tradition has seen this relation of contractual exchange as fundamental to law and political authority as well as to economic activity. And some contemporary moral philosophers see the contractual relation as the relation on which even morality itself should be based. The marketplace, as a model for relationships, has become so firmly entrenched in our normative theories that it is rarely questioned as a proper foundation for recommendations extending beyond the marketplace. Consequently, much moral thinking is built on the concept of rational economic man. Relationships between human beings are seen as arising, and as justified, when they serve the interests of individual rational contractors.

In the society imagined in the model based on assumptions about rational economic man, connections between people become no more than instrumental. Nancy Hartsock effectively characterizes the worldview of these assumptions, and shows how misguided it is to suppose that the relationship between buyer and seller can serve as a model for all human relations: "the paradigmatic connections between people [on this view of the social world] are instrumental or extrinsic and conflictual, and in a world populated by these isolated individuals, relations of competition and domination come to be substitutes for a more substantial and encompassing community."[10]

Whether the relationship between nurturing person (who need not be a biological mother) and child should be taken as itself paradigmatic, in place of the contractual paradigm, or whether it should be seen only as an obviously important relationship that does not fit into the contractual framework and should not be overlooked, remains to be seen. It is certainly instructive to consider it, at least tentatively, as paradigmatic. If this were done, the competition and desire for domination thought of as acceptable for rational economic man might appear as a very particular and limited human connection, suitable perhaps, if at all, only for a restricted marketplace. Such a relation of conflict and competition can be seen to be unacceptable for establishing the social trust on which public institutions must rest,[11] or for upholding the bonds on which caring, regard, friendship, or love must be based.[12]

The social map would be fundamentally altered by adoption of the point of view here suggested. Possibly, the relationship between "mother" and child would be recognized as a much more promising source of trust and concern than any other, for reasons to be explored later. In addition, social relations would be seen as dynamic rather than as fixed-point exchanges. And assumptions that human beings are equally capable of entering or not entering into the contractual relations taken to characterize social relations generally would be seen for the distortions they are. Although human mothers could do other than give birth, their choices to do so or not are usually highly constrained. And children, even human children, cannot choose at all whether to be born.

It may be that no human relationship should be thought of as paradigmatic for all the others. Relations between mothering persons and children can become oppressive for both, and relations between equals who can decide whether to enter into agreements may seem attractive in contrast. But no mapping of the social and moral landscape can possibly be satisfactory if it does not adequately take into account and provide appropriate guidance for relationships between mothering persons and children.

Between the Self and the Universal

Perhaps the most important legacy of the new insights will be the recognition that more attention must be paid to the domain *between* the self—the ego, the self-interested individual—on the one hand, and the universal—everyone, others in general—on the other hand. Ethics traditionally has dealt with these poles, trying to reconcile their conflicting claims. It has called for impartiality against the partiality of the egoistic self, or it has defended the claims of egoism against such demands for a universal perspective.

In seeing the problems of ethics as problems of reconciling the interests of the self with what would be right or best for everyone, moral theory has neglected the intermediate region of family relations and relations of friendship, and has neglected the sympathy and concern people actually feel for particular others. As Larry Blum has shown, "contemporary moral philosophy in the Anglo-American tradition has paid little attention to [the] morally significant phenomena" of sympathy, compassion, human concern, and friendship.[13]

Standard moral philosophy has construed personal relationships as aspects of the self-interested feelings of individuals, as when a person might favor those he loves over those distant because it satisfies his own desires to do so. Or it has let those close others stand in for the universal "other," as when an analysis might be offered of how the conflict between self and others is to be resolved in something like "enlightened self-interest" or "acting out of respect for the moral law," and seeing this as what should guide us in our relations with those close, particular others with whom we interact.

Owen Flanagan and Jonathan Adler provide useful criticism of what they see as Kohlberg's "adequacy thesis"—the assumption that the more formal the moral reasoning, the better.[14] But they themselves continue to construe the tension in ethics as that between the particular self and the universal. What feminist moral theory will emphasize, in contrast, will be the domain of particular others in relations with one another.

The region of "particular others" is a distinct domain, where it can be seen that what becomes artificial and problematic are the very "self" and "all others" of standard moral theory. In the domain of particular others, the self is already closely entwined in relations with others, and the relation may be much more real, salient, and important than the interests of any individual self in isolation. But the "others" in the picture are not "all others," or "everyone," or what a universal point of view could provide. They are particular flesh and blood others for whom we have actual feelings in our insides and in our skin, not the others of rational constructs and universal principles.

Relationships can be characterized as trusting or mistrustful, mutually considerate or selfish, and so forth. Where trust and consideration are appropriate, we can find ways to foster them. But doing so will depend on aspects of what can be understood only if we look at relations between persons. To focus on either self-interested individuals or the totality of all persons is to miss the qualities of actual relations between actual human beings.

Moral theories must pay attention to the neglected realm of particular others in actual contexts. In doing so, problems of egoism vs. the universal moral point of view appear very different, and may recede to the region of background insolubility or relative unimportance. The important problems may then be seen to be how we ought to guide or maintain or reshape the relationships, both close and more distant, that we have or might have with actual human beings.

Particular others can, I think, be actual starving children in Africa with whom one feels empathy or even the anticipated children of future generations, not just those we are close to in any traditional context of family, neighbors, or friends. But particular others are still not "all rational beings" or "the greatest number."

In recognizing the component of feeling and relatedness between self and particular others, motivation is addressed as an inherent part of moral inquiry. Caring between parent and child is a good example.[15] We should not glamorize parental care. Many mothers and fathers dominate their children in harmful or inappropriate ways, or fail to care adequately for them. But when the relationship between "mother" and child is as it should be, the caretaker does not care for the child (nor the child for the caretaker) because of universal moral rules. The love and concern one feels for the child already motivate much of what one does. This is not to say that morality is irrelevant. One must still decide what one ought to do. But the process of addressing the moral questions in mothering and of trying to arrive at answers one can find acceptable involves motivated acting, not just thinking. And neither egoism nor a morality of universal rules will be of much help.

Mothering is, of course, not the only context in which the salient moral problems concern relations between particular others rather than conflicts between egoistic self and universal moral laws; all actual human contexts may be more like this than like those depicted by Hobbes or Kant. But mothering may be one of the best contexts in which to make explicit why familiar moral theories are so deficient in offering guidance for action. And the variety of contexts within mothering, with the different excellences appropriate for dealing with infants, young children, or adoloscents, provide rich sources of insight for moral inquiry.

The feelings characteristic of mothering—that there are too many demands on us, that we cannot do everything that we ought to do—are highly instructive. They give rise to problems different from those of universal rule vs. self-interest. They require us to weigh the claims of one self-other relationship against the claims of other self-other relationships, to try to bring about some harmony between them, to see the issues in an actual temporal context, and to act rather than merely reflect.

For instance, we have limited resources for caring. We cannot care for everyone or do everything a caring approach suggests. We need moral guidelines for ordering our priorities. The hunger of our own children comes before the hunger of children we do not know. But the hunger of children in Africa ought to come before some of the expensive amusements we may wish to provide for our own children. These are moral problems calling to some extent for principled answers. But we have to figure out what we ought to do when actually buying groceries, cooking meals, refusing the requests of our children for the latest toy they have seen advertised, and sending money to UNICEF. The context is one of real action, not of ideal thought.

Principles and Particulars

When we take the context of mothering as central, rather than peripheral, for moral theory, we run the risk of excessively discounting other contexts. It is a commendable risk, given the enormously more prevalent one of excessively discounting mothering. But I think that the attack on principles has sometimes been carried too far by critics of traditional moral theory.

Noddings, for instance, writes that "To say, 'It is wrong to cause pain needlessly,' contributes nothing by way of knowledge and can hardly be thought likely to change the attitude or behavior of one who might ask, 'Why is it wrong?' . . . Ethical caring . . . depends not upon rule or principle" but upon the development of a self "in congruence with one's best remembrance of caring and being cared-for."[16]

We should not forget that an absence of principles can be an invitation to capriciousness. Caring may be a weak defense against arbitrary decisions, and the person cared for may find the relation more satisfactory if both persons, but especially the person caring, are guided, to some extent, by principles concerning obligations and rights. To argue that no two cases are ever alike is to invite moral chaos. Furthermore, for one person to be in a position of caretaker means that that person has the power to withhold care, to leave the other without it. The person cared for is usually in a position of vulnerability. The moral significance of this needs to be addressed along with other aspects of the caring relationship. Principles may remind a giver of care to avoid being capricious or domineering. While most of the moral problems involved in mothering contexts may deal with issues above and beyond the moral minimums that can be covered by principles concerning rights and obligations, that does not mean that these minimums can be dispensed with.

Noddings's discussion is unsatisfactory also in dealing with certain types of questions, for instance those of economic justice. Such issues cry out for relevant principles. Although caring may be needed to motivate us to act on such principles, the principles are not dispensable. Noddings questions the concern people may have for starving persons in distant countries, because she sees universal love and universal justice as masculine illusions. She refrains from judging that the rich deserve less or the poor more, because caring for individuals cannot yield such judgments. But this may amount to taking a given economic stratification as given, rather than as the appropriate object of critical scrutiny that it should be. It may lead to accepting that the rich will care for the rich and the poor for the poor, with the gap between them, however unjustifiably wide, remaining what it is. Some important moral issues seem beyond the reach of an ethic of caring, once caring leads us, perhaps through empathy, to be concerned with them.

On ethical views that renounce principles as excessively abstract, we might have few arguments to uphold the equality of women. After all, as parents can care for children recognized as weaker, less knowledgeable, less capable, and with appropriately restricted rights, so men could care for women deemed inferior in every way. On a view that ethics could satisfactorily be founded on caring alone, men could care for women considered undeserving of equal rights in all the significant areas in which women have been struggling to have their equality recognized. So an ethic of care, essential as a component of morality, seems deficient if taken as an exclusive preoccupation.

That aspect of the attack on principles which seems entirely correct is the view that not all ethical problems can be solved by appeal to one or a very few simple principles. It is often argued that all more particular moral rules or principles can be derived from such underlying ones as the Categorical Imperative or the Principle of Utility, and that these can be applied to all moral problems. The call for an ethic of care may be a call, which I share, for a more pluralistic view of ethics, recognizing that we need a division of moral labor employing different moral approaches for different domains, at least for the time being.[17] Satisfactory intermediate principles for areas such as those of international affairs, or family relations, cannot be derived from simple universal principles, but must be arrived at in conjunction with experience within the domains in question.

Attention to particular others will always require that we respect the particularity of the context, and arrive at solutions to moral problems that will not give moral principles more weight than their due. But their due may remain considerable. And we will need principles concerning relationships, not only concerning the actions of individuals, as we will need evaluations of kinds of relationships, not only of the character traits of individuals.

Birth and Valuing

To a large extent, the activity of mothering is potentially open to men as well as to women. Fathers can conceivably come to be as emotionally close, or as close through caretaking, to children as are mothers. The experience of relatedness, of responsibility for the growth and empowerment of new life, and of responsiveness to particular others, ought to be incorporated into moral theory, and will have to be so incorporated for moral theory to be adequate. At present, in this domain, it is primarily the experience of women (and of children) that has not been sufficiently reflected in moral theory and that ought to be so reflected. But this is not to say that it must remain experience available only to women. If men came to share fully and equitably in the care of all persons who need care—especially children, the sick, the old—the moral values that now arise for women in the context of caring might arise as fully for men.

There are some experiences, however, that are open only to women: menstruating, having an abortion, giving birth, suckling. We need to consider their possible significance or lack of significance for moral experience and theory. I will consider here only one kind of experience not open to men but of obviously great importance to women: the experience of giving birth or of deciding not to. Does the very experience of giving birth, or of deciding not to exercise the capacity to do so, make a significant difference for moral experience and moral theory? I think the answer must be: perhaps.

Of course birthing is a social as well as a personal or biological event. It takes place in a social context structured by attitudes and arrangements that deeply affect how women experience it: whether it will be accepted as "natural," whether it will be welcomed and celebrated, or whether it will be fraught with fear or shame. But I wish to focus briefly on the conscious awareness women can have of what they are doing in giving birth, and on the specifically personal and biological aspects of human birthing.

It is women who give birth to other persons. Women are responsible for the existence of new persons in ways far more fundamental than are men. It is not bizarre to recognize that women can, through abortion or suicide, choose not to give birth. A woman can be aware of the possibility that she can act to prevent a new person from existing, and can be aware that if this new person exists, it is because of what she has done and made possible.

In the past we have called attention to the extent to which women do not control their capacity to give birth. They are under extreme economic and social pressure to engage in intercourse, to marry, and to have children. Legal permission to undergo abortion is a recent, restricted, and threatened capacity. When the choice not to give birth requires grave risk to life, health, or well-being, or requires suicide, we should be careful not to misrepresent the situation when we speak of a woman's "choice" to become a mother, or of how she "could have done other" than have a child, or that "since she chose to become a mother, she is responsible for her child." It does not follow that because women are responsible for creating human beings, they should be held responsible by society for caring for them, either alone, primarily, or even at all. These two kinds of responsibility should not be confused, and I am speaking here only of the first. As conscious human beings, women can do other than give birth, and if they do give birth, they are responsible for the creation of other human beings. Though it may be very difficult for women to avoid giving birth, the very familiarity of the literary image of the woman who drowns herself or throws herself from a cliff rather than bear an illegitimate child should remind us that such eventualities are not altogether remote from consciousness.

Women have every reason to be justifiably angry with men who refuse to take responsibility for their share of the events of pregnancy and birth, or for the care children require. Because, for so long, we have wanted to increase the extent to which men would recognize their responsibilities for causing pregnancy, and would share in the long years of care needed to bring a child to independence, we have tended to emphasize the ways in which the responsibilities for creating a new human being are equal between women and men.[18] But in fact, men produce sperm and women produce babies, and the difference is enormous. Excellent arguments can be made that boys and men suffer "womb envy"; indeed, men lack a wondrous capacity that women possess.[19]

Of all the human capacities, it is probably the capacity to create new human beings that is most worth celebrating. We can expect that a woman will care about and feel concern for a child she has created as the child grows and develops, and that she feels responsible for having given the child life. But her concern is more than something to be expected. It is, perhaps, justifiable in certain ways unique to women.

Children are born into actual situations. A mother cannot escape ultimate responsibility for having given birth to this particular child in these particular circumstances. She can be aware that she could have avoided intercourse, or used more effective contraception, or waited to get pregnant until her circumstances were different; that she could have aborted this child and had another later; or that she could have killed herself and prevented this child from facing the suffering or hardship of this particular life. The momentousness of all these decisions about giving or not giving life can hardly fail to affect what she experiences in relation to the child.

Perhaps it might be thought that many of these issues arise in connection with infanticide, and that if one refrains from killing an infant, one is responsible for giving the infant life. Infanticide is as open to men as to women. But to kill or refrain from killing a child, once the child is capable of life with caretakers different from the person who is resonsible for having given birth to the child, is a quite different matter from creating or not creating this possibility, and I am concerned in this discussion with the moral significance of giving birth.

It might also be thought that those, including the father, who refrain from killing the mother, or from forcing her to have an abortion, are also responsible for not preventing the birth of the child.[20] But unless the distinction between suicide and murder, and between having an abortion and forcing a woman to have an abortion against her will, are collapsed completely, the issues would be very different. To refrain from murdering someone else is not the same as deciding not to kill oneself. And to decide not to force someone else to have an abortion is different from deciding not to have an abortion when one could. The person capable of giving birth who decides not to prevent the birth is the person responsible, in the sense of "responsible" I am discussing, for creating another human being. To create a new human being is not the same as to refrain from ending the life of a human being who already exists.

Perhaps there is a tendency to want to approve of or to justify what one has decided with respect to giving life. In deciding to give birth, perhaps a woman has a natural tendency to approve of the birth, to believe that the child ought to have been born. Perhaps this inclines her to believe whatever may follow from this: that the child is entitled to care, and that feelings of love for the child are appropriate and justified. The conscious decision to create a new human being may provide women with an inclination to value the child and to have hope for the child's future. Since, in her view, the child ought to have been born, a woman may feel that the world ought to be hospitable to the child. And if the child ought to have been born, the child ought to grow into an admirable human adult. The child's life has, and should continue to have, value that is recognized.

Consider next the phenomenon of sacrifice. In giving birth, women suffer severe pain for the sake of new life. Having suffered for the child in giving the child life, women may have a natural tendency to value what they have endured pain for. There is a tendency, often noted in connection with war, for people to feel that because sacrifices have been made, the sacrifice should have been "worth it," and if necessary, other things ought to be done so that the sacrifice "shall not have been in vain." There may be a similar tendency for those who have suffered to give birth to assure themselves that the pain was for the good reason of creating a new life that is valuable and that will be valued.

Certainly, this is not to say that there is anything good or noble about suffering, or that merely because people want to believe that what they suffered for was worthwhile, it was. A vast amount of human suffering has been in vain, and could and should have been avoided. The point is that once suffering has already occurred and the "price," if we resort to such calculations, has already been paid, it will be worse if the result is a further cost, and better if the result is a clear benefit that can make the price, when it is necessary for the result, validly "worth it."

The suffering of the mother who has given birth will more easily have been worthwhile if the child's life has value. The chance that the suffering will be outweighed by future happiness is much greater if the child is valued by the society and the family into which the child is born. If the mother's suffering yields nothing but further suffering and a being deemed to be of no value, her suffering may truly have been in vain. Anyone can have reasons to value children. But the person who has already undergone the suffering needed to create one has a special reason to recognize that the child is valuable and to want the child to be valued so that the suffering she has already borne will have been, truly, worthwhile.

These arguments can be repeated for the burdens of work and anxiety normally expended in bringing up a child. Those who have already borne these burdens have special reasons for wanting to see the grown human being for whom they have cared as valuable and valued. Traditionally, women have not only borne the burdens of childbirth, but, with little help, the much greater burdens of child rearing. Of course, the burdens of child rearing could be shared fully by men, as they have been partially shared by women other than natural mothers. Although the concerns involved in bringing up a child may greatly outweigh the suffering of childbirth itself, this does not mean that giving birth is incidental.

The decision not to have children is often influenced by a comparable tendency to value the potential child.[21] Knowing how much care the child would deserve and how highly, as a mother, she would value the child, a woman who gives up the prospect of motherhood can recognize how much she is losing. For such reasons, a woman may feel overwhelming ambivalence concerning the choice.

Consider, finally, how biology can affect our ways of valuing children. Although men and women may share a desire or an instinctive tendency to wish to reproduce, and although these feelings may be equally strong for both men and women, such feelings might affect their attitudes toward a given child very differently. In terms of biological capacity, a mother has a relatively greater stake in a child to which she has given birth. This child is about one-twentieth or one twenty-fifth of all the children she could possibly have, whereas a man could potentially have hundreds or thousands of other children. In giving birth, a woman has already contributed a large amount of energy and effort toward the production of this particular child, while a man has, biologically, contributed only a few minutes. To the extent that such biological facts may influence attitudes, the attitudes of the mother and father toward the "worth" or "value" of a particular child may be different. The father might consider the child more easily replaceable in the sense that the father's biological contribution can so easily and so painlessly be repeated on another occasion or with another woman; for the mother to repeat her biological contribution would be highly exhausting and painful. The mother, having already contributed so much more to the creation of this particular child than the father, might value the result of her effort in proportion. And her pride at what she has accomplished in giving birth can be appropriately that much greater. She has indeed "accomplished" far more than has the father.

So even if instincts or desires to reproduce oneself or one's genes, or to create another human being, are equally powerful among men and women, a given child is, from the father's biological standpoint, much more incidental and interchangeable: any child out of the potential thousands he might sire would do. For the mother, on the other hand, if this particular child does not survive and grow, her chances for biological reproduction are reduced to a much greater degree. To suggest that men may think of their children as replaceable is offensive to many men, and women. Whether such biological facts as those I have mentioned have any significant effect on parental attitudes is not known. But arguments from biological facts to social attitudes, and even to moral norms, have a very long history and are still highly popular; we should be willing to examine the sorts of unfamiliar arguments I have suggested that can be drawn from biological facts. *If* anatomy is destiny, men may be "naturally" more indifferent toward particular children than has been thought.

Since men, then, do not give birth, and do not experience the responsibility, the pain, and momentousness of childbirth, they lack the particular motives to value the child that may spring from this capacity and this fact. Of course, many other reasons for valuing a child are felt by both parents, by caretakers of either gender, and by those who are not parents, but the motives discussed, and others arising from giving birth, may be morally significant. The long years of child care may provide stronger motives for valuing a child than do the relatively short months of pregnancy and hours of childbirth. The decisions and sacrifices involved in bringing up a child can be more affecting than those normally experienced in giving birth to a child. So the possibility for men to acquire such motives through child care may outweigh any long-term differences in motivation between women and men. But it might yet remain that the person responsible for giving birth would continue to have a greater sense of responsibility for how the child develops, and stronger feelings of care and concern for the child.

That adoptive parents can feel as great concern for and attachment to their children as can biological parents may indicate that the biological components in valuing children are relatively modest in importance. However, to the extent that biological components are significant, they would seem to affect men and women in different ways.

Morality and Human Tendencies

So far, I have been describing possible feelings rather than attaching any moral value to them. That children are valued does not mean that they are valuable, and if mothers have a natural tendency to value their children, it does not follow that they ought to. But if feelings are taken to be relevant to moral theory, the feelings of valuing the child, like the feelings of empathy for other persons in pain, may be of moral significance.

To the extent that a moral theory takes natural male tendencies into account, it would at least be reasonable to take natural female tendencies into account. Traditional moral theories often suppose it is legitimate for individuals to maximize self-interest, or satisfy their preferences, within certain constraints based on the equal rights of others. If it can be shown that the tendency to want to pursue individual self-interest is a stronger tendency among men than among women, this would certainly be relevant to an evaluation of such theory. And if it could be shown that a tendency to value children and a desire to foster the developing capabilities of the particular others for whom we care is a stronger tendency among women than among men, this too would be relevant in evaluating moral theories.

The assertion that women have a tendency to value children is still different from the assertion that they ought to. Noddings speaks often of the "natural" caring of mothers for children.[22] I do not intend to deal here with the disputed empirical question of whether human mothers do or do not have a strong natural tendency to love their children. And I am certainly not claiming that natural mothers have greater skills or excellences in raising children than have others, including, perhaps, men. I am trying, rather, to explore possible "reasons" for mothers to value children, reasons that might be different for mothers and potential mothers than they would be for anyone else asking the question: why should we value human beings? And it does seem that certain possible reasons for valuing living human beings are present for mothers in ways that are different from what they would be for others. The reason, if it is one, that the child should be valued because I have suffered to give the child life is different from the reason, if it is one, that the child should be valued because someone unlike me suffered to give the child life. And both of these reasons are different from the reason, if it is one, that the child should be valued because the continued existence of the child satisfies a preference of a parent, or because the child is a bearer of universal rights, or has the capacity to experience pleasure.

Many moral theories, and fields dependent on them such as economics, employ the assumption that to increase the utility of individuals is a good thing to do. But if asked *why* it is a good thing to increase utility, or satisfy desire, or produce pleasure, or *why* doing so counts as a good reason for something, it is very difficult to answer. The claim is taken as a kind of starting assumption for which no *further* reason can be given. It seems to rest on a view that people seek pleasure, or that we can recognize pleasure as having intrinsic value. But if women recognize quite different assumptions as more likely to be valid, that would certainly be of importance to ethics. We might then take it as one of our starting assumptions that creating good relations of care and concern and trust between ourselves and our children, and creating social arrangements in which children will be valued and well cared for, are more important than maximizing individual utilities. And the moral theories that might be compatible with such assumptions might be very different from those with which we are familiar.

A number of feminists have independently declared their rejection of the Abraham myth.[23] We do not approve the sacrifice of children out of religious duty. Perhaps, for those capable of giving birth, reasons to value the actual life of the born will, in general, seem to be better than reasons justifying the sacrifice of such life.[24] This may reflect an accordance of priority to caring for particular others over abstract principle. From the perspectives of Rousseau, of Kant, of Hegel, and of Kohlberg, this is a deficiency of women. But from a perspective of what is needed for late twentieth century survival, it may suggest a superior morality. Only feminist moral theory can offer a satisfactory evaluation of such suggestions, because only feminist moral theory can adequately understand the alternatives to traditional moral theory that the experience of women requires.

Notes

1. See Virginia Held, *Rights and Goods: Justifying Social Action* (New York: Free Press, Macmillan, 1984).

2. See Genevieve Lloyd, *The Man of Reason: "Male" and "Female" in Western Philosophy* (Minneapolis: University of Minnesota Press, 1984).

3. Virginia Held, *Rights and Goods*, p. 272. See also V. Held, "The Political 'Testing' of Moral Theories," *Midwest Studies in Philosophy* 7 (1982): 343–63.

4. For discussion, see especially Nancy Hartsock, *Money, Sex, and Power* (New York: Longman, 1983), chaps. 10, 11.

5. Lawrence Kohlberg's studies of what he claimed to be developmental stages in moral reasoning suggested that girls progress less well and less far than boys through these stages. See his *The Philosophy of Moral Development* (San Francisco: Harper & Row, 1981); and L. Kohlberg and R. Kramer, "Continuities and Discontinuities in Child and Adult Moral Development," *Human Development* 12 (1969): 93–120. James R. Rest, on the other hand, claims in his study of adolescents in 1972 and 1974 that "none of the male-female differences on the Defining Issues Test . . . and on the Comprehension or Attitudes tests were significant." See his "Longitudinal Study of the Defining Issues Test of Moral Judgment: A Strategy for Analyzing Developmental Change," *Developmental Psychology* (Nov. 1975): 738–48; quotation at 741. Carol Gilligan's *In A Different Voice* (Cambridge: Harvard University Press, 1982) suggests that girls and women tend to organize their thinking about moral problems somewhat differently from boys and men; her subsequent work supports the view that whether people tend to construe moral problems in terms of rules of justice or in terms of caring relationships is at present somewhat associated with gender (Carol Gilligan, address at Conference on Women and Moral Thought, SUNY Stony Brook, March 21, 1985). Other studies have shown that females are significantly more inclined than males to cite compassion and sympathy as reasons for their moral positions; see Constance Boucher Holstein, "Irreversible, Stepwise Sequence in the Development of Moral Judgment: A Longitudinal Study of Males and Females." *Child Development* 47, no. 1 (March 1976): 51–61.

6. For suggestions on how Gilligan's stages, like Kohlberg's, might be thought to be historically and culturally, rather than more universally, based, see Linda Nicholson, "Women, Morality, and History," *Social Research* 50, no. 3 (Autumn 1983): 514–36.

7. See, e.g., Debra Nails, "Social-Scientific Sexism: Gilligan's Mismeasure of Man," *Social Research* 50, no. 3 (Autumn 1983): 643–64.

8. I have discussed this in a paper that has gone through several major revisions and changes of title, from its presentation at a conference at Loyola University on April 18, 1983, to its discussion at Dartmouth College, April 2, 1984. I will refer to it as "Non-Contractual Society: A Feminist Interpretation." See also Carole Pateman, "The Fraternal Social Contract: Some Observations on Patriarchy," paper presented at American Political Science Association meeting, Aug. 30–Sept. 2, 1984, and "The Shame of the Marriage Contract," in *Women's Views of the Political World of Men,* edited by Judith Hicks Stiehm (Dobbs Ferry, N.Y.: Transnational Publishers, 1984).

9. For discussion, see especially Nancy Hartsock, *Money, Sex, and Power.*

10. Ibid., p. 39.

11. See Held, *Rights and Goods,* chap. 5.

12. Ibid., chap. 11.

13. Lawrence A. Blum, *Friendship, Altruism and Morality* (London: Routledge and Kegan Paul, 1980), p. 1.

14. Owen J. Flanagan, Jr., and Jonathan E. Adler, "Impartiality and Particularity," *Social Research* 50, no. 3 (Autumn 1983): 576–96.

15. See, e.g., Nell Noddings, *Caring: A Feminine Approach to Ethics and Moral Education* (Berkeley: University of California Press, 1984) pp. 91–94.

16. Ibid., pp. 91–94.

17. Participants in the conference on Women and Moral Theory offered the helpful term "domain relativism" for the version of this view that I defended.

18. See, e.g., Virginia Held, "The Obligations of Mothers and Fathers," repr. in

Mothering: Essays in Feminist Theory, edited by Joyce Trebilcot (Totowa, N.J.: Rowman and Allanheld, 1984).

19. See Eva Kittay, "Womb Envy: An Explanatory Concept," in *Mothering,* edited by Joyce Trebilcot. To overcome the pernicious aspects of the "womb envy" she skillfully identifies and describes, Kittay argues that boys should be taught that their "procreative contribution is of equal significance" (p. 123). While boys should certainly be told the truth, the truth may remain that, as she states elsewhere, "there is the . . . awesome quality of creation itself—the transmutation performed by the parturient woman" (p. 99).

20. This point was made by Marcia Baron in correspondence with me.

21. In exploring the values involved in birth and mothering, we need to develop views that include women who do not give birth. As Margaret Simons writes, "we must define a feminist maternal ethic that supports a woman's right not to have children." See Margaret A. Simons, "Motherhood, Feminism and Identity," *Hypatia, Women's Studies International Forum* 7, 5 (1984): 353.

22. E.g., Noddings, *Caring,* pp. 31, 43, 49.

23. See Gilligan, *In a Different Voice,* p. 104; Held, "Non-Contractual Society: A Feminist Interpretation;" and Noddings, *Caring,* p. 43.

24. That some women enthusiastically send their sons off to war may be indicative of a greater than usual acceptance of male myths rather than evidence against this claim, since the enthusiasm seems most frequent in societies where women have the least influence in the formation of prevailing religious and other beliefs.

B. *Autonomy: Self and Other*

The Importance of Autonomy

THOMAS E. HILL, JR.

Summary

Thomas Hill outlines the importance that the concept of autonomy has played in numerous and varied approaches to moral theory. But recently, that importance has been questioned, especially by those such as Carol Gilligan who argue for the moral importance of the concept of compassion. In his analysis of autonomy, Hill brings out three senses of the concept that he argues are important for moral theory *and* compatible with the concept of compassion.

Hill first discusses autonomy as impartiality. While impartiality is important in the review and justification of moral principles, it does not follow from this that moral agents making decisions about specific actions should be cool, detached, and calculating. Hill next addresses the issue of rights and autonomy. He argues that persons should respect each other's freedom to deliberate and act on their moral problems. Although this principle of noninterference places certain constraints on the concept of compassion, the right to autonomy and the need for compassion are not incompatible theses. Lastly, Hill discusses the question of autonomy as a goal of self-fulfillment. He suggests that once properly understood, this is a morally important and worthy goal, one that is in keeping with a care perspective.

S.M.

For many years we have been hearing that *autonomy* is important.[1] Immanual Kant held that autonomy is the foundation of human dignity and the source of all morality; and contemporary philosophers dissatisfied with utilitarianism are developing a variety of new theories that, they often say, are inspired by Kant. Autonomy has been heralded as an essential aim of education; and feminist philosophers have championed women's rights under the name of autonomy.[2] Oppressive political regimes are opposed on the grounds that they deny individual autonomy; and respect for the autonomy of patients is a recurrent theme in the rapidly expanding literature on medical ethics. Autonomy is a byword for those who oppose conventional and authoritative ethics; and for some existentialists, recognition of individual autonomy is apparently a reason for denying that there are objective moral standards. Both new rights theorists and the modern social contract theorists maintain that their theories best affirm autonomy.[3] Finally, and not least in their esteem for autonomy, well known psychologists speak of autonomy as the highest stage of moral development.

Recently, however, the importance of autonomy has been questioned from a variety of sources. Utilitarian critics have struck back at the neo-Kantians, and a group of moral philosophers, sometimes labeled "personalists," have challenged the Kantian ideal that we should be moved by regard for impartial principles rather than concern for particular individuals.[4] A "different voice" is being heard, emphasizing aspects of morality too often ignored in the persistent praise of autonomy. Some suggest that, far from being the source and highest development of morality, autonomy may be the special ideal of a particular dominant group, and in fact an ideal which serves to reinforce old patterns of oppression.[5] If so, feminists who appeal to autonomy may be unwittingly adopting a dominant male ideology and ignoring the best in a feminine outlook on morals. Animal liberationists join the new feminists, personalists, and utilitarian critics in calling for a re-emphasis on the role of compassion in a moral life; for, as they point out, classic theories of autonomy attach no intrinsic importance to the suffering of animals.[6]

Out of this confusing morass of claims and counterclaims, I want to isolate three ways in which I believe that autonomy is important; or better, since "autonomy" means different things to different people, I should say that what I want to do is focus upon three *senses,* or ideas, of autonomy and explain why, despite recent critics, I still believe each of these ideas has an important place in an ideal conception of morality. Exaggerated reactions to extravagant praise of autonomy, I fear, have put us in danger of overlooking some elementary points embedded in the autonomy-glorifying tradition. These points should be rather obvious and nonthreatening once they are disentangled from certain unnecessary accompaniments; and they are fully compatible with recognition of the moral importance of compassion.

My point of view is that of moral philosophy, not that of developmental psychology; and so I will have little to say about the stages of moral development and whether autonomy represents a peculiarly masculine point of view, as Gilligan's work seems to suggest. My aim, instead, will be to explain three modest theses about autonomy, unencumbered with some of the more extreme Kantian baggage that usually travels with them. My hope is that, once properly understood, these points will be recognized as an important part of any complete conception of morality.

I. Autonomy as Impartiality in the Review and Justification of Moral Principles and Values

"Autonomy," like many philosophers' favorite words, is not the name of one single thing; it means quite different things to different people. None of these ideas is simple, and the relations among the different senses of autonomy are staggeringly complex. Little progress can be made in debates about autonomy until these different ideas are sorted out.[7] To begin this effort, let me consider first a classic idea of autonomy introduced by Immanual Kant and followed, with modifications, by John Rawls and others.

Autonomy, Kant held, is a property of the wills of all adult human beings insofar as they are viewed as ideal moral legislators, prescribing general principles to themselves rationally, free from causal determinism, and not motivated by sensuous desires. For present purposes, two points in this conception are crucial. *First,* having autonomy means considering principles from a point of view that requires temporary detachment from the particular desires and aversions, loves and hates, that one happens to have; *second,* autonomy is an ideal feature of a person conceived in the *role* of a moral legislator, i.e., a person *reviewing* various suggested moral principles and values, *reflecting* on how they may conflict and how they might be reconciled, and finally *deciding* which principles are most acceptable, and whether and how they should be qualified.

To elaborate the first point, the autonomy of a moral legislator means that, in debating basic moral principles and values, a person ideally should not be moved by blind adherence to tradition or authority, by outside threats or bribes, by unreflective impulse, or unquestioned habits of thought. More significantly, an autonomous moral legislator must try not to give *special* weight to his or her particular preferences and personal attachments. In debating the standards of arbitration between sheep herders and cattlemen, for example, one must try to discount one's particular aversion, or attraction, to sheep. In searching for the appropriate values regarding the relations between the sexes, one must try not to tailor the decision to the advantage of the sex one happens to be. Kant called this "abstracting from personal differences"[8], and Rawls refers to it as choosing "behind a veil of ignorance."[9] The central point for both is, that for purposes of trying to adjudicate fairly and reasonably among competing principles and values, certain considerations must be ruled out of court. For example, the fact that a principle would benefit *me, my* family, and *my* country instead of someone else, someone else's family and country, is not *in itself* a reason for anyone, as a moral legislator, to favor that principle. In other words, at the level of deliberation about basic principles, morality requires impartial regard for all persons.

The second point, however, states an extremely important qualification. Autonomy, as impartiality, is part of an ideal for moral legislation, or general debate about moral principles and values; it is not a recommended way of life. Unfortunately, some philosophers, including Kant, seem at times to conflate this legislative ideal with another idea, which does not really follow; namely, the idea that in facing the moral choices of daily life we should constantly strive to act on impartial principles, to free ourselves of particular attachments, and to ignore the distinguishing features of individuals. In fact, far from being a consequence of autonomy in legislation, this idea that we should live with our eyes fixed on abstract, impartial principles seems quite the opposite of what autonomous moral legislators would recommend. Even from an impartial perspective, which gives no special advantage to interests just because they are one's *own,* one can see good reasons for moral principles such as "Be compassionate," "Take responsibility, within limits, for your family, your country, and yourself," "Don't face concrete moral problems as if they were mathematical puzzles, but restructure them with sensitivity and find a 'caring' solution."

Now one might well wonder why impartiality in the review of basic principles has been called *autonomy,* especially since such impartiality seems to have little to do with the right of self-governance and other things that nowadays pass for autonomy. The explanation, I think, is rooted in Kant's idea that one's "true self," in a sense, is the way one is when free as possible from transitory concerns, personal eccentricities, and the particular attachments one is caused to have by nature and circumstance. In this conception, one is most fully oneself, expressing one's true nature, when one "rises above" the particular natural and conditioned desires that distinguish one from others; and one does this by adopting principles from an impartial point of view and acting from respect for these principles. In this way, it is thought, one is self-governing, or autonomous, i.e. governed by one's true (impartial) self.

While this seems to be the historical origin of the use of the word "autonomy" for the idea of impartiality in the review of basic principles, these originating associations are not an essential part of that idea. In other words, one can perfectly well reject the notion that a person is truly self-governing only when making and acting from impartial principles and yet still agree with the main point, namely, that autonomy as impartiality is a crucial aspect of the ideal perspective from which moral principles are to be reviewed and defended.

Once this point is seen clearly for what it is, who would want to deny it? Only those extreme relativists who believe that reasonable debate about basic moral principles is either impossible or presupposes a prior arbitrary personal commitment that cannot be rationally defended to anyone who happens to feel differently.[10] For all the impartiality thesis says is that, if and when one raises questions regarding fundamental moral standards, the court of appeal that one addresses is a court in which no particular individual, group, or country has *special* standing. Before that court, declaring "I like it," "It serves *my* country," and the like, is not decisive; principles must be defensible to anyone looking at the matter apart from his or her special attachments, from a larger, human perspective.

Is not this, in fact, just what most of us, men and women, believe? Of course, when faced with a concrete moral problem, we are guided by thoughts such as, "He is, after all, my friend," and "I have a responsibility to my family—and myself." But if the philosophical question is raised, "Why does one have such responsibilities and what are their limits?," do we really think we could get a satisfactory answer *solely* by reference to our own needs and wants or to the needs and wants of others (e.g. family), identified essentially by relation to ourselves? At this stage, when the moral grounds and limits of personal responsibility are called into question, the discussion moves to a more abstract level in which impartiality plays an important role. At this point if one says, "I don't care what impartial people would say," then one has simply given up the effort to find a reasonable moral adjudication and defense of one's beliefs.

To avoid misunderstanding, it is worth emphasizing again that the impartiality thesis we have been considering is not the same as its more controversial cousins. For example, it does not assert, with Kant, that basic moral principles are grounded in pure reason, independent of all contingent features of human nature, that they admit no exceptions, or that they command only our wills and not our feelings. Our thesis does not imply that self-sufficiency is better than dependence, or that the emotional detachment of a judge is better than the compassion of a lover. No one is urged to live with his or her eyes fixed on abstract moral principles, still less with concentration on their justification from an impartial perspective. Nothing is implied about which motives make acts morally commendable. Impartiality has its important place, but its place is not that of a model for moral sainthood.

A footnote here may be helpful. Modern philosophers sometimes talk rather loosely about "the moral point of view." It is frequently said that the moral point of view is an impartial point of view, detached from one's individual loves and hates.[11] But, in fact, there is not a single "moral point of view;" what point of view is morally appropriate depends upon what is being viewed and what the question about it is. When a conscientious mother faces the question of how to respond to her daughter's unwanted pregnancy, compassion and sensitivity to individual needs are crucial to a moral perspective. When, later, awareness of cultural differences leads her to question the nature and grounds of the moral values she has relied on, then her compassion and sensitivity alone will not settle the issue. Another point of view is called for, a perspective from which she could discuss these matters reasonably with others who have different particular attachments. It is here that impartiality becomes important. To talk as if there is a single "moral point of view" only confuses the issue.

II. Autonomy as a Right to Make Certain Personal Decisions

Often we hear the complaint that someone has violated the autonomy of another, for example, by trying to manipulate the other person with lies or improper threats. The idea here is quite different from the previous, philosophers' notion of autonomy. The autonomy in question here is not a feature of ideal moral legislators but a *right* that every responsible person has, a right to make certain decisions for himself or herself without undue interference from others. To respect someone as an autonomous person in this sense is to acknowledge that certain decisions are up to him or her and thus to refrain from efforts to control those decisions. To say that a person is autonomous, in this view, is not to *describe* the person (e.g. as mature, reflective, or independent); it is to *grant* the person a *right* to control certain matters for himself or herself. The operative analogy here is with autonomous nations. They may not be especially wise or well governed, but they have a right to determine their internal affairs without outside interference of various sorts.

Exactly what these rights of autonomy are is, of course, a matter of controversy. But, to focus discussion, let us think of a right of individual autonomy as follows: it is a right to make otherwise morally permissible decisions about matters deeply affecting one's own life without interference by controlling threats and bribes, manipulations, and willful distortion of relevant information. Like most rights, this right of autonomy may be defeasible—or overridden in special circumstances; but it is nonetheless important.

The right of autonomy is a right to freedom of a certain sort, but, of course, it is not an unlimited right to do as one pleases. It is limited, for example, by principles of justice, noninjury, contract, and responsibility to others. Autonomous persons are not free to cheat on their taxes, beat their children, or renege on their promises. Nor is autonomy a freedom to win in situations of fair competition: you do not violate my autonomy if you prevent me from having a place on a team by performing better than I do in the tryouts. Again, autonomy is not freedom to control others' lives in matters that mainly affect them, for example, a friend's choice of companions, jobs, and hairstyle. On the contrary, a person's right of autonomy protects certain decisions that deeply affect that person's own life so long as they are consistent with other basic moral principles, including recognition of comparable liberties for others.

When we say that a person has a right of autonomy, however, we are not simply saying that he or she is morally *permitted* to make his or her own decisions within the appropriate area of choice; we are also saying that others should not interfere in certain ways. What sorts of interferences are ruled out? Most obviously, physical coercion and threats that would be wrong to carry out in any case: e.g. threatening to slander someone if he or she does not vote as one wishes. But other interference can be illegitimate too. Consider, for example, the manipulative parent's threat, "If you move away, I will commit suicide." If designed solely to control another's choice rather than merely explaining one's "contingency plans," the threat represents an undue interference with that person's autonomy. Generally, when we try to manipulate others' choices of partner, career, or legitimate lifestyle by nonrational techniques, we unduly interfere with choices that are rightfully their own. Respecting individuals' autonomy means granting them at least the *opportunity* to make their crucial life-affecting choices in a rational manner. Concealing or distorting information relevant to such decisions can also be a way of depriving them of this opportunity, even if one's aim is not primarily to influence their choices. For example, a father, however well intentioned, might unduly interfere with his shy daughter's important life choices if, to comfort her, he tried to persuade her that women in law and other competitive professions are always unattractive.

The right of autonomy, as I see it, is not rooted in any idea that rational decision making is intrinsically valuable, or in the optimistic faith that people will use their opportunity to make the best possible choices. All the more, I would not want to say that people have a right of autonomy only to the extent that we expect they will make rational choices. Within limits, people should be allowed to make their own choices even if the choices are likely to be foolish. Questions about the justification and limits of the right of autonomy are difficult; but I hope that, on reflection, most would agree that we are not entitled to interfere with others' crucial life choices just because we believe they are likely to be nonrational or unwise.

Accepting this right of autonomy does not mean that we must accept more extreme views that are sometimes associated with the word "autonomy." For example, we can acknowledge the right without in any way implying that self-sufficiency, independence, and separation from others are goals worth pursuing. Respecting people's autonomy requires resisting the temptation to "take charge" of their lives without their consent, but it does not deny anyone the choice to share with others, to acknowledge one's dependency, to accept advice, or even to sacrifice for the interests of others. The right of autonomy allows people some room to make their own choices; it does not dictate what those choices should be.

Also acknowledging a right of autonomy does not mean that people are morally better, or at a higher stage of development, if they constantly think of moral problems as conflicts of individual rights rather than as occasions for sensitivity and compassion. Rights are just one aspect of complex moral problems, and fixation on this aspect to the exclusion of others can be as much a moral fault as overlooking rights altogether. To say that we should respect a right of autonomy is not to say that we should ignore everything else.

But, one may wonder, does not the right of autonomy often conflict with the compassionate response to a moral problem? Suppose, for example, that by a benevolent lie I can manipulate a friend away from a potentially disastrous choice, say, to reunite with an unworthy and incompatible exlover. Would not compassion advise me to tell the lie despite the invasion of my friend's autonomy? Or, again, would not the right of autonomy prevent a kindhearted doctor from compassionately distorting the truth regarding the progress of a patient's terminal illness?

Such conflicts, I think, are unavoidable; the question is how should we handle them? Should we deny that there is anything here but compassion to consider? Or should we rather acknowledge such conflicts as tragic choices between two competing values each important in its own right—the prevention of unnecessary suffering and the individual's opportunity to make his or her own crucial life choices? The latter, surely, would be the answer of a balanced moral conception which encompasses both the male and female perspectives described by Gilligan. This would mean that concern for rights at times constrains what a compassionate person may do; but in no way does it deny the moral importance of compassion.

III. Autonomy as a Goal for Personal Development

Neither of the previous ideas of autonomy implies that in general, being an autonomous person, or living autonomously, is a morally desirable goal. But many have felt that, in some sense, autonomy is such a goal. Some, for example, may think of autonomy as constantly being motivated by pure respect for impartial principles rather than by compassion; but, as I have said, I find it far from obvious that this is a moral ideal. At least, it is a more controversial ideal than the two autonomy theses I have presented so far. Others seem to think of autonomy as self-sufficiency, independence, "making it on one's own;" but, though some people may prefer this way of life, it is hard to see why it should be regarded a *moral* goal. Is a person morally worse for acknowledging his or her dependency and preferring close ties with others to self-sufficiency? Surely not; and, as Carol Gilligan suggests, any development theories that implied this would be naturally suspected of prejudice.

There is, however, a more limited idea of autonomy that might be recommended as a moral ideal; and this idea lies behind a third way I believe autonomy is important.

Suppose we focus on the situation of an ordinary person facing a real moral decision. The context is not, as before, general philosophical reflection or debate about the nature and justification of moral principles but rather an immediate need to decide what to do about an actual problem at hand. Is there any sense in which making the judgment as an autonomous person is a moral ideal, so that we should make it our goal to face such problems as autonomous persons.

Impartial detachment from particular concerns, I have suggested, is not such a goal; and the *right* of autonomy we have considered is concerned with how we affect others by our decisions rather than with how we make our moral choices. Is there, then, any other sense of autonomy in which we should strive to make particular moral decisions as autonomous agents?

A clue is provided by the very word "autonomy," which suggests "self-governance." People are not self-governing, in a sense, when their responses to problems are blind, dictated by neurotic impulses of which they are unaware, shaped by prejudices at odds with the noble sentiments they think are moving them. When we make decisions like this we are divided against ourselves. There is little profit in debating which is the "true self"—the "self" revealed in high-minded, consciously adopted principles, or the "self" of prejudice and neurotic impulse that really determines the outcome; there is no unified "self" here to govern the decision.

While it may be debated whether having a unified personality is in general a moral goal, surely we can agree that it is a morally worthy goal to try to face our important moral decisions with as few as possible of these self-fracturing obstacles. Ideally autonomous, or self-governing, moral agents would respond to the real facts of the situation they face, not to a perception distorted by morally irrelevant needs and prejudices. The principles and values they try to express in their decisions would be genuine guiding considerations and not mere epiphenomena unrelated to their real moral motivation. If compassion is the guiding value, it would be genuine compassion and not a self-deceptive mask for concern for reputation. If respect for rights is the guiding consideration, then it would be sincere respect and not fear of punishment. This is not to say that other motives are bad or inappropriate (though they may be), nor that approaching moral decisions with autonomy of this sort is sufficient for making the right decision. The point is rather that, ideally, moral agents face their moral choices with awareness of both the relevant features of the problem and effective understanding of their real values.

To say that autonomy in this sense is an ideal is not necessarily to condemn those who lack it; for it is far from the only moral ideal, and it is very hard to achieve.

Is this third idea of autonomy compatible with compassion? Of course, it is. Holding autonomy of this sort as an ideal is neutral in disputes about which is more important, compassion or respect for rights. What it tells us is merely that we should try to face moral decisions with integrity and self-awareness. Or, perhaps better, if it favors either side, the ideal of autonomy for particular moral decisions urges us to face such problems with compassion: for I suspect that without compassion one can never really become aware of the morally relevant facts in the situation one faces. The inner needs and feelings of others are virtually always relevant, and without compassion one can perhaps never fully know what these are—or give them their appropriate weight.

I conclude, then, that there are at least three modest but important ways that autonomy is needed in a complete conception of morality. None is incompatible with recognition of the importance of compassion; and, though one ideal of autonomy puts some constraints on the reliance on compassion alone, another ideal of autonomy itself seems to require compassion. If, as Carol Gilligan's work suggests, autonomy represents a male value and compassion a female value, then my conclusion is that we must get the sexes together.

Notes

1. This paper was written for presentation to students and faculty at Ripon College as a part of a colloquium on "Autonomy and Caring," which was inspired by Carol Gilligan's *In A Different Voice*. Thanks are due to the participants at that conference, and especially to Robert Hannaford, for their comments.

2. A noteworthy example of the latter is Sharon Bishop Hill's "Self-determination and Autonomy" in Richard Wasserstrom's *Today's Moral Problems* (Macmillan, Third Edition, 1985).

3. See, for example, John Rawls's A *Theory of Justice* (Cambridge: Harvard University Press, 1971) and Robert Nozick's *Anarchy, State and Utopia* (New York: Basic Books, Inc., 1974).

4. Notably among these are Lawrence Blum, whose *Friendship, Altruism and Morality* (London, Boston and Henley: Routledge & Kegan Paul, 1980) has stimulated much useful discussion.

5. This remark applies only to those who try to draw certain moral and political conclusions from Carol Gilligan's research. In her book, Gilligan herself claims only to have uncovered tendencies in male and female populations and not to have established any ideological generalizations.

6. See, for example, Peter Singer's *Animal Liberation* (New York: Avon Books, 1977).

7. For some discussion of these distinctions, see my "Autonomy and Benevolent Lies," *Journal of Value Inquiry* 18:251–67 (1984).

8. See *The Groundwork of the Metaphysics of Morals* translated by H. J. Paton (Harper), p. 101.

9. See John Rawls, A *Theory of Justice,* pp. 136–42.

10. Examples might be Nietzche, early emotivists, and more recently Andrew Oldenquist in his provocative paper "Loyalties" in the *Journal of Philosophy* 79 (1982), 173–93.

11. For example, Kurt Baier, *The Moral Point of View* (Ithaca: Cornell University Press, 1958).

8

The Socialized Individual and Individual Autonomy

An Intersection between Philosophy and Psychology

DIANA T. MEYERS

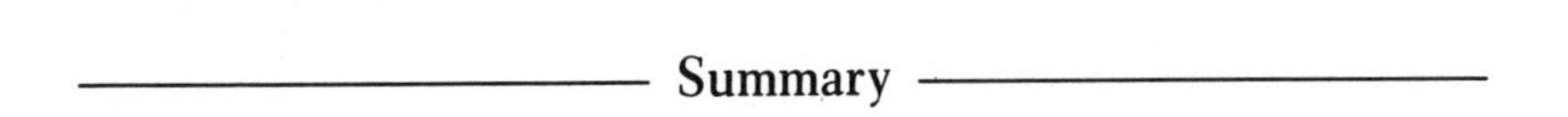

Summary

Diana T. Meyers asks whether exponents of the care perspective can be morally autonomous, that is, morally self-governing. There are three main reasons to think that the care perspective cannot support moral autonomy. First, since girls are socialized to be other-directed, it can be argued that conduct in accordance with the care perspective is a product of socialization rather than individual choice. Second, since adherents of the care perspective do not concern themselves with formulating and refining rules, it could be argued that adherents of this morality have no way of consulting themselves to discover their moral views. Third, since giving care requires subordinating one's interests to those of the recipient of care, it could be argued that the care perspective prevents people from acting on their own beliefs and desires. Meyers answers all of these charges and defends an account of moral autonomy as a competency that can be exercised in at least two ways: impartial reason—the method of the justice perspective; or responsibility reasoning—the method of the care perspective. Whereas impartial reason is motivated by rational self-interest and considers only those characteristics that all people share, responsibility reasoning is motivated by persons' sense of their own identity, along with their need for self-respect, and attends to unique individuals. D.T.M.

Autonomy is commonly taken to be incompatible with, indeed the antithesis of, socialization. People are thought to be autonomous only when they are free of social influence. Thus, autonomous people must somehow transcend the lessons that parents, teachers, religious leaders, and other authority figures instilled in them when they were children, as well as the pressures that peers and institutions continue to exert on them as adults. In the standard view, the true self is a self preserved from social taint, and autonomous conduct is action expressing the true self.

This picture of autonomy has spawned an extensive philosophical literature purporting to explain how people can circumnavigate their social backgrounds, and a psychological literature purporting to document the superior ability of men to carry out these maneuvers. However, I shall take a different approach in this paper. Instead of looking for a tear in the fabric of socialization through which a posited true self might emerge, I shall ask whether an alternative conception of autonomy can be defended. Specifically, I shall examine Carol Gilligan's recent research on the moral development of women and consider the challenge it poses to the traditional conception of moral autonomy developed by Kant and currently championed by John Rawls in philosophy and Lawrence Kohlberg in psychology. What I would like to suggest is that moral autonomy is a variegated phenomenon that depends on the exercise of a complex competency. Though the Kantian view of moral autonomy contributes to our understanding of this competency, it does not provide a complete account.

1. Gilligan's Research on Women's Morality

Carol Gilligan is a psychologist who studies moral development using the model that Lawrence Kohlberg pioneered in this field. Kohlberg holds that, on their way to moral maturity, people go through a series of six stages that can be grouped into three levels (Kohlberg 1981, pp. 409–12). Initially, children simply bow to the directives of external authorities, but in time, they realize that the rules they are expected to follow maintain a mutually advantageous social order. Eventually, people may advance to a postconventional, universalistic ethic of principles. People move from one stage to the next when their moral view proves inadequate to cope with novel predicaments that they are facing. Thus, cognitive dilemmas instigate progress through Kohlberg's hierarchy of stages and propel people towards increasingly comprehensive principles. Although the cognitive development model is vulnerable to serious objections, I shall set these problems aside, for my main concern is with Gilligan's and Kohlberg's alternative conceptions of moral maturity.

Gilligan accepts Kohlberg's basic theoretical apparatus, but her studies have led her to question Kohlberg's substantive account of the moral views prevailing at each stage of development (Gilligan 1982, pp. 100–105). Whereas Kohlberg contends that there is only one track leading to moral maturity and that this track terminates at a morality of justice founded on rights to noninterference, Gilligan contends that there is a parallel track with a different end-point. Her data suggest that many women develop towards a morality of care and responsibility.

The best way to succinctly sketch these two moral perspectives is to highlight the contrasts between them. For Kohlberg, morally mature individuals accept a system of universal rights along with their correlative duties. These rights protect people from others' interference, but, since they can conflict, they must be qualified and ranked according to their relative stringencies. Thus, morality involves discovering and complying with an ordered set of generally applicable, yet highly differentiated rules. In contrast, for Gilligan, moral maturity can be based on general injunctions to give care, to sustain interpersonal connections, and to secure one's own integrity. In this view, morally mature people are not preoccupied with articulating and refining rules, nor do they regard noninterference as morally sufficient. Rather, they concentrate on understanding other individuals and their particular circumstances in order to respond appropriately to these persons' needs and concerns. Concomitantly, they recognize and undertake to fulfill their own potential. Whereas Kohlberg's vision of moral maturity might be characterized as one of decent respect for others while pursuing one's own good, Gilligan's alternative might be characterized as a vision of concerned involvement with others while respecting oneself.

Gilligan illustrates the difference between these two perspectives with the rather poignantly contrastive solutions that exponents of the two perspectives give to the following problem (Gilligan, 1985). A group of industrious, prudent moles have spent the summer digging a burrow where they will spend the winter. A lazy, improvident porcupine who has not prepared a winter shelter approaches the moles and pleads to share their burrow. The moles take pity on the porcupine and agree to let him in. Unfortunately, the moles did not anticipate the problem the porcupine's sharp quills would pose in close quarters. Once the porcupine has moved in, the moles are constantly being stabbed. The question is, what should the moles do? On the one hand, subjects answering according to the rights perspective point out that the moles own the shelter and are therefore entitled to throw the porcupine out. When asked what the moles should do if the porcupine refuses to leave, some of these respondents favor shooting the porcupine. On the other hand, subjects answering according to the care perspective suggest solutions like covering the porcupine with a blanket. These respondents devise compromises that defuse conflict and secure everyone's interests.

Now, it is important to recognize not only that the solutions proposed by exponents of the rights perspective differ from those proposed by exponents of the care perspective, but also that the reasoning leading to these divergent solutions differs. Here, I shall idealize the two reasoning processes in order to highlight their differences.

Within the rights perspective, deliberators regard moral problems as analogous to mathematical equations with variables to compute. Accordingly, moral reflection consists of impartial, rational choice of principles and the application of these principles. People are bearers of rights that have varying degrees of moral force. In general, then, our moral task is to ascertain which rights people have, what the relative stringencies of these rights are, and which of the rights that are in play in the case at hand is the most weighty. In the process of working out a particular moral problem, the individual may find grounds for modifying prior moral conceptions or for articulating new relations between principles. By resolving tensions arising between their principles, people progress to higher stages of development.

At the highest stage, they are capable of electing principles from the standpoint of a Rawlsian original position (Rawls 1971, pp. 118–50). In short, they have become morally self-governing and hence free.

The care perspective places no premium on the codification of principles. A consideration that takes precedence over a second consideration in one context may be overshadowed by that selfsame consideration in another situation with a new cast of characters. Moreover, agents may be unable to specify the relevant distinction between the two contexts; in other words, they may be unable to reduce their moral conclusions to general rules. The care perspective allows for the possibility that human relations can involve deep and special emotional bonds that have a moral significance but that, nonetheless, cannot be universalized. (For a related discussion, see Jonathan Adler's paper in this volume.) Subjects who think in terms of the care perspective make moral progress, not by stepping outside their social context in order to generate ever more sophisticated systems of rules, but rather by expanding the scope of the injunctions to give care and to maintain connections. This is not to say that the care perspective altogether bars adherence to moral principles. But it is to say that the sense of responsibility at the core of the care perspective neither exacts rationality to the exclusion of emotionality nor imposes impartiality at the expense of ongoing attachment.

Which of these two orientations people are likely to adopt depends on their gender. Gilligan has found that, although all people are able to understand and even to use both moral approaches, the vast majority of males rely primarily on the rights-based morality; however, about one third of all females rely primarily on the care morality while another third rely primarily on the rights-based morality (Gilligan, this volume). In other words, many women think in terms of rights, but almost no men think in terms of care. This cleavage demands an explanation.

2. Socialization and Gender-Differentiated Morality

Gilligan cites Nancy Chodorow's account of differential feminine-masculine socialization to explain the discrepancy between women's and men's moral perspectives (Gilligan 1982, pp. 7–8). Using a psychoanalytic framework, Chodorow argues that the differences between feminine and masculine personalities emerge as a result of the child's need to establish a gender identity in a world in which women serve as children's primary caretakers. With regard to gender identity, there is an assymmetry between the developmental issues faced by girls and those faced by boys. Since girls are the same sex as their primary caretakers, they are not obliged to break off their emotional attachment to their mothers in order to secure their gender identity. Thus, girls' sense of themselves is compatible with a sense of embeddedness in relationships, and their capacity for empathy flourishes (Chodorow 1978, pp. 167–69). But since boys are the opposite sex of their primary caretakers, they must decisively break away from their mothers in order to secure their gender identity. Consequently, boys' sense of themselves depends on a sense of their separation from others, and their capacity for empathy is stifled while their capacity for independence is cultivated (Chodorow 1978, pp. 165 and 181–83).

The coincidence between Chodorow's and Gilligan's theories is striking. If rationality and impartiality are marks of independence, Chodorow's account affirms that boys would be driven to develop their rational skills and to assume an impartial stance. In contrast, Chodorow's account suggests that girls would have little or no need to gain this moral perspective, for their gender identities are not threatened by their immersion in a network of emotion-laden relationships. However, since many people have what I would agree are well-founded doubts about the empirical standing of psychoanalytic accounts like Chodorow's, I want to emphasize that studies based on a wide variety of theoretical approaches supply ample evidence that socialization plays a telling role in the evolution of moral perspectives. However, in the interest of space, I shall only sample the supporting evidence that could be adduced.

No one discounts the role of parents and peers in childhood socialization. A number of recent studies specify in considerable detail the way in which girls are sensitized to others and taught to respond to others' concerns while boys are taught to forge their own paths.

Studies show that adults are disposed to interact with children on the basis of gender-stereotypes. Left in a room with a baby said to be female, mothers offer the child a doll rather than a train. Told that an unknown baby is a boy, mothers offer the child the train instead of the doll (Weitzman 1984, p. 160). Although it is hard to assess the impact on babies of this disposition mothers have to guide their conduct on the basis of sex, one study suggests that differential treatment may have a discernible effect as early as the age of thirteen months. By that time, boys start spending less time in close proximity to their mothers, but girls continue to talk with and gaze at their mothers (Hunter College 1983, p. 145). These observations lend support to the contention that boys become more independent earlier than girls. Nevertheless, it is debatable why this difference appears. It may be partially due to differences in activity levels. Boys have been found to be more active than girls (Hyde 1985, p. 149), and greater activity would help to explain boys' more extensive forays. However, many students of development are convinced that their greater activity is stimulated, at least in part, by social forces.

There is evidence that fathers' attitudes strongly influence their children's developmental trajectory. This is noteworthy because fathers' conceptions of how their children should behave are more stereotypical than mothers', and fathers impose these conceptions on their children firmly and consistently (Weitzman 1984, p. 164). Moreover, fathers use enforcement methods to deal with their daughters different from those they use with their sons. Fathers tend to reward their daughters for feminine behavior, but they are apt to punish their sons for "sissyish" behavior (Weitzman 1984, p. 164). Since studies show that children are more compliant when punishments are administered by people with whom they identify, there is reason to believe that this mode of paternal insistence that boys be masculine is very effective. How responsive girls are to their fathers' approbation remains an open question.

Outside the home, children encounter numerous incentives to fit into gender roles. For example, it has been found that children are less tolerant of gender-inappropriate behavior than many adults are (Hyde 1985, pp. 110–11). Moreover, girls who are attuned to social approval are likely to be popular with their peers, but boys who are other-directed in this way are likely to be unpopular (Hunter College 1983, p. 153). Whereas boys benefit from independence, girls pay a price for going their own way. Thus, girls' self-interest strongly commends attending to others' wishes.

Since children imitate the models available to them, the information about social expectations conveyed by various media are an important factor in childhood socialization, and the media to which children are exposed—books and television—provide unrealistically polarized images of women and men (Weitzman 1984, pp. 165–66). An interesting sidelight in regard to children's media concerns their presentation of reactions to female characters. Whereas male characters are commonly shown being rewarded for their activities, female characters are simply ignored (Weitzman 1984, pp. 165–66). Female characters only elicit significant responses when they violate gender stereotypes and are punished for their transgressions (Weitzman 1984, p. 166). When books and television shows are not threatening girls with ostracism for gender-crossing behavior, they are instilling in girls the message that they should stay in the background and acquiesce in anonymity. It is hardly surprising, then, that many girls become reluctant to act assertively, and become, instead, willing to function only as facilitators and helpmates.

Whether or not there is any biological basis for observed behavioral differences between women and men is open to dispute, but it is clear that without differential gender socialization, these behavioral differences would be much less pronounced. As it is, self-sufficiency is encouraged in boys while other-directed pliancy is encouraged in girls. This assymmetry helps to explain the discrepancy Gilligan had found between women's and men's moral perspectives.

Nevertheless, it is important to recognize that feminine socialization is not monolithic. For example, despite the fact that women are not supposed to be achievers, young girls are rewarded for doing well in school (Weitzman 1984, p. 219). Thus, ambivalence is built into conventional feminine socialization processes. Moreover, many girls undergo unconventional socialization processes—either their mothers work and provide nontraditional role models, or their fathers actively support their nontraditional aspirations (Weitzman 1984, pp. 217–18). For this reason, it is not surprising that Gilligan has not found uniform adherence to the ethic of care among women.

What *is* surprising is the rarity of deviance from the ethic of rights among men. Social psychologists have noted profound tensions within the contemporary masculine role. While men are expected to be indomitably aggressive at work, they are expected to be tenderly affectionate at home (Hyde 1985, p. 107). Still, this split has not translated into weaker allegiance to the rights perspective among men. Perhaps, this is because the public activities of the provider and protector remain dominant in the masculine role, and the morality of rights remains dominant in the public sphere. Whatever the explanation of the virtual unanimity of men's commitment to this moral perspective, it is undeniable that socialization disposes them to neutralize the moral significance of emotional bonds and to rely instead on impartial reason.

3. Socialization and Autonomy

The Kantian model of moral autonomy maintains that reason enables people to achieve individual autonomy without sacrificing social cooperation. To be morally autonomous is to follow rules that one has chosen for oneself. Through reason, people conceive and adopt their own moral principles. Since they have freely and rationally elected these principles, people do what they really want to do when they act on them. Yet, since reason is universal, everyone chooses the same rules, and violence and anarchy are averted. On this model of autonomy, each person can be self-governing because all people have the same benign true self—we are all rational beings. Moreover, autonomous individuals transcend the limits of their respective socialization experiences since reason is not culture bound.

Given this model of autonomy, it is easy to see why women have acquired a reputation for heteronomy. Gilligan has documented many women's indifference to the project of formulating and abiding by a set of rules (Gilligan 1982, p. 44). Furthermore, these women acknowledge the primacy of emotional attachments in their moral deliberations, and emotional involvement is commonly regarded an inimical to rationality. Finally, notwithstanding the fact that there is no empirical support for the claim that women's reasoning ability is inferior to men's, thinkers otherwise as opposed as Aristotle and Simone de Beauvoir have retailed this prejudice (Aristotle *Politics*, 1260a and de Beauvoir 1953, pp. 437 and 580). Thus, the conclusion that femininity traps women in heteronomy may seem natural enough.

I would like to cast some doubt on this conclusion by considering whether masculine patterns of moral deliberation measure up to the Kantian ideal. First, it is important to recognize that men do not transcend their upbringings when they resort to impartial reason. We have seen that the socialization to which boys are subjected instills this approach in them. Nevertheless, it might be argued that impartial reason does enable men to transcend their socialization inasmuch as the principles chosen in this way are not beholden to any particular cultural milieu. However, this, too, is doubtful. John Rawls has granted that the concept of the person on the basis of which people choose principles in the original position may vary from society to society, and therefore that the principles that are chosen may vary as well (Rawls 1980, p. 569). On Rawls's Kantian view, practical reason is not universal, though it is uniform within each culture.

Although Rawls holds that moral conduct expresses the person's nature as a free and equal rational being, he concedes that all people may not have an identical nature. Still, he maintains that all of the members of a cultural group share the same true self that shapes their moral perspective. Thus, one way to read Gilligan's data would be to delineate two cultural groups corresponding to the two moral perspectives she has described. However, I do not consider this to be an especially promising avenue of inquiry.

Perhaps, a dual culture interpretation would be warranted if Gilligan had conducted her research in a prototypically patriarchal society. But in our own society, there is such extensive contact between women and men that it is hard to believe that the feminine and masculine realms constitute separate cultural spheres. Furthermore, a dual culture interpretation would overlook one of Gilligan's most striking findings, namely, that, regardless of their basic orientations, women and men alike readily understand and can be cued to use both moral perspectives (Gilligan, this volume). When the members of different cultural groups cease to baffle one another, either they have taken pains to familiarize themselves with one another's alien beliefs and practices, or their cultures have, to some extent, merged. Gilligan observes that women and men have common childhood experiences that would account for their mutual understanding (Gilligan, this volume). Thus, it is unnecessary for women and men to make anthropological studies of the opposite sex, and it seems doubtful that the distinctions between Gilligan's two moral perspectives are of the magnitude of cultural divides. This is not to gainsay the possibility that women and men once constituted distinct cultural groups, but it is to deny that they still do in Western societies today.

In my estimation, a more theoretically compelling reason to reject the dual culture interpretation is that, in effect, it would ratify the assumption that for purposes of morality true selves are uniform within each culture. But I, for one, have doubts about the wisdom of this assumption. Although it is plain that people have no choice but to assume a common stock of interests when they are deciding how to treat strangers—any other assumption would be an invitation to self-aggrandizing rationalization of the sort practiced by slave-owners who denied the humanity of their chattels—it is by no means obvious why this same assumption is appropriate in all interactions amongst intimates.

Limiting morality to consideration of only those interests that people have in common closes off the possibility of a more subtle, more humane morality. As I understand it, the morality of rights is primarily a morality of self-defense. It aims to protect people from aggression and severe deprivation. Paradoxically, to protect people from these woefully commonplace assaults on their individual integrity, rights must disregard individuality and concentrate on a general concept of human dignity. But hardly anyone thinks that rights exhaust morality. Even Kohlberg has conceded that his studies have investigated justice, that is, the part of morality that is most accessible to abstract reason (Kohlberg 1982, pp. 515–16). Accordingly, I take it to be uncontroversial that the ethic of rights stands in need of supplementation.

If the ethic of rights tells us how we must act in order to respect people's fundamental human dignity, it is left to the ethic of care (or some other ethical theory) to tell us how we must act to respect people's individuality. People can have atypical interest profiles, and I see no reason why a conscientious agent should not take solid information about such idiosyncracies into account, provided that no one's rights are violated. Moreover, people's close personal relationships can create special needs and interdependencies, which a conscientious person cannot ignore. To honor a person's distinctive qualities, while respecting this person's rights, is to morally address the whole of that individual's true self. To attend to one's own distinctive capacities and weaknesses, while refusing to allow the standards one sets for oneself to fall below the minimum set by others' rights, is to give moral expression to the totality of one's own true self.

Intimacy belies the claims that people's true selves are uniform and that morality need only address those parts of people's true selves that they share with others. How rich a moral life people have depends on their willingness and ability to look beyond common humanity and respond to others' unique personalities. That socialization differentially sensitizes women to the particularities of individuals and situations no more impugns their autonomy than the fact that socialization inclines men to reach for impartiality impugns theirs.

4. Moral Autonomy and Moral Competency

I have argued that no one's ethical view is independent of socialization and that basing one's ethics entirely on the assumption that all people have identical true selves impoverishes one's moral life. However, I have not yet confronted the question of whether the care perspective can sustain a form of moral reflection that can be dubbed autonomous. Against the possibility of autonomy within the care perspective, it could be pointed out that the care perspective relegates rules to a minor role and compromises reason with emotional attachments. Since Kantian autonomy is secured through adherence to rationally accepted rules, it is hard to see how exponents of the care perspective could be autonomous.

In approaching this issue, it is important to keep in mind that the Kantian conception of autonomy is not definitive. Moral autonomy requires that people be morally self-governing. I have already argued that adherence to rationally accepted impartial rules does not always guarantee that people will give full moral expression to their true selves. It is an open question whether some other mode of deliberation can provide a moral conduit for the true self. Preliminary to defending a conception of moral autonomy based on the care perspective, I shall examine Rawls's account of autonomy in more detail, for Rawls's moral epistemology allows for the possibility that his conception of reflective equilibrium is but one method of gaining moral autonomy.

Rawls's account of autonomy starts from the assumption that all people have a sense of justice that enables them to form judgments about the justice of various practices (Rawls 1971, p. 46). The sense of justice is not foolproof: such factors as self-interest, fear, and haste can yield distorted judgments (Rawls 1971, p. 47). However, under favorable circumstances, everyone is competent to assess the justice of actions and policies. In Rawls's view, a theory of justice is a set of principles that captures a person's considered convictions, that is, those judgments that the person affirms under favorable circumstances (Rawls 1971, p. 46). Broadly speaking, moral rules articulate and systematize a person's underlying moral sense.

Rawls compares people's moral sense with their sense of grammaticality (Rawls 1971, p. 47). Although there are many disanalogies between Rawls's moral theory and Chomsky's linguistic theory, some of the analogies are illuminating. For Rawls, morality is the expression of a competency similar to a realized linguistic competency, such as the ability to speak English, and a system of moral rules comprises a theory of a moral competency just as English syntax and semantics explicate a linguistic competency. For my present purposes, I propose to accept Rawls's insight that moral judgment depends on the exercise of a competency. But, in order to aviod begging any questions about autonomy, I shall sever my conception of moral competency from Chomsky's conception of an innate system of rules and instead rely on the conception of a competency that we find in ordinary usage. Let us, then, understand a competency to be a repertory of coordinated skills that enables a person to perform a specified task. Supposing that Rawls is correct in thinking that moral conduct stems from a competency, I shall explore the role of rules in competent moral interaction and in moral autonomy.

Kohlberg identifies moral conduct with following rules and holds that advanced moral stages are distinguished by gains in the agent's critical perspective on the rules. Thus, for Kohlberg, the most morally mature people not only grasp the theory that accounts for their moral competency, but they also assess the merits of this theory and alter it to meet new contingencies. In Rawlsian parlance, they achieve reflective equilibrium (Kohlberg 1981, pp. 195–97). Their principles in harmony with their considered judgments and their conduct in harmony with their principles, these people are morally autonomous—they act in accordance with self-chosen rules. My question is whether this is the only way moral competency can give rise to moral autonomy.

Now, it is clear that, in general, people can be competent without being able to state the rules that govern their performances. I long ago forgot many of the grammatical rules my elementary school teachers worked so hard to inculcate, but I did not lose my ability to speak and write standard English. And, in any event, those rules never did codify all of the legitimate moves we can make in the course of communicating in standard English. So competency does not presuppose one's ability to expound the theory of the competency.

In ethics, one of Gilligan's more interesting discoveries is that, given a choice, most people regard solutions stemming from the care perspective as better (Gilligan, 1985). If you recall the solutions to the problem of the moles and the porcupine, I think you will be inclined to confirm this result. Presumably, adherents of the rights perspective who make such judgments will then set about revising their principles to accommodate their beliefs, but I shall not go into the question of whether the care perspective can be successfully grafted onto the rights perspective. What I want to focus on is the status of care-based solutions. Since people consider care-based solutions satisfactory even though most people do not come up with them first, it seems doubtful that care solutions are just lucky guesses. In other words, it seems reasonable to regard them as genuine—possibly superior—exercises of moral competency. Nevertheless, since they are not produced through the mediation of rationally adopted rules, it is not clear that these solutions are produced autonomously.

From the standpoint of moral competency, two reasons to insist on moral codification stand out. In contexts in which predictability is important—interaction with strangers and child-rearing, for example—rules are needed, for mutual recognition of rules can foster stability and trust. Also, rules are indispensable when improvisation would lead to opprobrious solutions, or would only lead to satisfactory solutions erratically. If adherents of the care perspective had recommended that the moles anaesthetize the porcupine and pluck its quills, we would bemoan their indifference to the porcupine's rights, and we would want them to embrace some rules. But as long as care-based solutions do not undermine trust or violate anyone's rights, it is immaterial whether or not the agent refers to rules in the process of deliberation, and it is immaterial whether or not the agent's solutions could be captured in a system of rules.

Notice, also, that rules cannot fully account for solutions within the justice perspective. Among the well-established dicta of the justice perspective is one requiring us to tell the truth. Yet, honesty is no mechanical matter. In delicate situations, people can be tactfully candid or brutally frank, and brutal frankness can be morally condemnable. Yet, there may be no formula for generating the tactfully candid expression; it is left to the individual agent to invent it. Evidently, morality can require people to use their ingenuity in complying with rules. Thus, in several respects, the role of rules in moral competency can be sharply circumscribed.

But what of moral autonomy? Are rules necessary there? It is arguable that rules play a more crucial role in moral autonomy because the autonomous person must be able to monitor her conduct to make sure that it matches her true self. The process of selecting a set of principles affords an occasion for people to examine their moral convictions and to decide what they really believe. Furthermore, the coherence requirement implicit in Rawls's conception of reflective equilibrium can be understood as a standard indicating when a system of rules adequately embodies a person's true self. Thus, a rationally certified set of rules tells a person what she must do if her conduct is to express her true self, and the rules that a person embraces exhibit that individual's convictions in a readily usable fashion that makes it easy for her to check up on her conduct. To decide whether her actions express her true self, the individual need only measure them against the list of rules she has rationally chosen.

From this sketch of Rawlsian autonomy, two necessary conditions for moral autonomy can be extracted. First, autonomous people must use some procedure to discover and, perhaps, to adjust the contents of their moral sense. Second, they must act in accordance with the results obtained by using this procedure. With respect to this second condition, it is clear that rationally certified rules are nothing more than a convenience. They simplify the agent's self-monitoring activities. However, it is doubtful that anyone can bypass rationally certified rules and still fulfill the first condition. For Rawls, the procedure whereby people discover the contents of their moral sense is the process of bringing their intuitions into reflective equilibrium with the principles they deduce in the original position. Does the care perspective supply any comparable procedure?

I believe that the care perspective does include such a procedure. Instead of asking whether she has achieved reflective equilibrium, the exponent of the care perspective asks whether she can take responsibility for this or that action. This alternative conception of autonomy could be challenged in two main ways. First, it could be objected that taking responsibility is not a procedure at all but rather an admission of accountability. Second, it could be urged that responsibility is too elastic a concept to be used to distinguish right from wrong. I think that both of these charges can be answered.

The first of these criticisms rests on a misunderstanding. What I am suggesting is not that the mere act of avowing responsibility ensures moral autonomy. Plainly, we are sometimes responsible for acts that do not express our true selves and that we wholeheartedly regret. Rather, I am suggesting that the process of determining whether or not one could avow responsibility for an act while retaining one's self-respect may well ensure autonomy. Though it may not be possible to formalize this process in the way that Rawls has distilled the process of impartial reason into the decision procedure of reflective equilibrium, responsibility reasoning is a process that is sensitive to morally relevant concerns and that provides a touchstone for assessing alternative moral solutions.

In regard to the charge of excessive elasticity, it is necessary to recall that precisely the same charge has been leveled against Kant's universalizability criterion as well as Rawls's reflective equilibrium. Individuals who are genuinely unconcerned with their own welfare can sincerely universalize the most despicable practices. Likewise, Adina Schwartz has persuasively argued that Rawls's risk-averse agent will achieve reflective equilibrium over principles of justice befitting a liberal welfare state, whereas a less risk-averse individual will opt for libertarian principles (Schwartz 1981, pp. 127–43). Admittedly, what people can feature themselves taking responsibility for depends on what sort of people they are, but this liability is one that this mode of reasoning shares with impartial reason.

At this point, it might be conceded that there are no universally compelling arguments in ethics, yet it might be urged that any acceptable conception of moral autonomy must guarantee the elimination of the abominable solutions. The liberals and the libertarians can harmlesly continue to bicker, but the Nazis must be put out of the running. Here, it might be argued that Rawls's explication of impartial reason fares better than any other proposal. Behind the veil of ignorance, no one knows whether she is a member of an oppressed minority; therefore, it would be foolish to agree to principles that would institutionalize discriminatory oppression.

But here, again, there does not seem to be any way to prevent people with a very high tolerance for risk from taking a chance that they will come out on top. It seems a foolish risk to me, but, without introducing moral appeals, I see no way to dissuade the Russian roulette enthusiasts among us. Accordingly, if the safeguards built into responsibility reasoning are no less effective than the veil of ignorance, which curbs unbridled self-interest in the original position, it seems to me that we can reject the charge of undue elasticity. Thus, we need to consider what safeguards operate in the process of responsibility reasoning.

In responsibility reasoning, the individual's moral sense gains expression through an exercise in imaginative introjection. Instead of asking what one would believe if one were not in a position to skew arrangements to one's own advantage, one asks what choices are compatible with or reinforce desirable aspects of one's personal identity. Questions like "What would it be like to have done that?" and "Could I bear to be the sort of person who can do that?" are foremost. To answer these questions satisfactorily, the individual must be able to envisage a variety of solutions, must be able to examine these solutions open-mindedly, must be able to imagine the likely results of carrying out these options, must be attuned to self-referential responses like shame and pride, must be able to critically examine these responses, and must be able to compare various possibilities systematically along sundry dimensions. Each of these abilities represents a complex skill, and, together, these skills equip the individual to make a choice by consulting her self. Thus, it is plausible to say that people who deliberate in this way are self-governing.

In responsibility reasoning, the moral filter is the person's sense of her own identity. (For a related view, see Taylor 1976, pp. 289–96.) To do violence to this sense of oneself is to undermine one's self-respect. Just as the parties to the original position have the incentive of maximizing their own self-interest under the constraints of the veil of ignorance, the responsibility reasoner has the incentive of preserving or enhancing her self-respect. Though it cannot be denied that a base individual is unlikely to be converted to high moral ideals through responsibility reasoning—such a person may have no self-respect and may not miss it, or this person may gain self-respect through monstrous behavior—a basically decent individual is not likely to be tempted into monstrous behavior nor to choose a worse course of action by employing this mode of deliberation rather than impartial reason. If anything, obscuring morally suspect parts of the true self under the veil of ignorance may cripple moral invention. Tapping the true self directly, then, may encourage greater innovation and thereby promote better solutions. This may explain why people tend to prefer solutions issuing from the care perspective.

As with all competencies, the procedures of responsibility reasoning are just as good as the practitioner is skilled. And, as with impartial reason, responsibility reasoning relies on the honesty and humanity of the deliberator. What is necessary for moral autonomy is that the agent command some procedure for obtaining the guidance of the true self. Responsibility reasoning deploys a repertory of skills that anchor moral deliberation in the agent's personal identity without excluding any potentially relevant factors from consideration.

5. Moral Autonomy and Care

If I am right about the viability of responsibility reasoning as a form of autonomy, it follows that the care perspective supports moral autonomy without denying human connectedness. But this observation may bring to mind another doubt about the autonomy of responsibility reasoning. By definition, giving care requires attending to others' interests and demands. Thus, it would seem that giving care entails subordinating one's own self to the selves of others and abrogating self-governance.

This objection may seem more powerful than it is if one forgets that any moral view must serve as a curb on self-interest. No plausible moral position holds that moral autonomy is doing what you want to do regardless of others' needs and desires. Still, it might be countered that the care perspective does not merely curb self-interest; rather, it totally submerges self-interest. This reply overlooks two crucial facts. First, mature adherents of the care perspective embrace a dual injunction to be true to themselves—their own needs and desires—while giving care to others. Caring need not be servile (Friedman 1985, p. 145). Second, a person can identify with the interests of others and therefore most want to secure those interests. Caring need not be self-sacrificial. Thus, the care perspective in no way neutralizes concern with one's self.

I have argued that no form of autonomy can escape the charge that it is socially conditioned—that its adherents are reared to think the way they do. Furthermore, the care perspective and the rights perpective are both expressions of moral competency. Finally, I have urged that adherents of the care perspective use responsibility reasoning to deliberate and that this form of reasoning puts the individual in touch with her true self. Since these people's moral decisions stem from their selves, they are self-governing. Accordingly, I conclude that Kantian impartial reason is only one form of moral autonomy and that Carol Gilligan's research has alerted us to a second, equally tenable form.

References

Adler, Jonathan. "Moral Development and the Personal Point of View." In *Women and Moral Theory,* eds. Eva Feder Kittay and Diana T. Meyers. Totowa, N.J.: Rowman and Littlefield, 1987.

Aristotle. *Politics*. trans. Ernest Barker. Oxford: Oxford University Press, 1946.

Chodorow, Nancy. *The Reproduction of Mothering*. Berkeley: The University of California Press, 1978.

de Beauvoir, Simone. *The Second Sex,* trans. H.M. Parshley. New York: Bantam Books, 1953.

Friedman, Marilyn A. "Moral Integrity and the Deferential Wife." *Philosophical Studies* (1985), 47: 141–50.

Gilligan, Carol. *In a Different Voice*. Cambridge: Harvard University Press, 1982.

———. "Keynote Address." At the conference on Women and Moral Theory, S.U.N.Y. at Stony Brook, March 22–24, 1985.

———. "Moral Orientation and Moral Development." In *Women and Moral Theory*, eds. Eva Feder Kittay and Diana T. Meyers. Totowa, N.J.: Rowman and Littlefield, 1987.

Hunter College Women's Studies Collective. *Women's Realities, Women's Choices*. New York: Oxford University Press, 1983.

Hyde, Janet Shibley, ed. *Half the Human Experience: The Psychology of Women*. Lexington, Mass.: D.C. Heath and Company, 1985.

Kohlberg, Lawrence. *The Philosophy of Moral Development*. San Francisco: Harper and Row, Publishers, 1981.

———. "A Reply to Owen Flanagan and Some Comments on the Puka-Goodpaster Exchange." *Ethics* (1982) 92:513–28.

Rawls, John. *A Theory of Justice*. Cambridge: Harvard University Press, 1971.

———. "Kantian Constructivism in Moral Theory." *The Journal of Philosophy* (1980), 77:515–72.

Schwartz, Adina. "Against Universality." *The Journal of Philosophy* (1981), 78:127–43.

Taylor, Charles. "Responsibility for Self." In *The Identities of Persons*. Ed. Amelie Oksenberg Rorty. Berkeley: The University of California Press, 1976.

Weitzman, Lenore J. "Sex-Role Socialization: A Focus on Women." In *Women: A Feminist Perspective*, ed. Jo Freeman. Palo Alto, Calif.: Mayfield Publishing Company, 1984.

9

The Generalized and the Concrete Other
The Kohlberg-Gilligan Controversy and Moral Theory

SEYLA BENHABIB

Summary

Seyla Benhabib argues that the task of feminist critical theory is twofold: first it is necessary to undertake social scientific research in order to provide an "explanatory-diagnostic analysis" of the way in which gender-sex systems have contributed to the oppression and exploitation of women, and secondly, it is important to engage in normative, philosophical reflection that will allow for an anticipatory-utopian critique.

Benhabib contends that modern moral theory is founded on a dichotomy between justice and the good life. The former is associated with the realm of the public, the moral, and the historical; while the latter is associated with the private, the natural, and the atemporal. Attempts in contemporary moral theory to restrict the moral point of view to the perspective of the "generalized other" indicate that the dichotomy still functions within ethical theory. Benhabib suggests the need for the recognition of the concrete as well as the generalized other. She presents a model of a communicative ethic of need interpretations and the relational self as a paradigm that offers a critical, emancipatory alternative to "original position" justice models. S.M.

Can there be a feminist contribution to moral philosophy? Can those men and women who view the gender-sex system of our societies as oppressive, and who regard women's emancipation as essential to human liberation,

An earlier version of this paper was read at the Conference on "Women and Morality," SUNY at Stony Brook, March 22–24, 1985, and at the "Philosophy and Social Science" Course at the Inter-University Centre in Dubrovnik, Yugoslavia, April 2–14, 1985. I would like to thank participants at both conferences for their criticisms and suggestions. Larry Blum, Eva Feder Kittay, and Diana T. Meyers have made valuable suggestions for corrections. Nancy Fraser's commentary on this essay, "Toward a Discourse Ethic of Solidarity," read at the Women and Moral Theory Conference, has been crucial in helping me articulate the political implications of the position developed here. Both this article and Fraser's comments have appeared in *Praxis International*, special issue on *Feminism as Critique*, edited by Seyla Benhabib and Drucilla Cornell, vol. 5, no. 4 (January 1986).

criticize, analyze, and when necessary, replace the traditional categories of moral philosophy so as to contribute to women's emancipation and human liberation? By focusing on the controversy generated by Carol Gilligan's work, this essay seeks to outline such a feminist contribution to moral philosophy.

I. The Kohlberg-Gilligan Controversy

Carol Gilligan's research in cognitive, developmental moral psychology recapitulates a pattern made familiar to us by Thomas Kuhn.[1] Noting a discrepancy between the claims of the original research paradigm and the data, Gilligan and her co-workers first extend this paradigm to accomodate anomalous results. This extension then allows them to see some other problems in a new light; subsequently, the basic paradigm of the study of the development of moral judgment, according to Lawrence Kohlberg's model, is fundamentally revised. Gilligan and her co-workers now maintain that Kohlbergian theory is valid only for measuring the development of one aspect of moral orientation that focuses on the ethics of justice and rights.

In the 1980 article "Moral Development in Late Adolescence and Adulthood: A Critique and Reconstruction of Kohlberg's Theory," Murphy and Gilligan note that moral judgment data from a longitudinal study of twenty-six undergraduates scored by Kohlberg's revised manual replicate his original findings that a significant percentage of subjects appear to regress from adolescence to adulthood.[2] The persistence of this relativistic regression suggests a need to revise the theory. In this paper, they propose a distinction between "post-conventional formalism" and "post-conventional contextualism." While the post-conventional type of reasoning solves the problem of relativism by constructing a system that derives a solution to all moral problems from concepts like social contract or natural rights, the second approach finds the solution in the following way: "While no answer may be objectively right in the sense of being context-free, some answers and some ways of thinking are better than others." (Murphy and Gilligan 1980: 83) The extension of the original paradigm from post-conventional formalist to post-conventional contextual then leads Gilligan to see some other discrepancies in the theory in a new light, especially women's persistently low score when compared to their male peers. Distinguishing between the ethics of justice and rights, and the ethics of care and responsibility allows her to account for women's moral development and the cognitive skills they show in a new way. Women's moral judgment is more contextual, more immersed in the details of relationships and narratives. Women show a greater propensity to take the standpoint of the "particular other," and appear more adept at revealing feelings of empathy and sympathy required by this. Once these cognitive characteristics are seen not as deficiencies, but as essential components of adult moral reasoning at the post-conventional stage, then women's apparent moral confusion of judgment becomes a sign of their strength. Agreeing with Piaget that a developmental theory hangs from its vertex of maturity, "the point towards which progress is traced," a change in "the definition of maturity," writes Gilligan, "does not simply alter the description of the highest stage but recasts the understanding of development, changing the entire account."[3] The contextuality, narrativity, and the specificity of women's moral judgment is not a sign of weakness or deficiency, but a manifestation of a vision of moral maturity that views the self as a being immersed in a network of relationships with others. According to this vision, the respect for each others' needs and the mutuality of effort to satisfy them sustain moral growth and development.

When confronted with such a challenge, it is common for adherents of an old research paradigm to respond by arguing (a) that the data base does not support the conclusions drawn by revisionists, (b) that some of the new conclusions can be accomodated by the old theory, and (c) that the new and old paradigms have different object domains and are not concerned with explaining the same phenomena at all. In his response to Gilligan, Kohlberg has followed all three alternatives.

A. THE DATA BASE

In his 1984 "Synopses and Detailed Replies to Critics," Kohlberg argues that available data on cognitive moral development do not report differences among children and adolescents of both sexes with respect to justice reasoning.[4] "The only studies," he writes, "showing fairly frequent sex differences are those of adults, usually of spouse housewives. Many of the studies comparing adult males and females withough controlling for education and job differences . . . do report sex differences in favor of males." (Kohlberg 1984: 347) Kohlberg maintains that these latter findings are not imcompatible with his theory. [5] For, according to this theory, the attainment of stages four and five depends upon experiences of participation, responsibility, and role taking in the secondary institutions of society such as the workplace and government, from which women have been and still are, to a large extent, excluded. The data, he concludes, does not damage the validity of his theory, but shows the necessity for controlling for such factors as education and employment when assessing sex differences in adult moral reasoning.

B. ACCOMMODATION WITHIN THE OLD THEORY

Kohlberg now agrees with Gilligan that "the acknowledgement of an orientation of care and response usefully enlarges the moral domain." (Kohlberg 1984: 340) In his view, though, justice and rights, care and responsibility, are not two *tracks* of moral development, but two moral *orientations*. The rights orientation and the care orientation are not bipolar or dichotomous. Rather, the care-and-response orientation is directed primarily to relations of special obligation to family, friends, and group members, "relations which often include or presuppose general obligations of respect, fairness, and contract." (Kohlberg 1984: 349) Kohlberg resists the conclusion that these differences are strongly "sex related"; instead, he views the choice of orientation "to be primarily a function of setting and dilemma, not sex." (Kohlberg 1984: 350)

C. OBJECT DOMAIN OF THE TWO THEORIES

In an earlier response to Gilligan, Kohlberg had argued as follows:

> Carol Gilligan's ideas, while interesting, were not really welcome to us, for two reasons . . . The latter, we thought, was grist for Jane Loewinger's mill in studying stages of ego development, but not for studying the specifically moral dimension in reasoning . . . Following Piaget, my colleagues and I have had the greatest confidence that reasoning about justice would lend itself to a formal structuralist or rationalist analysis . . . whereas questions about the nature of the "good life" have not been as amenable to this type of statement.[6]

In his 1984 reply to his critics, this distinction between moral and ego development is further refined. Kohlberg divides the ego domain into the cognitive, interpersonal, and moral functions. (Kohlberg 1984: 398) Since, however, ego development is a necessary but not sufficient condition for moral development, in his view, the latter can be studied independently of the former. In light of this clarification, Kohlberg regards Murphy's and Gilligan's stage of "post-conventional contextualism" as being more concerned with questions of ego as opposed to moral development. While not wanting to maintain that the acquisition of moral competencies ends with reaching adulthood, Kohlberg nevertheless insists that adult moral and ego development studies only reveal the presence of "soft" as opposed to "hard" stages. The latter are irreversible in sequence and integrally related to one another in the sense that a subsequent stage grows out of and presents a better solution to problems confronted at an earlier stage.[7]

It will be up to latter-day historians of science to decide whether, with these admissions and qualifications, Kohlbergian theory has entered the phase of "ad-hocism," in Imre Lakatos's words,[8] or whether Gilligan's challenge, as well as that of other critics, has moved this research paradigm to a new phase, in which new problems and conceptualizations will lead to more fruitful results.

What concerns me in this paper is the question, what can feminist theory contribute to this debate? Since Kohlberg himself regards an interaction between moral philosophy and the empirical study of moral development as essential to his theory, the insights of contemporary feminist philosophy can be brought to bear upon some aspects of his theory. I want to define two premises as constituents of feminist theorizing. First, for feminist theory, the gender-sex system is not a contingent but an essential way in which social reality is organized, symbolically divided, and experienced. By the "gender-sex" system, I mean the social-historical, symbolic constitution, and interpretation of the differences of the sexes. The gender-sex system is the context in which the self develops an *embodied* identity, a certain mode of being in one's body and of living the body. The self becomes an *I* in that it appropriates from the human community a mode of psychically, socially, and symbolically experiencing its bodily identity. Societies and cultures reproduce embodied individuals through the gender-sex system.[9]

Second, the historically known gender-sex systems have contributed to the oppression and exploitation of women. The task of feminist critical theory is to uncover where and how this occurs and to develop an emancipatory and reflective analysis that aids women in their struggles to overcome oppression and exploitation. Feminist theory can contribute to this task in two ways: by developing an *explanatory-diagnostic analysis* of women's oppression across history, cultures, and societies, and by articulating an *anticipatory-utopian critique* of the norms and values of our current society and culture, which projects new modes of togetherness and of relating to ourselves and to nature in the future. Whereas the first aspect of feminist theory requires critical, social-scientific research, the second is primarily normative and philosophical: it involves the clarification of moral and political principles, both at the meta-ethical level with respect to the *logic of justification* and at the substantive, normative level with reference to their concrete content.[10]

In this chapter, I shall try to articulate such an anticipatory-utopian critique of universalistic moral theories from a feminist perspective. I want to argue that the *definition* of the moral domain, as well as of the ideal of *moral autonomy,* not only in Kohlberg's theory but in universalistic, contractarian theories from Hobbes to Rawls, lead to a *privatization* of women's experience and to the exclusion of its consideration from a moral point of view. In this tradition, the moral self is viewed as a *disembedded* and *disembodied* being. This conception of the self reflects aspects of male experience; the "relevant other" in this theory is never the sister but always the brother. This vision of the self is incompatible with the very criteria of reversibility and universalizability advocated by defenders of universalism. A universalistic moral theory restricted to the standpoint of the "generalized other" falls into epistemic incoherencies that jeopardize its claim to adequately fulfill reversibility and universalizability.

Universalistic moral theories in the western tradition from Hobbes to Rawls are *substitutionalist,* in the sense that the universalism they defend is defined surreptitiously by identifying the experiences of a specific group of subjects as the paradigmatic case of all humans. These subjects are invariably white, male adults who are propertied or professional. I want to distinguish *substitutionalist* from *interactive* universalism. Interactive universalism acknowledges the plurality of modes of being human, and differences among humans, without endorsing all these pluralities and differences as morally and politically valid. While agreeing that normative disputes can be rationally settled, and that fairness, reciprocity, and some procedure of universalizability are constituents, that is, necessary conditions of the moral standpoint, interactive universalism regards difference as a starting point for reflection and action. In this sense, "universality" is a regulative ideal that does not deny our embodied and embedded identity, but aims at developing moral attitudes and encouraging political transformations that can yield a point of view acceptable to all. Universality is not the ideal consensus of fictitiously defined selves, but the concrete process, in politics and morals, of the struggle of concrete, embodied selves, striving for autonomy.

II. Justice and the Autonomous Self in Social Contract Theories

Kohlberg defines the privileged object domain of moral philosophy and psychology as follows:

> We say that *moral* judgments or principles have the central function of resolving interpersonal or social conflicts, that is, conflicts of claims or rights. . . . Thus moral judgments and principles imply a notion of equilibrium, or reversibility of claims. In this sense they ultimately involve some reference to justice, at least insofar as they define "hard" structural stages. (Kohlberg 1984: 216)

Kohlberg's conception of the moral domain is based upon a strong differentiation between justice and the good life.[11] This is also one of the cornerstones of his critique of Gilligan. Although acknowledging that Gilligan's elucidation of a care-and-responsibility orientation "usefully enlarges the moral domain" (Kohlberg 1984: 340), Kohlberg defines the domain of *special relationships of obligation* to which care and responsibility are oriented as follows: "the spheres of kinship, love, friendship, and sex that elicit considerations of care are usually understood to be spheres of personal decision-making, as are, for instance, the problems of marriage and divorce." (Kohlberg 1984: 229–30) The care orientation is said thus to concern domains that are more "personal" than "moral in the sense of the formal point of view." (Kohlberg 1984: 360) Questions of the good life, pertaining to the nature of our relationships of kinship, love, friendship, and sex, on the one hand, are included in the moral domain but, on the other hand, are named "personal" as opposed to "moral" issues.

Kohlberg proceeds from a definition of morality that begins with Hobbes, in the wake of the dissolution of the Aristotelian-Christian world view. Ancient and medieval moral systems, by contrast, show the following structure: a definition of man-as-he-ought-to-be, a definition of man-as-he-is, and the articulation of a set of rules or precepts that can lead man-as-he-is into man-as-he-ought-to-be.[12] In such moral systems, the rules that govern just relations within the human community are embedded in a more encompassing concept of the good life. This good life, the *telos* of man, is defined ontologically with reference to man's place in the cosmos at large.

The destruction of the ancient and medieval teleological concept of nature through the attack of medieval nominalism and modern science, the emergence of capitalist exchange relations, and the subsequent division of the social structure into the economy, the polity, civil associations, and the domestic-intimate sphere, radically alter moral theory. Modern theorists claim that the ultimate purposes of nature are unknown. Morality is thus emancipated from cosmology and from an all encompassing world view that normatively limits man's relation to nature. The distinction between justice and the good life, as it is formulated by early contract theorists, aims at defending this privacy and autonomy of the self, first in the religious sphere, and then in the scientific and philosophical spheres of "free thought" as well.

Justice alone becomes the center of moral theory when bourgeois individuals in a disenchanted universe face the task of creating the legitimate basis of the social order for themselves. What "ought" to be is now defined as what all would have rationally to agree to in order to ensure civil peace and prosperity (Hobbes, Locke); or the "ought" is derived from the rational form of the moral law alone (Rousseau, Kant). As long as the social bases of cooperation and the rights-claims of individuals are respected, the autonomous bourgeois subject can define the good life as his mind and conscience dictate.

The transition to modernity does not only privatize the self's relation to the cosmos and to ultimate questions of religion and being. First, with western modernity the concept of privacy is so enlarged that an intimate domestic-familial sphere is subsumed under it. Relations of "kinship, friendship, love, and sex," indeed, as Kohlberg takes them to be, come to be viewed as spheres of "personal decision-making." At the beginning of modern moral and political theory, however, the "personal" nature of these spheres does not mean the recognition of equal, female autonomy, but rather the removal of gender relations from the sphere of justice. While the bourgeois male celebrates his transition from conventional to post-conventional morality, from socially accepted rules of justice to their generation in light of the principles of a social contract, the domestic sphere remains at the conventional level. The sphere of justice, from Hobbes through Locke and Kant, is regarded as the domain wherein independent, male heads-of-household transact with one another, while the domestic-intimate sphere is put beyond the pale of justice and restricted to the reproductive and affective needs of the bourgeois *pater familias*. Agnes Heller has named this domain the "household of the emotions."[13] An entire domain of human activity, namely, nurture, reproduction, love, and care, which becomes the woman's lot in the course of the development of modern, bourgeois society, is excluded from moral and political considerations, and confined to the realm of "nature."

Through a brief historical genealogy of social contract theories, I want to examine the distinction between justice and the good life as it is translated into the split between the public and the domestic. This analysis will also allow us to see the implicit ideal of autonomy cherished by this tradition.

At the beginning of modern moral and political philosophy stands a powerful metaphor: the "state of nature." At times this metaphor is said to be fact. Thus, in his *Second Treatise of Civil Government,* John Locke reminds us of "the two men in the desert island, mentioned by Garcilasso de la Vega . . . or a Swiss and an Indian, in the woods of America."[14] At other times it is acknowledged as fiction. Thus, Kant dismisses the colorful reveries of his predecessors and transforms the "state of nature" from an empirical fact into a transcendental concept. The state of nature comes to represent the idea of *Privatrecht*, under which is subsumed the right of property and "thinglike rights of a personal nature" (*auf dingliche Natur persönliche Rechte*), which the male head of household exercises over his wife, children, and servants.[15] Only Thomas Hobbes compounds fact and fiction, and against those who consider it strange "that Nature should thus dissociate, and render men apt to invade, and destroy one another,"[16] he asks each man who does not trust "this Inference, made from the passions," to reflect why "when taking a journey, he arms himself, and seeks to go well accompanied; when going to sleep, he locks his dores; when even in his house he locks his chests. . . . Does he not there as much accuse mankind by his actions, as I do by my words?" (Hobbes, *Leviathan*, 187) The state of nature is the looking glass of these early bourgeois thinkers in which they and their societies are magnified, purified, and reflected in their original, naked verity. The state of nature is both nightmare (Hobbes) and utopia (Rousseau). In it, the bourgeois male recognizes his flaws, fears, and anxieties, as well as his dreams.

The varying content of this metaphor is less significant than its simple and profound message: in the beginning man was alone. Again, it is Hobbes who gives this thought its clearest formulation. "Let us consider men . . . as if but even now sprung out of the earth, and suddenly, like mushrooms, come to full maturity, without all kind of engagement to each other."[17] This vision of men as mushrooms is an ultimate picture of autonomy. The female, the mother of whom every individual is born, is now replaced by the earth. The denial of being born of woman frees the male ego from the most natural and basic bond of dependence. Nor is the picture very different for Rousseau's noble savage who, wandering wantonly through the woods, occasionally mates with a female and then seeks rest.[18]

The state-of-nature metaphor provides a vision of the autonomous self: this is a narcissist who sees the world in his own image; who has no awareness of the limits of his own desires and passions; and who cannot see himself through the eyes of another. The narcissism of this sovereign self is destroyed by the presence of the other. As Hegel expresses it:

> "Self-consciousness is faced by another self-consciousness; it has come *out of itself*. This has a twofold significance: first, it has *lost* itself, for it finds itself as an *other* being; secondly, in doing so it has superseded the other, for it does not see the other as an essential being, but in the other sees its own self.[19]

The story of the autonomous male ego is the saga of this initial sense of *loss* in confrontation with the other, and the gradual recovery from this original narcissistic wound through the sobering experience of war, fear, domination, anxiety, and death. The last installment in this drama is the social contract: the establishment of the law to govern all. Having been thrust out of their narcissistic universe into a world of insecurity by their sibling brothers, these individuals have to reestablish the authority of the father in the image of the law. The early bourgeois individual not only has no mother but no father as well; rather, he strives to reconstitute the father in his own self-image. What is usually celebrated in the annals of modern moral and political theory as the dawn of liberty is precisely this destruction of political patriarchy in bourgeois society.

The constitution of political authority civilizes sibling rivalry by turning their attention from war to property, from vanity to science, from conquest to luxury. The original narcissism is not transformed; only now ego boundaries are clearly defined. The law reduces insecurity, the fear of being engulfed by the other, by defining mine and thine. Jealousy is not eliminated but tamed; as long as each can keep what is his and attain more by fair rules of the game, he is entitled to it. Competition is domesticized and channeled towards acquisition. The law contains anxiety by defining rigidly the boundaries between self and other, but the law does not cure anxiety. The anxiety that the other is always on the look to interfere in your space and appropriate what is yours; the anxiety that you will be subordinated to his will; the anxiety that a group of brothers will usurp the law in the name of the "will of all" and destroy "the general will," the will of the absent father, remains. The law teaches how to repress anxiety and to sober narcissism, but the constitution of the self is not altered. The establishment of private rights and duties does not overcome the inner wounds of the self; it only forces them to become less destructive.

This imaginary universe of early moral and political theory has had an amazing hold upon the modern consciousness. From Freud to Piaget, the relationship to the brother is viewed as the humanizing experience that teaches us to become social, responsible adults.[20] As a result of the hold of this metaphor upon our imagination, we have also come to inherit a number of philosophical prejudices. For Rawls and Kohlberg, as well, the autonomous self is disembedded and disembodied; moral impartiality is learning to recognize the claims of the other who is just like oneself; fairness is public justice; a public system of rights and duties is the best way to arbitrate conflict, to distribute rewards and to establish claims.

Yet this is a strange world: it is one in which individuals are grown up before they have been born; in which boys are men before they have been children; a world where neither mother, nor sister, nor wife exist. The question is less what Hobbes says about men and women, or what Rousseau sees the role of Sophie to be in Émile's education. The point is that in this universe, the experience of the early modern female has no place. Women are simply what men are not. Women are not autonomous, independent, and aggressive but nurturant, not competitive but giving, not public but private. The world of the female is constituted by a series of negations. *She* is simply what *he* happens not to be. Her identity becomes defined by a lack—the lack of autonomy, the lack of independence, the lack of the phallus. The narcissistic male takes her to be just like himself, only his opposite.

It is not the misogynist prejudices of early modern moral and political theory alone that lead to women's exclusion. It is the very constitution of a sphere of discourse that bans the female from history to the realm of nature, from public light to the interior of the household, from the civilizing effect of culture to the repetitious burden of nurture and reproduction. The public sphere, the sphere of justice, moves in historicity, whereas the private sphere, the sphere of care and intimacy, is unchanging and timeless. It pulls us toward the earth even when we, as Hobbesian mushrooms, strive to pull away from it. The dehistoricization of the private realm signifies that, as the male ego celebrates his passage from nature to culture, from conflict to consensus, women remain in a timeless universe, condemned to repeat the cycles of life.

This split between the public sphere of justice, in which history is made, and the atemporal realm of the household, in which like is reproduced, is internalized by the male ego. The dichotomies are not only without but within. He himself is divided into the public persona and the private individual. Within his chest clash the law of reason and the inclination of nature, the brilliance of cognition and the obscurity of emotion. Caught between the moral law and the starry heaven above and the earthly body below,[21] the autonomous self strives for unity. But the antagonism—between autonomy and nurturance, independence and bonding, sovereignty of the self and relations to others—remains. In the discourse of modern moral and political theory, these dichotomies are reified as being essential to the constitution of the self. While men humanize outer nature through labor, inner nature remains ahistorical, dark, and obscure. I want to suggest that contemporary universalist moral theory has inherited this dichotomy between autonomy and nurturance, independence and bonding, the sphere of justice and the domestic, personal realm. This becomes most visible in its attempt to restrict the moral point of view to the perspective of the "generalized other."

III. The Generalized versus the Concrete Other

Let me describe two concepts of self-other relations that delineate both moral perspectives and interactional structures. I shall name the first the standpoint of the "generalized"[22] and the second that of the "concrete" other. In contemporary moral theory, these concepts are viewed as incompatible, even as antagonistic. These two perspectives reflect the dichotomies and splits of early modern moral and political theory between autonomy and nurturance, independence and bonding, the public and the domestic, and more broadly, between justice and the good life. The content of the generalized as well as the concrete other is shaped by the dichotomous characterization, which we have inherited from the modern tradition.

The standpoint of the generalized other requires us to view each and every individual as a rational being entitled to the same rights and duties we would want to ascribe to ourselves. In assuming this standpoint, we abstract from the individuality and concrete identity of the other. We assume that the other, like ourselves, is a being who has concrete needs, desires, and affects, but what constitutes moral dignity is not what differentiates us from each other, but rather what we, as speaking and acting rational agents, have in common. Our relation to the other is governed by the norms of *formal equality* and *reciprocity:* each is entitled to expect and to assume from us what we can expect and assume from him or her. The norms of our interactions are primarily public and institutional ones. If I have a right to *x*, then you have the duty not to hinder me from enjoying *x* and conversely. In treating you in accordance with these norms, I confirm in your person the rights of humanity and I have a legitimate right to expect that you will do the same in relation to me. The moral categories that accompany such interactions are those of right, obligation, and entitlement; the corresponding moral feelings are those of respect, duty, worthiness, and dignity.

The standpoint of the concrete other, by contrast, requires us to view each and every rational being as an individual with a concrete history, identity, and affective-emotional constitution. In assuming this standpoint, we abstract from what constitutes our commonality. We seek to comprehend the needs of the other, his or her motivations, what he or she searches for and desires. Our relation to the other is governed by the norms of *equity* and *complementary reciprocity*: each is entitled to expect and to assume from the other forms of behavior through which the other feels recognized and confirmed as a concrete, individual being with specific needs, talents, and capacities. Our differences in this case complement rather than exclude one another. The norms of our interaction are usually private, noninstitutional ones. They are norms of friendship, love, and care. These norms require in various ways that I exhibit more than the simple assertion of my rights and duties in the face of your needs. In treating you in accordance with the norms of friendship, love, and care, I confirm not only your *humanity* but your human *individuality*. The moral categories that accompany such interactions are those of responsibility, bonding, and sharing. The corresponding moral feelings are those of love, care, sympathy, and solidarity.

In contemporary universalist moral psychology and moral theory, it is the viewpoint of the "generalized other" that predominates. In his article on "Justice as Reversibility: The Claim to Moral Adequacy of a Highest Stage of Moral Development," for example, Kohlberg argues that

> moral judgments involve role-taking, taking the viewpoint of the others conceived as *subjects* and coordinating these viewpoints . . . Second, equilibriated moral judgments involve principles of justice or fairness. A moral situation in disequilibrium is one in which there are unresolved, conflicting claims. A resolution of the situation is one in which each is "given his due" according to some principle of justice that can be recognized as fair by all the conflicting parties involved.[23]

Kohlberg regards Rawls's concept of "reflective equilibrium" as a parallel formulation of the basic idea of reciprocity, equality, and fairness intrinsic to all moral judgments. The Rawlsian "veil of ignorance," in Kohlberg's judgment, not only exemplifies the formalist idea of universalizability but that of perfect *reversibility* as well.[24] The idea behind the veil of ignorance is described as follows:

> The decider is to initially decide from a point of view *that ignores his identity* (veil of ignorance) under the assumption that decisions are governed by maximizing values from a viewpoint of rational egoism in considering each party's interest. [Kohlberg 1981: 200; my emphasis]

What I would like to question is the assumption that "taking the viewpoint of others" is truly compatible with this notion of fairness as reasoning behind a "veil of ignorance."[25] The problem is that the defensible kernel of the ideas of reciprocity and fairness are thereby identified with the perspective of the disembedded and disembodied generalized other. Now since Kohlberg presents his research subjects with hypothetically constructed moral dilemmas, it may be thought that his conception of "taking the standpoint of the other" is not subject to the epistemic restrictions that apply to the Rawlsian original position. Subjects in Kohlbergian interviews do not stand behind a veil of ignorance. However, the very *language* in which Kohlbergian dilemmas are presented incorporate these epistemic restrictions. For example, in the famous Heinz dilemma, as in others, the motivations of the druggist as a concrete individual, as well as the history of the individuals involved, are excluded as irrelevant to the definition of the moral problem at hand. In these dilemmas, individuals and their moral positions are represented by abstracting from the narrative history of the self and its motivations. Gilligan also notes that the implicit moral epistemology of Kohlbergian dilemma frustrates women, who want to phrase these hypothetical dilemmas in a more contextual voice, attuned to the standpoint of the concrete other. The result is that

> though several of the women in the abortion study clearly articulate a post-conventional meta-ethical position, none of them are considered principled in their normative moral judgments of Kohlberg's hypothetical dilemmas. Instead, the women's judgments point toward an identification of the violence inherent in the dilemma itself, which is seen to compromise the justice of any of its possible resolutions. [Gilligan 1982: 101]

Through an immanent critique of the theories of Kohlberg and Rawls, I want to show that ignoring the standpoint of the concrete other leads to epistemic incoherence in universalistic moral theories. The problem can be stated as follows: according to Kohlberg and Rawls, moral reciprocity involves the capacity to take the standpoint of the other, to put oneself imaginatively in the place of the other, but under conditions of the "veil of ignorance," the *other as different from the self* disappears. Unlike in previous contract theories, in this case the other is not constituted through projection, but as a consequence of total abstraction from his or her identity. Differences are not denied; they become irrelevant. The Rawlsian self does not know:

> his place in society, his class position or status; nor does he know his fortune in the distribution of natural assets and abilities, his intelligence and strength, and the like. Nor, again, does anyone know his conception of the good, the particulars of his rational plan of life, or even the special features of his psychology such as his aversion to risk or liability to optimism or pessimism.[26]

Let us ignore for a moment whether such selves who also do not know "the particular circumstances of their own society" can know anything at all that is relevant to the human condition, and ask instead, are these individuals *human selves* at all? In his attempt to do justice to Kant's conception of noumenal agency, Rawls recapitulates a basic problem with the Kantian conception of the self, namely, that noumenal selves cannot be *individuated.* If all that belongs to them as embodied, affective, suffering creatures, their memory and history, their ties and relations to others, are to be subsumed under the phenomenal realm, then what we are left with is an empty mask that is everyone and no one. Michael Sandel points out that the difficulty in Rawls's conception derives from his attempt to be consistent with the Kantian concept of the autonomous self, as a being freely choosing his or her own ends in life.[27] However, this moral and political concept of autonomy slips into a metaphysics according to which it is meaningful to define a self independently of *all* the ends it may choose and all and any conceptions of the good it may hold. (Sandel 1984: 47ff.) At this point we must ask whether the *identity* of any human self can be defined with reference to its capacity for agency alone. Identity does not refer to my potential for choice alone, but to the actuality of my choices, namely, to how I, as a finite, concrete, embodied individual, shape and fashion the circumstances of my birth and family, linguistic, cultural, and gender identity into a coherent narrative that stands as my life's story. Indeed, if we recall that every autonomous being is one born of others and not, as Rawls, following Hobbes, assumes, a being "not bound by prior moral ties to another,"[28] the question becomes: how does this finite, embodied creature constitute into a coherent narrative those episodes of choice and limit, agency and suffering, initiative and dependence? The self is not a thing, a substrate, but the protagonist of a life's tale. The conception of selves who can be individuated prior to their moral ends is incoherent.

If this concept of the self as a mushroom, behind a veil of ignorance, is incoherent, then it follows that there is no real *plurality* of perspectives in the Rawlsian original position, but only a *definitional identity.* For Rawls, as Sandel observes, "our individuating characterisitics are given empirically, by the distinctive concatenation of wants and desires, aims and attributes, purposes and ends that come to characterize human beings in the particularity." (Sandel 1984: 51) But how are we supposed to know what these wants and desires are independently of knowing something about the person who holds these wants, desires, aims and attributes? Is there perhaps an "essence" of anger that is the same for each angry individual; an essence of ambition that is distinct from ambitious selves? I fail to see how individuating characteristics can be ascribed to a transcendental self who can have any and none of these, who can be all or none of them.

If selves who are epistemologically and metaphysically prior to their individuating characteristics, as Rawls takes them to be, cannot be human selves at all; if, therefore, there is no human *plurality* behind the veil of ignorance but only *definitional identity* then this has consequences for criteria of reversibility and universalizability said to be a constituent of the moral point of view. Definitional identity leads to *incomplete reversibility,* for the primary requisite of reversibility, namely, a coherent distinction between me and you, the self and the other, cannot be sustained under these circumstances. Under conditions of the veil of ignorance, the other disappears.

It is no longer plausible to maintain that such a standpoint can universalize adequately. Kohlberg views the veil of ignorance not only as exemplifying reversibility but universalizability as well. This is the idea that "we must be willing to live with our judgment or decision when we trade places with others in the situation being judged." (Kohlberg 1981: 197) But the question is, *which* situation? Can moral situations be individuated independently of our knowledge of the agents involved in these situations, of their histories, attitudes, characters, and desires? Can I describe a situation as one of arrogance or hurt pride without knowing something about you as a concrete other? Can I know how to distinguish between a breach of confidence and a harmless slip of the tongue, without knowing your history and your character? Moral situations, like moral emotions and attitudes, can only be individuated if they are evaluated in light of our knowledge of the history of the agents involved in them.

While every procedure of universalizability presupposes that "like cases ought to be treated alike" or that I should act in such a way that I should also be willing that all others in a like situation act like me, the most difficult aspect of any such procedure is to know what constitutes a "like" situation or what it would mean for another to be exactly in a situation like mine. Such a process of reasoning, to be at all viable, must involve the viewpoint of the concrete other, for situations, to paraphrase Stanley Cavell, do not come like "envelopes and golden finches," ready for definition and description, "nor like apples ripe for grading."[29] When we morally disagree, for example, we do not only disagree about the principles involved; very often we disagree because what I see as a lack of generosity on your part, you construe as your legitimate right not to do something; we disagree because what you see as jealousy on my part, I view as my desire to have more of your attention. Universalistic moral theory neglects such everyday, interactional morality and assumes that the public standpoint of justice, and our quasi-public personalities as right-bearing individuals, are the center of moral theory.[30]

Kohlberg emphasizes the dimension of ideal role-taking or taking the viewpoint of the other in moral judgment. Because he defines the other as the generalized other, however, he perpetrates one of the fundamental errors of Kantian moral theory. Kant's error was to assume that I, as a pure rational agent reasoning for myself, could reach a conclusion that would be acceptable for all at all times and places.[31] In Kantian moral theory, moral agents are like geometricians in different rooms who, reasoning alone for themselves, all arrive at the same solution to a problem. Following Habermas, I want to name this the "monological" model of moral reasoning. Insofar as he interprets ideal role-taking in the light of Rawls's concept of a "veil of ignorance," Kohlberg as well sees the silent thought process of a single self who imaginatively puts himself in the position of the other as the most adequate form of moral judgment.

I conclude that a definition of the self that is restricted to the standpoint of the generalized other becomes incoherent and cannot individuate among selves. Without assuming the standpoint of the concrete other, no coherent universalizability test can be carried out, for we lack the necessary epistemic information to judge my moral situation to be "like" or "unlike" yours.

IV. A Communicative Ethic of Need Interpretations and the Relational Self

In the preceding sections of this chapter, I have argued that the distinction between justice and the good life, the restriction of the moral domain to questions of justice, as well as the ideal of moral autonomy in universalist theories, result in the privatization of women's experience and lead to epistemological blindness toward the concrete other. The consequence of such epistemological blindness is an internal inconsistency in universalistic moral theories, insofar as these define "taking the standpoint of the other" as essential to the moral point of view. My aim has been to take universalistic moral theories at their word and to show through an immanent critique, first of the "state of nature" metaphor and then of the "original position," that the concept of the autonomous self implied by these thought experiments is restricted to the "generalized other."

This distinction between the generalized and the concrete other raises questions in moral and political theory. It may be asked whether, without the standpoint of the generalized other, it would be possible to define a moral point of view at all.[32] Since our identities as concrete others are what distinguish us from each other according to gender, race, class, cultural differentials, as well as psychic and natural abilities, would a moral theory restricted to the standpoint of the concrete other not be a racist, sexist, cultural relativist, discriminatory one? Furthermore, without the standpoint of the generalized other, it may be argued, a political theory of justice suited for modern, complex societies is unthinkable. Certainly rights must be an essential component in any such theory. Finally, the perspective of the "concrete other" defines our relations as private, noninstitutional ones, concerned with love, care, friendship, and intimacy. Are these activities so gender-specific? Are we not all "concrete others"?

The distinction between the "generalized" and the "concrete other," as drawn in this essay so far, is not a *prescriptive* but a *critical* one. My goal is not to prescribe a moral and political theory consonant with the concept of the "concrete other." For, indeed, the recognition of the dignity and worthiness of the generalized other is a *necessary,* albeit *insufficient,* condition to define the moral standpoint in modern societies. In this sense, the concrete other is a critical concept that designates the *ideological* limits of universalistic discourse. It signifies the *unthought,* the *unseen,* and the *unheard* in such theories. This is evidenced by Kohlberg's effort, on the one hand, to enlarge the domain of moral theory to include in it relations to the concrete other and, on the other hand, to characterize such special relations of obligation as "private, personal" matters of evaluative life choices alone. Urging an examination of this unthought is necessary to prevent the preemption of the discourse of universality by an unexamined particularity. Substitutionalist universalism dismisses the concrete other, while interactive universalism acknowledges that every generalized other is also a concrete other.

From a meta-ethical and normative standpoint, I would argue, therefore, for the validity of a moral theory that allows us to recognize the dignity of the generalized other through an acknowledgment of the moral identity of the concrete other. The point is not to juxtapose the generalized to the concrete other or to seek normative validity in one or another standpoint. The point is to think through the ideological limitations and biases that arise in the discourse of universalist morality through this unexamined opposition. I doubt that an easy integration of both points of view, of justice and of care, is possible, without first clarifying the moral framework that would allow us to question both standpoints and their implicit gender presuppositions.

For this task a model of communicative need interpretations suggests itself.[33] Not only is such an ethic, as I interpret it, compatible with the dialogic, interactive generation of universality, but most significant, such an ethic provides the suitable framework within which moral and political agents can define their own concrete identities on the basis of recognizing each other's dignity as generalized others. Questions of the most desirable and just political organization, as well as the distinction between justice and the good life, the public and the domestic, can be analyzed, renegotiated, and redefined in such a process. Since, however, all those affected are participants in this process, the presumption is that these distinctions cannot be drawn in such a way as to privatize, hide, and repress the experiences of those who have suffered under them, for only what all could consensually agree to be in the best interest of each could be accepted as the outcome of this dialogic process.

One consequence of this communicative ethic of need interpretations is that the object domain of moral theory is so enlarged that not only rights but needs, not only justice but possible modes of the good life, are moved into an anticipatory-utopian perspective. What such discourses can generate are not only universalistically prescribable norms, but also intimations of otherness in the present that can lead to the future.

In his current formulation of his theory, Kohlberg accepts this extension of his Stage 6 perspective into an ethic of need interpretations, as suggested first by Habermas.[34] However, he does not see the incompatibility between the communicative ethics model and the Rawlsian "original position."[35] In defining reversibility of perspectives, he still considers the Rawlsian position to be paradigmatic. (Kohlberg 1984: 272, 310) Despite certain shared assumptions, the communicative model of need interpretations and the justice model of the original position need to be distinguished from each other.

First, in communicative ethics, the condition of ideal role-taking is not to be construed as a *hypothetical* thought process, carried out singly by the moral agent or the moral philosopher, but as an *actual* dialogue situation in which moral agents communicate with one another. Second, it is not necessary to place any epistemic constraints upon such an actual process of moral reasoning and disputation, for the more knowledge is available to moral agents about each other, their history, the particulars of their society, its structure and future, the more rational will be the outcome of their deliberations. Practical rationality entails epistemic rationality as well, and more knowledge rather than less contributes to a more rational and informed judgment. To judge rationally is not to judge as if one did not know what one could know, but to judge in light of all available and relevant information. Third, if there are no knowledge restrictions upon such a discursive situation, then it also follows that there is no privileged subject matter of moral disputation. Moral agents are not only limited to reasoning about primary goods, which they are assumed to want no matter what else they want. Instead, both the *goods* they desire and their *desires* themselves become legitimate topics of moral disputation. Finally, in such moral discourses, agents can also change levels of reflexivity, that is, they can introduce meta-considerations about the very conditions and constraints under which such dialogue takes place and evaluate their fairness. There is no closure of reflexivity in this model as there is, for example, in the Rawlsian one, which enjoins agents to accept certain rules of the bargaining game prior to the very choice of principles of justice.[36] With regard to the Kohlbergian paradigm, this would mean that moral agents can challenge the relevant *definition* of a moral situation, and urge that this very definition itself become the subject matter of moral reasoning and dispute.

A consequence of this model of communicative ethics would be that the language of rights and duties can now be challenged in light of our need interpretations. Following the tradition of modern social contract theories, Rawls and Kohlberg assume that our affective-emotional constitution, the needs and desires in light of which we formulate our rights and claims, are private matters alone. Their theory of the self, and, in particular, the Rawlsian metaphysics of the moral agent, does not allow them to view the constitution of our inner nature in *relational* terms.

A relational-interactive theory of identity assumes that inner nature, while being unique, is not an immutable given.[37] Individual need interpretations and motives carry within them the traces of those early childhood experiences, phantasies, wishes, and desires as well as the self-conscious goals of the person. The grammatical logic of the word "I" reveals the unique structure of ego identity: every subject who uses this concept in relation to herself knows that all other subjects are likewise "I"s. In this respect, the self only becomes an "I" in a community of other selves who are also "I"s. Every act of self-reference expresses simultaneously the uniqueness and difference of the self as well as the commonality among selves. Discourses about needs and motives unfold in this space created by commonality and uniqueness, generally shared socialization, and the contingency of individual life-histories.

The nonrelational theory of the self, which is privileged in contemporary universalist moral theory, by contrast, removes such need interpretations from the domain of moral discourse. They become "private," nonformalizable, nonanalyzable, and amorphous aspects of our conceptions of the good life. I am not suggesting that such concept of the good life either *can* or *should* be universalized, but only that our affective-emotional constitution, as well as our concrete history as moral agents, ought to be considered accessible to moral communication, reflection, and transformation. Inner nature, no less than the public sphere of justice, has a historical dimension. In it are intertwined the history of the self and the history of the collective.

To condemn it to silence is, as Gilligan has suggested, not to hear that other voice in moral theory. I would say more strongly that such discourse continues woman's oppression by privatizing their lot and by excluding a central sphere of their activities from moral theory.

As the second wave of the women's movement, both in Europe and the United States has argued, to understand and to combat woman's oppression, it is no longer sufficient to demand woman's political and economic emancipation alone; it is also necessary to question those psychosexual relations in the domestic and private spheres within which women's lives unfold, and through which gender identity is reproduced. To explicate woman's oppression, it is necessary to uncover the power of those symbols, myths, and fantasies that entrap both sexes in the unquestioned world of gender roles. Perhaps one of the most fundamental of these myths and symbols has been the ideal of autonomy conceived in the image of a disembedded and disembodied male ego. This vision of autonomy was and continues to be based upon an implicit politics which defines the domestic, intimate sphere as ahistorical, unchanging, and immutable, thereby removing it from reflection and discussion.[38] Needs, as well as emotions and affects, become mere given properties of individuals, which moral philosophy recoils from examining, on the grounds that it may interfere with the autonomy of the sovereign self. Women, because they have been made the "housekeeper of the emotions" in the modern, bourgeois world, and because they have suffered from the uncomprehended needs and phantasies of the male imagination, which has made them at once into Mother Earth and nagging bitch, the Virgin Mary and the whore, cannot condemn this sphere to silence. What Carol Gilligan has heard are those mutterings, protestations, and objections which women, confronted with ways of posing moral dilemmas that seemed alien to them, have voiced. Only if we can understand why their voices have been silenced, and how the dominant ideals of moral autonomy in our culture, as well as the privileged definition of the moral sphere, continue to silence women's voices, do we have a hope of moving to a more integrated vision of ourselves and of our fellow humans as generalized as well as "concrete" others.

Notes

1. Thomas Kuhn, *The Structure of Scientific Revolutions,* vol. 2., no. 2 of *International Encyclopedia of Unified Science* (Chicago: University of Chicago Press, 1970, second edition), pp. 52ff.

2. John Michael Murphy and Carol Gilligan, "Moral Development in Late Adolescence and Adulthood: A Critique and Reconstruction of Kohlberg's Theory," *Human Development* 23 (1980), pp. 77–104; cited in the text as Murphy and Gilligan, 1980.

3. Carol Gilligan, *In a Different Voice: Psychological Theory and Women's Development* (Cambridge: Harvard University Press, 1982), pp. 18–19; cited in the text as Gilligan 1982.

4. Lawrence Kohlberg, "Synopses and Detailed Replies to Critics," with Charles Levine and Alexandra Hewer, in L. Kohlberg, *Essays on Moral Development,*

vol. II, *The Psychology of Moral Development* (San Francisco: Harper & Row, 1984), p. 341. This volume is cited in the text as Kohlberg 1984.

5. There still seems to be some question as to how the data on women's moral development is to be interpreted. Studies that focus on late adolescents and adult males and that show sex differences, include J. Fishkin, K. Keniston, and C. MacKinnon, "Moral Reasoning and Political Ideology," *Journal of Personality and Social Psychology* 27 (1973), pp. 109–19; N. Haan, J. Block, and M.B. Smith, "Moral Reasoning of Young Adults: Political-Social Behavior, Family Background, and Personality Correlates," *Journal of Personality and Social Psychology* 10 (1968), pp. 184–201; C. Holstein, "Irreversible, Stepwise Sequence in the Development of Moral Judgment: A Longitudinal Study of Males and Females," *Child Development* 47 (1976), pp. 51–61. While it is clear that the available evidence does not throw the model of stage-sequence development into question, the prevalent presence of sex differences in moral reasoning does raise questions about *what* exactly this model might be measuring. Norma Haan sums up this objection to the Kohlbergian paradigm as follows: "Thus the moral reasoning of males who live in technical, rationalized societies, who reason at the level of formal operations and who *defensively intellectualize and deny interpersonal and situational detail,* is especially favored in the Kohlbergian scoring system," in "Two Moralities in Action Contexts: Relationships to Thought, Ego Regulation, and Development" (*Journal of Personality and Social Psychology* 36 (1978), p. 287; emphasis mine). I think Gilligan's studies also support the finding that inappropriate "intellectualization and denial of interpersonal, situational detail" constitutes one of the major differences in male and female approaches to moral problems. This is why, as I argue in the text, the separation between ego and moral development, as drawn by Kohlberg and others, seems inadequate to deal with the problem, since formalist ethical theories do seem to favor certain ego attitudes like defensiveness, rigidity, inability to empathize, and lack of flexibility over others like a nonrepressive attitude toward emotions, flexibility, and presence of empathy.

6. L. Kohlberg, "A Reply to Owen Flanagan and Some Comments on the Puka-Goodpaster Exchange," in *Ethics* 92 (April 1982), p. 316. Cf. also Gertrud Nunner-Winkler, "Two Moralities? A Critical Discussion of an Ethic of Care and Responsibility Versus an Ethics of Rights and Justice," in *Morality, Moral Behavior and Moral Development,* edited by W. M. Kurtines and J. L. Gewirtz (New York: John Wiley and Sons, 1984), p. 355. It is unclear whether the issue is, as Kohlberg and Nunner-Winkler suggest, one of distinguishing between "moral" and "ego" development or whether cognitive-developmental moral theory does not presuppose a model of ego development that clashes with more psychoanalytically oriented variants. In fact, to combat the charge of "maturationism" or "nativism" in his theory, which would imply that moral stages are a priori givens of the mind unfolding according to their own logic, regardless of the influence of society or environment upon them, Kohlberg argues as follows: "Stages," he writes, "are equilibriations arising from interaction between the organism (with its structuring tendencies) and the structure of the environment (physical or social). Universal moral stages are as much a function of universal features of social structure (such as institutions of law, family, property) and social interactions in various cultures, as they are products of the general structuring tendencies of the knowing organism." (Kohlberg, "A Reply to Owen Flanagan," p. 521) If this is so, then cognitive-developmental moral theory must also presuppose that there is a *dynamic* between self and social structure whereby the individual learns, acquires or internalizes the perspectives and sanctions of the social world. But the mechanism of this dynamic may involve learning as well as resistance, internalization as well as projection and fantasy. The issue is less whether moral development and ego development are distinct—they may be concep-

tually distinguished and yet in the history of the self they are related—but whether the model of ego development presupposed by Kohlberg's theory is not distortingly *cognitivistic* in that it ignores the role of affects, resistance, projection, phantasy, and defense mechanisms in socialization processes.

7. For this formulation, see J. Habermas, "Interpretive Social Science vs. Hermeneuticism," in *Social Science as Moral Inquiry,* edited by N. Haan, R. Bellah, P. Rabinow, and W. Sullivan (New York: Columbia University Press, 1983), p. 262.

8. Imre Lakatos, "Falsification and the Methodology of Scientific Research Programs," in *Criticism and the Growth of Knowledge,* edited by I. Lakatos and A. Musgrave (Cambridge: Cambridge University Press, 1970), pp. 117ff.

9. Let me explain the status of this premise. I would characterize it as a "second-order research hypothesis" that both guides concrete research in the social sciences and that can, in turn, be falsified by them. It is not a statement of faith about the way the world is: the cross-cultural and transhistorical universality of the sex-gender system is an empirical fact. It is also most definitely not a normative proposition about the way the world *ought* to be. To the contrary, feminism radically challenges the validity of the sex-gender system in organizing societies and cultures, and advocates the emancipation of men and women from the unexamined and oppressive grids of this framework.

10. For further clarification of these two aspects of critical theory, see my *Critique, Norm, and Utopia: A Study of the Foundations of Critical Theory* (New York: Columbia University Press, 1986), Part Two, "The Transformation of Critique."

11. Although frequently invoked by Kohlberg, Nunner-Winkler, and also Habermas, it is still unclear *how* this distinction is drawn and how it is justified. For example, does the justice/good life distinction correspond to sociological definitions of the public vs. the private? If so, what is meant by the "private"? Is women-battering a "private" or a "public" matter? Another way of drawing this distinction is to separate what is universalizable from what is culturally contingent, dependent upon the specifics of concrete life-forms, individual histories, and the like. Habermas, in particular, relegates questions of the good life to the aesthetic-expressive sphere; cf. "A Reply to My Critics," in *Habermas: Critical Debates,* ed. by John B. Thompson and David Held (Cambridge: MIT Press, 1982), p. 262; "Moralbewusstsein und kommunikatives Handeln," in *Moralbewusstsein und kommunikatives Handeln* (Frankfurt: Suhrkamp, 1983), pp. 190ff. Again, if privacy in the sense of intimacy is included in the "aesthetic expressive" sphere, we are forced to silence and privatize most of the issues raised by the women's movement, which concern precisely the quality and nature of our "intimate" relations, fantasies, and hopes. A traditional response to this is to argue that in wanting to draw this aspect of our lives into the light of the public, the women's movement runs the risk of authoritarianism because it questions the limits of individual "liberty." In response to this legitimate political concern, I would argue that one must distinguish two issues: on the one hand, questioning life-forms and values that have been oppressive for women, and making them "public" in the sense of making them accessible to reflection, action, and transformation by revealing their *socially constituted* character; and on the other hand, making them "public" in the sense that these areas become subject to legislative and administrative state-action. The second may, but need not, follow from the first. Because feminists focus on pornography as an "aesthetic-expressive" mode of denigrating women, it does not thereby follow that their critique should result in public legislation against pornography. Whether there ought to be this kind of legislation needs to be examined in the light of relevant legal, political, or constitutional arguments. Questions of political authoritarianism arise at this level, but not at the level of a critical-philosophical examination of traditional distinctions that have privatized and silenced women's concerns.

12. Alasdair MacIntyre, *After Virtue* (Notre Dame: University of Notre Dame Press, 1981), pp. 50–51.

13. Agnes Heller, *A Theory of Feelings* (Holland: Van Gorcum, 1979), pp. 184ff.

14. John Locke, *The Second Treatise of Civil Government* in *Two Treatises of Government,* edited and with an introduction by Thomas I. Cook (New York: Haffner Press, 1947), p. 128.

15. Immanuel Kant, *The Metaphysical Elements of Justice,* translated by John Ladd (New York: Liberal Arts Press, 1965), p. 55.

16. Thomas Hobbes, *Leviathan* (1651), edited and with an introduction by C. B. Macpherson (Middlesex: Penguin Books, 1980), p. 186. All future citations in the text are to this edition.

17. Thomas Hobbes, "Philosophical Rudiments Concerning Government and Society," in *The English Works of Thomas Hobbes,* edited by Sir W. Molesworth, vol. II (Darmstadt, 1966), p. 109.

18. J. J. Rousseau, "On The Origin and Foundations of Inequality Among Men," in J. J. Rousseau, *The First and Second Discourses,* edited by R. D. Masters, translated by Roger D. and Judith R. Masters (New York: St. Martin's Press, 1964), p. 116.

19. G. W. F. Hegel, *Phänomenologie des Geistes,* edited by Johannes Hoffmeister (Hamburg: Felix Meiner, 1952), 6th ed., p. 141, (Philosophische Bibliothek, Bd. 114), translation used here by A. V. Miller, *Phenomenology of Spirit* (Oxford: Clarendon Press, 1977), p. 111.

20. Sigmund Freud, *Moses and Monotheism,* translated by Katharine Jones (New York: Vintage, Random House, 1967), pp. 103ff.; Jean Piaget, *The Moral Judgment of the Child,* translated by Marjorie Gabain (New York: Free Press, 1965), pp. 65ff. Cf. the following comment on boys' and girls' games: "The most superficial observation is sufficient to show that in the main the legal sense is far less developed in little girls than in boys. We did not succeed in finding a single collective game played by girls in which there were as many rules and, above all, as fine and consistent an organization and codification of these rules as in the game of marbles examined above." (p. 77)

21. Kant, "Critique of Practical Reason" in *Critique of Practical Reason and Other Writings in Moral Philosophy,* translated and edited with an introduction by Louis White Beck (Chicago: University of Chicago Press, 1949), p. 258.

22. Although the term "generalized other" is borrowed from George Herbert Mead, my definition of it differs from his. Mead defines the "generalized other" as follows: "The organized community or social group which gives the individual his unity of self may be called the "generalized other." The attitude of the generalized other is the attitude of the whole community." George Herbert Mead, *Mind, Self and Society: From the Standpoint of a Social Behaviorist,* edited with introduction by Charles W. Morris (Chicago: University of Chicago Press, 1955), tenth printing, p. 154. Among such communities, Mead includes a ball team as well as political clubs, corporations, and other more abstract social classes or subgroups such as the class of debtors and the class of creditors (*ibid,* p. 157). Mead himself does not limit the concept of the "generalized other" to what is described in the text. In identifying the "generalized other" with the abstractly defined, legal and juridical subject, contract theorists and Kohlberg depart from Mead. Mead criticizes the social contract tradition precisely for distorting the psycho-social genesis of the individual subject, cf. *ibid,* .p. 233.

23. Kohlberg, "Justice as Reversibility: The Claim to Moral Adequacy of a Highest Stage of Moral Judgment," in *Essays on Moral Development,* vol. I, *The*

Philosophy of Moral Development (San Francisco: Harper & Row, 1981), p. 194, cited in the text as Kohlberg 1981.

24. Whereas all forms of reciprocity involve some concept of reversibility, these vary in degree: reciprocity can be restricted to the reversibility of actions but not of moral perspectives, to behavioral role models but not to the principles which underlie the generation of such behavioral expectations. For Kohlberg, the "veil of ignorance" is a model of perfect reversibility, for it elaborates the procedure of "ideal role-taking" or "moral musical chairs" where the decider "is to successively put himself imaginatively in the place of each other actor and consider the claims each would make from his point of view." (Kohlberg 1981, p. 199) My question is: are there any real "others" behind the "veil of ignorance" or are they indistinguishable from the self?

25. I find Kohlberg's general claim that the moral point of view entails reciprocity, equality, and fairness unproblematic. Reciprocity is not only a fundamental *moral* principle, but defines, as Alvin Gouldner has argued, a fundamental *social norm*, perhaps, in fact, the very concept of a social norm ("The Norm of Reciprocity: A Preliminary Statement," *American Sociological Review*, vol. 25 (April 1960), pp. 161–78). The existence of ongoing social relations in a human community entails some definition of reciprocity in the actions, expectations, and claims of the group. The fulfillment of such reciprocity, according to whatever interpretation is given to it, would then be considered fairness by members of the group. Likewise, members of a group bound by relations of reciprocity and fairness are considered equal. What changes through history and culture are not these formal structures implicit in the very logic of social relations (we can even call them social universals), but the criteria of inclusion and exclusion. Who constitutes the *relevant* human groups: masters vs. slaves, men vs. women, Gentiles vs. Jews? Similarly, *which* aspects of human behavior and objects of the world are to be regulated by norms of reciprocity: in the societies studied by Levi-Strauss, some tribes exchange sea shells for women. Finally, *in terms* of what is the equality among members of a group established: would this be gender, race, merit, virtue, or entitlement? Clearly Kohlberg presupposes a *universalist-egalitarian* interpretation of reciprocity, fairness, and equality, according to which all humans, in virtue of their mere humanity, are to be considered beings entitled to reciprocal rights and duties.

26. John Rawls, *A Theory of Justice* (Cambridge: Harvard University Press, 1971; second printing, 1972), p. 137.

27. Michael J. Sandel, *Liberalism and the Limits of Justice* (Cambridge: Harvard University Press, 1982; reprinted 1984), p. 9; cited in the text as Sandel 1984.

28. Rawls, *A Theory of Justice*, p. 128.

29. Stanley Cavell, *The Claims of Reason* (Oxford: Oxford University Press, 1982), p. 265.

30. A most suggestive critique of Kohlberg's neglect of interpersonal morality has been developed by Norma Haan in "Two Moralities in Action Contexts: Relationships to Thought, Ego Regulation, and Development," pp. 286–305. Haan reports that "the formulation of formal morality appears to apply best to special kinds of hypothetical, rule-governed dilemmas, the paradigmatic situation in the minds of philosophers over the centuries." (p. 302) Interpersonal reasoning, by contrast, "arises within the context of moral dialogues between agents who strive to achieve balanced agreement, based on compromises they reach or on their joint discovery of interests they hold in common." (p. 303) For a more extensive statement see also Norma Haan, "An Interactional Morality of Everday Life," in *Social Science as Moral Inquiry*, pp. 218–51. The conception of "communicative need interpretations,"

which I argue for below, is also such a model of interactional morality which, nonetheless, has implications for *institutionalized* relations of justice or for public morality as well, cf. note 37.

31. Cf. E. Tugendhat, "Zur Entwicklung von moralischen Begründungs-strukturen im modernen Recht," *Archiv für Recht und Sozialphilosophie*, vol. LXVIII (1980), pp. 1–20.

32. Thus a Rawlsian might object that while the epistemic information pertaining to the standpoint of the concrete other may be relevant in the application and contextualizing of general moral and political principles, it is unclear why such information need also be taken into account in the original choice or justification of such principles. For the moral point of view only concerns the constituents of our common humanity, not those differences which separate us from each other. I would like to distinguish here between the normative standpoint of *universalism*, which I share with Rawls and Kohlberg, and the methodological problem of *formalism*. Although the two have often gone together in the history of moral and political thought they need not do so. A formalist method, which also proceeds via an idealized thought-experiment, is subject to certain epistemic difficulties which are well known in the literature critical of social contract theories. And as Rawls himself has had to admit in his later writings, the device of the "original position" does not justify the concept of the person from which he proceeds, rather it presupposes it (cf. "Kantian Constructivism in Moral Theory"). Once this admission is made, however, and the device of the "original position" with its "veil of ignorance" is said to presuppose a concept of the person rather than justify it, then the kinds of criticisms raised in my paper that concern moral identity and epistemology must also be taken into account. Rawls's concepts of the moral person and autonomy remain restricted to the discourse of the "generalized other." I would like to thank Diane T. Meyers for bringing this objection to my attention.

33. Although I follow the general outline of Habermas' conception of communicative ethics, I differ from him insofar as he distinguishes sharply between questions of justice and the good life (see note 11 above), and insofar as in his description of the "seventh stage," he equivocates between concepts of the "generalized" and the "concrete other"; cf. J. Habermas, "Moral Development and Ego Identity," in *Communication and the Evolution of Society*, translated by T. McCarthy (Boston: Beacon Press, 1979), pp. 69–95. The "concrete other" is introduced in his theory through the back door, as an aspect of ego autonomy, and as an aspect of our relation to inner nature. I find this implausible for reasons discussed above.

34. See Habermas, *ibid.*, p. 90, and Kohlberg's discussion in Kohlberg 1984: 35–86.

35. In an earlier piece, I have dealt with the strong parallelism between the two conceptions of the "veil of ignorance" and the "ideal speech situation"; see my " The Methodological Illusions of Modern Political Theory: The Case of Rawls and Habermas," *Neue Hefte für Philosophie* (Spring 1982), no. 21. pp. 47–74. With the publication of *The Theory of Communicative Active*, Habermas himself has substantially modified various assumptions in his original formulation of communicative ethics, and the rendition given here follows these modifications; for further discussion see my "Toward a Communicative Ethics," in *Critique, Norm, and Utopia*, chap. 8.

36. Cf. Rawls, *A Theory of Justice*, pp. 118ff.

37. For recent feminist perspectives on the development of the self, cf. Dorothy Dinnerstein, "*The Mermaid and the Minotaur: Sexual Arrangements and Human Malaise* (New York: Harper, 1976); Jean Baker Miller, "The Development of Women's Sense of Self," work-in-progress paper published by the Stone Center for

Developmental Services and Studies at Wellesley College, 1984; Nancy Chodorow, *The Reproduction of Mothering* (Berkeley: University of California Press, 1978); Jessica Benjamin, "Authority and the Family Revisited: Or, A World Without Fathers?" in *New German Critique* 13 (1978), pp. 35–58; Jane Flax, "The Conflict Between Nurturance and Autonomy in Mother-Daughter Relationships and Within Feminism," in *Feminist Studies*, vol. 4, no. 2 (June 1981), pp. 171–92; and I. Balbus, *Marxism and Domination* (Princeton: Princeton University Press, 1982).

37. The distinction between the public and the private spheres is undergoing a tremendous realignment in late-capitalist societies as a result of a complicated series of factors, the chief of which may be the changing role of the state in such societies in assuming more and more tasks that were previously more or less restricted to the family and reproductive spheres, e.g., education, early child care, health care, care for the elderly, and the like. Also, recent legislation concerning abortion, wife battering, and child abuse, suggests that the accepted legal definitions of these spheres have begun to shift as well. These new sociological and legislative developments point to the need to fundamentally rethink our concepts of moral, psychological, and legal autonomy, a task hitherto neglected by formal-universalist moral theory. I do not want to imply, by any means that the philosophical critique voiced in this paper leads to a wholly positive evaluation of these developments or to the neglect of their contradictory and ambivalent character for women. My analysis would need to be complemented by a critical social theory of the changing definition and function of the private sphere in late-capitalist societies. As I have argued elsewhere, these social and legal developments not only lead to an extension of the perspective of the "generalized other," by subjecting more and more spheres of life to legal norms, but create the potential for the growth of the perspective of the "concrete other," that is, an association of friendship and solidarity in which need interpretations are discussed and new needs created. I see these associations as being created by new social movements like ecology and feminism, in the interstices of our societies, partly in response to and partly as a consequence of, the activism of the welfare state in late-capitalist societies; cf. *Critique, Norm, and Utopia*, pp. 343–353. I am much indebted to Nancy Fraser for her elaboration of the political consequences of my distinction between the "generalized" and the "concrete" other in the context of the paradoxes of the modern welfare state in her "Feminism and the Social State." (*Salmagundi*, April 1986) An extensive historical and philosophical analysis of the changing relation between the private and the public is provided by Linda Nicholson in her book, *Gender and History: The Limits of Social Theory in the Age of the Family.* (New York: Columbia University Press, 1986).

C. *Debating the Challenge of Difference to Theory*

Other Voices, Other Rooms? Women's Psychology and Moral Theory

GEORGE SHER

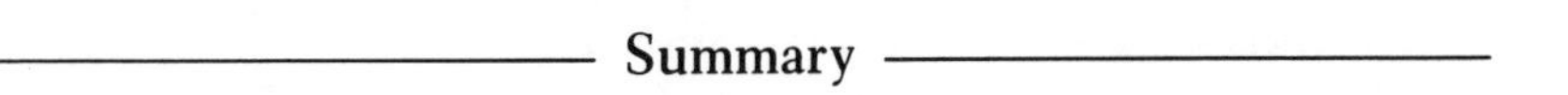

Summary

In his essay "Other Voices, Other Rooms?" George Sher explores the significance of Gilligan's empirical findings for moral theory. According to Sher, Gilligan's study reveals a number of oppositions: the contrasts between concrete and abstract, personal and impersonal, and care and duty. Sher argues that these oppositions have historically constituted the moral problematic. Given this fact, the women's articulation of a morality that emphasizes the concrete, the personal, and a care orientation is a voice that has been heard before. Sher concludes that, contrary to what some have argued, Gilligan's findings do not suggest the need for a radical reformulation of moral theory. Rather, Gilligan's research provides some guidelines as to how we might balance these oppositions within moral theory. S.M.

Of all the reasons for the recent surge of interest in Carol Gilligan's work, not the least is the idea that her findings may have important implications for moral theory. Although this idea is not always made explicit, its overall thrust is clear enough. By showing that women and men construe moral problems differently, and by demonstrating that their moral development traverses different stages, Gilligan is thought to have uncovered an imbalance in existing moral theories. She is thought to have shown that their standard categories and questions embody a subtle bias—a male bias—and thus to have opened our eyes to alternative possibilities.[1] Here I want to register some skepticism about this idea. Despite their undeniable importance, I believe Gilligan's findings open few new doors for moral theory. Women's moral judgments may be expressed in a different voice, but that voice echoes through some quite familiar rooms.

For an initial sense of what is at stake, let us briefly review Gilligan's reconstruction of women's moral thought. Her conception of the prevailing paradigms, and her views about how women deviate from them, are interwoven with her discussion of the three empirical studies around which her book[2] is built. Thus, I shall begin by citing a few representative passages:

> Claire's inability to articulate her moral position stems in part from the fact that hers is a contextual judgment, bound to the particulars of time and place, contingent always on "that mother" and that "unborn child" and thus resisting a categorical formulation. To her the possibilities of imagination outstrip the capacity for generalization [pp. 58–59].
>
> Hypothetical dilemmas, in the abstraction of their presentation, divest moral actors from the history and psychology of their individual lives and separate the moral problem from the social contingencies of its possible occurrence. In doing so, these dilemmas are useful for the distillation and refinement of objective principles of justice and for measuring the formal logic of equality and reciprocity. However, the reconstruction of the dilemma in its contextual particularity allows the understanding of cause and consequence which engages the compassion and tolerance repeatedly noted to distinguish the moral judgments of women [p. 100].
>
> Seeing in the dilemma not a math problem with humans but a narrative of relationships that extends over time, Amy envisions the wife's continuing need for her husband and the husband's continuing concern for his wife and seeks to respond to the druggist's need in a way that would sustain rather than sever connection. Just as she ties the wife's survival to the preservation of relationships, so she considers the value of the wife's life in a context of relationships [p. 28].
>
> Women's construction of the moral problem as a problem of care and responsibility in relationships rather than as one of rights and rules ties the development of their moral thinking to changes in their understanding of responsibility and relationships, just as the conception of morality as justice ties development to the logic of equality and reciprocity [p. 73].
>
> Thus it becomes clear why a morality of rights and noninterference may appear frightening to women in its potential justificatiion of indifference and unconcern. At the same time, it becomes clear why, from a male perspective, a morality of responsibility appears inconclusive and diffuse given its insistent contextual relativism [p. 22].

In these and many similar passages, Gilligan elaborates her conception of women's distinctive moral "voice" through a series of oppositions. She can be read as saying that women's morality is concrete and contextual rather than abstract; that it is nonprincipled rather than principled; that it is personal rather than impersonal; that it motivates through care rather than through awareness of duty; and that it is structured around responsibilities rather than rights. There is room for debate over which of these claims Gilligan regards as fundamental, and, indeed, over which she is committed to at all. But if our question is whether any aspect (or plausible extension) of Gilligan's findings can lead to a recasting of moral theory, then we will do well to examine each opposition.

Thus, consider first the suggestion that women's moral decisions are concrete and contextual rather than abstract. Taken literally, the opposition here seems spurious, for at least *prima facie,* it is hard to see either how all contextual features could ever be *irrelevant* to a moral decision, or how they all could be *relevant* to it. Even the most unbending absolutist, who believes that (say) no promises should ever be broken, must allow moral agents to pay enough attention to context to ascertain whether a particular act *would* break a promise; and additional attention to context is required by the notorious problem of conflict of duty. Yet, on the other hand, even the most ardent proponent of "situation ethics" must acknowledge that moral decision-making requires some selectivity of attention, and thus too, some abstraction from total context. The woman who agonizes over an abortion may be influenced by a myriad of "particulars of time and place"; but given the uncountable number of such particulars, she plainly cannot consider them all. *A fortiori,* she cannot assign them all weight. Thus, the proper question is not so much *whether* context is relevant, but rather how many, and which aspects of it are pertinent to our moral decisions, and how these interact to generate moral duties. But when the role of context is thus tamed,[3] it no longer represents a new discovery for moral theory. Instead, the questions it raises are the very stuff of orthodox normative ethics.[4]

Not surprisingly, these *a priori* remarks are borne out by the reports of Gilligan's own subjects. Despite Gilligan's claim that these women make moral decisions contextually and concretely, their words often evidence a well developed sense of differential relevance. Moreover, this sense emerges not only in their responses to Kohlberg's hypothetical dilemmas, but also in their formulations of dilemmas from their actual lives. Thus, for example, Claire, whose doubts about her activities as an abortion counselor were the occasion for the first passage quoted, remarks that "yes, life is sacred, but the quality of life is also important, and it has to be the determining thing in this particular case" (p. 58). One might quarrel with Claire's characterization of life as "sacred" when she takes its value to be overridden by other considerations; but she is undeniably trying both to isolate the relevant features of her situation and to impose an order upon them.

This is, of course, not to deny that women may in general be more attuned than men to context; nor is it to deny that such receptivity may be extremely important in shaping women's moral assessments. Certainly genetic or environmental factors may have conspired to make women especially sensitive to what their acts really mean to the persons they affect. It is also conceivable that women may care more than men about this. Indeed, given Gilligan's data, such differences seem far more than mere possibilities. Furthermore, any reasonable theory will acknowledge that both the rightness of one's acts and one's moral goodness are heavily influenced by how accurately and fully one assesses one's situation and the possibilities for action within it. For a deontologist, one's attentiveness to context determines how well one appreciates the nature, and so too the right-making characteristics of the available acts; for a consequentialist, it determines how well one appreciates those acts' potential consequences. Yet even taken together, these concessions imply at most that women may be better than men at one aspect of a multifaceted common enterprise. They surely do not imply that women operate within a "morality of context" while men do not. If Kohlberg's "masculine" stage-sequence construes moral development only as movement toward greater abstraction, and ignores the possibility that persons may also develop in sensitivity to context, then so much the worse for its pretensions to measure all aspects of moral progress. So much the worse, too, for its claim to capture all that is importantly common among traditional competing theories.

This way of dismissing the contextual/abstract distinction may seem too quick. Even if we agree that every moral decision requires both sensitivity to context and abstraction from it, we need not agree about the form such abstraction must take. More specifically, even if persons cannot make moral decisions without selectively focusing on some features of their situations, there remains a question about whether the selected features can license decisions all by themselves, or whether they can do so only in concert with more general moral principles. It is a commonplace of most moral theories that if a given constellation of facts is to be a good reason for a person *X* to do *A*, then a similar constellation must be equally good reason for another person *Y*, or for the same person *X* at a different time.[5] Putting the point slightly differently, most theories agree that all moral justification involves at least tacit appeal to principle. Yet Gilligan can be read as taking her findings to show that women's decisions are often *not* backed by universal principles.[6] Hence, her results may seem to point the way to a new view of what constitutes a moral reason.

With this, we have shifted from the first to the second of our contrasts. Underlying the opposition between the contextual and the abstract, we have found a further opposition between the principled and the nonprincipled. This second opposition is, for us, the more interesting; for the role of principle in moral thought is far less clear than the mere need for abstraction. There have, of course, been many attempts to show that nonprincipled decisions are irrational, or in other ways deficient. But when pitted against these, Gilligan's findings may seem to carry considerable weight. For if women commonly do make nonprincipled decisions, then to reject such decisions as unacceptable would be to dismiss the standard moral *modus operandi* of half the world's population.

It is, in fact, a nice question of metatheory how heavily such empirical findings should weigh against other, more nearly *a priori* arguments about standards of rationality. To philosophers sympathetic to naturalism, who operate in the spirit of Nelson Goodman's suggestion that "[t]he process of justification is the delicate one of making mutual adjustments between rules and accepted inferences,"[7] the empirical findings will presumably matter a lot. To others, more a prioristically inclined, they will presumably matter less. But in fact, and fortunately, we need not resolve the general problem of method here. For, despite appearances to the contrary, Gilligan's results show very little about the role of principle in women's decisions.

To see why, we must keep our attention firmly fixed on what acting on principle is. As we saw, to act on principle is just to act for reasons that one takes (or perhaps: would take) to apply with similar force to any others who were similarly situated. But, given the counterfactual element of this formulation, the mere fact that women's responses are rarely *couched* in terms of principle provides little evidence about the underlying structure of their decisions. Even persons who fail to mention principles in reconstructing their deliberations, and indeed even persons who explicitly disavow them, may well have decided on principled grounds. Their omissions or disavowals may reflect, not a lack of commitment to principles, but rather an imperfect appreciation of what such commitment amounts to. Whether one acts on principle depends not just on what one says about principles, but rather on what one does or would say (or do) about a variety of other matters. There are, of course, difficult problems here—problems about which questions would best elicit a person's considered views, about what distinguishes deviations from principles from lack of commitment to them, and about which acts or assertions would best show that persons regard their reasons as fully general. However, given our purposes, we need not resolve these problems. Instead, we need only note that *whatever* resolution one adopts, no one can establish the role of principle in a subject's deliberations without some focused and directive counterfactual inquiry. Since Gilligan's questions do not take this form, the responses she elicits do not show that women's decisions are generally nonprincipled (or even that they are less often principled than men's).

This is, I think, not quite to say that Gilligan's data provide *no* evidence for such a conclusion. Since that conclusion is one possible explanation of women's reluctance to appeal explicitly to principles, it does draw some confirmation from Gilligan's data. But because the same data can be explained in many other ways, the degree of confirmation is minimal. Of the plausible competing explanations, one—that Gilligan's subjects lack the somewhat recondite understanding of principled action that figures in philosophical debates—has already been noted. But there are also others. Women's principles may be hedged with more qualifications than men's, and so may be more difficult to articulate, and thus less ready at hand. Women, being more attuned to the need for qualification, may be more aware of the inadequacies of the principles that first come to mind, and so more hesitant to assert them. Women may attach comparatively less importance to the generality of their reasons, and comparatively more to the reasons' complete specification. Given these and other possibilities, the fact that women seldom explicitly invoke moral principles implies little about whether their actual decisions are principled.

This is still not the end of the story. A further aspect of Gilligan's account is that women's moral decisions tend in two ways to be more personal than men's. For one thing, her female subjects often represent moral dilemmas as problems in balancing the needs of specific individuals (who sometimes, but not always, include themselves). For another, they often represent the proper resolutions to these dilemmas as stemming not from impersonal duty, but rather from personal sympathy and care. Since there is at least a *prima facie* tension between the duty to implement an impersonal principle and the concern that stems from a personal relationship, these findings may seem to lend further (if indirect) support to the view that women's decisions are nonprincipled. In addition, they may seem to add further dimension to the claim that women approach problems of conflicting interests differently than men. If these things are true, then our earlier question of how heavily to count actual practice in establishing standards of moral reasonableness will return with a vengeance.

Yet before concluding this, we must look more closely at the tension between personal relationship and impersonal principle, and at the prospects for resolving it within something like the traditional framework. Let us begin by asking why that tension should be thought to exist at all. Although there are surely many contributing factors, one obvious reason is the unique and unrepeatable nature of personal relationships. Because such relationships are rooted in particular histories of transactions between particular persons, any demands they impose must apply to those persons alone. Even if other persons are similarly situated, their different histories will insure that they are not subject to similar demands. Moreover, if personal relationships do impose demands, then those demands must apparently not just differ from, but also sometimes conflict with, the demands of impersonal principle. In particular, such conflict must arise whenever relationship and principle call for incompatible acts.

Thus interpreted, the opposition between the personal and the impersonal is at least *prima facie* plausible. Yet on this account, its challenge to the familiar body of theory invites at least two objections. Most obviously, even if historically rooted relationships do raise questions about the hegemony of a morality of principle, they cannot possibly provide a comprehensive alternative to it; for many pressing moral choices affect only persons with whom the agent *has* no personal relationship. This may be obscured by the prominence of parents, husbands, and lovers in the reports of Gilligan's subjects; but it emerges as soon as we scrutinize the "relationships" between newly pregnant women and the fetuses they carry. It emerges yet more clearly when we consider such cases as that of Hilary, who as a trial lawyer has discovered that the opposing counsel has

> overlooked a document that provided critical support for his client's "meritorious claim." Deliberating whether or not to tell her opponent . . . Hilary realized that the adversary system of justice impedes not only "the supposed search for truth" but also the expression of concern for the person on the other side. Choosing in the end to adhere to the system, in part because of the vulnerability of her own professional position, she sees herself as having failed to live up to her standard of personal integrity as well as to her moral ideal of self-sacrifice [p. 135].

Whatever Hilary's compromised ideal amounts to, it is plainly *not* an ideal of responsiveness to personal relationships; for no such relationships here exist.[8]

Of course, even if decisions like Hilary's cannot be guided by the demands of personal relationships, they may still be motivated and guided by care and sympathy for all the affected parties. That this is part of what Gilligan takes Hilary to have sacrificed is suggested by her observation that the adversary system impedes "the expression of concern for the person on the other side." Yet as soon as care and concern are detached from the demands of unique and historically rooted relationships—as soon as they are said to be elicited merely by the affected parties' common humanity, or by the fact that those parties all have interests, or all can suffer—the care and concern are once again viewed as appropriate responses to shared and repeatable characteristics. By so regarding them, we completely lose the contrast between the particularity of relationship and the generality of principle. Having lost it, we seem to be left with an approach that seeks to resolve moral dilemmas through sympathetic identification with all the affected parties. Yet far from being novel, this approach—which is at least closely related to that of the familiar impartial and benevolent observer—is central to the existing tradition.[9]

There is also a deeper difficulty with the suggestion that a morality that is sensitive to the demands of relationship must be incompatible with a morality of duty and principle. As I have reconstructed it, the incompatibility arises when the demands of relationship and principle conflict. Yet the assumption that such conflict is inevitable should itself not go unquestioned. Even if we concede that relationships impose demands which *differ* from the demands of moral principles—and I think we ought to concede this—it remains possible that each set of demands might be adjusted to, and might be bounded by, the other. It is, on the one hand, not at all farfetched that friendship might never demand that one betray the trust of another, or that one do anything else that is seriously wrong. It is also not farfetched that the demands of some impersonal moral principles might be contingent on the prior demands of personal relationships. For one thing, we may sometimes be morally permitted, or even required, to give our friends and loved ones preference over others. For another, even where we are not forced to choose whom to help, we may be morally required to produce just the responses that our relationships demand. Such a convergence of demands upon a single action would be no more anomalous than the convergence that occurs when a given act is demanded both by (say) an obligation one has incurred by undertaking a public position and one's natural duty to support just institutions. In general, the demands of relationship and principle may be so interwoven that there is no theoretical bar to our being fully responsive to both.

Needless to say, there are many questions here. It is one thing to suggest that the demands of relationship and impersonal principle might be reconciled, and quite another to tell a plausible detailed story about how this would work. Of all the problems facing such an account, perhaps the most familiar is the objection that the motive of duty is in some sense alienating, and that persons who act merely on principle are *ipso facto* not displaying the affection and care appropriate to personal relationships. Bernard Williams has put this worry well in his influential discussion of the suggestion that a moral principle might license a decision to save one's wife rather than a stranger when only one can be saved. Williams remarks that "this construction provides the agent with one thought too many: it might have been hoped by some (for instance, by his wife) that his motivating thought, fully spelled out, would be the thought that it was his wife, not that it was his wife and, that in situations of this kind, it is permissible to save one's wife."[10] Yet Williams' worry, though provocative, is far from decisive. In an interesting recent essay, Marcia Baron has argued that the worry draws its apparent force partly from our tendency to associate acting from duty with motives that really are inimical to care and affection, but that have no intrinsic connection with duty, and partly from a failure to see that moral principles may operate not as independent sources of motivating force, but rather as filters through which other motives must pass.[11] Since I find Baron's diagnosis convincing, I shall not discuss this problem further. Instead, I shall briefly take up another, less familiar problem that the reconciliationist project faces.

In a nutshell, the further problem is that of justification. It is the problem of finding, within the standard repertoire of justificatory approaches, resources sufficient to ground not merely principles of impartial morality, but also principles licensing the sort of partiality that reconciliationism requires. Put (too) briefly, the difficulty here is that both deontologists and consequentialists have standardly tried to justify their favored principles from some abstract and general perspective. For this reason, the impersonality of their starting points may itself seem to guarantee the rejection of any principles which acknowledge the demands of personal relationships. As Williams notes, this point seems to obtain

> even when the moral point of view is itself explained under conditions of ignorance of some abstractly conceived contracting parties . . . For while the contracting parties are pictured as making some kind of self-interested or prudential choice of a set of rules, they are entirely abstract persons making this choice in ignorance of their own particular properties, tastes, and so forth.[12]

If this is right, and if Gilligan is right to say that women often resolve dilemmas precisely by responding to the demands of personal relationships, then we will indeed be forced to choose between denying that women's decisions are made on moral grounds and radically altering our conceptions of what counts as well grounded morality.

But *does* the impersonality of the familiar justificatory approaches rule out the justification of principles that accomodate the demands of personal relationships? Although we obviously cannot examine all the possibilities, it will be worth our while to look more closely at one familiar strategy. Since the Rawlsian approach has already been mentioned, I shall stick with it. In this approach, a principle is justified if it would be chosen by rational and self-interested persons who were ignorant of the particulars of their situations, and thus were prevented from making biased choices. Although I am no particular friend of hypothetical contractarianism, I cannot see that its difficulties lie where Williams say they do. It is true that Rawls himself says little about personal relationships, and true also that Richards' adaptation of his framework leads to such "righteous absurdities" as that persons should not base their relationships on "arbitrary physical characteristics alone."[13] But none of this implies that Rawlsian contractors could not, in fact, agree on more sensible principles concerning relationships. It does not imply that they could not agree on principles that prescribe compliance with the demands of personal relationships under certain conditions, or that permit or require some partiality to friends and loved ones. In particular, the choice of such principles seems plainly *not* to be ruled out merely by the ignorance of the contracting parties. The contractors' ignorance does rule out the choice of principles that name either specific agents who are allowed or required to be partial or the specific recipients of their partiality. However, this is irrelevant; for the question is not whether any *given* person may or should display partiality to any other, but rather whether *all* persons may or should be partial to their wives, husbands, or friends. The relevant principles, even if licensing or dictating partiality, must do so impartially. Hence, there is no obvious reason why such principles could not be chosen even by contractors ignorant of the particulars of their lives.

Can we go further? Is there any positive reason for rational, self-interested, but ignorant Rawlsian contractors to opt for principles that adjust duties and obligations to the demands of personal relationships? To answer this question fully, we would have to say far more about the demands of relationships than can be said here. But given present purposes, which are merely dialectical, there is indeed something to be said. Our question about the Rawlsian contractors has arisen because their failure to choose principles adjusted to the demands of relationships would support the broader claim that *all* impersonal justificatory strategies yield principles that sometimes conflict with the demands of relationships. This, in turn, would combine with Gilligan's findings to suggest a reconceptualization of the moral point of view in more personal and relationship-oriented terms. But this last move will only be plausible if the demands of personal relationships are in themselves sufficiently compelling to warrant description as moral demands. Hence, for us, the question is not what the Rawlsian contractors would choose *simpliciter*, but rather what they would choose *on the assumption that the demands of relationships are this compelling.*

When the issue is framed in these terms, I think the Rawlsian contractors might well have good reason to choose principles that conflicted as little as possible with the demands of personal relationships. To see why, consider what the demands of relationships would have to be like to be compelling enough to qualify as moral demands. At a minimum, they would have to be so urgent that persons could not violate them without at the same time violating their own integrity. The demands would have to grow out of the kind of deep personal commitment that, as Williams puts it, "compels . . . allegiance to life itself."[14] In addition, when viewed from the perspective of the other parties to relationships, the demands would have to dictate responses that were not merely optional, but were in some sense owed. The demands' nonfulfillment would have to be real grounds for complaint. Just how relationships can generate such demands is of course a large part of the mystery about them. But if they can—and I believe they not only can but often do—then the satisfaction of those demands, when they arise, must itself be a good that transcends mere personal preference. Like liberty and other Rawlsian primary goods, a general ability both to give and to receive such satisfaction must be something it is rational to want whatever else one wants. But if so, then rational contractors endowed with full general information about human psychology could hardly avoid wanting to protect this ability. Since protecting it requires choosing principles whose prescriptions are adjusted to the demands of important relationships, I conclude that they would indeed be motivated to choose such principles.

This conclusion might be challenged through appeal to the last of Gilligan's oppositions. As derived, the conclusion rests on the premise that morality is fundamentally a matter of what persons owe to others. It thus appears to presuppose that any genuinely moral principle must specify people's *rights*. Yet one of Gilligan's most persistent themes is that a preoccupation with rights rather than responsiblities is itself a typically male construction. As she often notes, her female subjects think less about what they are entitled to than about what they are responsible for providing. Thus, it may seem illegitimate for us to say that only demands that specify responses that are owed can qualify as moral. For, if we do say this, we may seem to beg the question against those who see Gilligan's work as prefiguring a new vision of morality.

Yet, here again, the worry is overdrawn. Let us simply grant that women, at least in the earlier stages of their development, think more readily of what they are responsible for providing than of what they are entitled to receive. Even so, nothing follows about the status of the responsibilities they acknowledge. Indeed, one very reasonable suggestion is that they regard themselves as responsible for providing sympathy, care, and help to others precisely *because* they regard themselves as owing these things. Putting the point in terms of rights, and ignoring the complexities and differing interpretations of that notion, we can say that nothing rules out the possibility that women regard others as having a *right* to their sympathy, care, and help. To suppose otherwise would be to conflate the well supported claim that women are less concerned than men with the protection of *their* rights with the quite different claim that women are less inclined than men to think that people *have* rights (or to hold views functionally equivalent to this).

All things considered, Gilligan's findings seem neither to undermine nor decisively to adjudicate among the familiar options of moral theory. They may edge us in certain theoretical directions, but the movement they compel takes us nowhere near the boundaries of the known territories. This is not to deny that the findings suggest that women are, in some respects, better equipped than men to reach morally adequate decisions; but it is to deny that that result requires any exotic recasting of our familiar understanding of "morally adequate." To all of this, the still-hopeful revisionist might finally complain that I have interpreted the received body of theory so broadly that it is not clear what *could* show that it needs radical revision. But this, though true, is precisely the point I want to make. The oppositions of concrete and abstract, personal and impersonal, duty and care are not recent empirical discoveries, but generic determinants of the moral problematic. We have always known that an adequate theory must assign each its proper place. What we have not known, and what Gilligan's findings bring us little closer to knowing, is what those places are.

Notes

1. Thus, for example, Linda J. Nicholson writes, in an issue of *Social Research* devoted to Gilligan's work, that "many feminists have responded that the masculinity of the authors has affected the very content of the theory itself . . . I agree with the feminist argument" (Linda J. Nicholson, "Women, Morality and History," *Social Research,* 50, 3 (Autumn 1983), p. 514). I do not mean to imply that either Nicholson or the other contributors to that issue subscribe to the specific views I criticize below.

2. Carol Gilligan, *In a Different Voice* (Cambridge: Harvard University Press, 1982). All page references in the text are to this volume.

3. That it must be so tamed is one of the few points of agreement between Owen Flanagan and Lawrence Kohlberg in their interchange on moral development. See Owen J. Flanagan, "Virtue, Sex, and Gender: Some Philosophical Reflections on the Moral Psychology Debate," *Ethics* 92 (April 1982), pp. 499–512; and Lawrence Kohlberg, "A Reply to Owen Flanagan and Some Comments on the Puka-Goodpaster Exchange," *Ethics,* 92 (April 1982), pp. 513–28.

4. Moral philosophers have proposed a variety of approaches to the question of which aspects of one's context are morally relevant. Some focus exclusively on a single factor, such as the happiness or preference-satisfaction that available acts would produce. See, for instance, John Stuart Mill, *Utilitarianism* (Indianapolis: Hackett Publishing Company, 1979). Others hold that more than one factor is relevant, but that some factors take priority over others. This approach is exemplified by John Rawls' "lexical ordering" of his principles of justice; see his *A Theory of Justice* (Cambridge: Harvard University Press, 1971). Still others say that more than one factor is relevant, and that there are no priority rules to adjudicate conflicts. See, for example, W. D. Ross, *The Right and the Good* (Oxford: Oxford University Press, 1973), and William Frankena, *Ethics,* 2nd Edition (Englewood Cliffs: Prentice-Hall, 1973). Again, R. M. Hare has argued that a factor's moral relevance for an agent depends on his willingness to universalize a principle in which it appears; see his *Freedom and Reason* (Oxford: Oxford University Press, 1963).

5. For two of the many statements of this view, see Henry Sidgwick, *Methods of Ethics,* 7th Edition (London: Macmillan, 1922), Book III, Chap. 1; and J.L. Mackie, *Ethics: Inventing Right and Wrong* (Harmondsworth, England: Penguin, 1977), chap.4.

6. As the editors of this volume have suggested to me, Gilligan's point may be not that women's decisions are nonprincipled, but only that their principles tend not to be couched in such terms as fairness and justice. I agree that this interpretation is available, but continue to regard the stronger interpretation as at least as plausible. More importantly, even if Gilligan herself does not hold the stronger view, the questions of its tenability and relation to her data remain worth discussing.

7. Nelson Goodman, *Fact, Fiction, and Forecast* (Indianapolis: Bobbs-Merrill, 1965), pp. 64.

8. In a recent public presentation, Gilligan has distinguished between the view that care rests on attachment, and the view that care rests on knowledge gained

through attachment. If she holds that personal relationships are important primarily because they provide a sort of knowledge that can guide and inform our dealings even with strangers, her view is of course not vulnerable to the objections just mounted. It is, however, then vulnerable to the objection to follow.

9. Two classical representatives of this approach are: David Hume, *Treatise of Human Nature,* L. A. Selby-Bigge, ed. (Oxford: Oxford University Press, 1960), bk. III, pt. III, sec. 1; and Adam Smith, *The Theory of Moral Sentiments,* in L.A. Selby-Bigge, *The British Moralists* Vol. 1 (Oxford: Oxford University Press, 1897), pp. 257–77. For a more recent treatment, see R. M. Hare, *Moral Thinking* (Oxford: Oxford University Press, 1981), part II.

10. Bernard Williams, "Persons, Character, and Morality," in Amelie Rorty, ed., *The Identities of Persons* (Berkeley: University of California Press, 1976), pp. 214–15.

11. Marcia Baron, "The Alleged Moral Repugnance of Acting from Duty," *The Journal of Philosophy* LXXXI, 4 (April 1984), pp. 197–220. For related discussion, see Peter Railton, "Alienation, Consequentialism, and the Demands of Morality," *Philosophy and Public Affairs,* 13, 2 (Spring 1984), pp. 134–171.

12. Williams, "Persons, Character, and Morality," pp. 198–99. The approach to which Williams alludes is of course that developed by Rawls in *A Theory of Justice.*

13. David A. J. Richards, *A Theory of Reasons for Action* (Oxford: Oxford University Press, 1971), p. 94. The apt phrase "righteous absurdity" is used by Williams in "Persons, Character, and Morality," p. 212.

14. Williams, "Persons, Character, and Morality," p. 215.

Care and Context in Moral Reasoning

MARILYN FRIEDMAN

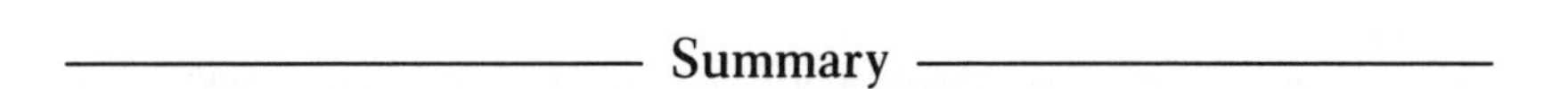

Marilyn Friedman explores the philosophical dimensions of two major features of the framework of moral reasoning that Gilligan's critique of Kohlberg provides. In the first half of her paper, Friedman assesses the importance of the consideration of care and relationships in moral reasoning. She does this by using a series of hypothetical narratives: the story of Abraham, Plato's *Euthyphro,* and modified versions of the Heinz dilemmas. These stories serve to illustrate the need for attention to special relations and the inadequacy of Kohlberg's insistence on the primacy of the justice perspective. In the second half of her paper, Friedman takes up the second major feature of Gilligan's framework, the importance of contextual thinking. Friedman argues that the crucial element of this form of reasoning lies not, as Gilligan seems to think, in the difference between hypothetical and real dilemmas, but rather in how much detail is provided in the construction and presentation of the problem. Complex, richly specified situations allow for a way of breaking out of Kohlberg's narrow perspective so that broader issues of social justice can be raised. Friedman concludes that these two elements of Gilligan's research, care and context, point to two philosophically significant limitations in Kohlberg's theory of moral development. S.M.

A number of researchers[1] have claimed that a moral "gender gap" is revealed by Lawrence Kohlberg's research into the stages of development in moral judgment: that women do not score as high as men on Kohlberg's scale of moral reasoning. If sound, such evidence would appear to imply that women's moral judgment, on average, is deficient when compared to that of men. Carol Gilligan has become the most well known of Kohlberg's critics

Earlier versions of this paper have appeared as a monograph, entitled "Care and Context in Moral Reasoning" (Bath, England: University of Bath, 1986), and as a chapter entitled "Abraham, Socrates, and Heinz: Where Are the Women? (Care and Context in Women's Moral Reasoning," in *Moral Development: Philosophical and Psychological Issues in the Development of Moral Reasoning,* edited by Carol Harding (Chicago: Precedent, 1985), pp. 25–42.

on this issue. The first chapter of her book, *In a Different Voice,*[2] compares the purported gender gap in Kohlberg's work to a number of other theorists and researchers in psychology whose results all proclaimed the moral and/or psychological deficiency of women relative to men, for example, Freud and Erikson.[3] Although highly controversial, Gilligan's research has nevertheless generated intense interest in a number of issues which are as important for moral philosophy as they are for moral psychology. Both of these fields are legitimate targets of Gilligan's accusation that there has been little serious study of what she regards as the distinctive moral reasoning of women—women's "different voice."

Gilligan argues that instead of regarding women's moral reasoning as an immature form of the development which men attain, we should recognize that women exhibit a *different* moral development altogether, one which she characterizes as a "morality of care," a "morality of responsibility." This alternative framework, this "different voice" for dealing with moral dilemmas, is contrasted with Kohlberg's stage sequence of moral reasoning which centers around the notions of justice and rights. Two of the major features which differentiate Gilligan's alternative, purportedly female, moral framework are: first, that relationships predominate as the central moral consideration; and second, that moral reasoning is permeated by what Gilligan calls "contextual relativism."[4]

As Gilligan explains it, the importance of relationships as women's central moral concern makes care and responsibility to persons the major categories of moral thinking for women, rather than rights and rules. She identifies the concern not to hurt as a major theme of women's moral reasoning, thereby suggesting, without actually saying so, that she regards this concern as absent from Kohlberg's moral stages. Also, according to Gilligan, feelings of empathy and compassion abound for women, the expression of care is considered the fulfillment of moral responsibility, and principles of justice and rights are lacking.

The "contextual relativism" that Gilligan attributes to women's moral judgment actually encompasses two distinct features: one, a great sensitivity to the details of situations; and two, a reluctance to make moral judgments. The feature that I shall emphasize is that of sensitivity to detail. Gilligan suggests that women, more often than men, will respond to stories such as the Heinz dilemma by evading a forced choice betweeen the two proffered alternatives and seeking more details before reaching a conclusion. Women are likely to seek the detail that makes the suffering clear, and that engages compassion and caring. In Gilligan's view, such responses have often been misunderstood by interviewers who administered the tests in their studies of moral reasoning. Such responses were often regarded as showing a failure to comprehend the dilemmas or the problem to be solved. On the contrary, Gilligan has said, these responses represent a *challenge* to the problem as it is posed: a rejection of its adequacy in allowing any real or meaningful choice.

In this chapter, I will explore some philosophically important dimensions of the sort of reasoning to which Gilligan has drawn our attention. In the next part of the chapter, I will attempt to show, through a sequence of hypothetical narratives, that considerations of care and relationships are more important in overall moral reasoning than Kohlberg, at any rate, has yet appreciated. The subsequent, and final, part of the chapter contains a discussion of the role of contextual detail in moral reasoning. This, I believe, is the philosophically important core of the "contextual relativism" that has caught Gilligan's attention. In both sections, I will ignore the controversy over whether it can be empirically confirmed that *women's* moral reasoning shows greater concern with care and contextual detail than that of men. I will deal simply with the philosophical importance of these two features of moral reasoning which Gilligan's gender-based studies have highlighted.

Care

Gilligan's claims about the differences between men's and women's moral judgments have become highly controversial. Most of the controversy has centered around two claims: one, the claim that women tend to score lower than men when measured according to Kohlberg's moral reasoning framework; and two, the claim that Kohlberg's framework is male-biased and fails to take account of the distinctly different moral orientation of women. Lawrence Walker, a psychologist from the University of British Columbia, has recently surveyed all the empirical studies that were supposed to have revealed sex differences in scorings; his conclusion is that there is no significant difference.[5] Some studies do show that adult males score higher on Kohlberg's scale than adult females, but these differences appear to be explicable by differences in level of education and occupation, rather than by differences in gender. In particular, it seems that housewives are the women who tend to score lower on Kohlberg's scale. In one of his most recent books, *Moral Stages: A Current Reformulation and Response to Critics,*[6] Kohlberg reminded us of his ongoing contention that the attainment of the higher stages of moral reasoning, stages 4 and 5 "depend upon a sense of participation, responsibility, and role-taking in the secondary institutions of society such as work and government" (ibid., 129), all of which, we are evidently supposed to presume, are unavailable to housewives.

If women do not score significantly differently than men on Kohlberg's scale when matched against men of similar educational and occupational background, then there would be a good deal less evidence for a gender gap in moral reasoning. There would also be a good deal less evidence for the second controversial claim, namely, that Kohlberg's framework is male-biased for ignoring the distinctly different moral orientation of women. However, and more importantly, even if there is no gender gap, a substantial bias in Kohlberg's framework seems to have been uncovered by Gilligan's work, not necessarily a bias toward male moral reasoning, but a bias toward certain particular moral considerations that comprise only a part of the whole range of our moral reasonings.

Kohlberg himself has acknowledged (ibid., 20, 122–23) that Gilligan's research prompted him to take account of the importance, to overall moral development, of notions of care, relationships, and responsibility, and to consider how *these* moral concerns augment his own prior emphasis on reasoning having to do with justice and rights. He has suggested that his previous concern has been with "justice reasoning" only, and that it is unfortunate that it was simply called "moral reasoning" as if it represented the whole breadth and substance of the moral cognitive domain. Kohlberg has supported his contention that there is no gender gap in moral reasoning by arguing that both sexes use justice and care orientations, and that the type of orientation used depends on "the type of moral problem defined" and the environment in which the problem is located (ibid., 132). Moral dilemmas located, for example, in a family context are more likely to invoke caring considerations from both sexes, whereas dilemmas located in a secondary institution of society, such as government, are more likely to invoke justice considerations from both sexes.

I leave to psychologists the task of assessing the empirical claim about differences in the moral reasoning of the two sexes. My interest is in the relationship between the two different moral perspectives that are now recognized by Kohlberg as well as Gilligan. In *Moral Stages: A Current Formulation and Response to Critics,* Kohlberg argued that justice and caring are *not* "two different tracks of moral development which are either independent or in polar opposition to one another" (ibid., 137), that "many moral situations or dilemmas do not pose a choice between one or the other orientations, but rather call out a response which integrates both orientations," and that considerations of caring need not conflict with those of justice "but may be integrated into a response consistent with justice, especially at the post-conventional level." (Ibid., 134) Several decades ago, we learned that "separate" was inherently unequal; however, we cannot assume that integration is inherently *equal.* In Kohlberg's most recent formulation, even though it is claimed that care can be integrated with justice, considerations of justice are still taken to be "primary in defining the moral domain." (Ibid., 91)

Kohlberg has portrayed a morality of care as pertaining to special relationships among particular persons, in contrast to the universalistic relationships handled by justice reasoning. He has suggested that "central to the ethic of particularistic relationships are affectively-tinged ideas and attitudes of *caring, love, loyalty, and responsibility.*" (Ibid., 20–21) In Kohlberg's estimation, special relationships should be regarded as supplementing and deepening the sense of generalized obligations of justice. For example, in the Heinz dilemma, Heinz's care for his wife would be regarded as supplementing the obligation that he has to respect her right to life. However an ethic of care cannot, in Kohlberg's view, supplant a morality of justice for "an ethic of care is, in and of itself, not well adapted to resolve justice problems; problems which require principles to resolve conflicting claims among persons, all of whom in some sense should be cared about." (Ibid.) Furthermore, "morally valid forms of caring and community presuppose prior conditions and judgments of justice." (Ibid., 92)

Kohlberg has admitted that the primacy of justice has not been "proved" by his research, and that, instead, it has been a guiding assumption of the research, based on certain methodological and metaethical considerations.

(Ibid., 93–95) First, it is based on a "prescriptivist conception of moral judgment"; that is, moral judgment is treated not as expressing the interpretation of situational fact, but rather as the expression of universalizable "ought"-claims. Second, it derives from a search for moral universality, for "minimal value conceptions on which all persons could agree." Third, the primacy of justice has stemmed from Kohlberg's cognitive, or rational, approach to morality. In Kohlberg's words, "justice asks for 'objective' or rational reasons and justifications for choice rather than being satisfied with subjective, 'decisionistic', personal commitments to aims and to other persons." (Ibid., 93) Finally, Kohlberg has claimed that the most important reason for the primacy of justice is that it is "the most structural feature of moral judgment." "With the moral domain defined in terms of justice," wrote Kohlberg, "we have been successful in . . . elaborating stages which are structural systems in the Piagetian tradition." (Ibid., 92) Kohlberg has suggested that care reasoning may not be capable of being represented in terms of the criteria that he takes to define Piagetian cognitive stages.

Kohlberg's reasons for according primacy to justice reasoning are dissatisfying, for several reasons. First, the methodological considerations to which he has appealed, at best, entitle us to infer that justice is primary in that domain of morality that *can* be represented in terms of Piagetian hard stages, but not that justice is primary to morality as such. Second, his appeal to certain meta*ethical* considerations is controversial at best, question-begging at worst. Whether moral judgments express universalizable prescriptions rather than interpretations of situational facts, whether there are "minimal value conceptions on which all persons could agree," whether "personal commitments to aims and to other persons" are excluded as rational justifications of choice, as Kohlberg has seemed to suggest—are all issues that cannot be resolved simply by *assuming* the primacy of a type of reasoning that has these features. Each of these issues is controversial and calls for considerably more reflection than this.

Kohlberg's primacy of justice in defining the moral domain is troubling for a third reason. I have noted Kohlberg's suggestion that higher scores on his scale of moral development are correlated with participation in the secondary institutions of society, such as government and the workplace outside the home. By contrast, care reasoning is supposed to be relevant only to special relationships among "family, friends, and group members." (Ibid., 131) It is tempting to characterize these two sorts of moral reasoning as pertaining, respectively, to the "public," or "political," realm and to the so-called "private," or "personal," realm. It seems that Kohlberg's primacy of justice reasoning coincides with a long-standing presumption of western thought that the world of personal relationships, of the family and of family ties and and loyalties—the traditional world of women—is a world of lesser moral importance than the public world of government and of the marketplace—the male-dominated world outside the home.

Considerations of justice and rights have to do with abstract persons bound together by a social contract to act in ways that show mutual respect for rights that they possess equally. Considerations of justice do not require that persons know each other personally. Relatives, friends, or perfect strangers all deserve the same fair treatment and respect. In Kohlberg's view, considerations of special relationship and of caring seem merely to enrich with compassion the judgments that are based on *prior* considerations of justice. In no way would considerations of special relationship, for Kohlberg, override those of justice and rights. Unless caring and community presupposed prior judgments of justice, they would seem, in Kohlberg's terms, not to be "morally valid." (Ibid., 92) In the discussion to follow, I shall only *begin* to challenge Kohlberg's emphasis on the primacy of justice. I shall do so by telling some stories, the point of which is to suggest that sometimes considerations of justice and rights *are* legitimately overridden by considerations of special relationship. My stories will not, of course, show that special relationships *always* override considerations of justice; indeed, I do not believe that to be the case. But I hope to begin delineating in some detail just what the priorities and interconnections are between these apparently diverse moral notions.

My first story is the biblical story of Abraham having just been asked by God to sacrifice Isaac, Abraham's only son. In this familiar tale, Abraham shows himself willing to carry out the command; and only at the last moment does God intervene to provide a sacrificial ram and permission for Abraham to sacrifice it in place of Isaac. Abraham's faith in God has been tested and has proved unshakeable. Both Carol Gilligan (ibid., 104) and Owen Flanagan[7] referred to this story in their discussions of the controversy about sex-differences in moral reasoning. They each used it as an illustration of what can go wrong with Kohlberg's highest or principled stage of moral reasoning, a stage, as Flanagan puts it, "where 'principle' always wins out in conflicts with even the strongest affiliative instincts and familial obligations."[8] Kohlberg has disagreed with the Gilligan/Flanagan interpretation of the Abraham story:

> By no stretch of the imagination could Abraham's willingness to sacrifice Isaac be interpreted by Gilligan or myself as an example or outcome of principled moral reasoning. It is, rather, an example of an action based on reasoning that the morally right is defined by authority (in this case God's authority) as opposed to universalizable moral principles. For both Gilligan and myself, such judgment based on authority would represent conventional (stage 4) moral judgment, not postconventional (principled) moral judgment.[9]

However, there is at least one more way to interpret the Abraham story, and it is an interpretation that regards Abraham's choice to sacrifice Isaac as deriving from the considerations of a special relationship that is taken to override the duties derived from justice and rights. This third interpretation is suggested by Soren Kierkegaard in *Fear and Trembling.*[10] Kierkegaard reminds us that Abraham's faith in and love for God were being tested by God's command that Abraham sacrifice his only son. In Kierkegaard's view, "to the son the father has the highest and most sacred obligation."[11] Thus Kohlberg is wrong, given this interpretation, to think that Abraham's act derives from the stage 4 reasoning that whatever God says is right. There must be *some* sense in which what Abraham is asked to do remains morally *wrong*. The supreme test of the faith of a moral person is to ask that person to commit what they continue to regard as a grave moral wrong; only this sort of act would be the greatest sacrifice that such a person could be asked to make. If the command of God made the sacrifice of Isaac right in *all* senses, then it would be no sacrifice for a moral person such as Abraham to perform it, and hence, no test of the faith of such a moral person. Thus, one way of construing the story of Abraham, derived loosely from Kierkegaard's interpretation, is that it represents the moral dilemma of someone having to choose to uphold the right to life, thereby sacrificing relationships with a Supreme Being, or, rather, choosing relationship with a Supreme Being, thereby sacrificing considerations of rights.

My second story is taken from Plato's dialogue, the *Euthyphro*.[12] In this dialogue, Socrates encounters Euthyphro who has just arranged to prosecute his father for murder. The victim was a slave in Euthyphro's home who had killed another domestic servant in a drunken fit. Euthyphro's father tied up the slave who had done the killing, threw him into a ditch, and went to seek advice about what to do with him. Before the father could return, the slave died in the ditch from the cold, the hunger, and the chains. Socrates is astonished that Euthyphro would prosecute his own father for bringing about such a death. Socrates' reaction is complicated by certain troubling suggestions: an emphasis on the servant status of the man left to die by Euthyphro's father, and an emphasis on the father's status as "master," as if this role conferred privileges of life and death over servants. In this discussion, I will ignore these suggestions and focus only on Socrates' concern that a charge of murder is being brought against a father by his own son. Euthyphro tries to defend his action by appeal to universal rules, in particular, a rule of piety, which is something that both Socrates and Euthyphro agree to be a part of justice. The rule, in Euthyphro's view, calls for "prosecuting anyone who is guilty of murder, sacrilege, or of any other similar crime—whether he be your father or mother, or some other person, that makes no difference—"[13] Against this universalizable, impartial injunction, Socrates continues to express strong reservations, as if the responsiblities deriving from family relationships outweigh even considerations of justice.

Socrates has been singled out by Kohlberg as one of the few human beings ever to have reached the highest stage of moral reasoning, now called the "hypothetical" sixth stage. It is, therefore, especially poignant to recall the story of the *Euthyphro*, in which it is the figure of Socrates who suggests that impartial and universalizable considerations of justice may be overridden by personal responsibilities arising out of familial relationships, relationships that are particular and nonuniversalizable.

It might be argued that the responsibilites deriving from particular relationships *are* universalizable. For example, if it is true that certain behavior is owed to someone simply because that person is my father, then such behavior is owed *by anyone* to whomever happens to be that person's father. Thus, more needs to be said in order to differentiate the responsibilities entailed by personal relationships from the duties that are based upon considerations of justice and rights. I have two suggestions to make about the differences between them. First, many of the personal relationships that matter to us do not originate in mutual consent, or with anything that can suitably be represented by the metaphor of a social contract—this is particularly true of most kinship ties. Yet, as one moves up Kohlberg's scale of moral reasoning, social contract becomes increasingly important as the justification of universalizability in moral reasoning. Therefore, the reponsibilities arising out of personal relationships still cannot be derived from Kohlbergian justice principles. Second, it hardly makes sense to construe, as a universalizable principle of *justice*, a maxim requiring that one's kin be treated as *exempt* from the principles of justice that are to apply to all (other) persons. Thus, even if responsibilities to one's kin could be subsumed under universalizable requirements of justice, they could hardly include the Socratic recommendation to Euthyphro that considerations of justice be *overridden* for the sake of one's kin.

Thus far my stories have all been about men. Yet Gilligan's work on *women's* moral development was the original stimulus for my investigation. My remaining stories will, therefore be about women. I shall take the liberty of performing a sex-change operation on the Heinz dilemma, the most famous of the dilemmas used by Kohlberg to measure the level of moral reasoning of interview subjects. The original dilemma is as follows:

> In Europe, a woman was near death from cancer. One drug might save her, a form of radium that a druggist in the same town had recently discovered. The druggist was charging $2000, ten times what the drug cost him to make. The sick woman's husband, Heinz, went to everyone he knew to borrow the money, but he could only get together about half of what it cost. He told the druggist that his wife was dying and asked him to sell it cheaper or let him pay later. But the druggist said, "No." The husband got desperate and broke into the man's store to steal the drug for his wife. Should the husband have done that? Why?[14]

Of course, there is already a woman in the Heinz dilemma, namely, Heinz's wife. She is easy to forget since, unlike Heinz, she has no name, and unlike both Heinz and the also unnamed druggist, she is the only person in the story who does not act. Instead she is simply the passive patient who is there to be saved, the one whose presence provides both Heinz and the druggist with their moral opportunities for heroism and villainy. Let us remove her from this oblivion. First, she needs a name: I will call her Heidi. Next, let us change her role from that of patient to that of agent. Finally, let us suppose that the druggist, another unnamed character in the original dilemma is also a woman; I will call her Hilda. Now we are ready for our new story: the "Heidi dilemma":

> In Europe, a man was near death from cancer. One drug might save him, a form of radium that a druggist in the same town, a woman named Hilda, had recently discovered. The druggist was charging $2000, ten times what the drug cost her to make. The sick man's wife, Heidi, went to everyone she knew to borrow the money, but she could only get together about half of what it cost. She told Hilda, the druggist, that her husband was dying and asked Hilda to sell the drug cheaper or let her, Heidi, pay later. But

> Hilda said, "No." Heidi got desperate and broke into the woman's store to steal the drug for her husband. Should the wife have done that? Why?

It would be interesting to speculate whether any of our responses to the dilemma have changed as a result of the sex-change operation and the emergence of women as protagonists. For surely there are new questions to ask: What risks does theft pose for a woman which are not posed for a man? What unique indignities are inflicted on a woman who is arrested of street crime? And if the druggist is a woman, is the druggist's intransigence in the face of someone's likely death still so believable as it was in the original dilemma? Gilligan's portrayal of women's moral concerns finds striking hypothetical applicabiilty in this "context" of sorts: for would not a female druggist *care* about the dying patients who can't afford her medication? Wouldn't she spare some of the drug if only she could afford to do so? Wouldn't she spare some of the drug even if she *couldn't* afford to do so? In any event, she would hardly refuse another woman outright on a matter of life and death. Two women, it strikes many of us, would keep talking and work something out.

With women as the protagonists, the very plausibility of the "Heinz" dilemma as an exercise in forced choice diminishes dramatically. However this change is not my real concern. An even more modified version of the original dilemma brings me closer to my main point; version #1 was just a transitional stage. Consider Heidi dilemma #2:

> In Europe, a man was near death from cancer. One drug might save him, a form of radium that a druggist in the same town, a woman named Hilda, had recently discovered. The druggist was charging $2000, ten times what the drug cost her to make. A perfect stranger, a woman named Heidi, chanced to read about the sick man's plight in the local newpaper. She was moved to act. She went to everyone she knew to borrow the money for the drug, but she could only get together about half of what it cost. She asked the druggist to sell the drug more cheaply or to let her, Heidi, pay for it later. But Hilda, the druggist, said, "No," Heidi broke into the woman's store to steal the drug for a man she did not know. Should Heidi have done that? Why?

If Kohlberg's dilemma can indeed be resolved through impartial considerations of justice and rights, then the solution to the dilemma should not depend upon the existence of any special relationship between the person who is dying of cancer and the prospective thief of the drug. However, I suggest that the conviction, which many of us have, that Heinz should steal the drug for his nameless wife in the original dilemma, rests at least in part on our notion of responsiblities arising out of the special relationship called marriage, and that without this relationship, our conviction that theft ought to be commited might well—on grounds provided simply by the story—be much weaker than it is. If the patient and the prospective thief were absolute strangers, I suspect that we would be far less likely to say that a serious personal risk should be taken to steal the drug, break the law, and harm the druggist—even to save a life.

In *Moral Stages,* Kohlberg has already responded to the question of whether the solution to the original dilemma depends only upon considerations of justice or rather upon considerations of special relationship as well. Kohlberg first explained why the issue is important; he wrote, "A universalizable judgment that appeals to norms implies a fair or impartial application of the norms."[15] He then produced excerpts from an interview with an 11-year-old boy who was asked whether a "man" should steal a drug to save the life of a stranger, "if there was no other way to save his life." The 11-year-old first responded that it does not seem that one should steal for someone whom one doesn't care about. But then the boy revised his judgment and said: "But somehow it doesn't seem fair to say that. The stranger has his life and wants to live just as much as your wife; it isn't fair to say you should steal it for your wife but not for the stranger."[16] For Kohlberg, this example illustrates the way in which a concern for universalizing a moral judgment leads to a preference for justice reasoning rather than reasoning in terms of care and special relationship.

I shall conclude this section with several comments on Kohlberg's sample 11-year-old. First, the boy's reasoning is actually quite perceptive: it is *not* fair to steal the drug for one's spouse but not for a stranger. Considerations of *fairness* would not lead to this distinction among needy persons. If there is a distinction of this sort between what is owed to one's kin and what is owed to strangers, the distinction would likely derive from the special nature of the relationship to one's kin. If my duty to steal in order to save a life is owed to my kin in virtue of my kinship relationship to them, then the fact that it's *not fair* that I don't have this duty toward strangers does *not* entail that I therefore *have* the same duty toward strangers as I do toward my kin. The main point of my stories was to suggest that we cannot presuppose that considerations of justice have moral primacy, never to be outweighed by considerations of special relationship. Considerations of justice and rights do not necessarily lead to the conclusion that we owe to all persons the special treatment that is due to our families and friends. It may not be "fair"; but, as I have been trying to suggest, fairness may not be our only moral concern.

Second, the authenticity of Kohlberg's 11-year-old respondent is suspect. Few persons, even at the higher stage of justice reasoning, would judge, in a manner that informs their behavior, that (any) one ought to steal to save the life of a stranger. If you are not persuaded that this is so, then please consider one final modified form of the Heinz dilemma: the "You" dilemma:

> *You* are the perfect stranger who has just read in your morning paper of a man dying of cancer and of the only drug that can save him, yet which he cannot afford. *You* are the stranger who fails to convince the druggist to sell the drug more cheaply. Will *you* take the risk of stealing the drug to save the life of someone you don't know? What moral judgment will you make in *this* dilemma?

How many of those who endorse the judgment that, "You should steal to save the life of a stranger," actually act on it? Yet this failure to act does *not* stem from any *absence* of impoverished, medically needful persons in our society. The "You" dilemma confronts us with the gap betweeen moral reasoning and moral behavior. It discloses the limited bearing, on true moral maturity, of those moral judgments upon which we do not act.

In addition, the "You" dilemma alerts us to another factor that may differentiate the universalistic reasoning of a justice orientation from the particularistic reasoning of a care orientation. With our verbalized moral judgments, we lay claims to our moral identities, to the sorts of persons we, morally, aspire to be—and wish others to think we are. We express the purported sweep of our moral visions and our moral aspirations. A justice orientation, with its strict impartiality and grandiose universality, lends itself to a more "heroic"[17] form of moral expression than does a care orientation. Judgments based upon considerations of justice and rights, *rather than* considerations of "my husband," "my wife," "my child," or "my body," seem permeated with an impersonal nobility of moral concern.

Nobility of moral concern is especially easy to affect when one is merely responding to a test interviewer or, for some other reason, when real commitment is not measured and deeds need not follow upon words. Of course, some individuals in our world really do steal to save the lives of strangers. But most people who judge that "one" should do so are not in fact displaying a genuine readiness to act. Most such judgments are cut off from any link with practice. At best, such judgments are sincere and betoken failed moral ambitions; at worst, they are insincere and exhibit moral hypocrisy. Perhaps, as well, such judgments are rarely acted upon because those who so judge have a gnawing suspicion that the impartial demands of justice do not necessarily override all other moral concerns.

Context

The second point raised by Gilligan, which I wish to explore, is the importance to moral reasoning of a sensitivity to contextual detail. Gilligan suggests that women, more so than men, respond inadequately to such dilemmas as the Heinz dilemma because the dilemmas themselves are problematic. In Gilligan's view the problem is that they are hypothetical rather than real dilemmas; they are too abstract and, as she puts it, they separate "the moral problem from the social contingencies of its possible occurrence."[18] I shall try to strengthen Gilligan's insight by putting the point somewhat differently. What matters is not whether the dilemmas are real or hypothetical, but rather whether they are spelled out in great detail or simply described in a very abbreviated form. A substantial work of literature can portray a moral crisis with enough detail to make most of us feel comfortable that we know enough to judge what should be done by the protagonist; when Nora leaves her marriage home, her "Doll's House," many of us support her decision wholeheartedly; the hypothetical nature of her moral dilemma is simply unimportant.

Perhaps Gilligan has been distracted by the fact that when we learn of real moral dilemmas, we typically know the people and a good bit about their lives and their current situations. We rely upon our background information to help ourselves generate alternative possible solutions for those problems. Hypothetical dilemmas have no social or historical context outside their own specifications; lacking any background information, we require longer stories in order to feel comfortable that we know most of the pertinent information that can be expected in cases of this sort. What matters is having *enough* detail for the story at hand—whether the story is of a real or a hypothetical moral dilemma.

Gilligan herself provides an example of how the hypothetical Heinz dilemma would be significantly altered were it to be enriched by some very plausible details. Commenting on the response to the Heinz dilemma given by one subject, Gilligan says:

> Heinz's decision to steal is considered not in terms of the logical priority of life over property, which justifies its rightness, but rather in terms of the actual consequences that stealing would have for a man of limited means and little social power.
>
> Considered in the light of its probable outcomes—his wife dead, or Heinz in jail, brutalized by the violence of that experience and his life compromised by a record of felony—the dilemma itself changes. Its resolution has less to do with the relative weights of life and property in an abstract moral conception than with the collision between two lives, formerly conjoined but now in opposition, where the continuation of one life can occur only at the expense of the other.[19]

In order to make clear just how important contextual detail is, let us elaborate the Heinz/Heidi dilemma even further.

The woman who is dying of cancer is weary and depressed from the losing battle that she has been fighting for several years. It all began with cancer of the colon, and her doctors convinced her to resort to a colostomy. Now, several years later, it is clear that the malignancy was not stopped by this drastic measure. Disfigured in a manner that she has never been able to accept, weakened, and in pain from the cancer that continues to poison her system, bedridden and dependent on others for her daily functioning, she has lost hope and grown despondent at a fate which, to her, is worse than death. How does this woman really measure the value of her own life?

And perhaps there is more to the druggist's story as well. Her husband deserted her and her three children years ago, and has paid not a penny of his court-ordered child support money. So the druggist struggles mightily day after day to keep her family together and tends a small pharmacy that barely meets the material needs of her children, let alone her own. Moreover, she lives in a society that jealously guards the private ownership of its property. Were she and her children to fall into poverty, that society would throw her a few crumbs of welfare support, but only after she had exhausted all other resources, and at the cost of her dignity and the invasion of her privacy.

In this society, the tiny share of goods on which she can labor and whose fruits she can sell are the slender means of livelihood for her and her family. The notion of property does not mean the same thing to a single mother with dependent children, living at the margin under the constraints of a capitalist economy, as it does to the major shareholders of General Dynamics. The druggist, too, is a person of flesh and blood with a story of her own to tell.

There are other contingencies that could be explored. I have already referred to one of the interviews highlighted by Gilligan in which the subject ponders the risks and uncertainties of theft for a person who hasn't the skill or experience to bring the job off successfully—burglary is no mean accomplishment. Then there are the possible deleterious side-effects of drugs *proclaimed* as cancer cures in all the glittering hyperbole of the mass media, before they have been adequately tested. When the story is filled out with such additional considerations, it is no longer possible to resolve the dilemma with a simple principle asserting the primacy of life over property. A restrictive economic context can turn property into a family's only means to life, and can force a competition of life *against* life in a desperate struggle that not all can win. Indeed, the most pervasive and universalizable problems of justice in the Heinz dilemma lie entirely outside the scope of its narrowly chosen details.

The significance of the *real* justice problem in the Heinz dilemma has apparently been missed or ignored by Kohlberg, whose construction of the dilemma as a problem in moral reasoning forces a choice between two alternatives that, in fact, are identical in at least one important respect: neither of them threatens the institutional status quo in which the situation occurs. The significance of this more fundamental justice problem has also not been commented on by Gilligan, even though she perceptively sees the importance of grasping the situation in terms of rich contextual detail. For Gilligan appears to think that contextual detail is a concern only of people whose moral reasoning centers on care and relationships. She does not appear to realize that in reasoning about justice and rights, it is equally inappropriate to draw conclusions from highly abbreviated descriptions of situations. Gilligan's position would be strengthened, I believe, by incorporating this insight.

In the Heinz situation, there are broad issues of social justice at stake in the delivery of health care. These issues cannot be resolved nor even properly understood from the scanty detail that is provided in any of Kohlberg's formulations of the so-called "dilemma." We must have background knowledge about the inadequacy of health care provided for people without financial resources, in a society that allows most health care resources to be privately owned, privately sold for profit in the market place, and privately withheld from people who cannot afford the market price. And before we can resolve the problem, we must know what the alternatives are, and must assess them for the degree to which they approximate an ideal of fair and just health care available to all, and the degree to which they achieve, or fall short of, other relevant moral ideals.

For example, should we allow health care resources to remain privately owned while we simply implement a Medicaid-like program of government transfer payments to subsidize the cost of health care to the needy? Or, should the government provide mandatory health insurance for everyone, with premiums taken from those who can pay, as a kind of health care tax, and premiums waived for those who cannot pay, as an in-kind welfare benefit? Or, should we instead abolish private ownership of health care resources altogether, and, if so, should our alternative be grass-roots-organized health care cooperatives, or state-run socialized medicine? Selecting an answer to these questions and resolving the *real* justice dilemma, which the Heidi/Heinz situation merely intimates, requires an inordinate amount of detail as well as a complex theoretical perspective on matters of economics, politics, social and domestic life. Thus, contextual detail matters overridingly to matters of justice as well as to matters of care and relationships.

There is a second feature of Gilligan's emphasis on contextual detail in moral reasoning that I would change. Gilligan believes that a concern for contextual detail moves a moral reasoner away from principled moral reasoning in the direction of "contextual relativism." She suggests that persons who exemplify this form of moral reasoning have "difficulty at arriving at definitive answers to moral judgments" and show a "reluctance to judge" others.[20] Obviously, many people experience this reluctance at some time or other, and some people experience it all the time. But we misunderstand moral reasoning if we regard this as a necessary or inevitable outcome of becoming concerned with contextual detail.

At the same time, Kohlberg's response to Gilligan on this point is simplistic and unhelpful. In Kohlberg's view, the notion of a principle is the notion of that which guides moral judgment in a way that allows for the exceptions. On this construal, a responsiveness to contextual details and a willingness to alter moral judgments depending upon the context does not, therefore, imply an abandonment of moral principles or a genuine moral relativism.[21] For Kohlberg, an increasing awareness of context need only indicate an increasing awareness of the difficulties of applying one's principles to specific cases. There is something to this: sensitivity to contextual detail need not carry with it the relativistic view that there *are no* moral rights or wrongs, nor the slightly weaker view that *there is no way to decide* what is right or wrong. It need only be associated with uncertainties about *which* principles to apply to a particular case, or a concern that one does not yet *know* enough to apply one's principles, or a worry that one's principles are too *narrow* to deal with the novelties at hand.

However, this last alternative is quite significant. It is precisely the possibility of this narrowness of principles that Kohlberg seems not to appreciate. A rich sense of contextual detail awakens one to the limitations in moral thinking that arise from the *minimalist* moral principles with which we are familiar. A principle that asserts the primacy of life over property is obviously not wrong; in the abstract, few of us would be reluctant to make the judgment. But its relevance to a particular situation depends on countless details about the quality of *those particular* lives at stake, the meaning of *that particular* property, the identity of those whose lives and/or property are at stake, the range of available options, the potential benefits and harms of each, the institutional setting that structures the situation and the lives of its participants—and the possibility of changing that institutional context. These details are ordinarily very complex; some sway us on one direction, some in another. In no time at all, we will need principles for the *ordering* of our principles. Kohlberg's suggestion that contextual detail helps one to figure out which principle to apply simply does not get us very far in understanding how we finally decide what ought to be done in the complex, institutionally-structured situations of our everyday lives. And this is true whether the reasoning is about care and relationships or about matters of social justice.

Kohlberg has already acknowledged a variety of ways in which his scale of moral development does not measure the whole of moral reasoning; it is limited to what he calls structural stages in the development of reasoning about justice and rights. Drawing upon Gilligan's gender-based critique of Kohlberg, I have discussed two other limitations which I regard as highly significant: first, the absence of any real integration of moral considerations having to do with care and relationships; and second, the absence of an adequate account of how people reason about complex and richly specified situations in terms of moral rules and principles. I have explored some of the philosophical significance of these two prominent problems suggested by Gilligan's study of women's moral reasoning.

Notes

1. Cf. Constance Holstein, "Development of Moral Judgment: A Longitudinal Study of Males and Females," *Child Development* 47 (1976), pp. 51–61.
2. Carol Gilligan, *In a Different Voice* (Cambridge: Harvard University Press, 1982).
3. Cf. Sigmund Freud, "Female Sexuality" (1931), Vol, XXI of *The Standard Edition of the Complete Psychological Works of Sigmund Freud,* trans. and ed. by James Strachey (London: The Hogarth Press, 1961); and Erik Erikson, *Childhood and Society* (New York: W. W. Norton, 1950). References are taken from Gilligan.
4. *Op. cit.*, p. 22.
5. Lawrence J. Walker, University of British Columbia, "Sex Differences in the Development of Moral Reasoning," *Child Development,* vol. 55, no. 3 (1984), pp. 677–91.
6. Co-authored with Charles Levine and Alexandra Hewer (Basel: S. Karger, 1983). All references to Kohlberg's views are drawn from this book.
7. "Virtue, Sex, and Gender: Some Philosophical Reflections on the Moral Psychology Debate," *Ethics,* vol. 92, no. 3 (April 1982), p. 501.
8. West, op. cit., p. 320.
9. Ibid.
10. Trans. by Walter Lowrie (Princeton, N.J.: Princeton University Press, 1941).
11. Ibid., p. 39.
12. Trans. by Benjamin Jowett. In: Irwing Edman, ed., *The Works of Plato* (New York: The Modern Library, 1928), pp. 35–55.
13. Ibid., pp. 34–40.
14. Lawrence Kohlberg, "Stage and Sequence: The Cognitive-Developmental Approach to Socialization," in D. A. Goslin, ed., *Handbook of Socialization Theory and Research* (Chicago: Rand McNally, 1969), p. 379.
15. Op. cit., p. 92.
16. Ibid.
17. I am grateful to Eva Kittay for suggesting the relevance of "heroism" to this part of my discussion.
18. *In a Different Voice,* p. 100.
19. Ibid., p. 101.
20. Ibid.
21. *Moral Stages,* pp. 145–48.

Moral Development and the Personal Point of View

JONATHAN E. ADLER

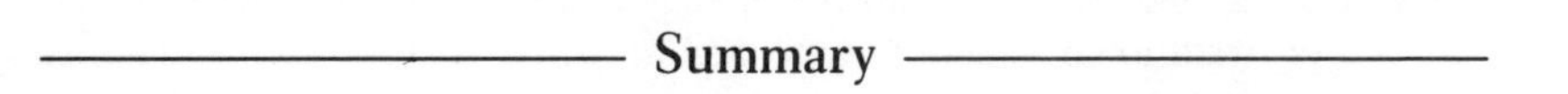

Summary

According to Jonathan Adler, an important contribution of Gilligan's research is that it alerts us to the personal point of view in morality and to a number of difficulties that arise when we focus too exclusively on abstract criteria of moral adequacy. Based on these concerns, Adler develops an extended critique of Lawrence Kohlberg's stress on autonomy, comprehensiveness, and consistency in moral reasoning.

First, Adler urges that people wisely assume a fund of established principles and values when they address moral problems, and that it is a mistake to regard these principles and values as constantly open to challenge and revision. Second, Adler questions Kohlberg's contention that people can be expected to rank all moral considerations in a way that applies to all situations. Third, Adler urges that a person's commitment to morality can, in fact, be undermined by an excessively stringent demand for consistency. If research on moral development is to exhibit a coincidence between good reasoning and good conduct, our conception of good reasoning must be adjusted to the exigencies of the practical sphere. D.T.M.

I. Introduction: Moral Life and Moral Action.

1. The different moral voice that Carol Gilligan[1] hears parallels recent challenges to traditional moral theory—Kantian or utilitarian—for their failure to respect the personal point of view.[2] The demands of impersonal morality, critics allege, interfere with (1) an individual's pursuit of his or her own ends, (2) commitment to certain deeply cherished beliefs, and (3) devotion or loyalty to particular people, groups, or traditions. It is also claimed that impersonal morality requires of us enormous control over our

I am grateful to Catherine Elgin, Marcia Lind, Georges Rey, Paul Taylor, Stephen White and the editors of this volume for comments. Discussions with Gareth Matthews and George Sher also helped.

character and motivation. Finally, it is charged that in its aspiration to a purely objective or impartial point of view, which places no *a priori* constraints on acceptable moral positions, traditional moral theory allows us so many possibilities for choice as to stymie rational judgment and action. In short, the challenge is to show that the ideals of traditional moral theory can be embodied in a human life.[3]

That challenge looms large for Gilligan. She delves into moral conflicts that are embedded in a person's life, noting that an ethic that values personal relations, responsibility for others, and care can conflict with one of rights.

Emphasizing the question of the place of morality in one's life leads Gilligan and those who raise the problem of the personal point of view to query the methodology of moral psychology and moral theory, respectively. Critics of traditional moral theory are at pains to give richly detailed examples, often taken from history of realistic works of literature. In part, this is meant to counter the methodology of presenting and modifying principles in response to unrealistic hypothetical counter-examples. The lack of realism undermines the critical import of our intuitive judgments on such cases, and concentrates moral discussion on finding principles of ever greater scope. The result is a further abstraction from situational factors, and a widening of the gap between theory and our actual moral practices.

Parallel to these criticisms, Gilligan has us linger over the detailed responses of her subjects. She cautions psychologists who focus only on easily controlled and generalizable variables leads to hasty judgments of moral irrelevance for a multiplicity of factors that influence actual moral judgments. In both cases, Gilligan and the critics of "modern moral philosophy" are claiming that methodology biases theory, instead of serving as a relatively neutral court of adjudication among competing views.

Gilligan's studies are set against the background of the powerful and important theory of moral reasoning developed by Lawrence Kohlberg[4] over the last three decades. Kohlberg construes the central points of intersection of Kantian and utilitarian philosophies—autonomy, universalizability, and the moral equality of persons—as generating criteria for higher stages of moral reasoning. For Kohlberg "each higher stage is more autonomous, universalizable, prescriptive and reversible."[5]

In light of Gilligan's observations and these recent challenges in moral theory, it is natural to inquire into how well Kohlberg's theory respects the personal point of view. I shall argue that, on this score, it fares poorly. In particular, I shall argue that the kind of principled (autonomous, universalizable) reasoning that Kohlberg, following traditional moral theory, takes as the aim of moral education and development, cannot and should not have the dominant role he accords them in our lives. Nor, so I shall claim, should it play the role he ascribes to it as criteria for judging the comparative adequacy of different types of moral reasoning, *even* for those who accept traditional moral theory.

2. One form my criticism takes is a plausibility argument concerning the likely effects upon character and action of accepting the Kohlbergian goals. While I offer only limited empirical backing for my claims, they do not

run afoul of those claims of Kohlberg's that are most deeply rooted in empirical research, e.g., the *reliability* of the scoring manuals for assigning stages.[6] In the area of moral action, however, where my argument does heavily infringe on empirical questions, Kohlberg's support is weak or actively challenged.[7]

Kohlberg has urged for a long time, particularly in discussing the early work of Hartshorne and May,[8] that higher-stage reasoners are more likely to be consistent in judgment and action. The Hartshorne and May studies, as Kohlberg understands them, came to the disappointing conclusion that there was no positive correlation between the ethical concerns students evidence in their avowals, and their willingness to engage in moral behavior (e.g. cheating). Kohlberg summarizes this finding: "People's verbal moral values about honesty have nothing to do with how they act. People who cheat express as much or more moral disapproval of cheating as those who do not cheat."[9] This finding continues to be widely accepted. We expect that persons may avow all manner of high moralizing, but fail to do anything when the issue calls on them to act. The main, but not the only reason we don't expect such a connection, is that acting on, rather than merely reasoning with, high moral principles typically entails a sacrifice of self-interest. And, by contrast, we each know people who lead remarkably moral lives, though they can offer little in the way of theorizing to explain it. However, Kohlberg boldly claims: "true knowledge of principles of justice does entail virtuous action."[10]

If Kohlberg could demonstrate that higher moral reasoning leads persons to act better ethically, he would have provided the most serious support for the prescriptive features of his theory. For example, one major alternative approach to moral education, which Kohlberg derides as the 'bag of virtues' approach, calls for rather direct inculcation of values, particularly, through practice in acting morally. (This approach receives renewed support from the Aristotelian ideas that inspire the problems of the personal point of view). One argument for this approach is that the gap between reasoning and action is large, and if we agree on the end—namely, better moral behavior—then we must take a rather direct route to that end.

Of course, all other things being equal, we would prefer an approach that showed more respect for enlarging the child's autonomy. If Kohlberg could show that his autonomy based approach would also lead to more moral behavior, he would have confirmed his own educational program, while undermining a central argument for a main competitor. My own criticisms, similarly, would be greatly undermined. They claim that serious threats to moral character and behavior are likely consequences of enforcing in training the dominant role that Kohlberg accords to higher reasoning as opposed, say, to the inculcation of virtues.

The extensive studies of moral action are hard to compare, yielding results that are confused, inconsistent, and difficult to replicate.[11] But in his recent paper, "The Relationships of Moral Judgments to Moral Action,"[12] Kohlberg claims to have clear, operational support for the thesis that higher stage moral reasoners become more practically consistent. The study is not reported in depth, and it has certainly not been widely replicated, but what it appears to show is that higher stages correspond to greater willingness to act beneficiently under controlled conditions. Subjects scored for their level of reasoning find themselves confronted with someone pleading for help. Those who score higher appear more willing to offer assistance.

While I find this study promising and believe it to be the right direction for Kohlberg to take, there is a crucial weakness. The weakness undermines the inference from the greater willingness to act morally to the higher-stage reasoning as putative cause, even if the two are positively correlated. For reaching the higher stages is itself correlated with greater care or concern for personal morality.

But moral concern is not constitutive of different stages as Kohlberg repeatedly defines them. Higher-stages of moral reasoning are marked by a greater willingness to examine moral issues from an impersonal perspective in which we attribute rights to persons, as such. We can surely understand and use this reasoning, as students who take courses in moral philosophy sometimes do, without having any greater concern with moral issues than those who do not so reason.

If the higher stages of reasoning will *cause* one to have greater concern for behaving morally, and a greater sense of responsibility for one's actions and the lives of others, that would indeed be a dramatic confirmation of Kohlberg's theory. However, this recent study of Kohlberg's only indicates, for all we are told, that a greater degree of concern or care is itself a *cause* of movement to higher stages, or more plausibly, that both result from some general *common cause.*[13] In any case, it is intriguing, but not too surprising, to discover that co-variation in stages and degree of concern should lead to a co-variation of beneficent judgment with consistency in action.[14]

II. Conservatism, Autonomy, and Commensurability

> Littlewood, the Cambridge mathematician, tells a story of a schoolmaster who began stating a problem: 'Suppose *y* is the number of eggs—' 'But sir, please sir, suppose *y* isn't the number of eggs?[15]

> When Socrates is asked some large and exciting question, it was characteristic of him to find some other question that would have to be answered first. For example, when he was asked whether virtue could be taught, he said that he was unable to answer the question because he did not know what virtue was. He meant, of course, that he did not know exactly what it was. It is understandable that many people found his way of doing philosophy maddening. For consecutive thought is such a difficult achievement that it is natural to feel resentment when someone takes up the first word and questions its exact application. He is not playing the game. But of course he is not. That is his whole point.[16]

> Eleven year-old Amy's response to whether in the 'Heinz dilemma' the husband should steal the drug in order to save his wife's life: 'Well, I don't think so. I think there might be other ways besides stealing it, like if he could borrow the money or make a loan or something.'[17]

3. The broad claim of Piaget and Kohlberg that children move from heteronomous to autonomous behavior and reasoning is plausible and well

supported empirically. Developmentally, we expect increasing reliance on one's own reasons to rest on a bedrock of prior dependence on external sources. Children must first bend to authority in order to learn values, attitudes, and habits that allow a gradual increase in the exercise of a responsible freedom. So far, this seems innocuous enough. The obvious (psychological) dependence of freedom on prior heteronomous action should, however, caution us about any single-minded pursuit of autonomy. Where the stability provided by a heteronomous bedrock weakens, the freedom gained may be empty or chaotic.[18]

Kohlberg contrasts preconventional and conventional morality with the autonomous reasoning of a Kantian-utilitarian postconventional morality. In preconventional morality, the source of reasons is simply that these are the rules given (e.g. by the parents), and not to obey them will lead to punishment. At the conventional level, rightness is in terms of loyalty to the laws and to culturally approved standards of good behaviour. These laws and standards are themselves construed as ultimate. We reach the postconventional level when no particular source, external to morality, ultimately justifies the moral rightness. At the level of autonomous or principled reasoning

> there is a clear effort to define moral values and principles that have validity and application apart from the authority of the groups or people holding these principles and apart from the individual's own identification with these groups.[18a]

Kohlberg is strongly influenced by Kant in the idea that true moral reasoning seeks its source of reasons, and its motivation for moral action, only in morality itself. This occurs when maxims are tested by their form alone. Kant writes:

> What else, then, can the freedom of the will be but autonomy, i.e., the property of the will to be a law to itself? The proposition that the will is a law to itself in all its actions, however, only expresses the principle that we should act according to no other maxim than that which can also have itself as a universal law for its object. And this is just the formula of the categorical imperative and the principle of morality. Therefore a free will and a will under moral laws are identical.[19]

Kohlberg's ideals only go part of the way with Kant: everything must be open to question (i.e. no possibility is ruled out due to a source external to morality or reason itself), but Kohlberg doesn't want to hold that the wrong judgment implies less principled reasoning. In particular, even though he holds (against relativists) that there is a right or wrong in many of the dilemmas he presents, his method of assigning stages is meant to depend purely on the reasoning, not on the judgment reached. In principle, any judgment is possible consistent with a given assignment of stage.

I bring this up not to explore the possibilities for developing a selectively Kantian ethics, but rather to focus on the great demands made upon the principled reasoner. One may be able to appeal to universal rights owed to all persons merely by virtue of being persons (and thus reason near stage 6), while yet not coming to the right judgment. Once we admit this reasoning/

right-judgment gap—a consequence of the unequal development of the abilities and knowledge that inform sound moral judgment—we should go on to ask, specifically, about the previous identification of post-conventional reasoning with a refusal to allow any external limitations on the possibilities for choice.

In science, a hypothesis has the praiseworthy quality of *conservatism* (methodological, not political) when it is less in conflict with prior beliefs than its alternatives.[20] One important advantage of a conservative hypothesis is that it avoids challenging fundamental beliefs—beliefs, which if renounced, would lead to rejection of a wide range of other beliefs that the hypothesis binds together. As a feature of rational belief changes, conservatism seems broadly applicable to individual systems of belief, as well as to scientific ones, and I shall so assume.

If this assumption is correct, there is a *prima facie* tension between conservatism and autonomy: to be autonomous in action is to be motivated to act on one's own freely accepted reasons. (This, for Kohlberg, would show itself in one's engaging in a "role-reversal" test. This test forces one to weigh equally everyone's interests involved, and thereby not permit certain possible ways of distributing harms and benefits to be unfairly excluded.) But conservatism can justify one's action for reasons that are accepted arbitrarily (hence, in some way, not real reasons), and that are supported by considerations external to the immediate inquiry.[21] Moreover, because the reasons that favor conservatism stem from considerations at a very general justificatory level, removed from issues in a particular dilemma, one may be (rightly) relying on conservatism without being able to cite it, or its rationale, as a reason.

Despite its paradoxical nature, there is little controversy surrounding conservatism as a rational constraint on scientific theorizing. Nor is it considered an impediment to radical scientific change. As Rorty puts it: "a 'new theory' is simply a rather minor change in a vast network of beliefs."[22] While *a priori,* it cannot be demonstrated that the more conservative hypothesis is more likely to be true, it certainly sacrifices less of what we take to be true. Such a demonstration is unnecessary anyway, once we appreciate how much inquiry is facilitated by relying on a large body of accepted beliefs. The virtues of conservatism are especially striking in the case of the individual knowledge-seeker whose very self-identity may depend upon maintaining a set of deep personal commitments. By contrast, the scientific system of beliefs, rather than the beliefs of individual scientists, is impersonal. Fundamental anamolies for a well-entrenched theory are not to be resisted for the devotion of persons to them, nor do they ever strike at more than a small portion of the total fabric of empirical knowledge. Further, whereas the proper interests of the scientific enterprise are simply for comprehensive truth, the moral agent has numerous other interests (social, personal) besides truth. These other interests depend much more on stability, continuity, and familiarity in his (evaluative) beliefs than does the search for truth alone.

Thus, I shall urge that conservatism in ethics is a necessary force, not only to protect our beliefs against constant potential threats, but also in order to preserve our ties with the traditions that give meaning to our central moral vocabulary.[23]

In this light, the law gives us a better model for a normative theory of actual moral reasoning than moral theory alone does. For in the law, we are trying to guide our judgments through the wisdom of inherited judgment. A precedent provides a *presumptive* justification—we do not have to seek sufficient reasons for it—to be rejected only if there is a serious challenge such as a conflict with constitutional principles. I will develop this comparison with legal reasoning in the next section.

4. There is an important distinction between the moral agent as judge and as legislator, introduced in one form by John Rawls[24] and interestingly extended in a recent article by Conrad Johnson.[25]

Johnson develops the distinction by analogy with the law: the judge has a limited authority to promote goals. He can decide cases and pass on laws only according to already existing laws and precedent. But it is not within his authority to pass new laws. This is a legislative function that he, *qua* judge, does not have. So similarly, Johnson wants to say for the moral agent: "in this 'division-of-labor' conception, moral reasoning takes place within a framework in which the moral agent is confronted with a genuinely external authority which has the authority, within some bounds, to limit the competence of moral agents."[26] This conception is at odds with the view that "the whole foundation of right is at all times within the agent's purview, and even constraints resting on that foundation are in principle always open to reconsideration."[27]

Kohlberg's methodology and theory strive to make the moral agent view himself at all times as judge and legislator. Precedents do not matter except insofar as we can extract from them independently justifiable principles. Indeed, Kohlberg's dilemmas are created to highlight conflicts between fundamental principles. Consequently, each occasion that inspires moral reflection is one in which moral foundations are open to questioning and doubt.

One aspect of Gilligan's different voice, by contrast, is that moral judgments are somehow bound to the social context, especially to personal relationships. The moral voice she attempts to recover often is more uncertain about, and resistant to, generalizing across cases. While we are familiar with these as weaknesses, we can now see some clear strengths. These fatures do not permit judgment regarding a particular case to reverberate throughout the system of beliefs. The judge forms an opinion on the case, but there is so much that she finds in the specifics that there is a diminished basis for extrapolating to other domains. Conflicts loom large, and are not necessarily eliminated in the act of judging. It is recognized that action responds, in part, to practical exigencies.

Similarly, Johnson's use of the judge as a model for moral reasoning implies that the interpreter and arbiter of the (moral) law is not simultaneously the creator of the law. Moreover, a judge can neither initiate nor enact legislation by way of "judicial review." Cases have to be presented to him. Where possible, major issues are decided on narrow, technical, and undramatic grounds. Threats to basic principles are thereby minimized.[28]

One way an individual moral agent might minimize threats to her moral beliefs is by blunting the force of a dilemma or suggesting compromises so that principles do not have to be rejected or ranked. It is thus noticeable how some of the females in Gilligan's studies attempt, in the Heinz dilemma for example, to find alternatives beyond the limited choices of stealing the drug or letting the wife die.

In Amy's response quoted at the beginning of this section, is there something insightful that can be gleaned from it, or does she just miss the point. If a moral dilemma is analogous to a problem in algebra, then we expect that contained within the statement of the problem are the few bits of data necessary and sufficient for a complete solution to the problem. Since the formalism applies universally, it matters not at all what content is chosen. For example, given we are told that one set is included in another, this is sufficient, no matter what sets we are talking about, to decide which set has more members. Consequently, we find in Piagetian problems that, once the problem is solved by a subject, subject and observers then feel it is solved forever. Once a child reaches the point of understanding why, for example, pouring water between two differently shaped containers does not alter the amount of water, it can be applied to any number of other manipulations. The decisive factors are clear and complete (i.e., the reversibility of the oeprations is all that matters). And there is no turning back here to preconservationist responses.[29]

However, this clarity and completeness is bought at the cost of exposing a basic principle to refutation should an experience arise where reversibility seems to fail. In the ethical domain, where challenges and conflicts, which touch our personal lives deeply, are common, this disadvantage poses a serious problem. Refusal to permit closure on a dilemma, i.e., keeping the details of the case open to further exploration, creates a buffer against hasty rejection or modification of principles.

Of course, one cannot and should not always try to avoid testing one's principles and facing conflicts of principles. Similarly, one can only defer to authorities or traditions so much before one genuinely undermines autonomy. Johnson recognizes that the moral agent cannot always remain ensconced as judge. The equal autonomy of citizens resides in their each having

> the freedom or fair opportunity to participate in a *collective* enterprise of legislation, the equal autonomy of moral agents is governed by the ideal that no person's moral opinions and judgments have greater standing simply because they emanate from that person.[30]

Johnson declines to answer the question of when it is proper to switch from a judicial to a legislative role for the agent. Obviously, this question is crucial if the issue is whether the "equal autonomy" protected is autonomy enough.[31]

When then does conservatism turn into slavish adherence to a group or culture or tradition? When is the agent, in sticking to his judicial role, abdicating his legislative responsibilities by comfortably maintaining established norms? When should moral reflection on difficult cases lead to fundamental changes in principles?[32] I cannot here answer these questions much beyond noting that nothing in the way I praise conservatism is meant to deny either the ideal of autonomy, rather than certain ways of embodying that ideal, or the potential dangers of conservatism. If my discussion exaggerates praise of one at the expense of the other, that is a question of focus, not substance. It is an attempt to begin to redress the current imbalance.

One circumstance in which such a change in role is demanded is when one's current moral values lead to unacceptable consequences. Perhaps Kohlbergian dilemmas are meant to simulate circumstances of "revolutionary" rather than "normal" moral life, to use Kuhn's well-known distinction, where one should switch to a legislative role. Of course, such circumstances do not represent the main moral issues facing one in a relatively stable community. It might be asked, though, why does "stability" matter? The moral code can be equally bad whether there is active opposition or not. The first point to note is that examples of radical moral action, with respect to the prevailing moral code, are often not matters of the adoption of new principles, but the application of already held principles, rules, or precepts. For example, our moral practice with respect to the treatment of animals for food, research, clothing, and hunting had been, until about the 70s, mainly, one of indifference. Those who have attempted recently to change this—whether solely in their personal lives or in the form of political action—were moved to do so, I believe, by following out the consequences of simple evaluative beliefs that they already had. (In part, I draw this inference because Peter Singer's work, *Animal Liberation,*[33] which is generally given much credit for inspiring this change, is especially forceful due to the unexceptionable simplicity of one of its basic premises: one should not cause unnecessary pain or suffering.)[34] Second, the important fact is that we hold a person more *morally* culpable for failure to critically examine or challenge a prevailing code where there is a real voice calling it into question. Here there are well-known political analogues. For example, the arguments for foreign divestiture of holdings in South Africa are much stronger now that there is an active revolt than previously.

5. If conservatism is a virtue in moral reasoning despite its tension with autonomy, must it be possible to display this preference in a person's own justification? That is, if a subject's reasoning was best understood as relying on conservatism, but then he was made to confront his own or others more autonomous or principled reasoning, what preferences will he show? Such a test misunderstands, I think the kind of justification conservatism offers, as well as being methodologically suspect.

The virtue of conservatism is something we appreciate in considering the course that moral or scientific inquiry may take. It is not easy to offer it as a reason for judgment in any instance because it invites the reply: "So such-and-such answer preserves more of our system of beliefs, but is it right?" This question must be answered through broad reflections on epistemology. But even then the answer, as applied to the specific case, is awkward. It bases a conclusion that a statement is to be accepted as true on the seemingly arbitrary fact that one hypothesis had been accepted before equally plausible (at the time) alternatives had been considered. In the moral domain, a conservative appeal might be one that points to a tradition (or precedent) as a basis for a judgment without justifying that tradition, i.e. without offering a fundamental principle that backs the judgment (thereby rendering the original appeal as superfluous). Nonetheless, conservatism is accepted as one of the pillars of scientific methodology. If there is an analogous quality in (personal) moral reasoning, it is likely to show itself not as a justification or explicit reason an agent offers, but rather in the implicit deference of the agent to the collective and inherited wisdom of the community to which he belongs.[35]

6. I want to argue that the comparisons that Kohlbergian interviews are meant to engender among different types of moral justifications, rules, or principles, are not sound bases for inferring real preferences. Fundamental values may not be commensurate, even when we appear to engage in comparison of them.

The issue is central. Kohlberg emphasizes that subjects are asked to respond not simply to the dilemma but to a systematic set of queries aimed at eliciting the subject's own best judgment, i.e., the highest stage of reasoning he or she has reached.[36] Thus, in reply to Gilligan's charge of sex-bias in the method of scoring, Kohlberg notes that his method "pulls for the justice orientation."[37] Under these circumstances, once a higher stage is elicited, subjects seem content with it as the best representative of their answer. In fact, for Kohlberg, this "hierarchy of perceived moral adequacy" is partially definitive of moral stages.

A recent review of cross-cultural studies in moral reasoning, cited in support by Kohlberg, illustrates his claim, but also leads to conclusions divergent from his.[38] The study used the following version of one of Kohlberg's nine standard dilemmas:

> Joe is a fourteen-year-old boy who wanted to go to camp very much. His father promised him he could go if he saved up the money for it himself. So Joe worked hard at his paper route and saved up the forty dollars it cost to go to camp, and a little more besides. But before camp was going to start, his father changed his mind. Some of his friends decided to go on a special fishing trip, and Joe's father was short of the money it would cost. So he told Joe to give him the money he had saved from the paper route. Joe didn't want to give up going to camp, so he thinks of refusing to give his father the money.[39]

Now consider the following interview on this dilemma from a Taiwanese study:

> Q. Should Joe refuse to give his father the money? Why or why not?
>
> A. No. In terms of parent-child relations, he has the role as father, and the son should fulfill whatever his father wants. This is because the father has reared Joe for such a long time and given him affection and protection. So Joe should give his father the money to show how much he appreciates his father's caring.
>
> Q. The father promised Joe he could go to camp if he earned the

money. Is the fact that the father promised the most important thing in the situation? Why or why not?

A. Yes, though Joe is just a kid, he has his own rights and should be respected. The father should not treat his son as a means to fulfill his own wishes.

Q. What do you think is the most important thing a son should be concerned about in his relationship to his father? Why?

A. Understanding his parents' intent. Parents' expectations for their child are derived out of their own experiences, and with the purpose for the child's own good. Though the child need not do everything his parent's demand, considering their intention and affeciton, the child should eliminate conflict with parents to as few as possible by standing up on his own position [only] if he truly believes he is right. But later on he should compensate his parents loss in other respects. . . . Camping is not an important thing. [What] I am talking about [is that] one should not sacrifice one's basic principles for other people's happiness.[40]

At first, the subject sides with the father; then, after the second question, which emphasizes his promise, he supports the son's rights as decisive. So this subject would be scored higher on the basis of his second reply than he would on the basis of his initial response (or on his final reply that emphasizes happiness). If the second response dominates in the final assignment of stages,[41] we have an illustration, of Kohlberg's claim that his method "pulls for the justice orientation." But in so doing, we are assuming that the queries are neutral and the responses commensurate. Are they?

David Lewis has interpreted a phenomenon that suggests we must be cautious here.[42] Lewis's domain is vastly different from ours: he is criticizing Peter Unger's argument[43] for radical skepticism. Unger's argument turns on showing us that when what he calls "absolute terms" are true of an object, there cannot be anything to which that term applies to a higher degree. If my desk is *really* flat, there can be no surface flatter. If the room is empty, there can no space emptier. It follows that to be truly empty or flat is like beng perfectly circular: no objects at all can be in a perfectly empty room; a surface that is truly flat cannot contain even the slightest bump.

Lewis wants to show how certain implicit or contextual boundaries explain away the *prima facie* incoherence between maintaining that (1) a room is empty; (2) empty is an absolute term; and that consequently (3) the room can have nothing at all in it. Lewis accepts all these implications drawn by Unger. But where he disagrees is in the assumption that, if the room is empty, then it contains no physically extended material at all (not even atoms!). For when we say that the room is empty, we have an implicit sense of what count as things in that room. On this contextual constraint, the presence of boxes or furniture count; but the presence of air, molecules, or atoms does not. Rooms can be empty, though there are molecules of air floating about.[44]

Lewis's claim is that Unger has improperly shifted the appropriate standards for being flat, empty, etc. This shift occurs in the very act of applying Unger's comparative proof of nonabsoluteness: if *O* is more *X* (e.g.

flatter, emptier, more circular) than *O*′, then *O*′ is not really *X*. So if a laboratory chamber that has been made into a vacuum is emptier than my room where all furniture, books, carpets, have been removed, then my room is not really empty. Lewis claims that in making the comparison, Unger does not show that the judgment that the room is empty is false, for that statement is true within its *appropriate* contextual standard. But the very comparison itself subtley shifts us to a new level—one of raised standards. Lewis observes that the "raising of standards always goes more smoothly than lowering." He notes that this is a natural, albeit nonrational, fact about us which he cannot explain. He writes, "Raising of standards . . . manages to seem commendable even when we know that it interferes with our conversational purpose. Because of this asymmetry, a player who is so inclined may get away with it if he tries to raise the standard of precision as high as possible."[45]

The mere comparison of objects with different standards (in the context created by the particular question) is enough to raise doubts about how meaningful the evaluation is. This meaningfulness is not then assured by virtue of our answering the particular comparative question: Is *O* more *X* than *O*′? Nor is it secured by our responding without hesitation and converging on the same judgment.

Is it meaningful to compare, with respect to the same judgment, filial loyalty, the obligations of promise-keeping, and the importance of a person's happiness? By "meaningful" here I simply mean, does the normal range of experience or learning provide a basis for well-informed judgment? And does such a judgment demonstrate a general preference or scale for ranking? Lewis's line of argument gives us a basis for casting doubt on such comparisons without forcing us to deny that these diverse considerations may all be relevant to the agent's judgment.

We may actually make such comparisons, though I doubt that they are frequent. First, conservatism would strain against construing those occasions in which we are forced to choose ones where the results indicate a general preference. For such ranking increases the vulnerability of our moral rules: it announces conditions under which one rule is to be subordinated to another, and admits the reality of conflicts between them.[46] Second, implicit contextual bounds are easy to ascribe to moral judgments, thereby limiting the range of cases to which any particular comparison is meant to apply. If, in one situation, I say the person acted wrongly because one should not steal, but then I am confronted with the Heinz dilemma, I may quickly indicate that the previous judgment was really based on the qualified rule that "one should not steal, unless . . ."[47]

Third, and finally, there is a good deal of psychological evidence from different sources that we are highly disposed to compartmentalize information. Our comparisons and categorizations, even when they are stated without qualification, implicitly contain restrictions to specific dimensions of comparison or categorization. Such compartmentalization diminishes the generalizability of any comparison.[48] There is a specific kind of compartmentalization—involving Gilligan's emphasis on contextual versus abstract approaches to moral dilemmas—that follows on an observation about Unger's comparisons: the objects that can be meaningfully introduced for deciding the emptiness of vacuum chambers include those for empty rooms but not vice versa. More generally: if *O* is more *X* than *O'*, then everything ordinarily judged to be *X* within the domain of *O'* will be so within *O's* domain but not vice versa, i.e., *O* has greater scope with respect to *Xness than O'*. I infer, consequently, that one symptom of an upwards shift in standards will be the comparison of judgments where one has a much narrower scope than the other.

The next step in the argument seems obvious. The particularity of filial obligations and loyalties and, in general, the fundamental diversity of goods contrasts sharply in scope with the unbounded applications of principles of promise-keeping or rights.[49] Consequently, we have a *prima facie* case for saying that the inferences Kohlberg draws from the justice pull of his interviews are questionable. They enforce comparisons where there is no appropriate scale. However, this conclusion needs qualification, for there are significant complications that have been glossed over.

The first complication is this: I do not find neat analogues in the moral case for the clear, contextual bounds of terms like "empty," i.e. nothing analogous in the moral domain to the inappropriateness of offering the existence of air molecules as evidence for the nonemptiness of the living room. So I have been using a misleadingly clear, simple, and supportive case. For the thesis of Lewis I have been relying on is much more general and radical in scope, implying as it does, contextual bounds for the application of terms like "certain," which lack the domain specificity of terms like "flat" or "empty." "Certain" (more accurately, "*X* is more certain of . . . than ———") seems to be the kind of scaling term, like "preference," that allows everything to be layed out on the same dimension.

If, though, Lewis's more general and radical thesis is correct, then my application of it to the moral domain is even more compelling. His thesis points to an enormous degree of contextual sensitivity that comparisons of objects or judgments of different ranges of scope have. It is because of this sensitivity that we can find the meaning of comparing these very different moral values, rules, or principles unclear even when we are all willing not only to make those comparisons, but to reach consensus on their outcomes. (How, or whether these comparisons could become more meaningful, i.e., when is it appropriate for different standards of precision to be combined or imposed, is a difficult question that has not been addressed.)

The second point concerns the issue of whether there is a place in traditional moral theory for respecting special personal relations—for respecting their particularity. Those who have doubted this have done so because the demands for impartiality seems to imply that no moral favoritism can be shown merely because someone is in a particular personal relations to the agent (e.g. friend, lover, brother). These personal relations by themselves confer no moral privilege, they are morally accidental or external.

But from the point of view of moral theory, this is just too simplistic. One can surely find in the impoverishment of a human life without strong personal relationships or loyalties a basis in either utilitarian or Kantian philosophies for according these relationships a protective place. Doubts can still be voiced as to whether the standard impartial bases (e.g. hypothetical contracts behind a 'veil of ignorance') are sufficiently sensitive and fine-grained to generate all the moral asymmetries in judgment. This is a topic of much current debate.

However, this dispute can be pushed a little to one side. For the question we are addressing is empirically constrained by the resources of the subjects we are studying. What is sufficient for my purposes is that there are significant differences for most subjects in the scope of their judgments founded on personal relations or filial loyalties and those founded on basic rights. Consequently, I assume that at some points in the above interview the crucial factor for the subject is the particular nature of Joe's relationship to his father (first response: "because the father has reared Joe for such a long time and given him affection and protection."), rather than parent-child relations generally. (I do not want to rest too much on the example, which is, at best, illustrative).

Assuming then, that there is a level for most subjects of particularistic reasoning about filial loyalties that is morally significant and not to be assimilated to principled inference, its scope will be quite narrow. The scope of higher-stage (principled) understanding of promise-keeping or rights is supposed to be universal and exceptionless. Specifically, with each new query in the interview above, there is a forced comparison between judgments with narrower and much wider scope of application. (A similar point could be made about forced comparisons of a care-based with a rights-based response). This is indicative of a Lewis-like shift in standard, and therefore is not a secure basis for generalization.

The "structured wholeness" of a stage from the agent's point of view—his preference for reasoning at a higher level across similar problems with different content—cannot be extrapolated from this data. Since contextual restrictions can become so familiar as to go unnoticed, we may attribute these restrictions to subjects even when they themselves do not articulate them.

The commentator in the above study tells us that "In the third question, when the two ideas confronted each other, the subject solved the dilemma by maintaining both values in a hierarchy."[50] But this interpretation looks biased by a Kohlbergian ideology. The subject does not seem to be offering principled grounds for saying that obedience to parents is a strong value that nonetheless can be outweighed by the child's rights, if both the child is sure of them and his happiness is at stake. Rather, the subject offers a prudential strategy: keep your parents as content as possible until it threatens to be unbearable, and, even then, try to make it up to them. The subject is not trying to hierarchically integrate the diverse moral and social pulls. He is trying to negotiate his way through, without upsetting too much in the process.

A parallel result should obtain if Unger-like questioning in the domain of objects was really pressed. Such questioning forces persons into a *prima facie* incoherence: *X* is a circle, a circle is 360 degrees, *X* is not 360 degrees. This particular incoherence quickly generalizes to the assertion and denial that any objects in our world can be circular (or flat, that any spaces can be empty, that any judgments can be certain). Under such questioning, though, the agent is not likely to withdraw acceptance of these basic beliefs. He is likely to attempt a conservative tack, where the incoherence is finessed, not confronted. After all, in the person's own normal range of experience, these beliefs have worked out pretty well. So too our respondent above does not so much try to resolve the conflicts in the various principles or beliefs he holds, he attempts to finesse the problem. His final answer blunts any direct (conflictual) comparison or ranking of the values he favors.

III. Ethical Consistency: Weaknesses in Everyday Reasoning

> The child's reactions to the interrogatory—i.e., his theoretical reflections—are always a year or two behind his life reactions, that is to say, his effective moral feelings. (Jean Piaget, *The Moral Judgment of the Child*, Free Press, 1965, p. 274)
>
> You are eating a hearty meal, while somewhere a baby is starving. As the charitable appeals point out, you might have saved it. But pleading guilty to the charge does not give you license to strangle a neighbour's infant with your bare hands, as though to say 'What's the difference? Both babies are dead, aren't they?'[51]

7. Consistency, in two ways, is one of the major pillars of higher reasoning for Kohlberg: first, practical consistency in that principles and actions match; and, second and crucially, consistency in the sense of the test of universalizability—acts that are right for one must be right for anyone *similarly situated*. With regard to universalizability, the characteristic form of argument is that of analogy. The characteristic criticism is that of inconsistency. You say it is permissible for you to do A, but it is not permissible for someone else to do A. Yet, there is no relevant difference between your circumstances and the other person's with respect to A. Hence, your original set of judgments is inconsistent. (The inconsistency, as stated, is not logical inconsistency. Perhaps, "arbitrary" might be the better term). The two kinds of inconsistency are related because by one's actions one represents oneself as holding certain moral beliefs. Where these run counter to professed principles, it is reasonable to challenge the agent for treating similar cases differently, i.e. being morally inconsistent or arbitrary.

The test of universalizability has bite provided that cases are not too easily distinguished. As more differences make a moral difference, it is less likely that a charge of inconsistency can be made to stick—for that charge depends upon showing that similar cases have been judged dissimilarly. In moving to more abstract levels, (levels that remove more potential differentiating factors), we come closer to moral judgments being tested purely on the basis of form irrespective of content—an ideal to which Kohlberg aspires.[52]

A well-known problem in moral theory is to show that the test of universalizability can be nontrivial, while still retaining its claim as constituitive of our idea of morality. On purely formal grounds, the worst kinds of injustice and evils are universalizable. Stronger kinds of universalizability—taking other points of view, or becoming an ideal, impersonal observer—are harder to justify on *a priori* grounds. People who refuse to universalize at these stronger levels cannot necessarily be said to have opted out of morality. And those who do universalize in these more powerful ways derive judgments of what should be done so distant from their own position that they do not see these principles as giving them, in particular, reasons to act.[53]

A second side to applying the test of universalizability is crucial, but often unnoticed. To show that two cases are dissimilar, one must be able to offer *explicit reasons* to distinguish them. Judgments that one cannot support by reasons are mere prejudices. There is no distinction from the point of view of Kohlberg's methodology between failing to be able to offer a good reason and the failure to have a good reason to offer.[54] (In defending this distinction, I believe we reach a point where the moral-judge/legal-judge analogy breaks down. For justificatory purposes, the legal judge's reasons for his decisions are to be identified with those that he explicitly offers.)

8. A common issue of justice is the potential conflict between the right of property, and positive rights to education, welfare, and perhaps, cultural activities. This issue is not tapped, as far as I know, by Kohlberg's dilemmas, yet it helps expose some limitations to the test of universalizability as we expect it to be used in everyday reasoning.

Is infringement on one's *(prima facie)* fairly acquired possessions for the sake of other's or the community's welfare an infringement on liberty? Robert Nozick[55] has offered well-known and powerful libertarian arguments against Rawls's[56] liberal principles of justice along such lines. One of the simplest types of argument that Nozick urges against patterned theories of justice generally and Rawls's in particular is a universalizability argument: if we can redistribute money, then to be consistent, we must redistribute beauty. For it is not implausible to believe that (money, beauty) each can be (1) strongly desired by individuals, (2) significant in potential benefits, while yet (3) the degree of possession of either is unrelated to moral desert. But we would never seek, even in principle, to redistribute beauty, so we cannot consistently redistribute money. For a different use of this reasoning, consider Nozick's reply to Williams's claim that medical need is the "only proper criterion" for distributing medical care. Nozick simply responds with the higher-order charge of inconsistency: if this is so, why do't we say "that the only proper criterion for the distribution of barbering services is barbering need."

The question before us is this: if a principled response is unavailable to a person, either because there is none or because it has not become public fare, where does this leave a good moral reasoner? Must this individual give up or modify his or her beliefs? Again, notice the elegance and symmetry of form in Nozick's criticisms.

If the principled response is unavailable, the reasoner will rely on an intuitive exclusion of far-out possibilities, a practical understanding that we want to distribute as few types of things as possible (that is, to evade problems of requiring a unitary scale of measurement), human sympathy for those in need of health services rather than barbering services, and a sense of cultural traditions as to how goods have been distributed.[57] Or the reply might involve a common-sense insistence that health care is vital, whereas barbering services are not; or that it is ridiculous to suggest we redistribute beauty. Or finally, the reply may involve a recognition of an issue that others, such as liberal theoreticians, are better able to answer, that is, the response may involve deferring to experts.

From Kohlberg's perspective, these do not appear to be principled responses. The responses hover, at State 2 or 3. They do not offer principled distinctions among these types of good, and at places, they resemble a stance, not the offering of well-grounded reasons. My claim is that they are not inadequate responses, in everyday moral reasoning, to this type of quite common libertarian challenge. (Once this challenge has been raised, it should inspire inquiry, as it has in philosophy, toward re-examining the foundation of those judgments that reject the libertarian challenges. But, a citizen's reasoning is not to be denigrated pending the outcome of that reexamination.) The adequacy of these responses remains despite their lack of the across-the-board consistency and the generality of Nozick's simple principle of entitlement. So if liberal thinkers are not to be paralyzed when they seek reasonable replies to their libertarian peers' challenges, they must gain a healthier respect for less abstract appeals in reasoning and for distinctions among goods that may not be determined by general principles.

9. I want to shift our focus slightly from the danger of a paralysis of reason in according the test of consistency a dominating role in everyday moral reasoning to that of action. This danger takes on special significance for two reasons. First, if we are to lead ethical lives, they will be filled with practical inconsistency. For even the least objectionable, though still substantive, ethical rules and principles demand more from us than we are (or should be) willing to live up to.

Second, there is a prevalent tendency toward 'extremism' defined as a tendency to form attitudes that are polarized with respect to the wide variety of options realistically open. Under pressure for higher moral reasoning, the natural fact of both practical inconsistency and the tendency toward extremism can lead to moral indifference as the only path to consistency. In the philosophical story and text *Lisa,*[58] the main character is offended when a man hits his dog with a switch. Lisa, a young teen-ager, goes home to a chicken dinner. Later, she wonders how she can get angry at the man for hitting his dog, but then go on to eat chicken. She senses here, perhaps erroneously, inconsistency or hypocrisy.

We can expect such inconsistency to face us continually for a reason already discussed: our judgments and actions represent us as holding principles that apply to a large number of cases that haven't been considered as falling under this principle (for example, eating chicken and concern for the welfare of animals). We may be morally too weak to change many of these actions (such as Lisa's eating of chicken), though we do not want to renounce the principles that we appear to be violating. In fact, one of the central objections to traditional moral theory, as we have noted, is that it is too demanding. In particular, ethical concerns for equality, justice, or suffering enjoin a seriousness that expose many of our actions as frivolous.

As Susan Wolf aptly observes in a related contest: "No plausible argument can justify the use of human resources involved in producing a *pâté de canard en croûte* against possible alternative beneficient ends to which these resources might be put."[59]

Before proceeding, let me again offer caution. As above I did not deny that autonomy was a constituitive ideal of morality; so now, I am not asserting that some requirement of ethical consistency can be dispensed with. If Lisa cannot reconcile the conflicting judgments she takes herself to be committed to by her actions, she is obliged to try to find the relevant disanalogy. If she cannot, so that the charge of inconsistency that she ascribes to herself sticks, then she will conclude that restoration of consistency requires either her beliefs or actions to be changed.[60]

But even if she reaches this conclusion, she still may find, as many of us have, that we cannot fully live up to the demands of morality. Isn't it preferable—if consistency for Lisa can only be realized by denying legitimacy to her immediate reaction to the man who hit the dog—that she accept the inconsistency, and continue to protest the abuse of a pet? Moral behavior can evidence compromises and inconsistency, while yet being preferable to a do-nothing consistency.

Many of us have reduced our eating of meat, wearing clothing of animal skins, using make-up tested on animals, or supporting non-medical research done on animals. It *may* be that by our principles we are inconsistent: we should be vegetarians. Nonetheless, even with our 'dirty hands,' we seem to be acting better, by virtue of coming nearer to our ideals, than if we resigned ourselves to one of the other alternatives.[61]

10. The problem of the weakness of universalizability and the prevalence of practical inconsistency is exacerbated by the tendency toward extremism. Although the issues are too far-reaching for extended discussion here, I want briefly to offer support for the claim that this is a human tendency.[62] Assuming that this is true, I want to suggest that Kohlberg's prescriptions will encourage extremism beyond its tolerable bounds.

First, if one maintains a less than extreme position, it forces one to be more cognizant of alternatives and objections. Not only does that put our beliefs more in question, but it hinders action. Typically, actions are forced upon us well before a thorough inquiry into the alternatives has been made. A non-extreme position makes us more aware of just how weak our basis for action is. Alternatively, it may promote Hamlet-like indecision on behalf of a craving for certainty.

Second, there is a good deal of psychological evidence that individuals do not well integrate divergent bits of evidence. Rather, they tend unconsciously to ignore or interpret evidence, contrary to their own beliefs, so as to provide a rationale for those beliefs.[63] This makes it easier for people to maintain extreme positions in the face of counter-arguments.

Third, on a more philosophical plane, we have unfulfillable expectations or desires for various forms of ultimate justification. The failure to meet our expectations—the frustration of those desires that seek something like a rationalist foundation for knowledge—leads us to an opposite pole where all possibility of justification, however modest, is renounced.

Recently, James Fishkin[64] has reported studies that confirm the extremism hypothesis in ethics. (This is not his aim, which is mainly to criticize Kohlberg for failure to incorporate meta-ethical considerations into his largely normative theory of ethics.) Fishkin found that students moved from a position that seeks absolute certainty about moral issues to some form of subjectivism. Fishkin pinpoints their conversion to their holding some combination of six overly high expectations for a correct ethical system. (I would include Kohlberg's demand for consistency as an analogue in normative ethics to these overly high expectations in meta-ethics). For example, an objectively valid moral position must have a basis that is rationally unquestionable.[65] Frustration of these unrealizable expectations leads them to the coherent nihilism of subjectivism. However, in this conversion they ignore a range of reasonable alternatives such as a modest form of objectivism about ethics.[66]

In moral matters, where self-interest is frequently challenged, the extreme is often the place where one is more comfortable. Either we are absolutists of one form or another, so that morality is too demanding for anyone and thus, no one *can* live up to it. Or we switch to some strong form of relativism—subjectivism or nihilism—so that everything is justified and consequently, there is nothing we *have* to live up to. In either case, our actions and judgments are defended.

Here extremism converges with the inevitability of practical inconsistency. If we are not strong enough to be vegetarians, for those whose principles commit them to it, isn't it comforting to know that we are at least consistent in completely ignoring animal concerns in our consumer habits? We can therefore stave off the threat, not from those whom we view as saintly in sticking tightly to principle, but from those who compromise—who cut down somewhat on their meat consumption, accept some animal experimentation for medical research, and do not purchase fur. Once we can dismiss this group as inconsistent or, preferably, hypocritical, we can relax in our extremist indifference.

11. If my argument is correct, then given the premium that Kohlberg places on ethical consistency, there are empirical consequences that should support or undermine my position. Specifically, I would doubt whether Kohlberg's claim for the *structured wholeness* of stages and the greater *adequacy* of higher stages can be maintained in the strong form in which he presents it. For those who are initial ascendants to a higher stage, whose logical abilities exceed their depth of experience, the weakness of universalizability and the tendency toward extremism should lead to instability.[67]

We should expect, first, "decalage" as a set of judgments are made in one dilemma, which are then confronted by apparently similar situations where considered intuitive judgments go differently. I presume that there are many such situations (for reasons already given in section 9). 'Decalage' represents a failure of homogenity in reasoning within a stage, given variation merely in the content of dilemma.[68] The destabilization that will ensue would be followed, so my speculations continue, by some regression to a lower stage. This lower stage then offers a kind of extremist stability—subjectivism or relativism being one form of this regressive stability.

Although the research literature offers some empirical support for my conjectures, I am not conversant enough with it to claim strong corroboration. However, aside from Fishkin's own data,[69] it is worth observing an important epicycle in Kohlberg's theory that involves an admission of a transitional stage 4½ in which "choice is personal and subjective. It is based on emotions, conscience is seen as arbitrary and relative, as are ideas such as 'duty' and 'morally right.' "[70]

With this worrisome change comes another. Kohlberg now ascribes stage 6 to very few, to only the most philosophically sophisticated. Even at stage 5 or earlier, there are rudiments of the abstract reasoning that he favors, and my conjecture is, that pushed in the right ways, the need for further transitional stages, or the admission of "decalage" and regression would be clear.

However, Kohlberg's methodology does not facilitate crucial tests. What is needed is (a) extensive variation in the order of presentation of dilemma and queries (following my discussion of Lewis above); (b) realism in the dilemmas sufficient to enhance the subject's sense that they are moral actors, not just moral judges;[71] and, most importantly, (c) an attempt to systematically vary the dilemmas so as both to test hard subjects' conception of a relevantly similar situation, and to force them to apply the principles recently invoked to unanticipated action. My conjecture is that under this kind of critical scrutiny, the responses of neophyte higher-stage subjects' responses would show disequilibrium with respect to that stage; and it would elicit great variation in the reasoning of different subjects putatively assigned this same stage.

IV. Conclusion

12. When one comes to Kohlberg's ideas from the study of moral theory, it is hard not to believe that on its most fundamental points it must be right. And, correlatively, we are prejudiced into believing that there must be something deeply flawed with that part of Gilligan's work that proposes a different moral voice with a coherent structure. How can there even be a mature approach to moral issues that can conflict with a "rights-based" one, but is nonetheless not to be rejected for that reason?

My criticisms of the Kohlbergian ideals of autonomy and universalizability aim to show, albeit not focusing on the particular virtues of care and responsibility, how Gilligan's alternative is possible and its normative claims plausible.

(On the issue of sex-differences, which has seemed to many to be the most important part of Gilligan's work, I have had little to say, except indirectly. I find implausible the thesis sometimes ascribed to Gilligan that one orientation goes exclusively with men and the other with women. I also doubt that this finding of extreme sex-differences, if it did hold, should be "normative for women," so that "only a woman who fully embraces such a moral orientation, to the exclusion of other ethical positions, reasonably can be called a fully developed woman."[72] But I question this presentation of

Gilligan's ideas. She clearly states views inconsistent with these positions, quite consonant with what I take her central discoveries to be.[73] Even if both voices coexist in males and females, the crucial claim is one of their dissonant co-existence and the relative dominance of one over the other along sex lines. Some of the evidence offered against this latter, weaker, claim seems to me to depend upon the kind of contrived comparisons—confronting "care" with "rights" responses to a dilemma—that I disparaged above (section 6).

In developing my critique of Kohlberg, I have used the problem of the personal point of view as a guide without, though, acceding to its rejection of traditional moral theory. Quite the contrary: Kohlberg's failure lies not with his adherence to traditional moral theory within its appropriate domain. Similarly, one can assimilate Gilligan's "different voice," as it relates to Kohlberg's views, with the challenge of the personal point of view, while holding onto a Kantian or utilitarian ethics. I have tried to note how the problems I raise concerning autonomy and universalizability are compatible, albeit uneasily, with traditional moral theory. My objections to Kohlberg do not then imply any corollary criticism of the project of attempting to extend the utilitarian-Kantian framework so it can sensitively answer the problems of the personal point of view.[74]

However this position looks unstable. For, on one hand, traditional moral theory claims a comprehensivenss in the moral domain that implies that all valid moral factors can ultimately be subsumed under the theory. And, on the other hand, the challenge of the personal point of view has been cast as generating conflicts between our intuitive judgments in various moral situations and the judgments implied by traditional moral theory. So is even partial reconciliation a viable project?

There are at least three directions this reconciliation project can take. First, it can simply deny that the job of traditional moral theory—to provide the foundations for the moral law—must be constrained by the needs and limits of human lives. Second, traditional moral theory can be viewed as an idealization (or competence model for moral reasoning). The problems of the personal point of view raise questions of application under nonidealized performance conditions. Third, there remain unmined resources within traditional moral theory, such as Hare's distinction between intuitive and critical thinking.[75] for allaying some of these concerns.

One resource is to recognize that the moral principles that should guide a human life will be quite complex. For example, one prescription that rapidly leads morality to seem too demanding is Singer's for helping the starving: "If it is in our power to prevent something bad from happening without thereby sacrificing anything of comparable importance, we ought, morally to do it."[76] Singer briefly documents facts about the extensive amount of worldwide poverty and starvation. It takes little to recognize that most of us could help "without sacrifice of anything of comparable importance." However, we ourselves would have to come pretty near this subsistence level before our sacrifice would be commensurate to their condition. Morality is now starting to look too demanding, even while beginning from such a weak-seeming principle. One suggestion for how to answer this problem—a suggestion involving significant, but not vast, sacrifices—is to formulate a more complex principle of obligations to the starving that is a *prima facie* one and applies primarily to groups (e.g. the United States might be obligated to give extensive aid, but not each of us individually).[77]

What I want to observe is that if stage 6 is reached by hardly any of us, then even fewer of us will be able to formulate the complex principles that traditional moral theory might ultimately use as a defense. For even principles formulated at stage 6 are still too simple to respond to the challenge to respect the personal point of view. However, the challenge itself is appreciable well before this point. We need to face these problems, though in Kohlberg's view we cannot have the resources for doing so. That is why, I argue, that striving for more abstract moral principles, for more autonomous reasoning, for greater consistency in judgment and action, are not singular virtues, and in fact, can be dangerous, when experience lags behind formal powers.

Since the main question of traditional moral theory is to articulate and defend fundamental moral principles, assuming that they are applied in the best possible ways, they abstract away from those limitations that my argument presupposes. Consequently, my objections to Kohlberg's promotion of the higher stages are not intended to reflect back in the moral theories that are the models for his construction. Nor then does it reflect back unfavorably on much of what Kohlberg says on behalf of the moral preferability of the higher stages. It is his failure to give due weight to or to denigrate other perspectives (e.g. 'the bag of virtues' approach), that is my target.

13. Kohlberg recently has retreated to claiming that he is interested only in questions of justice in a fairly narrow sense, not in moral development more generally. In regard to this strategy, there are approving references in Kohlberg to a study that assimilates the moral perspective of care as corresponding to Kant's "imperfect duties," with "perfect duties" being "negative duties of noninterference with the rights of others."[78]

But even if Kant's duty of benevolence is assimilated solely to an imperfect duty, Kohlberg clearly has benevolence as part of both Stage 5 and Stage 6 reasoning. At Stage 5, "The social welfare orientation reflects a rule-utilitarian philosophy in which social institutions, rules, or laws are evaluated by reference to their long-term consequences for the welfare of each person or group in society." (Kohlberg ibid., 637) At stage 6, we have a Rawlsian difference principle, and "the principle of benevolence or utility, that is, act so as to maximize the welfare of all individuals concerned, the attitude of universal human care or agape."[79] Kohlberg explicitly notes that the general principles at stage 6 are "positive prescriptions rather than negative proscriptions."

Further, although Kohlberg now emphasizes the limited ambitions of his theory, this does not square with some of the implications he has drawn. First, the issues of justice themselves, once benevolence is included, are very broad. The problem of morality being too demanding, central to the challenges from the personal point of view, immediately arises once benevolence is admitted. Second, Kohlberg has drawn explicit attention to the connections of his theory with cognitive-developmental theory generally, personality theory and moral action. He has opposed the "bag of virtues" approach whose central domain is character. Third, he wants his stage theory to be the center of projects on moral education; and he has promoted "Development as the Aim of Education."[80]

A related tack of moderating claims, mentioned above, would have Kohlberg conceive his model itself as an idealization or competence model. The first difficulty for this maneuver is that all the data he offers are data of performance. Second, he would need to offer an account of approximation to his idealization since it is to be applied to real moral reasoners engaging with real moral problems. And such an account would have to allow for "decalage" and regression.

But there is a principled objection to this defense. Imagine we listed on one side the ideals of traditional moral theory such as autonomy and consistency, and on the other (arguably derivative) side ideals such as care, concern, conservatism, altruism, responsibility, or other "virtues" (e.g. trust). Let us assume that we held that the former list could ultimately account for, and absorb, the latter. Still it could not be claimed that any reasoning more dominated by ideals from the former list must be better than reasoning dominated by factors from the latter. This should be clear enough from the above arguments and examples already considered. But let me add to that discussion because it takes us full circle to the Aristotelian approach that inspires concern with the personal point of view.

We cannot transfer our normal preference for good reasoning to wrong conclusions (behavior) over poorer reasoning to the right conclusions (behavior), assuming now, for the sake of argument, Kohlberg's favored criteria for better reasoning. The moral domain is crucially different from the favored Piagetian domain of scientific reasoning. We recognize, in the former, a gulf between reasoning toward a judgment and acting on that judgement caused by strong conflicting (personal) interest. But we do not find strong personal interests in, say, Piagetian conservation tasks that would pull one away from acting on the judgment that the amount of water is the same in the two glasses of different heights. But motivational problems are central in ethics. Aristotle, in his moral psychology, recognized the importance of imitating moral "role-models" because of his realistic approach to human motivation. If the kind of *modeling* he favored is fundamental to developing moral character, then our evaluation of the worth of a judgment is significant for our evaluation of the reasoning toward that judgment, even though the two can be theoretically distinguished.

There is, in fact, much in contemporary psychology, particularly social cognition theories, that supports Aristotle's assumptions.[81] For a central claim of those theories is that people's attitudes shift toward falling in line with actions as part of their attempt to give rational explanations of their own behavior. Appropriate attitudes and reasons move in the direction of justifying action, rather than always according with the rationalist account of belief justifying action. So as a matter of fact, wrong judgment or immoral action can infect and undermine reasoning that is seemingly apt by the standards of the relevant age group.

14. In sum, Kohlberg cannot continue to shield his own views under the banner of contemporary moral philosophy. On the one hand, the forcefulness of the recent challenges to traditional moral theory demonstrates at the very least that there is less agreement than he alleges. But on the other hand, where there is convergence, it is at a level of idealization distant from his applications.

Notes

1. Carol Gilligan, *In a Different Voice* (Harvard University Press, 1982).

2. See B.A.O. Williams, A *Critique of Utilitarianism* in *Utilitarianism: For & Against* J.J.C. Smart & Bernard Williams (Cambridge University Press, 1973); the early essays in his *Moral Luck* (Cambridge University Press, 1983); and his recent *Ethics and the Limits of Philosophy* (Harvard Universial Press, 1985). See also G.E.M. Anscombe, "Modern Moral Philosophy," *Philosophy* 33 (1958): 1-19; Alasdair MacIntyre, *After Virtue* (University of Notre Dame Press, 1981); Michael Stocker, "The Schizophrenia of Modern Ethical Theories," *The Journal of Philosophy* 73 (1976); 453-466; Lawrence A. Blum, *Friendship, Altruism, and Morality* (Routledge and Kegan Paul, 1980). I lump together here a number of different routes to criticizing traditional moral theory. For some of the distinctions see Lawrence Blum, "Particularity and the Doman of the Moral," forthcoming.

3. The most important appreciation and response to the problem of the personal point of view is in the work of Thomas Nagel. See his collection, *Mortal Questions* (Cambridge University Press, 1979); "The Limits of Objectivity," The Tanner Lectures (Oxford University, 1979); and "The Unreasonable Demands of Morality," unpublished. Assimilating Gilligan's work to the personal point of view allows me to rely on Nagel's arguments in "Subjective and Objective" that no mere annexation or reduction (in Nagel's terms) of the subjective to the objective point of view is viable. One of Kohlberg's responses to Gilligan's work is just such an attempt at annexation. See L. Kohlberg, "A Reply to Owen Flanagan and Some Comments on the Puka-Goodpaster Exchange," *Ethics* 92 (1982): 513-528.

4. His papers have recently been collected in two volumes (the third to be published soon): *Essays on Moral Development: Volume I, The Philosophy of Moral Development: Moral Stages and the Idea of Justice* and *Volume II, The Psychology of Moral Development: The Nature and Validity of Moral Stages* (Harper & Row, 1981 and 1984, respectively).

5. Kohlberg, *Essays on Moral Development* Vol. II op. cit., p. 393.

6. Reliability concerns whether there is consistency among scorers in how they assign stages on the basis of the moral dilemma interviews. Validity, whether the tests measure what they are supposed to measure, is a separate and less purely an empirical question.

7. For an extensive review, see Augosto Blasi, "Bridging Moral Cognition and Moral Action: A Critical Review of the Literature," *Psychological Bulletin* Vol. 88 (1980); 1-45.

8. Hartshorne, H. and M.A. May, *Studies in the Nature of Character.* Vol. 1, *Studies in Deceit* (New York: Macmillan, 1928). For discussion of these studies in relation to Kohlberg's views, and for other issues relating to moral stage theory see Owen Flanagan, *The Science of Mind* (Bradford Books: M.I.T. Press, 1984).

9. L. Kohlberg, "Stages of Moral Development," in *Moral Education: Interdisciplinary Approaches,* C.M., Beck, B.S. Crittenden, and E.V. Sullivan, eds. (Newman

Press, 1971) 23-92. Quote on p. 75. Similarly, Kohlberg claims support for his stage-action hypothesis in studies correlating the level of moral reasoning with the willingness of students to participate in the demonstrations at Berkeley in the 60s, and the resistance of subjects to giving electric shocks in Milgram's obedience experiments.

10. Ibid. p. 78.

11. See Blasi, op. cit. Blasi concludes: "The body of research reviewed here seems to offer considerable support of the hypothesis that moral reasoning and moral action are statistically related. This statement, however, should be qualified as soon as one looks at the findings in more detail." (ibid. p. 39)

12. In Kohlberg, *Essays on Moral Development* Vol. II, op. cit. See especially pp. 562-64.

13. More generally, we expect that the type of reasoning used is connected in complex ways to many other features of personality and behavior as Kohlberg notes in his discussion of stages and measures of ego-strength. See also Gilligan's, op. cit., discussion of Chodorow's work as a psychological background to sex-related differences in moral reasoning. Gilligan, op. cit. Chap. 1. See also Blasi, op. cit., p. 9

14. Compare to Piagetian stages. Attaining a grasp of conservation or class-inclusion seems fairly independent, beyond some minimal motivation, of how much you care about such problems. However, in the face of serious evidence of decalage for supposedly formal operational thinkers, Piaget adopted the maneuver that "we can retain the idea that formal operations are free from their concrete content, but we must add that this is true only on condition that for the subjects the situations involve equal aptitudes or comparable vital interests." See Jean Piaget "Intellectual Evolution from Adolescence to Adulthood," in *Thinking*, P.N. Johnson-Laird and P.C. Wason, eds. (Cambridge University Press, 1977) p. 165. This article has been taken as a retreat from Piaget's classical stage theory (see Johnson-Laird and Wason's introductory discussion). In particular, Piaget does not extend this concession to his account of stage development for younger children, though his explanation seems equally applicable.

15. P.T. Geach, *Reason and Argument* (University of California Press, 1976) p. 26.

16. David Pears, "Wittgenstein and Austin," in B.A.O. Williams and A. Montefiore, *British Analytical Philosophy* (Humanities Press, 1966) 17-39, quote on p. 24.

17. Gilligan, ibid. p. 28.

18. The case of adolescence, Kohlberg's main subject pool, is particularly important. Some of the main struggles of adolescent development involve difficulties in trying to find the right balance between a healthy freedom and external, especially parental, guidance. And, if a balance is found, a teen-ager's reasoning is not thought the worse for its relying on authority. See Kohlberg, Vol. II, op.cit. p. 18. On this point and its bearing on the autonomy issue in moral education, see George Sher and William Bennett, "Moral Education and Indoctrination," *The Journal of Philosophy* Vol. LXXIX (1982) 665–77.

18a. Kohlberg, Vol. I, op.cit. p. 18.

19. Immanuel Kant, *Foundations of the Metaphysics of Morals*, Lewis White Beck, translation in R.P. Wolff, ed., *Kant: Foundations of the Metaphysics of Morals. Text and Critical Essays* (Bobbs-Merrill, 1969) p. 74.

20. See W.V. Quine and J. Ullian, *The Web of Belief* (Random House, 1970). Their account is modest. For defenses of conservatism that conceive it more radically, see Lawrence Sklar "Methodological Conservatism," *Philosophical Review*, Vol. 84 (1975) 374–399; Michael Slote in "Conservatism and Confirmation," *American Philosophical Quarterly* Vol. 18 No. 1 (1981) 79–84.

21. Anscombe and MacIntyre, op.cit., have defended a kind of traditionalism (or communitarianism) that partly depends upon conservative arguments, e.g. about the need to arbitrarily or coercively limit possible choices for an agent. A clear parallel in science exists with the need to rule out certain possible hypotheses *a priori* lest inquiry be overwhelmed by options. Contrast this perspective with Piaget's. The mark of the formal-operational reasoner is his attaining the ability to systematically reason with all possibilities.

22. Richard Rorty, *Philosophy and the Mirror of Nature* (Princeton University Press, 1979) p. 284. See also, Slote op.cit.

23. The relationship between a tradition and the meaning of our moral vocabulary is a central theme in MacIntyre, op.cit., and Anscombe, op.cit. Consider also Dworkin's adoption of a major position in the philosophy of language to justify a distinction between a concept (e.g. justice, fairness, cruel and unusual punishment) and a specific conception (e.g. that capital punishment does not fall under the restrictions against cruel and unusual punishment). See Ronald Dworkin, "Constitutional Cases," in his *Taking Rights Seriously* (Harvard University Press, 1977). Our autonomy is not threatened, if we are bound to the same ideals, presuming these are freely consented to, but not thereby to the specific embodiments (in legislation) that others (e.g. the founding fathers) may have given to these ideals. On the foundations for this point in the philosophy of language, see Hilary Putnam. "The Meaning of 'Meaning' " in his collection *Mind, Language, and Reality: Philosophical Papers* Vol. 2 (Cambridge University Press, 1975) 215–271.

24. John Rawls, "Two Concepts of Rules," *The Philosophical Review* 64 (1955) 3–32.

25. Conrad D. Johnson, "The Authority of the Moral Agent," *The Journal of Philosophy* Vol. LXXXII, no. 8 (1985) 391–413.

26. Johnson, ibid. p. 397.

27. Johnson, ibid. p. 397.

28. Perhaps, my claims drawn from a broad noncontroversial conception of legal reasoning are, in fact, quite arguable. On some legal theories sufficient discretion is allowed judges to create new law. But even on these theories this is only true for so-called "hard cases."

29. Here I am speaking as if the paradigm Piagetian stages worked out smoothly in practice. I ignore the serious content-effects that have been found in Piagetian studies. For review, see Rochel Gelman, "Cognitive Development," *Annual Review of Psychology* 29: 297–332. Also, a problem analogous to Piaget's class-inclusion tests that children solve after age 7 is regularly "failed" by adults. For discussion see J.E. Adler, "Abstraction is Uncooperative," *The Journal for the Theory of Social Behaviour* Vol. 14 (1984) 165–181.

30. Johnson, op.cit. p. 399.

31. This is not a criticism of Johnson whose interests are more theoretical than ours. He seeks to defend a "two-tiered" conception of moral justification (deontological for rules and consequentialist for systems). However, it is worth noting that whether Johnson can block a reduction to act-utilitarianism, as he hopes, may turn on an account of when it is proper to switch from a judicial to a legislative role.

32. For a recent criticism of the dangers of one kind of moral conservatism, see Amy Guttman, "Communitarian Critics of Liberalism," *Philosophy and Public Affairs* 14 (1985) 308–322.

33. Peter Singer, *Animal Liberation* (New York Review/Random House 1975).

34. I believe that one can accept this precept without (a) holding it as a principle in Kohlberg's sense, (b) adhering to Singer's utilitarian defense of it and (c) even if one rejects Singer's general allegation of "speciesism" for our failure to accord equality of treatment to animals.

35. Compare to Putnam's notion of the "division of linguistic labor" in Putnam, op.cit. How do we distinguish good from bad implicit deference to the community? The answer is similar to the answer that would be right for the analogous question in the philosophy of language: the distinction turns on whether the best explanation for the person's having the moral beliefs he does is by appeal to values of the community that imply such a judgment, but do not require each agent in the community to appreciate these values (or their justification) as such.

36. John Snarey, "Cross-Cultural Universality of Social-Moral Development: A Critical Review of Kohlbergian Research," *Psychological Bulletin* Vol. 97 (1985) 202–32, observes that "the current (Kohlbergian) method of calculating an interview's global stage score requires that 25% of a person's reasoning be at a particular stage for that stage to be included in the subject's global stage score." (p. 206).

37. Kohlberg, Vol. II op.cit., p. 349.

38. Snarey, op.cit.

39. Kohlberg, Vol. II op.cit., p. 643.

40. Snarey, Ibid. p. 224. Snarey takes this study from T. Lei and S.W. Cheng, *An Empirical Study of Kohlberg's Theory and Scoring System of Moral Judgment in Chinese Society,* unpublished manuscript (Harvard University, Center for Moral Education, 1984) 12–13.

41. It is unclear from Snarey what is assigned as the stage. Snarey, op.cit. p. 225. There is the claim that the third reply has no place in the scoring manual. But the second response clearly does, and it could very well have been decisive.

42. D. Lewis, "Scorekeeping in a Language Game," *Journal of Philosophical Logic* 8 (1979).

43. Peter Unger, *Ignorance: A Case for Skepticism* (Oxford University Press, 1975). Unger now accepts Lewis' criticism to the extent of finding it in conflict with his position in *Ignorance*. However, Unger's position now is that neither position is rationally preferable to the other. See his recent *Philosophical Relativity* (University of Minnesota Press, 1984). Discussions with Unger were instrumental in my starting to think about extending Lewis' argument.

44. A similar line of response to Unger is pursued by Fred Dretske in *Knowledge and the Flow of Information* (Bradford Books: The M.I.T. Press, 1981). However, Lewis's contextualism is more radical than Dretske's, a point we return to below. See also Unger's discussion of Dretske's "sortalism" (in Unger's phrase) in *Philosophical Relativity* op.cit.

45. Lewis, op.cit. p. 353.

46. Again, let me mention that this pull of conservatism can be overridden. In science, obviously, we often want to put forward the bolder, more general, more precise theory even though this more readily invites refutation. Notice, though, that Karl Popper, who is the most forceful and persistant advocate of bold conjectures and refutation as the methodology of good science, clearly distinguishes between refutation and rejection (i.e. actually abandoning a theory). See his "Reply to Lakatos" in *The Philosophy of Karl Popper* Vol. II (Open-Court, 1974).

47. See further discussion of consistency in part III.

48. See Amos Tversky, "Features of Similarity," *Psychological Review* Vol. 84, (1977) 327–352. See also E. Rosch and C.B. Mervis, "Family Resemblances: Studies in the Internal Structure of Categories," *Cognitive Psychology* Vol. 7 (1975) 573–605.

49. For discussion of the moral significance of personal relations, see Blum, *Friendship, Altruism, and Morality* op.cit. See also Christina Hoff Sommers, "Filial Loyalty" (this volume) George Sher "Other Voices, Other Rooms? Women's Psychology and Moral Theory" (this volume) attempts to show that traditional moral theory, in particular, the Rawlsian 'original position,' can justify moral asymmetries due to personal relationships. My paper evolved from a commentary on Sher, ibid.

50. Snarey, op.cit. p. 225.

51. Mary McCarthy, *Medina*. The quote is taken from Jonathan Glover, *Causing Death and Saving Lives* (Penguin, 1977) p. 92.

52. But not Rawls. For a clear, recent statement on this point, see John Rawls, "Justice as Fairness: Political not Metaphysical," *Philosophy and Public Affairs* Vol. 14 (1985) 223–251.

53. In this paragraph, I mainly summarize well-known *prima facie* difficulties with the test of universalizability. (For a clear, fair-minded, and critical discussion see J.L. Mackie, *Ethics: Inventing Right and Wrong* (Penguin, 1977) Chap. 4. However, Alan Gewrith, for example, in *Reason and Morality* (University of Chicago Press, 1978) argues that logic (and universalizability) forbid agents from not extending rights to freedom and well-being to others. Critics of Gewirth have contended that it is possible for someone to claim the necessity of freedom and well-being for himself without claiming a right to them. See, for example, MacIntyre's discussion in After Virtue, op.cit. Some issues related to Kohlberg's theory and the problem of giving content to universalizability are discussed in O. Flanagan and J.E. Adler, "Impartiality and Particularity," *Social Research* Vol. 50 (1983) 576–96.

54. So principled reasoning must be displayed in the reasons offered. This point is crucial. I agree with those, like Sher, op.cit. that we have to be quite cautious in ascribing nonprincipled reasoning in response to dilemmas. Behind such responses might be general principles. So when I speak of nonprincipled reasoning I mean to be following Kohlberg's and Gilligan's usage, though I do not necessarily agree with their characterization. However, the implicit principles view can be easily overstated, if the principles are a matter only of a subject's competence, rather than his just not stating them. What we are concerned with is the actual kind of critical thinking a moral reasoner engages in. A person who offers explicit principles would commit himself to judgments in a wide variety of moral situations beyond those that elicited his initial response.

55. Robert Nozick, *Anarchy, State, And Utopia* (Basic Books, 1974), especially part 7, sections I and II.

56. John Rawls, *A Theory of Justice* (Harvard University Press, 1971). MacIntyre, op.cit. provides a plausible setting for a Rawls-Nozick type debate within everyday social life. It is a separate question whether MacIntyre's skepticism about the chances for resolving this dispute within the framework of the "Enlightment Project" is correct. I actually believe that Rawls, in particular, does not require the kind of *a priori* foundational justification that MacIntyre ascribes to the Enlightment Project. See Rawls's "Justice as Fairness: Political not Metaphysical," op.cit.

57. On the importance of recognizing the plurality of goods in a theory of justice, see M. Walzer, *Spheres of Justice* (Basic Books, 1983).

58. Matthew Lipman, *Lisa* (Institute for the Advancement of Philosophy for Children).

59. Susan Wolf, "Moral Saints," *The Journal of Philosophy* 79 (1982) 419–39 quote from p. 422. My introductory paragraph summarizes some of the alleged problems of morality being too demanding. See also Jonathan Glover, op.cit. Instead of adopting the acts and omissions distinction, which would lighten his moral burden, Glover adopts the utilitarian view, thereby being forced to acknowledge a "huge discrepancy between professed beliefs and actual conduct." He concludes: "This is not very admirable either." (Glover, ibid. p. 110).

60. Or she may ascribe to herself more complex principles than she first thought. For example, she may want to distinguish the gratuitous infliction of pain from the (hopefully) painless killing of animals for food.

61. Consider here an analogous problem of critical thinking in nonmoral contexts. The persuasiveness of some slippery slope arguments usually depends upon

getting us to focus on a contrast of drawing an arbitrary line vs. being principled. How can we draw a line at point X, but not at point Y, when there is no significant difference? However, such arguments are fallacious if the proper contrast is between different arbitrary lines to draw. For example, where one draws a cut-off line between a B and a B+ final grade. The crucial point to notice is that arbitrariness in where we draw the line is quite compatible, where antecedent judgments that a line must be drawn are firm, with reasoned disagreement over better or worse places to draw the line.

62. Note that "tendency" here is deliberately meant as a weak word—extremism is controllable, labile, and comes in degrees. In some unpublished work ("Toward a Naturalistic Skepticism") I discuss this topic within philosophy, especially epistemology.

63. See here the extensive review of a varied set of experiments in R.E. Nisbett and L. Ross, Human Inference: Strategies and shortcomings of social judgment (Cambridge University Press, 1980). See also Jon Elster, *Sour Grapes: Studies in the Subversion of Rationality*(Cambridge University Press, 1983) (especially references to the views of P. Veyne). On the integration of different types of information, see the discussion of the base-rate experiments of A. Tversky and D. Kahneman reported in a number of essays in D. Kahneman, P. Slovic, and A. Tverksy, eds. *Judgment Under Uncertainty: Heuristics and Biases* (Cambridge University Press, 1982). These studies have come in for important criticism by L. Jonathan Cohen. See his "Can Human Irrationality Be Experimentally Demonstrated?" *The Behavioral and Brain Sciences* Vol. 4 (1981) 317–31. I discuss these studies in "Abstraction is Uncooperative," op.cit.

64. James Fishkin, *Beyond Subjective Morality* (Yale University Press, 1985). I regret that Fishkin's book came to my attention too late for detailed consideration. Many of his themes bear directly on the arguments presented here.

65. Fishkin, ibid., p. 52.

66. My differences with Fishkin surface in how optional one considers these expectations, how forced the move is from failure of these expectations to subjectivism, and to what extent the articulation and public dissemination of alternatives can lead to a serious change in everyday meta-ethics. I tend to be much more skeptical on these questions than Fishkin.

67. Kohlberg, of course, does insist on the importance of experience and practice for moral development. But if his theory is to retain its distinctive claims, the point of this experience and practice is reducible to what can be abstracted for learning about certain very high-order principles and formal properties.

68. Kohlberg, in one of his foundational articles, (Lawrence Kohlberg and Rochelle Mayer, "Development as the Aim of Education," in *Stage Theories of Cognitive and Moral Development, Harvard Educational Review* Reprint No. 13, 1978 123–70.) claims that decalage is more relevant to education than movement between stages. I find this surprising, since Piaget's admission of decalage is generally taken as undermining the strong claims of structured wholeness for stages. See ibid. p. 164.

69. See Fishkin, ibid., especially Appendix A.

70. Kohlberg, Vol. I. op.cit. p. 411. For a critique see Fishkin, Appendix A.

71. The dilemmas usually end by asking whether someone should have done something. But this still misses the crucial issue of the personal point of view: whether *I* should do it, if actually in that situation. Consider the remarkable indifference to this question in assigning stage 2 to the following response to the Heinz dilemma: "Q. Should the husband have stolen the food? A. Yes. Because his wife was hungry . . . otherwise she will die. Q. Suppose it wasn't his wife who was starving but his best friend. Should he steal the food for his friend? A. Yes, because

one day when he is hungry his friend would help . . . Q. What if he doesn't love his friend? A. No, [then he should not steal] because when he doesn't love him it means that his friend will not help him later." (Snarey, op.cit. p. 221). Is this subject's attempt to offer a sensible balance between duty and motivation really to be characterized as merely "self-interested," or "instrumental?" (ibid. p. 222) Is a reasoner better who draws none of these distinctions?

72. John M. Broughton, "Women's Rationality and Men's Virtues," *Social Research* Vol. 50 (1983) 597–642. Quote on p. 602.

73. See, for example, Gilligan, op.cit. p. 174.

74. This is the kind of project—one not anticipating complete resolution or dissolution—I find in Nagel's writings mentioned above. See also Wolf op.cit. However I find Wolf too quick to dismiss the possibilities of traditional moral theory lessening the too great demands of morality. This possibility is explored hesitantly by Nagel or (with greater confidence) in R.M. Hare *Moral Thinking: Its Levels, Method, and Point* (Oxford University Press, 1981). On the other hand, I do not believe that these moral theories are as distant from offering ideals of proper human development as she does.

75. See R.M. Hare, op.cit. The distinction is (roughly) between dispositions to judge in fairly immediate time-pressured circumstances, and those unpressured moments of extended reflection when we can decide what sort of intuitive responses we should have. So some of the *prima facie* judgments that go counter to utilitarianism, e.g. asymmetries on behalf of personal relationships, can be explained as intuitive responses that serve broader utilitarian interests—interests that we recognize only at a critical level, where we decide to develop these intuitions. Notice that while moral development would include recognizing some such distinction—even in so rudimentary form as a difference between when we consider only the short-run and when we can evaluate options in terms of much longer-range goals—it appears too sophisticated for use by Kohlbergian subjects. As Hare invokes it, it is a tool of meta-ethics that first accepts a set of *prima facie* counter-examples to a complex theory (one easily represented in simplistic form) and then reinterprets these examples so it perfectly fits that theory. For a different attempt to respond to some other counter-examples from the personal point of view—ones involving the conflicting between acting from duty and acting out of friendship, see Marcia Baron, "On the Alleged Conflict Between Acting from Duty and Acting from Friendship" *The Journal of Philosophy* Vol. LXXXI, No. 4 (1984) 197–220. Her basic idea, similar to Hare's, is that the two are compatible once we see that in the counter-examples the right thing for a Kantian to say is that we act out of duty by developing dispositions to treat friends a certain way. Friendship is then our salient motive in going to see a friend in the hospital, though it arises from a much earlier recognition of our duty to act certain ways toward friends. I have strong doubts about this as a Kantian defense since, among other reasons, the ability to so create proper dispositions would not be available to us all. Hence it could not be a Kantian duty.

76. Peter Singer, "Famine, Affluence, and Morality," *Philosophy and Public Affairs* Vol. 1, 1972.

77. For such a suggestion see Michael McKinsey, "Obligations to the Starving," *Nous* Vol. XV, (1981) 309–23. Contrast McKinsey's use of the impossibility of our fulfilling Singer's principle as a reductio with Wolf's, op.cit., existential resignation to our failure.

78. Kohlberg, *Essays in Moral Development* Vol. II p. 358. See also, on imperfect duties in Kant, Wolf, op.cit.

79. Kohlberg, ibid. p. 637.

80. See Kohlberg and Mayer, op.cit.

81. For a simple and comprehensive account see, Susan Fiske and Shelley Taylor, *Social Cognition* (Random House, 1984); see also Nisbett and Ross, op.cit.

PART IV

Beyond Moral Theory: Political and Legal Implications of Difference

Remarks on the Sexual Politics of Reason

SARA RUDDICK

Summary

Sara Ruddick assesses some of the political difficulties and implications of the claim that each gender has its own distinctive cognitive style and mode of reasoning. Any claim to difference, whether between genders or within one, is not simply an epistemological thesis, but a political one. For example, the assertion often carries with it a charge of exclusion.

In a way that addresses, and is sensitive to, possible political misinterpretations and/or political misuses of this claim, Ruddick affirms female difference: "that women's moral reasoning yields a morality of love and that women's work gives rise to 'maternal thinking.' " Ruddick argues that although women's standpoint has been shaped by a variety of forces, including traditional relegation to the private domain, feminist acknowledgement and critique of women's reason allows for the productive use of "women's difference" in the public domain.

In the second part of her paper, Ruddick illustrates just how this can occur in her analysis of maternal thinking and the peace movement. Since maternal work is distinct from military work, it yields a different perspective on violence and nonviolent action. In contrast to contractual "just war" approaches to peace, the maternal view understands the fragility of strengths and weaknesses, and emphasizes the importance of "giving and receiving while remaining in connection." This perspective, derived from the morality of love, provides a critique of, and an alternative to, peacekeeping policies which foster aggressive "defensive" weaponry buildup. S.M.

Do prevailing standards of rationality and objectivity transcend sexual difference? If women reason differently from men, does this difference cast doubt upon women's (or men's) rationality or upon the conception of reason as sexless? Among feminists, there is widespread distrust in the idea of a

I am grateful to Virginia Held, Alison Jaggar, Evelyn Keller, Eva Kittay, Elizabeth Minnich, and Marilyn Young for helpful suggestions on an earlier draft.

reason that knows no sex. Several feminist theorists have argued that rationality and objectivity, as "we" understand them in Western philosophy, "might after all be thoroughly 'male.' " According to these theorists, since men have predominated in activities we call 'rational,' they have devised standards of 'rationality' shaped (and from a human perspective distorted) by masculine affective, sexual, and social histories. Although philosophers differ in the degree to which they hope and allow that women can become 'rational,' the attainment of reason for both women and men tends to depend upon overcoming what is identified, within particular philosophical and cultural contexts, as female—body, change, emotion, and particular affections.[1]

That ideals of reason are thought of as "male" does not mean that rationality so defined is useless, or that women cannot or should not be rational. Many women have shown themselves to be reasonable philosophers and scientists in ways indistinguishable from men. Nor does the maleness of reason in itself imply that there are distinctively female forms of reasoning. Although women's reasoning appears eccentric when judged by male standards, sex-neutral criteria might reveal reasoning that transcends sex. It might be, however, that women have not only been assigned, but have actually developed distinctive modes of cognition and conceptions of rationality and objectivity.

Among attempts to identify a distinctive female reasoning, two theories currently predominate. One, derived from psychology, takes as its subject morality. It claims to have found differences in women's and men's moral development that lead to differences in reasoning. The other is derived from philosophy. It argues, that given the social character of reason, the sexual division of labor, the formative place of work in human lives, and the processes of identification that occur in families, we should expect women to develop a distinctive "standpoint" comprised of metaphysical attitudes, epistemological principles, cognitive styles, and values.[2]

Although claims about the maleness of reason and distinctive female reasoning do not carry their politics with them, they are entwined in political angers and fears, claims and counterclaims. The assertion of difference usually includes a charge of exclusion. In the case of sexual difference, some women charge that distinctively male standards of rationality work to exclude them from conferences, journals, universities, defense departments, law courts, and other places where "reason" prevails. Without doubting the fact or pain of women's exclusion, many theorists reply that the concept of *women's* reason can itself become an exclusionary abstraction. Women differ from each other culturally, and within a culture, by class, race, and ethnicity. What is to keep female concepts of rationality from being as arrogant and as coercive as their male counterparts? Can women charge exclusion as women, and remain sensitive to the many different kinds of exclusion that women and most men suffer?

'Difference' is suspect in the eyes of liberals and many feminists. Transcendant ideals of reason are meant to apply to any rational being. 'Difference,' by contrast, is often invoked by the strong who thereby justify exclusion and exploitation of the weak. As feminists note, a belief in women's different nature has been used to keep women in the service of others, both at home and in public. According to many feminists, if women reason differently, this is a consequence of long years of discriminatory education and opportunity. To welcome the difference that has emerged is to welcome oppression itself. On a more intellectual level, it is difficult even to state women's difference without adopting the dichotomies that male reason has invented. To say that women are intuitive, personal, emotional, particularistic is not a critique of male reason, but an endorsement of its categories. The suggestion that there are ideals of reason appropriate to "women's work" can seem oppressively dismissive, both of women doing work traditionally considered male and rational, and of men doing work that has been historically considered female.

Despite these and other misgivings, many feminists believe that it is more dangerous to ignore than to explore the maleness of reason and women's different reasoning. They argue that because western ideals of rationality exclude what is simultaneously defined as irrational and female—"attachment to individual bodies, private interests, and natural feeling"—these ideals lead to and legitimate domination. Since objectivity demands separation from and control over whatever is emotional and physical, and therefore female, the objective knower is driven to dominate, and entitled to exploit actual females and those associated with them as well as whatever is threateningly female within himself (or herself).[3] Some feminists go on to argue that the "standpoint" that arises from women's experience, and that is misdescribed as irrational, includes politically useful values and perspectives. According to these theorists, although women's standpoint is marked by the oppression in which it originated, it not only survives its origins, but takes on new political usefulness when transformed by feminist consciousness and politics.[4]

My aim is to present certain claims about women's different reasoning in a way that avoids political misinterpretation, addresses political controversies, and makes political use of the differences claimed. In the first part, I set out the claims that women's moral reasoning yields a "morality of love" and that women's work gives rise to "maternal thinking"; I associate myself with the charge that male standards of rationality have excluded those who speak in women's different voice from rational discourse and the power it bestows, and address (though I do not pretend to resolve) feminist fears of cultural arrogance and misogynist uses of women's difference. In the second part, I outline and endorse the claim that the morality of love and maternal thinking should inform peace politics.

The Politics of Women's Different Voice

The psychological and philosophical claims of women's difference were derived independently. They are supplementary and mutually confirming. Neither is simply 'true.' Both depend upon psychological, psychoanalytic, philosophical, feminist, and other theoretical frameworks to derive differences and then to explain the difference derived. Each of the claims has been contested (as well as supported) within its own methodological discipline. Each has also been indirectly confirmed both informally, by the responses of women, and formally by those who take the claims as lively hypotheses, and then find them usefully illuminating in disciplines ranging from psychology, to philosophy of science, to literary theory, ethics, and psychology. It is notorious that belief or disbelief in differences between women and men tends to be self-confirming. Those who believe in differences tend to see what they believe in; what they see reinforces their beliefs. I set out claims for differences, not to persuade, but to indicate the structure of the arguments in a way sufficient for addressing political issues.

The psychological claim[5] identifies two kinds of moral reasoning, each of which is connected to distinctive conceptions of self. In one, the mode of reasoning is abstract and hypothetical, the subject of reason is rights and duties. One's duty is to accord people their rights, which are themselves determined according to fair, principled procedure. The primary virtue of individuals and institutions is fairness; the primary defects are isolated egoism and aggrandizing aggression; the primary conflicts are between competing rights. One can call this, in short, the morality of justice. This morality is connected to a conception of mature or "developed" selves as autonomous individuals related through hierarchical connections which, though threatened by egoism and aggression, are stabilized by the restraints of justice. In the second moral voice, the mode of reasoning is contextual and narrative, its subject is responsibility and response. One's moral aim is to respond to peoples' real needs. The primary virtues of individuals and institutions are caring and the realistic perception of needs; the primary defects are misperception of needs, failure to respond, and sacrifice of one's self; the primary conflict is between incompatible responsibilities. One can call this the morality of love.[6] It is connected to a conception of "developed" selves as individuals related through overlapping networks of mutual dependencies which, though threatened by parochialism and self-sacrifice, are stabilized by the responsibilities of care.

The two moral voices are identified, not by gender, but by cognitive modality, moral theme, and a conception of self. The central finding of the work—that there are at least two moral voices and that moral concepts vary with distinctive conceptions of self—is not a finding about or dependent upon gender. Yet these voices are strongly associated with gender both historically and empirically. The different voices were discovered in the course of research designed to include women's experience. This research was motivated, at least partly, by the desire to remedy the exclusion of women as a group from earlier psychological research, to redress mischaracterization of women's experience in dominant theories, and to contest the finding that women were morally less "developed" than men. It was in looking at women's experience with this motivation that the central concepts of care, responsibility, and relational selves were identified. Although the voice of care was discovered from studying women, the variance of the two voices among men and women is neither dichotomous nor symmetrical. Almost every person reasons in both the voice of justice and the voice of love. For some people neither voice predominates. Most women and men, however, tend to favor one kind of reasoning as they identify, interpret, and resolve moral dilemmas. Among men for whom one voice is predominant, the voice is, with few exceptions, the voice of justice. When one voice is predominant for women, it may be either the voice of justice or of love. But whenever the voice of love predominates in some one, that person, with few exceptions, is a woman. Briefly, men employ justice reasoning, and many women do too, but the voice of care is predominantly a woman's voice.[7]

For both women and men, the capacity to reason, both according to justice and according to love, is explained in terms of early childhood experiences of inequality and of attachment. The relatively greater salience of inequality and justice for men, and of attachment and love for women is partly explained in terms of early child-parent relations. In societies in which mothering is almost always done by women, boys tend to take separation as a goal and define themselves in opposition to others, while girls take, as a goal, the maintenance of connection, and define themselves in relation to others.[8] Difference is also explained in terms of permanent inequalities between women and men that ascribe to women responsibility for relationships, caring, and service.[9]

The second claim of difference[10] derives from a conjunction of practicalist and feminist views of reason. Practicalists hold that reason, rather than transcending history, is socially constructed by people living at particular times, engaged in their distinctive projects. The projects in which people engage are partly defined by, and in turn demand, distinctive ways of thinking, which include metaphysical attitudes, epistemological principles, and the identification of virtues. There is no ahistorical, asocial privileged vantage from which to assess either the projects or the constructions of reason that arise from them.[11] It follows that, to the extent that women and men engage in different kinds of work, their thinking should be expected to differ. However, if the attainment of rationality depends upon overcoming the "female," and if ideals of objectivity select for and reward "manliness," women's thinking will not appear as reason but as a deficiency of reason. Because ideals of reason inappropriate to women's (and most men's) lives are culturally dominant and pervasive, it is difficult even to articulate a "standpoint" appropriate to women's work, let alone formulate and assess ideals of reason presumed by the standpoint.[12]

I develop a version of the philosophical claim by considering the fundamental work of bearing and caring for children.[13] The work of mothering is defined by the demands to protect children, to nurture their growth, and train them to behave in ways acceptable to the social group.[14] Anyone who takes responsibility for maternal care, and makes the work of mothering a primary part of his or her working life is a 'mother' in this sense. Acting upon the demands for preservation, growth, and acceptability, reflecting upon their actions, articulating and sharing principles of action, mothers develop a distinctive standpoint. They ask certain questions rather than others, identify criteria for satisfactory answers, establish appropriate ways of knowing, develop fundamental attitudes to what is known, and identify virtues appropriate to their work. To give one example, child care prompts mothers to question the meaning and techniques of *control*. Persistent questions about control lead to maternal concepts which can be compared to concepts of control in scientific, religious, agricultural, militaristic, and other kinds of thinking. Protecting, training, and fostering growth require that a mother control her child, the child's world, and herself. Simultaneously, this work requires relinquishing control and accepting its limits so that the child can grow without fear or shame and, when alone, can keep herself safe and rely upon her own moral judgement. In the aid of limited, reflective control, mothers develop forms of concrete, rather than abstract cognition—scrutinizing and attentive love, for example—that allows them to see what endangers a particular child at a particular time. They develop a fundamental metaphysical attitude that I have called "holding." A mother "holds" whatever is useful for maintaining a child's life in safety. Mothers also develop a fundamental attitude to what they cannot control, including their children, that expresses itself in a respect for the limits of their own best will, and a "welcoming" attitude that expects change and can change with changes. Mothers identify virtues required or elicited by appropriate control such as clear-sighted cheerfulness, proper trust, and truthfulness that respects feeling.

Although "mother", in my sense, designates work that can be performed by any responsible adult, in most cultures, throughout most of history, the responsibility and work of child care has been borne largely by women. Some mothers are men; numerous women choose not to bear or care for children, and many more would do so if they could without penalty. Nonetheless, many women are, or expect to become, mothers, and more important, throughout most of the world, the majority of mothers are and have been women. It is, therefore, now impossible to separate, intellectually or practically, the female from the maternal condition. The persistent connection of women to mothering is explained, in part, by biology. Females give birth; giving birth is resonant with deep symbolic meaning as well as with practical consequences that shape women's and men's work in culturally specific ways. Women's willing participation in maternal work after birth is partly explained by versions of psychoanalytic theory supplemented by accounts of the centrality of work in human lives. Both sexual identity and "work," the ability to undertake and complete projects with which one is pleased, are central to human self-definition and self-respect. Since girls and boys learn that the work most central to their lives is done by women, girls learn that they are mother-like. Boys, by contrast, learn that they are not mothers, and have an open if not oppositional relation to maternal thinking. Girls may reject vehemently the very idea of mothering, and yet know that the work and its thinking are part of a gender identity that is theirs, if only to repudiate.[15]

Neither the psychological nor the philosophical claim is intended to be taken as universal. The psychological claim is derived primarily from studies on primarily middle-class white women living in the United States in the last quarter of the 20th century. The philosophical claim underlines the nearly universal sexual division of work, but also notes that the particular work assigned to women or to men varies radically, although child care is almost always assigned primarily to women. Although, in nearly every culture, women may reason differently from men, it is an open question how women's different reasonings differ from each other. Because there are commonalities of childhood and social life, it is possible to speak of a human work of child care constituted by the demands of preservation, growth, and acceptability. This means it is possible to compare, which means to contrast, strikingly different practices of child care within or between cultures. For example, all children need protection. However, the character and perception of danger, techniques of protection, distribution of resources necessary to protect, and the degree of commitment to protect vary among cultures and classes, and among groups within cultures. Both the philosophical and the psychological claims are supported by variants of psychoanalytic theory that were formulated in Western cultures, characterized at the least, by a sexual division of labor, male dominance, the assignment of mothering to women, and an ideological commitment to heterosexuality. The philosophical claim is further explained in terms of the centrality of work in people's developing sense of who they are. The relevant concepts of work and identity are also formulated in Western, technologically advanced, primarily capitalist cultures.

Although the claims of different reasoning are not intended to be universal, it is not possible to set in advance either their cultural limits or the ways in which they would have to be modified or scrapped in changed circumstances. There is no transcendant, acultural vantage from which to identify, let alone transcend, the limits of culture. Claims of difference are extended by asking questions of disparate cultures of which the following are only examples: Under what social circumstances do men and women tend to develop a morality of justice or, as in our culture, to lose a morality of love? Wherever you find (something like) a justice morality, do you also find (something like) a morality of love? Where something like the two moralities or maternal thinking can be identified, is the prevalence and content of each related to gender? Where you find a notion of "maternal work" does the work include (something like) protecting a child, however different the techniques of protection? How does the morality of love and/or maternal thinking change when mothering is undertaken by both women and men, or where most children are not expected to survive childhood?

In this paper, I do not concern myself with the extension of difference claims. I limit the two claims I consider to late 19th and 20th century, technologically advanced societies characterized by female mothering, an ideology of heterosexual parenting that affects lesbian and heterosexual mothers, and male dominance. In regard to maternal thinking, I have in mind only societies where most children are expected to survive into adulthood and the number of children in a family tends to be fewer than ten. In limiting the range of these claims, I do not imply that they do *not* hold in other circumstances, only that I make no predictions about finding similar differences or about the explanations that would be given for differences discovered. What I ask and learn about different groups within the domains in which my claims are applicable is shaped by my social and sexual experience. Although I attempt to understand others' experience, my understanding arises from a particular vantage with distortions for which I cannot, from some neutral place, compensate.

The issue of universality is political as much as it is epistemological. In recent decades, many groups of people have *asserted* that they differ in ways that include difference in reasoning. Whether or not difference derives from race, ethnicity, class, or gender, and whatever the evidential status of the differences asserted, the mere assertion that there are differences in reasoning has constituted a challenge to prevailing ideals of transcendant reason. The charge is that these ideals, although meant to include any "rational" person, serve as instruments of exclusion. Excluding is directed, negative activity, stronger than opposition. It depends upon enterprises sufficiently important and excluders sufficiently powerful to reward the efforts that exclusion requires. In the United States, women are excluded from active combat, men are not (usually) excluded from garden clubs. Excluding is not a simple or obvious act. People of good will exclude others without knowing that they are excluding or how exclusion works. For example, feminist women asserting difference derived from gender have meant their claim to have a wider applicability. Knowing that many women speak from exclusions at least as deep as gender, feminists have hoped that once gender difference was spoken and heard, other differences, other exclusions, would be made manifest. The very idea of letting difference be heard was meant to be an invitation to a multiplicity that excludes no one. Yet the most well-intentioned feminist generalizations continue to distort or ignore the experiences of class, or race, or religion—of social life.

There are many techniques of exclusion. One common to intellectuals is the *placing* of difference within a governing theory without recognizing its challenge to the theory's fundamental assumptions. Thus, Kohlberg allegedly scored what was later recognized as a morality of love at a lower stage of moral development than that of justice. If women then scored low, that was a difficulty with them, not with the theory within which they were placed. In political theory, women's perspectives were placed within an illusory "private sphere" and valued there. Since "public," "impersonal," "objective," and "rational" were reciprocally defined, women's perspectives, however valuable, became subjective, personal and nonrational. Freud at one time compared boys' and girls' development, noted the differences, then placed girls' development within the general theory as a puzzling deviation from the "human" norm. If women, then, had an inadequate sense of justice, or were unable to separate themselves from their families, this was not evidence for conflicts of loyalty and love to which the theory was blind. Rather, women were unable to recognize the claims of morality and maturity.[16] Similarly, some feminists have propounded theories about women's nature, relegating differences in class and race to footnotes, then devising concepts that are inapplicable to many women. We have acknowledged our limitations—white, middle class, or Protestant—but then have not looked to see, or waited to hear how these limitations restrict our inquiry. Even as we have criticized them, we have also relied upon theories—from psychoanalysis, to

Marxism, to deconstruction—without questioning or reflecting upon their class, national, cultural, or racial bias.[17]

Philosophers, too, sometimes "place" claims of difference by evaluating them by methods that are alleged to have excluded difference in the first place. If the "different" voice is narrative and particularistic, to argue abstractly that its concepts can be absorbed by the dominant concepts of rationality is to decide in advance that differences in cognitive style make no difference to truth. If, in the morality of love, speakers look for ways of changing the circumstances in which dilemmas arise rather than abstracting from circumstance in order to sharpen principles, then the abstract and hypothetical reasoning associated with justice and philosophical inquiry will preclude the initial statement of moral concepts within the language of love. Maternal knowledge tends to be expressed in stories whose maxims make sense of individual and community life, but are not universal laws. The virtues of a "good" maternal story include a truthfulness that respects feeling, and a narrative style that neither intrudes upon a person's sense of privacy, nor dominates or precludes their active response. These are not the virtues of philosophical "analysis" as it has been defined in western culture.

To hear difference without "placing" it requires careful listening and a suspension of judgement that the active stance of excluding makes difficult. For the excluded, it is a struggle to articulate *as reason* a way of reasoning that has been characterized as "irrational" in the dominant "rational" culture. To say that certain forms of reasoning prevail hegemonically is to say that they structure the conversations in which "rational" people participate. That is, to adapt to these forms of conversation is part of being what is called rational. If difference is to emerge, there must first be silence, a willing suspension of habitual speech, and then a patient struggle requiring of speaker and listener an attentive respect for different reasonings.

This prescription has the ring of circularity. It seems, that in order for difference to emerge, speaker and listener must already believe that difference exists. From the perspective of care, this admitted circularity is benign. To be heard speaking, to be heard as coherent, sensible, and rational, is a real human need. It is therefore a matter of care to hear differences wherever people *feel* silenced or coerced by forms of reason that are not theirs. This means attending to any person speaking out of a sense of exclusion and listening for different reason to the best of one's ability. However, by any standards of reason, individuals will vary in their ability to reason. The deeper challenge, simultaneously intellectual and moral, arises when the speaker is both a member of a *group* that has been excluded from public discourse and power, and a person whom that group deems to be representative of them, and rational. It is then that members of the dominant group, if they are either intellectually honest or caring, will engage in active, cooperative listening until the excluded themselves declare that they have been heard. This is a judgement only the excluded can make.[18]

Neither the claim that there are differences in reasoning, nor the charge that different reason has been deliberately or unwittingly excluded by allegedly objective criteria of "rationality," nor the insistence that it is only the excluded who can say that their difference had been heard, is tantamount to ascribing superiority to the excluded. Yet those who speak of women's difference are almost always heard as ascribing moral superiority to women. This is partly the fault of particular groups of articulate middle class women who celebrated a distinctively domestic morality.[19] Today's theorists, by contrast, explicitly disavow any such view of women's superiority. Even if the morality of love is associated with women, even if most mothers are women, on neither the psychological nor the philosophical view are women "loving" or "good mothers." Moral thinking is related in complex ways to moral action as is reflective maternal thinking to effective maternal love. Both the morality of love and maternal thought include *conceptions* of virtue. One may fail to be virtuous, whatever account of virtue one works with. Men's moral reasoning may focus upon justice, but the world, although dominated by men, is not just.

Rather than claiming superiority for women, both the psychological and philosophical claims critically reflect upon women's reasoning from a feminist perspective. They attribute specific defects in women's reasoning to women's subordination. More generally they claim that gender ideology prevents even the accurate description of women's moral lives. Reality is sentimentalized and temptations are redescribed so that defects emerge as virtues. Maternal love, for example, is said to be gentle and unconditional when, in fact, it is erotic, inseparable from anger, fierce, and fraught with ambivalence. Self-sacrifice is taken as a virtue rather than the defect it is.[20] The temptation to deny suffering that seems unalterable, especially the pain of those whom you love and for whom you are responsible, is exacerbated for women by powerlessness. It is an ongoing task within maternal practice and the morality of love to see and speak truly while conceptualizing a "truth" that is caring. Since the morality of love and maternal practice have been infected by denial, they will be affected by truthful inquiry; what is seen will be transformed in the seeing. When, for example, women no longer regard self-sacrifice as a virtue, or when mothers avow the complexities of maternal love, not only the idea of love, but love itself will change.[21] It is a transformed seeing, and therefore a transformed love, which I believe, could become a resource for peace.

Using Women's Difference: The Case of Mothers and Peace

If there is a kind of reasoning more common to women than men, it should be revealed in women's thinking about war. The maleness of military minds, unlike the maleness of reason, is virtually uncontested. The great preponderance of the world's soldiers, generals, industrial entrepeneurs, chiefs of staff, and heads of state have been and still are men. Many militaries explicitly rely upon a masculinist ideology to define soldierly behavior and to reward soldiers. What is becoming increasingly clear is that there is a "language of warriors,"a "technico-strategic rationality" that is shared by armers and disarmers, chiefs of staff, and chief negotiators. This abstract, quantitative mode of discourse that dominates our thinking about both war and peace is imbued with sexual metaphor, fear of the female, and celebration of "male" virtues. It exhibits, in near caricature, the concepts of objectivity and rationality that have, in other contexts, been identified as male.[22]

Just as the maleness of reason does not in itself ascribe distinctive conceptual standpoints to women, so too the maleness of the warrior mentality does not imply that women's thinking is "peaceful." There is a widely acknowledged *prima facie* opposition between maternal and military work. Mothering begins in birth and promises life; military thinking is characterized by its justification of organized, deliberate death. A mother preserves the bodies, nurtures the psychic growth, and disciplines the conscience of children she cares for; the military deliberately endangers the same body, mind, and conscience in the name of abstract causes and victories. Mother-identified men and women draw upon this opposition between maternal and military work when they set images of birth and hope against the barbed wire of military bases.

Yet, there is no doubt that women, whether or not they are mothers, can be militaristic. There is some evidence that women are more skeptical of military thinking than men. Nonetheless, where ever battles are fought, in the vilest and noblest of causes, on both sides of the battle lines, women support the warriorhood of sons, lovers, friends, and mates. Some mothers, and many daughters of mothers, are proud to fight as fiercely as their brothers in whatever battles their state or cadre enlists them.[23] When women do think against the grain of violence, their "peacefulness" plays much the same role in military reasoning that their partiality and emotionality play in reason generally. Women's "peacefulness," like women's "reason," has been misdescribed and sentimentalized. Like "emotion," "peacefulness" is kept within the boundaries that reasoned militarism and militarized rationality have set. Women preserve feelings and values that reason and war overrun precisely so they may continue to be overrun.[24] If women's "peacefulness" is to be grasped, let alone used, it is necessary to look through the sentiments that gender has created, to reveal, under the mask of "peacefulness," a kind of peacemaking that can oppose to war a resilient nonviolent fighting of its own.

Elsewhere,[25] I address this task in several ways: by highlighting the masculinism of war; by developing a feminist analysis of military and economic violence; by articulating a maternal understanding of conflict that contributes distinctively to theories of nonviolent activism; by identifying distinctive female sources of military enthusiasm and compliance with military authority; and by developing a critique of militarist thinking from a maternal perspective and the vantage of the morality of love. Overall, my aim is to use feminist critique in order to identify distinctive sources of women's compliance and resistance to militarism in ways that will undermine the former while strengthening the latter. In the remainder of this chapter, I will outline two aspects of the peacemaking I am trying to reveal. I will briefly describe maternal nonviolence, including sources of its potential militarization in order to suggest a kind of reasoning about conflict that could emerge from maternal practice. I will then compare a conception of peacemaking derived from maternal thinking that is consistent with the morality of love but different from the conception assumed by most warriors and negotiators.

Three words of caution. To speak of mothers' peacefulness is to address only one aspect of the relation between women and peace. Although the maternal and female are practically and conceptually connected, not all women are mothers, nor are all mothers women. Second, in attributing peacefulness to mothers, I do *not* mean that mothers raise antimilitarist children. Mothers have little control over the decisions their late adolescent children make about when or how to fight. In saying that mothers could come to think about conflict "peacefully," I mean that the work of caring for children gives rise to ways of thinking about the world and its battles, and if mothers themselves recognized and endorsed these ways of thinking, they would themselves tend to become antimilitarist and nonviolent. It is true that if mothers themselves became consciously antimilitarist, their ways of training would change and so presumably would the children they trained. But I myself make no predictions about mothers' children. To do so might burden mothers once again with responsibility for evils of *others* over which they have little control.

Finally, in speaking of "mothers" I limit my claims to the technological and social domains I specified earlier. Whenever I write about nonviolence, my primary reference is to renunciation of violence and alternative nonviolent resistance within the United States and by its government. In speaking of maternal nonviolence, I am more than ever aware that my perspective is limíted. Once again, however, I make no predictions about the applicability of my claims to mothers whose experience is quite different from my own. I do not say, therefore, (as I am often asked to do) that maternal nonviolence is an artifact of affluence and privilege. What I see, from my limited perspective, is that maternal violence occurs in all classes and groups; that poverty is a violence and makes the renunciation of violence and nonviolent resistance heartbreakingly difficult; and that, nonetheless, mothers engage in nonviolent struggle with their children and on their behalf with courage and resilience in the face of poverty, bigotry, and violence.

THINKING ABOUT PEACE MATERNALLY

Although mothers might wish it otherwise, conflict is an integral part of maternal life. Mothers are embattled with their children and on their behalf. They are also the arbiters and judges of their childrens' battles with each other, with their friends, and with authorities and institutions. Mothers know conflict from a double and shifting position of power and powerlessness. A mother experiences herself as powerless, certainly in the world, often in the home, and frequently, in relation to her children whose desires and will she can neither predict nor control. She is, nonetheless, powerful in relation to her children both physically and psychologically. Her children, too, are alternately powerful and powerless depending upon circumstances.

In living through the conflicts endemic to their work, mothers develop a practice of nonviolent action.[26] Children are vulnerable creatures and the vulnerable generally tend to elicit either aggression or care. Recalcitrance and anger tend to provoke aggression, and children are provocative. Simultaneously powerless and powerful, provoked and exhausted, many mothers are frequently tempted to violence against their children. Almost every mother I speak to (myself included) believes that she was more than once physically or verbally abusive toward her children. There are pathologically abusive mothers, and cultures in which normal practices seem pathologically abusive to outsiders. For children and mothers, violence is apt to be sharply etched. We remember the moment of abuse rather than the hour of patience, the day of rage rather than the habits of peace. Given the vulnerability of children, this is exactly as it should be. Yet responses of care predominate in many mothers' work and in maternal practice as a whole. Otherwise, children would not survive, let alone thrive. Whatever the failures, deliberate damaging of children counts as failure since it is in direct contradiction to the protection and nurturance that define maternal work.

It is an ongoing task of nonviolent theorists to define "violence" in such a way that violent policies and acts can be identified wherever they occur—on a battlefield, in a schoolroom or factory, in the bedroom, or boardroom. For mothers, it is a daily task first to identify, and then to resist violence inflicted upon their children as well as the violence their children inflict either on themselves (the drug abusing or anorexic child), or on others (the cruel bully). Mothers are powerful people who try to restrain their own violence toward the vulnerable; they develop precepts and strategies of restraint so that they can train their "powerful" children—the older sibling, healthy athlete, popular friend, successful student—to do likewise. Mothers are also socially powerless and were once children themselves. They can imagine for their children nonviolent strategies for resisting the strong, for *fighting* nonviolently when they are enraged by weakness. In attending to their strong and weak children as well as to their own shifting powers, mothers learn that advantage is inpredictable. No one can count on strength or on weakness. This lesson like many in maternal practice, is learned over time, through failure at least as much as through success.

Fighting is part of a mother's life. She must learn to fight on behalf of her children and teach her children to fight for themselves. It is right that people learn to *fight* to protect what they love and to get what they need. "Peace and quiet" can mask many kinds of violence or ill-advised compliance with harmful authorities. Yet, it is not easy for mothers, either to teach their children to resist hurtful authorities, or to resist on their children's behalf. It is, after all, part of a mother's job to train her children to comply with appropriate edicts, including her own. Not surprisingly, it is sometimes hard to recognize the unjust demand and illegitimate authority; it is far easier to urge upon children at least half-hearted compliance. Even when an authority demeans her child, it is often easier for a mother to correct the child than to challenge authority, especially when "authority" is someone—teacher, priest, pediatrician—who the mother herself fears or respects. Mothers often misidentify obedience as a virtue, rather than a proper trust that makes appropriate distrust and timely resistance possible.[27] Nonetheless, mothers do resist, and recognize their failure to resist as failure. Most striking is the notorious resistance, in the face of real danger, against enormous odds, by mothers who live in poverty, tyranny, and slavery.[28] In quieter times, more fortunate mothers exhibit their own barely visible courage as they get for their children what they need, and learn to say no to those who would hurt them.

Although mothers teach children how to fight, fighting is rarely their wish. Nonviolent battles escalate unpredictably into violence, hatred hurts both hater and hated, and even the most Spockian nonviolent strategy can leave its scars. Because they appreciate the cost of fighting, mothers keep the peace, ending and avoiding battles whenever possible. More important, they make a peace worth keeping by identifying and removing causes for battle and teaching principles and techniques of self-respecting cooperation.

As I have argued elsewhere, the understanding of "battle," which mothers develop, is akin to, though suggestively different from, that of nonviolent activists.[29] There is, however, a critical difference between the non-violent activism of, say, Gandhi and King, and that of mothers. Gandhi and King see and honor the universal in the particular—the soul, or goodness, in every individual person. All persons should be treated nonviolently. *No* life should be destroyed. By contrast, maternal work is embedded in particular passions for particular children and for the particular people and groups of people on whom those children depend and to whom they belong. The "sanctity of life" is grounded in myriad positive obligations to protect and sustain the members of a particular group.

Of the many ways in which the boundaries of maternal violence are drawn, at least two lend themselves to maternal militarism. One is to teach children to renounce violence unless and until it is enlisted in a collective enterprise such as a war, which the mother has endorsed, or one that has been sanctioned by those who have authority over her and her children. Although adept in the practice and sometimes in the articulation of nonviolence within her sphere, such a mother does not imagine a politics of nonviolent action. Another is more serious. It is seen in mothers' liability to distinctive and virulent forms of self-righteous hatred and fear of the outsider, sometimes issuing in a racism that fuels and is fueled by violence. Mothers work with life-gripping passion on behalf of particular people, often in social isolation, and at the cost of nonmaternal projects that might allow them battles and anger of their own. Whatever nonviolence they practice in their own domain, a possible threat from a threatening outsider evokes rage and fear. Militarists find in this self-righteous hatred and fear a potent ally.

This is the underside of maternal nonviolence, but it is not the only side. Mothers extend the range of their nonviolence when they identify proper (dis)trust of allegedly legitimate authority as a virtue and develop habits of resistance. Although liable to self-righteous protection of their own, mothers also develop distinctive ways of combatting their fear and ignorance. Frequently, mothers widen their vision by finding in other particular mothers, children and families, passions and responsibilities akin to their own. They justify an injunction against killing by pointing to the particularities of lives and life—connections, to the many kinds of past work and present hope that killing destroys. Even for these mothers, it is an ongoing task to sustain the tension between passionate loyalties to their particular children and a less personal imaginative grasp of what other children mean to other mothers.

Nonviolent action, the ideals of renunciation, resistance and peacekeeping, govern maternal practice. Although violence, passivity, and timidity, are temptations, they are recognized as such by mothers themselves. Renunciation, resistance, and peacekeeping are not exceptions to but the rule of maternal practice.[30] But to say that an ideal "governs" is not to mark an achievement but rather to identify a kind of struggle. For mothers, violence, passivity, timidity, and parochialism are liabilities of their work. Even if many mothers are generally more successful than not in resisting the violence they recognize, in every culture there are some mothers who fail to *see* violence in approved customs and therefore do not even struggle to resist it or renounce its strategies. In short, maternal nonviolence is a reality in the making, or to borrow a phase from Merleau-Ponty, a vérité-à-faire, a truth-to-be made.[31]

The making of the truth of maternal nonviolence is, in part, a task of reason. Central to that task is an adequate expression of the governing ideals, one that identifies the violence in sanctioned custom and the nonviolence of angry, yet disciplined love. In the making of maternal nonviolence, as in maternal thinking generally, it is an ongoing task to see clearly, speak responsibly, to develop a conception of "objective" sight and speech that is both truthful and caring. Although the intellectual capacities for generalizing through particulars are latent in maternal attentive love, it will require reasoned imagination to extend nonviolence in practice or theory.

Maternal nonviolence cannot be directly translated into political speech. I believe, however, that as maternal nonviolence is articulated, it will offer a distinct perspective upon justifications for war. It is my contention that theories of "just" and "necessary" wars depend upon a view of selves and reason presupposed in justice reasoning.[32] These theories of war include within them a practice of peacemaking and a conception of peace. In the space remaining, I will suggest that this conception of peace is at odds with maternal thinking yet consonant with the morality of love.

The prevailing concept of peacemaking is familiar through decades of treaty making and arms negotiation. W.B. Gallie has given it a name—"conflict resolution through mutual concessions"—and given it an acronym of its own—CRTMC.[33] In its ideal form, CRTMC consists of negotiation between equals, each of whom gives up as little as seems to be necessary in order to get what he wants. (Optimally, they give up nothing but the bargaining chips that were invented solely to be given up.) CRTMC is allegedly successful when each partner is free from fear of the other and can live alone, independently, in peace. I take it this account of peacemaking is sufficiently familiar to any newspaper reader to allow some comment.

Even when no visible agreement results, the mere practice of CRTMC serves to preserve the status quo, providing the occasion for public competitive bargaining that indirectly expresses while also containing the desire to dominate. Yet though CRTMC contains, or at least postpones, outright violence, it is both exploitative and inherently unstable. It is exploitative because the "equal," strong partners bargain over the heads and with the lives of persons or nations that are weak enough to be excluded. Although sometimes the weaker are promised safety or a particular form of government in return for submitting to protection, often, they are not even consulted. Since fortune is fickle, and the weak develop effective forms of resistance, treaty negotiations that turn upon others' armies, crops, or land are not only exploitative but also unstable. The instability is at least as serious, even if one considers only the active partners. Among them, equality is rightly perceived as fragile; anyone's power is dependent upon physical, political, and economic conditions that are difficult to control. Equality is, in any case, an abstraction. The search for quantitative measures of strength ignores the meanings people attribute to their own and others' needs and strategies. Actual people and nations have histories; "power" is not a possession but a changing relation some have to others in particular social and political contexts in which their fears and desires make sense.

The presuppositions of CRTMC are remarkably like those of "realist" justifications for defense and conquest. Realists claim that people and nations will, if they can, dominate and exploit those who are weaker. "They that have odds of power exact as much as they can, and the weak yield to such conditions as they can get" (Thucydides).[34] The weak are not less domineering than the strong; they are only people who have not yet gathered the strength needed to retaliate and, in turn, dominate. Moreover, at least some realists claim that the strong should get what they can, so long as what they get is in the interest of State or Cause. In this view, the relentless pursuit of greater strength, and the domination of others that strength allows, in fact, serves the good of the Whole or the Good.

In the realist view, as in CRTMC, anyone's greater strength is perceived as a threat. One's own strength, by contrast, is unthreatening. Either one is an exception, whose strength is in the service of safety rather than domination, or one's domination is justified, as another's is not, in the name of the Cause or the State. What looks like "peacemaking" actually justifies building up one's relative strength in defense and in the service of justified domination. Given these presuppositions, equality is not a resting point, but an invitation to fear and aggression. The practice of CRTMC is essentially negative: partners moved by fear and frustration, concede and compromise in order to be left alone in safety. At its best, CRTMC leads to a stasis of separate but equal partners each with cause to doubt whether the other will persist in renouncing violence if and when they become able to profit by it. Its best, then, is a result, which on the assumptions of its theory, is second best and inherently unstable.

Maternal thinking articulates a different perspective on relationships, a perspective expressed independently and therefore confirmed in the morality of love. To mothers, the ideal of equality is a phantom. Mothers are not equal to their children; siblings and childhood friends are not equal to each other. Differences in strength cannot be wished away—they are the stuff of childhood and of family life. Power relations are shifting and complex. Weakness in one context (physical strength, for example) may be irrelevant in another. In any case, the weak have powers to resist and to seduce that belie any absolute division between strong and weak. Because they live through and witness shifting power relations, because they watch firsthand the anxieties of children driven to be equal, mothers would be slow to wish upon themselves or anyone they care for the fearful pursuit of equality. In the maternal view of conflict, it is not necessary to be equal in order to resist violence. Most mothers try to teach their children when self-respect demands a fight. Their own peacemaking—their attempt to create conditions of peace—includes training for active, engaged nonviolent fighting. Rather than depending upon an illusory state of equality, they aim to fight as they live, within communities that attend to and survive shifting differences in power.

Maternal practice includes many moments of CRTMC, between parents and children, between parents, between parents and authorities, between sibling and childhood friends. But these are only moments in an ongoing practice of peacemaking that is radically different. Peace is not a precarious equilibrium in which everyone is somewhat warily left alone—(though this certainly describes many "peaceful" respites in maternal life). Battles provoke and are provoked by fear and rage, lust, greed, jealousy, shame and guilt, and certainly by loyalty and love. Peace, like the maternal life that it blesses, includes ambivalences, ambiguities, and compromise. Peace is a way of living in which participants counting on connection demand a great deal of each other. The peacemaker asks of herself and those she cares for, not what they can afford to give up, but what they can give; not how they can be left alone, but what they can do together. It is all too easy to sentimentalize maternal peacemaking. It is *not* easy to give what can be usefully received or to receive what can be willingly given. Mothers become addicted to giving, create addicted receivers, misperceive others' desires, deny and project their own desires, demand from others what they cannot give while refusing to receive what can willingly be given. In short, mothers, like other humans, fail. But the task of making peace by giving and receiving, while remaining in connection, is radically different from CRTMC and less dangerous.

From a maternal perspective, CRTMC seems partly a sweet dream of objective, impersonal, rule-governed reason. Yet, it is also a nightmare in which 'reason' obscures passion, and passion suggests violence. Taking an objective distance from the rage and fear of battle, negotiators are left without resources to understand the failure that leads to war and preparations for war; nor can they manage the emotions of peace, i.e. of life. Given their realist assumptions about strength, weakness, and unstable equality, to look at fear, anger, loyalty, and love, to look at history, is to see violence. And indeed, violence is everywhere to be seen, a public, documented, indeed "realistic" nightmare.

Mothers know another history. Passion is often destructive, but it is the material for a discipline of love and for the maternal thinking that is love's reason. Mothers learn first hand, as agent and spectator, in the position of the stronger and of the weaker, that the cost of dominating is paid in the fear and hatred of the dominated and anyone who sympathizes with them. Mothers have their dominating moments (to understate the case!) and therefore experience what it means to lose the trust of the dominated and to watch those they dominate lose pleasure in themselves. Most mothers also know what it is to be dominated. They watch as their children stumble in their efforts to learn to love, suffering sometimes the pain and loss that comes from dominating, other times the pain and humiliation of the dominated. But pain is not the only history a mother tells. Even siblings and rivalrous children learn to take strength from each others' strength rather than primarily from their weakness. Nor does the radical inequality of mother-child relations preclude a mutuality and respect for another's lively being. Without being atypically "unselfish," a mother may measure her power in terms of her ability to nurture a child whom she *cannot* dominate, a child lively with her or his own desires and projects.

It would be sentimental foolishness to claim for all mother-child relations such mutuality. It would be equally sentimental cynicism to deny that many mothers and children together create an ongoing, changing, approximation of mutuality. Out of their failures as well as successes, mothers develop a conception of relationships that undermines the paranoid conception of individuality that fuels conquest as well as provocative "defense." They not only modify aggression in the interest of connection but develop connections that limit aggression before it arises. The self who *desires* other selves to persist in their own lively being is a self at least capable of respecting the lives and life-connections of quite different others.

I shouldn't need to repeat the point that there are mothers whose nonviolence is limited to their own group and who therefore defend conquest justified by that group's interest. Nor am I claiming that a mother-child relationship is easily generalized. It does seem, however, that maternal peacemaking both depends upon and fosters the conceptions of the self and human nature that we find in the morality of love. In this view, individuals are not primarily centers of dominating and defensive activity trying to achieve a stable autonomy in threatening heirarchies of strength. An individual's sense of herself is inseparable from connection, and therefore inseparable from the ability to give and to receive. Although women may be more apt than men to hold this conception of human nature, women hold it to be true, not only of children and other women, but of anyone.

A view of "human" nature is not a view of "state" nature, nor can I here take up the question of states. Some people argue that states are inherently violent, and some also argue that they are "male." If so, women, appreciative of their own nonviolence and skeptical of authority, might endorse Virginia Woolf's now famous remark: "As a woman I want no country, as a woman I have no country, my country is the whole world."[35] It could be said with equal plausibility, that since women have been responsible for maintaining and appreciating extended connection, they will be especially loyal to states and to the causes of their people. Such women might subject state policies to maternal critique. Can states suffer pain and loss of domination? Can states take pleasure from the lively, independent, well being of other states? Is the fearful pursuit of equality the best a state can manage? Can we define states, as we are learning to define families, not in terms of extent and possession, but in the lives they make possible? If we look at the histories of states, at the real needs and angers of a state's citizens, will it be possible to devise ways of nonviolent fighting that will shape and satisfy legitimate need? Whether states are suspect or objects of loyalty, state relations, like their personal analogues, would look different from a maternal perspective or the morality of love.

To look closely at maternal nonviolence in the making, adopting consciously the morality of love, yields insights for anyone attempting to develop nonviolent practice and theory. Mothers are not peaceful, still less are they "good." Nonetheless, maternal struggle to achieve nonviolence parallels and illuminates the struggle to achieve a sturdy peace, one that demands resistance to violence and that depends upon continuing relationships that include anger, disappointment, difference, conflict and nonviolent battle. It is because mothers struggle in familiar, unheroic circumstances, with at best partial success, that their practice is useful. Mothers are everywhere; some people everywhere identify with the maternal tasks of preserving, healing, enabling, and teaching. Children everywhere are capable of hope and suffering. There are material, social bases for a maternal mode of reasoning which can grasp and attend to another mother's pain in a way that enables mothers to join in resistance to the violences their children suffer. Yet mothers differ radically from each other. Maternal thinkers, as much as any philosopher, must *learn* to hear difference, then learn what it takes to enable different people to grow. This is only to say that maternal rationality is like the rationality that philosophers envision, a difficult attainment. Yet the ideal of attainment differs markedly from the philosophical ideals of transcendance and objectivity. Maternal reason is fueled by and extends itself through particular passions; it emerges from and requires of itself the actions of love.

Notes

1. The phrase "might after all be thoroughly 'male' " comes from Genevieve Lloyd, *The Man of Reason: "Male" and "Female" in Western Philosophy* (Minneapolis: University of Minnesota Press, 1984), p. viii. "Maleness," in her and my use, is not an essential quality of human males, but a social construction whose character varies with the historical and intellectual context in which it appears. Evelyn Fox Keller, *Gender and Science,* (New Haven: Yale University Press, 1985), discusses the ways in which the ideologies of science and gender inform each other and produce "male" standards of rationality. An excellent collection of essays on gender and reason is Sandra Harding and Merrill B. Hintikka, editors, *Discovering Reality,* (Dordrecht: Reidl, 1983). In *Human Nature and Feminist Politics,* (Totowa, New Jersey: Rowman and Allanheld, 1983), Alison Jaggar explicates and expands upon philosophical critiques of traditional standards of rationality. Dorothy Dinnerstein has inspired an extensive critique of "male" reason from a psychoanalytic perspective: *The Mermaid and the Minotaur,* (New York: Harper & Row, 1977). The literature on reason and

gender is extensive and includes the following writers of many disciplines and styles: Susan Okin, *Women in Western Political Thought,* (Princeton: Princeton University Press, 1978); Susan Griffin, *Women and Nature: The Roaring Inside Her,* (New York: Harper & Row, 1980); Jean Bethke Elshtain, *Public Man, Private Women,* (Princeton: Princeton University Press, 1981); Audre Lorde, *Sister Outsider,* (Crossing Press: 1982); Nancy Hartsock, *Money, Sex and Power,* (New York: Longman Inc., 1983); Josephine Donovan, *Feminist Theory: The Intellectual Traditions of American Feminism,* (New York: Unger, 1985).

2. To the best of my knowledge, any theorist arguing for distinctive "female" forms of reasoning also argues that allegedly neutral standards of rationality are "male" biased. The best known exponent of the psychological claim is Carol Gilligan. See *In a Different Voice,* (Cambridge: Harvard University Press, 1982); "The Conquistador and the Dark Continent: Notes on the Psychology of Love," *Deadalus,* 1984, vol. 113, 75–95; "Remapping the Moral Domain: New Images of Self in Relationship," lecture at Stanford University, 1984. Claims supportive of Gilligan have been made by other psychologists. See especially, Jean Baker Miller, *Toward a New Psychology of Women,* (Boston: Beacon Press, 1973) and Mary Belenky, Blythe Clinchy, Nancy Goldberger, and Jill Tarule, *Women's Ways of Knowing,* (forthcoming, Basic Books, 1986). The series of papers issued by Jean Baker Miller and her colleagues from the Stone Center, Wellesley College, expand upon and tend to confirm Gilligan's work, especially her conception of a relational self. No single voice predominates among those making philosophical claims, as Gilligan's does among psychologists. The central article among analytic philosophers is Nancy Hartsock, "The Feminist Standpoint," a chapter in *Money, Sex and Power,* and collected in Harding and Hintikka, *Discovering Reality.* Jaggar discusses the "feminist standpoint" and associates it with socialist feminism in *Human Nature and Feminist Politics.* Iris Young has a valuable piece identifying those who recognize and welcome a feminist standpoint, "Humanism, Gynocentrism and Feminist Politics" in *Hypatia,* vol. 3, printed as a special issue of *Women's Studies International Forum,* vol. 8, 1985. See also Virginia Held, "Feminism and Moral Theory," this volume. For many years, Dorothy Smith has been insisting upon the existence and value of a feminist standpoint. See "A Sociology for Women" in *The Prism of Sex: Essays in the Sociology of Knowledge,* edited by Julia Sherman and Evelyn Beck, (Madison: University of Wisconsin, 1979). For two examples of what I consider philosophical claims made in 'different voices' that take the matter of voice seriously, see Lorde, *Sister Outsider,* and Griffin, *Women and Nature.* Many French feminists explore the maleness of reason and some also explore distinctive female reasoning. See *New French Feminisms,* Elaine Marks Isabelle de Cortivron, editors, (Amherst: University of Massachusetts, 1980).

3. The quoted phrase is from Genevieve Lloyd, "Selfhood, War, and Masculinity," in *Feminist Challenges,* eds. E. Gross and C. Pateman, Allen and Unwin, in press. Most of the authors cited in note I make this claim. I rely especially on Keller, *Gender and Science.*

4. This claim is made explicitly in Hartsock, "The Feminist Standpoint" and by me in "Maternal Thinking," *Feminist Studies,* vol. 6, 1980, and "Preservative Love and Military Destruction," in *Mothering: Essays in Feminist Theory,* edited by Joyce Trebilcot (Totowa, New Jersey: Rowman and Allenheld, 1984).

5. I present the psychological claim almost entirely in the words of Carol Gilligan, but I may well have misconstrued her intentions as I expand upon her actual words. (See Note 2.)

6. My account of the morality of justice follows Kohlberg and Gilligan and is not meant to represent the range of philosophical views on justice. The central elements of the voice (as I hear it) are fairness and universality. In speaking of a morality of

love instead of a morality of care, I differ from Gilligan's commentators and perhaps from Gilligan herself, although her most recent work suggests the appropriateness of this label. In my parlance, care is the primary virtue of the morality of love. To speak of love is provocatively sentimental and, for some ears, provocatively religious. It is central to the use I make of maternal thinking to confront sentimentality, to reconnect love with sexuality and anger, to show connections as well as differences between maternal and religious thinking. For these and other purposes I find "love" more useful than the quieter, less ambivalent "care."

7. I take this formulation from a lecture by Gilligan, Stonybrook, March 1985. This research is both developing and contested. In her 1984 articles, and in several forthcoming articles, Gilligan provides references to relevant studies. Gilligan herself provides precise measures of sexual variation but I have deliberately avoided a precision that I am in no position to assess. Without predicting the outcome of debates in psychology, I would make only three points. Given that she speaks within a context of gender dichotomy, Gilligan's claims about gender are misheard as dichotomous, symmetrical, and simple. Each of the psychological studies cited in Note 2 stress women's *development* and, therefore, women's changes over time, and differences from each other. Gilligan and others attempt to identify those situations in which the voice of "love" tends to be lost or can be heard (for example, when Gilligan hears the "subtext of care" in the reasoning of inner city children of both sexes who have been scored stage one in the Kohlberg scale). That a voice of "love" is found primarily in women, marks not an essentialist ending but an invitation to look both at the distinctive development of those women and at the silencing of the voice in men and women. A second point: the methods involved in gathering data are themselves indicted by Gilligan's findings, i.e. the methods used to test the findings are, if the findings are correct, themselves in need of testing by some quite different methods. Third, Gilligan's work is more or less directly confirmed by other psychologists, especially Belenky et. al., and Miller and her colleagues (see Note 2) whose methods differ from hers.

8. This account of the effect of child-parent relations is best known from the work of Nancy Chodorow, *The Reproduction of Mothering, Psychoanalysis and the Sociology of Gender,* (Berkeley; University of California Press, 1978). A similar account, which like Chodorow's, is indebted to the version of psychoanalytic theory known as "object relations," was developed independently by Keller, *Gender and Science.* In several articles, Jessica Benjamin has developed her own variant of this view. See especially, "The Oedipal Riddle: Authority, Autonomy and the New Narcissism" in *The Problem of Authority in America,* John P. Diggens and Mark E. Kahn, editors, (Philadelphia; Temple University Press, 1982). A more psychoanalytically traditional, though socially radical acount, of gender development makes up part of Dorothy Dinnerstein's *The Mermaid and The Minotaur.*

9. The phrase "permanent inequality" comes from Jean Baker Miller, *Toward a New Psychology of Women,* passim. She does not mean that these inequalities are inevitable, but that they are social and structural rather than personal. Social explanations of women's reasoning predominate in feminist writings.

10. In formulating the philosophical claim, I rely most directly upon Hartsock, "The Feminist Standpoint" and my own "Maternal Thinking." See notes 1 and 4 for full reference.

11. The stance that I am labelling "Practicalist" is associated with several philosophers. For me, the works of Kuhn, Wittgenstein, Habermas, Marx, Winch, and R. Rorty have been especially important.

12. See Hartsock, "The Feminist Standpoint," for a fuller account of the hegemonic character of prevailing ideals.

13. See Ruddick, "Maternal Thinking" and "Preservative Love and Military

Destruction." Throughout this paper, I am summarizing rather lengthy work still very much in progress.

14. Of the three demands that structure maternal work, that for protection is most invariant. Although criteria of "acceptability" and techniques of discipline are notoriously variant, the demand that children be trained in "acceptable" behavior seems universal. The demand for nurturance is, by contrast, historically and culturally specific. I myself share a belief widely prevalent in my culture: *all* children are complicated creatures whose development requires "nurturance."

15. See the references in note 8. On the centrality of work in the formation of identity, see Erik Erikson, especially *Identity and the Life Cycle*, and *Childhood and Society*, (New York: Norton, 1980, 1963, originally 1959, 1950); Marx, see especially *Economic and Philosophical Manuscripts*, (New York: International Publishers, 1964); David Meakin, *Man and Work*, (New York: Holmes and Meier, 1976); Simone Weil, see especially *The Need for Roots*, (New York: G.P. Putnam, 1953), *Oppression and Liberty*, (Amherst: University of Massachusetts Press, 1973), "Factory Work" collected in *Simone Weil Reader*, edited by George Panichas, (New York: McKay, 1977).

Although men can be mothers, in the cultures I consider, most male parents tend to be Fathers and Fathers tend to be men. Whether women or men, Fathers are not mothers. Fathers are meant to provide the material support for child care and to defend mother and child from external threat. They represent the "world" (language, culture) and are the arbiters of a child's suitability for the world they represent. I follow linguistic custom in treating "mother" and "father" as correlative terms, but capitalize "Father" to challenge the correlation. Fatherhood is more a role determined by cultural demands than a kind of work determined by childrens' needs. For women without connection to providers and defenders, or for men impoverished and disenfranchized, Fatherhood is an elusive goal and a cruel mystification of real choices.

16. On Kohlberg, see Gilligan, especially *In a Different Voice;* on women and public discourse see Elshtain, *Public Man, Private Woman*, and Okin, *Women in Western Political Thought*. The literature on Freud's treatment of women is vast. On this particular point see Gilligan, "The Conquistador and the Dark Continent."

17. See Lorde, *Sister Outsider;* Bell Hooks, *Feminist Theory: From the Margin to the Center*, (South End Press, 1984); Gloria Joseph and Jill Lewis, *Common Differences, Conflicts in Black and White Feminist Perspective*, (New York: Anchor Press, 1981); Maxine Bacon Zinn, Lynn Weber Cannon, Elizabeth Higginbotham, and Bonnie Thornton Dill, "The Costs of Exclusionary Practices in Women's Studies" (forthcoming, Signs); Angela Davis, *Women, Race and Class*, (New York: Random House, 1981); Marilyn Frye, "On Being White" in *The Politics of Reality*, (New York: The Crossing Press, 1983), Mary C. Lugones and Elizabeth V. Spelman, "Have We Got a Theory for You! Feminist Theory, Cultural Imperialism and the Demand for "The Woman's Voice" in *Women's Studies International Forum*, vol. 6, no. 6, 1983.

18. Indifference to the speaker—to the bodies and histories of speakers—is one element of a conception of "rationality" that separates mind from body, reason from life story. From the perspective of the morality of love, it matters who speaks. In the case of gender, it matters whether a speaker is a woman, that is, whether the speaker's body and history are female. Men can speak from deep knowledge of and sympathy with women's lives; they can say the "same things" that women do. (See for example, Annette Baier's "Hume as the Women's Moral Philosopher," this volume). But men cannot *now* speak out of the historical condition of being female; they do not, and have not, lived in women's bodies, lived women's lives; they have not been

and therefore cannot now become "women." Whatever exclusion men have suffered—in virtue of class, race, sexuality, or in certain places and cultures, of gender—men have not been excluded as women and cannot redress in their own voice that particular exclusion.

19. I am thinking here of later 19th and early 20th century writers who praised women's virtue. Ellen Kay, Olive Schreiner, and Jane Addams come to mind. Although these women did not articulate the same kind of feminist critique that I myself am developing and applaud in others, their thinking was far more complex and nuanced than their detracters suggest.

20. Gilligan and I, along with other writers, identify certain "failures" of women that are partly explained by the demands of the work. When women fail to take their own needs as legitimate, or confuse caring for others with pleasing them, or deny truths about themselves and the world that are hurtful, or delegate to others authority over their childrens' lives, this is partly because the strains and conflicts of obligation prompt those who care to tempting resolutions of daily conflicts that arise in responding to real people's real needs. But these temptations are much stronger when the care taker, in fact, has little power to affect the lives of those she cares for and is not encouraged to take her own needs, or ultimately even their needs, seriously. The perversion of value arises because these temptations have not been recognized as temptations, but instead those who succumb to them are described as virtuous—unselfish, obedient, cheerful, even innocent.

21. There are many feminist attempts to capture the reality of maternal work. Among those that particularly grapple with ambivalence and the passions of maternal love are Jane Lazarre, *The Mother Knot,* (Boston: Beacon Press, 1986); Audre Lorde, "Man Child, A Black Lesbian Feminist's Response" in *Sister Outsider;* Alta, *Momma: A Start on all the Untold Stories,* (New York: Times Change Press, 1974); Adrienna Rich, *Of Woman Born,* (New York: Norton, 1976).

22. The phrase, "The language of the warriors," used to include the language of arms controllers, comes from Freeman Dyson, *Weapons and Hope,* (New York: Harper & Row, 1984). The concept of technico-strategic reasoning comes from Carol Cohn who has developed a feminist and antimilitarist critique of technological language in two unpublished papers: "Technological Expertise in Anti-Nuclear Politics: Help or Hindrance," and "White Men in Ties Discussing Missile Size." The feminist critique of the language and concepts of war is extensive and growing. See especially, Genevieve Lloyd, "Selfhood, War and Masculinity," Jean Bethke Elshtain, "Reflections on War and Political Discourse: Realism, Just War and Feminism in a Nuclear Age," *Political Theory,* February 1985; Mary Seegers, "A Feminist Critique of the Bishop's Letter" *(Feminist Studies); Fall, 1985, Joel Kovel, Against the State of Nuclear Terror,* (London: Pan Books, 1983).

23. This should not be surprising. Women share human reasons for welcoming war: rage, excitment, and the pleasures of communal and self-righteous action. Historically, women have special reasons to welcome war's offer of training, wider experience, paid employment, and escape from domestic confinement. War's evident manliness still includes and excites its own brand of self-congratulatory femininity, a parodic caricature of womanliness. Doing the wash keeps the home fires burning, a kiss inspires a soldier, and daily child care is suffused with a patrio-erotic glow. As Virginia Woolf exclaimed in 1941, "No I don't see what's to be done about war. Its manliness; and manliness breeds womanliness—both so hateful." Virginia Woolf, *Letters,* (London: Harcourt Brace, Hogarth Press, vol. 6, 1984), p. 464.

24. "The absurd self-importance of his striving has been matched by the abject servility of her derision, which has on the whole been expressed only with his consent and within boundaries set by him, and which on the whole worked to

support the stability of the realm he rules." Dorothy Dinnerstein, "Toward the Mobilization of Eros," in *Face to Face,* edited by Meg Murray, (West Port, Conn.: Greenwood Press, 1982).

25. Ruddick, "Preservative Love and Military Destruction."

26. The difficulties in defining violence are legion. Briefly, I call violent any strategies, practices, or weapons that intentionally or predictably damage a person; by damage I mean serious and indefinitely lasting physical or psychological harm without compensatory benefit *for the person damaged.*

27. See Annette Baier, "Trust and Anti-Trust," *Ethics,* forthcoming, and Sissela Bok, "Distrust, Secrecy and the Arms Race," *Ethics,* April, 1985.

28. The long record of mothers' resistance includes mothers in Argentina, El Salvador, and Guatemala protesting the "disappearance" of children; mothers in slavery who fought for the survival and freedom of their children; mothers in ghettos and camps who shielded their children or comforted them when protection was no longer possible; mothers in South Africa fighting for their children's lives and spirits while simultaneously trying to protect them from the ravages of fighting; "welfare" mothers in the United States fighting for minimal health and security;' probably to mothers anywhere that poverty and tyranny endanger children and others for whom they care.

29. For pacifist theory, see Gandhi, *Nonviolent Resistance,* (Shocken Books, 1961; Martin Luther King, "Loving Your Enemies," (New York: A.J. Muste Foundation, 1981); H.J.N. Horsburgh, *Nonviolence and Aggression,* (London: Oxford University Press, 1978); Barbara Deming, *We are All Part of One Another,* (Philadelphia: New Society Publishers, 1984); and the series of pamphlets published by the A.J. Muste Foundation and available from the War Resister's League, 339 Lafayette St. NYC. For a provisional comparison of maternal thinking and pacifist theory, see Ruddick, "Preservative Love and Military Destruction."

30. The second criterion of governing—that rule and exception not be of equal frequency—is suggested by Wittgenstein, see for example *Philosophical Investigations,* especially paragraphs 142, 241–42.

31. Quoted in Raymond Geuss, *The Idea of a Critical Theory,* (Cambridge: Cambridge University Press, 1981).

32. Just war theory, to take the primary example, seems an abstract fiction in the aid of an illusory control not so much of killing but of thought about killing. See Note 22.

33. W.B. Gallie, "Three Main Fallacies in the Discussion of Nuclear Weapons" in Nigel Blake and Kay Pole, editors, *Dangers of Deterrence,* (London: Routledge, & Kegan Paul Inc., 1983).

34. Quoted by Michael Walzer, *Just and Unjust Wars,* (New York: Basic Brooks, 1977), p. 5.

35. Woolf, *Three Guineas,* (New York: Harcourt Brace, 1966), p. 109, (Original, London 1937). For the beginnings of a feminist analysis of states, see the works I have already cited by Elshtain, Hartsock, Lloyd and Okin and in addition, Nancy Hartsock, "The Barracks Community in Western Political Thought: Prologomena to a Feminist Critique of War and Politics" in *Women's Studies International Forum,* 1982, vol. 5.

Politics, Feminism, and the Ethics of Caring

MARY FAINSOD KATZENSTEIN & DAVID D. LAITIN

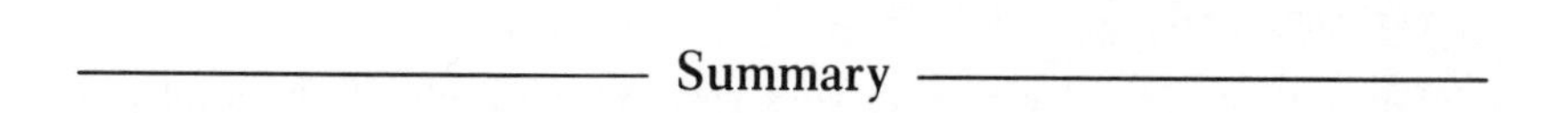

There has been a recent trend among women, both from the right and the left, to appeal to an ethics of caring as a focal point for feminist politics. Opponents of this strategy argue that it is reactionary, enforcing existing systems of gender stratification. Rather than simply accept this critique, authors Katzenstein and Laitin outline three criteria that they deem necessary if an ethics of care is to be conjoined with a progressive feminist politics. Using these three standards, Katzenstein and Laitin analyze two political movements that appeal to an ethics of care: the women's suffrage campaign at the turn of the century, and the recent antipornography movement. The authors find that on the whole, the women's suffrage movement was a progressive one, and that the battle against pornography includes both reactionary and progressive possibilities. The point of these analyses however, is not simply to condemn or endorse either movement, but rather to demonstrate the complexity of all such movements, and to show the effectiveness of the suggested criteria for assessing the political promise of each. The progressive tendencies in both movements are evidence of the politically productive possibilities implicit in Gilligan's research. S.M.

Carol Gilligan's *In a Different Voice* (Gilligan 1982) offers the argument that two moral systems coexist: one based on the preservation of personal ties, contextualized judgments, and values of caring; the other based on a more abstract axial systemization of general rules. Theorists of moral development such as Lawrence Kohlberg, Gilligan maintains, wrongfully identify these different moral systems not as coequal but as lesser or more fully matured developmental stages. Kohlberg might well take comfort from the existence of hundreds of years of political theory on his side. The heroes, rulers, princes, and virtuous citizens of Western political theory are not those who

The authors thank Joan Brumberg, Zillah Eisenstein, Davydd Greenwood, Peter Katzenstein, and the volume's editors, Eva Feder Kittay and Diana Meyers for their useful comments.

gave up lives, throne, and kingdom for the love of woman, friend, neighbor, or child. If the heroes of Western political theory sacrificed their personhood, it was in the pursuit of a "larger" glory—the conquest of nations or the well-being of the state. The hero was to be above family or personal ties. "Ties" after all, bind, limit, and constrict. The hero devoted himself to serving a cause greater than the well-being of self, or by extension, lover or family. Hanna Pitkin writes:

> From the political ideals of ancient Athens to their recent revival by Hannah Arendt, republican activism seems to be linked to 'manly' heroism and military glory and to disdain for the household, the private, the personal and the sensual. [1984, p. 5]

Were a morality of caring to be a core principle of a fully developed political theory, it would challenge the republican "disdain for the household, the private . . ." Feminist political theory, as it now stands, is hardly homogeneous. It is built on different theories of human nature, different conceptions of material and ideological forces, different views of the proper role of the state. (Jagger 1983). But a common thread in these theories is a shared refusal to ignore the household or to trivialize the personal. Those theories based on gender difference rather than gender sameness have, not surprisingly, given much attention to family and personal life (of both the psyche and the body).

In an important way, then, Gilligan's portrayal of the female mode of moral reasoning is in part confirmed by the very history and rhetoric of feminist politics. Summarizing the ideological history of the contemporary women's movement in the United States from a perspective of its moral "voice," we note two trends: (1) As has been accurately and vividly described elsewhere (H. Eisenstein 1980), feminism has moved from an attachment to ideals of androgyny to a debate over norms of difference; (2) the movement has also shifted from a commitment to ideals of individual rights to an insistence on moralities of caring.

In the earliest period of feminism's second wave (the mid- to late 1960s), feminists spoke the language of androgyny and sounded the rhetoric of abstract rights. The National Organization of Women (NOW) and feminist lobbies in Washington focused, during their first decade, on equal opportunities in employment and education. Matters traditionally defined as family issues were given little attention. Indeed, both the larger national groups (NOW, Women's Equity action League, and others) and the smaller consciousness-raising groups seemed to harbor a "disdain for family" that Pitkin speaks of as characterizing centuries of Western theory. But there was reason why this had to be the case. Before the family could be discussed in ways that could recreate intimacy free of women's subordination, the family had to be "deconstructed." As this project of "deconstruction" proceeded (with its attention to women's personal feeling and sexual experiences, with its analysis of heterosexuality and homosexuality) discussions of family and motherhood could once again become legitimate. By the mid-1970s, Adrienne Rich could thus criticize the experience of motherhood as found in patriarchy, but see in women's maternity the potential for unique joy and richness of life. (Rich 1976).

In search of new moralities of caring, feminism turned increasingly from arguments of sameness to ideas of difference. (Costain, forthcoming; Eisenstein 1980). By the mid- to late 1970s, the amount of writing that developed the thesis of women's difference expanded substantially within varied political concerns: spiritual feminism explored the possibility of women's alternative consciousness—what Mary Daly called the "spring into free space" (Echols 1984, p. 53).[1] Ecofeminism and pacifist feminists traced women's abhorrence of violence and aggression to their connection to nature and maternal experience. Conservative feminists sought to reclaim women's domestic role in the name of feminism. And a new body of radical feminist writing saw men and women defined by their sexuality into political opposites (with men driven by aggressive, irresponsible genital sexuality). This view was, in turn, vehemently criticized by other feminists (sometimes termed "pro-sex") who denounced these radical feminists as antisex and as absolutist, preaching a prescriptive morality that obscured individual differences in sexual tastes and preferences.[2]

Thus, there has been nothing simple about the evolution of contemporary feminist theory. Early ideas of androgyny that underlay the mobilization around equality at the work place appeared inattentive to issues of family and personhood. And yet arguments of difference embraced moralities of caring that had ambiguous implications for feminism. On the one hand, antifeminist Phyllis Schlafly's exhortation that women's special service to society lay with mothering and wifehood promised to return women to past inequalities.[3] On the other hand, spiritual, ecological, radical and conservative feminists insisted that they were speaking for difference in the name of feminism. Prosex feminists, to complicate the picture further, spoke against feminist advocates of sexual difference also in the name of difference. The issue of who spoke for women, who could claim to be on the side of feminist progress, and who spoke the language of political reaction became completely contested territory.

Despite these polemics, the political debate itself lent confirmation to a central Gilligan theme: all sides seemed to have agreed that caring and responsibility formed a focal point for feminist politics. Fundamental to this shared moral perspective was the conviction that the care and responsibility owed was not preeminently to principles of right or justice abstracted from their social context but was to ideas conjoined with named (and hence contextualized) persons—family, lovers, schoolchildren, victims of sexual violence, etc. Central to this conviction was the belief that the private and public spheres could not be set apart. To foster mutual caring and responsibility in the private domain required the exercise of political power on the public stage. To achieve responsibility and caring in public life demanded that values learned and exercised in personal relationships and family life had to be transported into public arenas of authority.

It is the feminist commitment to moralities of caring *based on gender and sexual difference*[4] that engages us most directly in this chapter. On the one hand, arguments of difference (rather than sameness) seem to promise to evoke a female world of caring relationships and, yet, on the other hand, difference implies too readily a continuation of female subordination. We turn therefore to two particular cases that will allow us to question how moralities of caring based on gender difference have in fact been incorporated into political programs and events.

We propose, then, to focus our attention on the political manifestations of moralities of caring in two very different political contexts. The first is the movement among suffragists at the turn of the century that argued for enfranchisement on grounds that giving women voting rights would, among other things, strengthen the family, and permit greater attention to the needs of education, home, and children. These suffragists did not overtly challenge the long standing authority of separate spheres. Rather, they saw in women's separate and special place in society the possibility for creating a new morality and a reformed world. In our second case, we look at the present day antipornography movement that expresses a morality of caring by its insistence that the personal is political. Their appeal has been based on the moral premise that care and responsibility can only take place when sexual relationships are nonviolent, making possible equal dignity for both sexes. Antipornography proponents, too, have built their arguments around assumptions of gender and sexual difference, viewing pornography as the outcome of and instrument to preserve a sexually dichotomous and gender-stratified world. Women's sexual gentleness and capacity for intimacy, it is argued, can be practiced only when male sexual violence has been countered.

Our concern is with the question of where these gender-defined moralities of caring leave women. We come to this concern because as students of politics, we know the deep antagonisms that result from an aggrieved group claiming its moral perspectives to be equally valid to those held by the dominant group of society. These claims have been made in the past by representatives of ethnic groups (blacks in the United States; Basques in Spain; French in Canada; Tamils in Sri Lanka), and they have usually been associated with intergroup suspicions and violence. An oft-cited study in political science (Rabushka and Shepsle 1972) argues that democratic societies cannot survive when groups make claims based on their distinctive cultural or moral outlook; and a prominent anthropologist has claimed that such appeals to difference are exemplifications of a sick society, one which hasn't reached "civil" status. (Geertz 1973)

But the claims of moral difference hold other threats as well. For women (as for Basques, blacks, etc.) an emphasis on a moral perspective that is gender- or culture-related may obscure the differences between the haves and the have-nots within each group. So too, as Marxists have pointed out, such claims to moral difference may make alliances between have-nots of different groups more difficult to construct. But claims to moral or cultural difference (or superiority) have for women a particularly reactionary potential. Particular to women is the problem that claims of moral difference, based on the importance of family and personal ties, carries the ever present possibility of reinforcing rather than challenging existing systems of gender stratification. The question is then presented: under what formulations are arguments of moral difference likely to serve progressive ends and when are they likely to fulfill counter-progressive or reactionary purposes?

Thus, we are alerted to a major question in feminist political theory. Can an ethic of caring (for family, close friends) and can an effort to recreate the capacity for intimacy be combined with a commitment to a political program that delinks the "natural" and binding association of women to domestic roles? To answer this question, we must reconceptualize it. Rather than inquire whether moralities of caring based on gender difference are (simply) progressive or reactionary, we need to ask what conditions must be met in order for such moralities to be considered more (or less) of the former than of the latter?

The cases we have picked to discuss are, in a sense (and this is what makes them especially interesting), biased towards a more reactionary "outcome." Both cases advance arguments of gender difference rather than sameness and both are thus more likely to invite a return to old patterns, modes, and values that associate women with domestic, private concerns. We will thus need to ask to what extent the moral arguments to support suffrage in the early twentieth century or the movement of the 1980s to repress pornography can be seen, from an historical point of view, as progressive forces. To answer this question, we work to specify some preliminary criteria as to what would constitute a progressive or rectionary claim and examine these two particular claims of moral difference with an eye to whether their political programs meet such criteria.

Consider the following criteria:

(1) *Claims to moral distinctiveness by a group are progressive when they portray the group's social and political role in a dynamic, not static manner.* The idealization of a group's past may help to mobilize it into a reassertion of rights and privileges. But for a movement to be progressive, it must focus on the expansion of opportunities, the enrichment of autonomy, and not merely on the recalibrating of opportunity and autonomy at past levels. Moralities of caring tied to gender difference must attempt to foster intimacy and caring in personal relations among and between adults and children but, in so doing, cannot continue to restrict women to the primary caretaking role in these relationships.

(2) *Claims to moral distinctiveness by a group are progressive when its leaders seek to nurture and promote diversity across its ranks and to remedy differences in mobility prospects vertically among its members.* To promote diversity of tastes, interests and culture among a group's membership cannot be confused with or obscure the need to address inequality of well-being among a group's membership. The organizing of feminist events by both black and white women, for instance, may help to promote horizontal diversity. But vertical equality will be served only if both speak for the least privileged and only if they are ready to act on those claims.

(3) *Claims to moral distinctiveness by a group are progressive when its political project involves entry into an alliance or historical bloc that is committed to the expansion of opportunities and political power for other disadvantaged classes or groups.* While coalitions with some nonprogressive groups that have re-

sources and power are often necessary for tactical reasons, a movement that compromises its autonomy (or alternatively simply sustains its independence) by an alliance with a group committed to political suppression of other low-strata groups cannot be considered progressive.

These criteria constitute, in our judgment, the defining characteristics of a culturally or gender-based political movement that seeks to play a progressive role in the politics of its society. However tentative or arbitrary, we shall move on to examine our two cases in the American women's movement with an eye to sorting out their progressive and reactionary strands. In general, the suffrage arguments will be found to have a progressive slant, more so than is generally presumed; similarly, the antipornography movement will be found to have progressive possibilities as well as an ominous reactionary dimension. Our overall conclusion is that a morality of caring based on ideas of difference—despite a nervousness by many political scientists and anthropologists—should not be too easily dismissed as reactionary ideology.

Suffrage, Social Housekeeping, and Moralities of Caring

Support for suffrage came out of several different theoretical positions. Some argued for enfranchisment on the basis of individual rights; others on the basis of the special contribution women might make in the public sphere. But no argument made by suffragists ignored the family. Elizabeth Cady Stanton (often seen as the leading proponent of an individual rights approach) devoted considerable thought to how the family might be changed to accommodate values of equality. Those who argued the case of women's special morality took a seemingly more conservative perspective on the family that appeared to invite the perpetuation of women's and men's separate spheres. This more conservative version of a caring morality is what we concern ourselves with here: what was it, and was it in its time, in fact, reactionary?

> DO YOU KNOW that extending the suffrage to women increases the moral vote; that in all states and countries that have adopted equal suffrage the vote of disreputable women is practically negligible, the slum wards of cities invariably having the lightest women vote and the respectable residence wards the heaviest; that only one out of every twenty criminals are women; that women constitute a minority of drunkards and petty misdemeanants; that for every prostitute there are at least two men responsible for her immorality; that in all the factors that tend to handicap the progress of society, women form a minority, whereas in churches, schools and all organizations working for the uplift of humanity, women are a majority? [Catt 1913, p. 9]

The elitist voice in Catt's appeal runs alongside the parallel appeal to women's special moral vision. Later, we take up the issue of racism and class exclusiveness. But first, we turn to the claims of women's moral voice. The "social housekeeping" dimension of the suffrage argument maintained that women's particular concerns with child labor, the exploitation of working mothers, decent standards of housing, and corruption in government constituted the preeminent reason for bringing women into the public domain. But was this social housekeeping argument, tied as it appeared to be to the distinction between the sexes, bound to maintain women's subordinate place in society? We turn to the three criteria offered earlier by which we argue that progressive and reactionary claims can be distinguished.

Did the argument of social housekeeping constitute a dynamic rather than static argument about women's place in American society? This "stasis" view would contend that as long as the argument for suffrage came out of a world view that posited women's and men's nature as different, the basic separation of spheres would go unchallenged. This first response relates to what suffragists may have *hoped* to achieve. The second argument is largely about what women did or did not achieve. Here, it has been argued that women did not "win" the vote but were "given" it for reasons unrelated to the recognition of gender claims. (Ginsberg 1982). This argument suggests further that, once "given" suffrage, women did little with it to venture outside the confines of the private sphere (as evidenced in part by the low percentages of women voting upon enfranchisement). (O'Neill 1969) We argue against these interpretations of suffrage.

On the first point, it seems clear that when exponents of social housekeeping referred to the difference in women's and men's natures, they did not feel tht these differences need confine women to the home. The social housekeeping argument grew naturally out of, but was very different from, the cult of domesticity which Charlotte Perkins Gilman had so scathingly criticized. (O'Neill 1969, p. 43) What the social housekeeping argument demanded was a place for women in the public domain. This was its radical contribution. From the vantage point of the 1980s, it is too easy to dismiss the nineteenth century demand for the vote as asking for something that could scarcely be termed radical. But at the turn of the century, the recognition of the right to a public voice—to participate in the affairs of men—constituted a radical break from the social order of the past. (Katzenstein 1984)

Had suffrage meant less, it would likely not have involved seven decades of active organization and the mass mobilization of women. (Catt 1923, p. 107). It is that long-waged extraordinary campaign that makes us reject the second "conservative argument"—that suffrage was bestowed, not won. This argument about the bestowal of suffrage by elites has been advanced in a provocative study of electoral institutions by political scientist Ben Ginsberg. (Ginsberg, 1982). He contends that enfranchisement often occurs because political elites seek to assert political control over new constituencies. Thus, he argues (convincingly) that there is reason to be skeptical when the Democratic party urged on the nation a lowering of the voting age in the 1960s since no such demand was forthcoming from the student movement. But the suffrage movement wanted *suffrage*—and it took over half a century and

> fifty-six campaigns of referenda to male voters, 480 campaigns to urge legislatures to submit suffrage amendments to voters; 47 campaigns to

> induce state constitutional conventions to write women suffrage into state constitutions; 277 campaigns to persuade state party conventions to include women suffrage planks; 30 campaigns to urge presidential party conventions to adopt women suffrage planks in party platforms and 19 campaigns with 19 successive Congresses. [Catt 1923, p. 107]

No doubt there were political elites who thought they could benefit from women's enfranchisement. Some elites probably took seriously the suffragist "promise" that women's enfranchisement would help to counter the black and immigrant vote. Others, whether or not they were influenced by the feminist "extremists" who chained themselves to the White House fence, fasted, and publicly burned Wilson's speeches on democracy, no doubt felt that women's support and labor were needed for the war effort and that enfranchisement would be a reasonable *quid pro quo*. But the point is that all nations at war needed the support of their female populations; and yet, it was England and the United States (where the feminist movement had been extremely active), rather than France or Italy (where feminists were less conspiciously organized), that "gave" women the vote. What this suggests is that the mobilization of women, at the least, worked to shape elite perceptions of how they might "control" women's support.[6]

Suffragists, we thus argue, won the right to vote. And although they did not immediately fall headlong into active participation in electoral politics, women certainly used their right to fuller participation in the public sphere. The final point that must be made here is that it is likely that only particular suffrage arguments would have mobilized the multitude of women whose numbers made the issue of wartime support in exchange for suffrage a bargaining point: it was the incorporation of the "morality of caring" into the suffrage claim that helped to turn the movement from its limited size at the turn of the century into a mass effort. (O'Neill 1969, pp. 50-51) Like temperance campaigns that had always drawn numbers far in excess of the suffrage movement in the latter half of the century, the social housekeeping phase of the suffragist movement was able to attract women into the campaign who otherwise might have found suffrage threatening their attachment to the family. (Degler 1980, p. 359)

Although women did not vote in the numbers expected they were hardly passive actors in the political arena. Women were the major force behind preventive health legislation, the long fought (and still unsuccessful) campaign for equal rights, and the move to establish protective legislation. The movement of women into the public domain, begun in the nineteenth century, was thus given constitutional authority with the 19th amendment.[7]

Our second criterion—that women's claims advance diversity without aggravating class inequality—is more controversial. The suffrage movement made room for ideological diversity across the movement's leadership. In the nineteenth century, suffragists included those who supported temperance and those who did not; those who were ready to support advocates of free love and those who were not; those who were critical of the churches and those who were not. There were debates, then, and sometimes tempestuous ones. But there was still room for considerable diversity. Social housekeeping suffragists were generally critical of, but did not set out to undo, the activities of the extremists. While Carrie Chapman Catt sought to work with President Wilson to win over his support of the vote, members of the Woman's Party demonstrated feverishly outside the White House, fasted, and went to jail. But the diversity of views and/or tactics was tolerated and militant homogeneity eschewed.

But on issues of race and social class, suffragist spokeswomen were less ready to be open-minded. Carrie Chapman Catt joined social housekeeping arguments with strong expressions of elitism. Insisting that women had learned invaluable capacities for love and service as rearers and caretakers of children, she then maintained that government faced a great danger from

> votes possessed by the males in the slums of the cities and the ignorant foreign vote. . . . There is but one way to avert the danger—cut off the vote of the slums and give to women . . . the power of protecting herself that man has secured for himself—the ballot. [Kraditor 1965, pp. 110, 125]

In the twenty years before passage of the 19th amendment, suffrage was all too often advanced on grounds that the illiterate, Negro, and foreign male vote could be countered through the enfranchisement of educated women. Even working-class advocates like Florence Kelley, who railed against treating poor and foreign women as an undifferentiated mass, argued for the imposition of an educational requirement at the ballot place. (Kraditor 1965, p. 139)

In other respects, however, suffrage proved an avenue that connected the lives of middle-class and working women. The need to mobilize large numbers of supporters made it possible for individuals like Gertrude Barnum to argue against the xenophobia of her suffragist, middle-class sisters. At the 1906 convention of the National American Women Suffrage Association (NAWSA). Barnum insisted, "We have been preaching to wage earning women, teaching them, rescuing them, doing almost everything for them except knowing them and working with them for the good of the country." (Rothman 1978, p. 129). Eventually, some working-class advocates like Harriet Stanton Blatch left NAWSA to found independent local suffrage societies that would address working-class women directly. Historian Ellen Dubois (1984) makes an interesting case that the "militant" strategies of the suffrage movement (parades, street corner rallies) were actions middle-class suffragists learned from their working-class associates.

Although working-class issues were not seriously addressed by most suffragists, and although the participation of working-class women in suffrage organizations was erratic, it would be wrong to see suffrage simply as the political vehicle of white middle-class women.

Suffrage did, for example, lead indirectly to the participation of lower middle-class women in programs designed to assist the poor. In 1921, erstwhile suffragist supporters of the Sheppard-Towner Act won a stunning victory. The legislation not only brought the state into the business of preventive medicine with its funding of community health centers, but in the process, the act gave numbers of women a primary position as midwives and public health nurses in community health care.[8]

Suffragists, then, were not made from a single mold. Support for enfranchisement came from those who were advocates of different causes and different strategies. And suffrage found its spokeswomen among some who were quick to use arguments of racism and elitism and some whose values were far less easily seen as self-serving.

Although the racist and xenophobic strain of suffragist rhetoric remains a counter to the claim that social housekeeping was clearly progressive, this reactionary dimension of the suffragist argumentation can be better understood—although not explained away—by an understanding of the suffragists' political position. Had the suffragists been able to locate powerful allies in its claim to women's voting rights, it might have been less readily drawn to reactionary appeals. Suffragists had formed successful alliances with the Progressives. But (despite the very late concession of the Republican and Democratic parties to include suffrage in their platforms), no major political party had thrown itself behind women's enfranchisement. As Elizabeth Cady Stanton's daughter, Harriet Stanton Blatch commented, Negro enfranchisement had been championed by a major political party; so had the farm labor enfranchisement in England where Blatch saw the Liberal party under Gladstone extend the vote despite the fact that "only a few of the disfranchised class were active." She writes: "What a contrast the women suffrage movement! Perhaps some day men will raise a tablet reading in letters of gold: "All honor to women, the first disfranchised class in history who unaided by any political party won enfranchisement by its own effort alone." (Blatch/Lutz 1940, p. 293)

As Catt too described it, the effective alliances were the ones against the suffragist cause—the alliances of the brewers interest, workingmen, immigrants, etc. Had the suffragists found responsive allies in either of the major political parties, perhaps they would have felt it less necessary or expedient to use the appeals of race and class snobism in their effort to woo public opinion to their cause. The lack of support from party quarters helped edge suffragists into other opportunistic positions. NAWSA, Mary Ryan observes, withdrew from women's peace organizations at the outbreak of World War I, in order not to alienate President Wilson and potential supporters in Congress. (Ryan 1975, p. 245) These kinds of political pressure did not force suffragists into positions they found totally alien. But it would be naive on our part to think that suffrage organizers, at their cause for so long and with so little evidence of success, might not have tried, lawyer-like, a range of arguments, including reactionary ones, in the hope that something might move the deeply resistant political powers in American society.

The three criteria set out above help us to offer an historical account of social housekeeping and the use of a gender-linked caring morality that avoids a characterization of the movement as *either* progressive *or* reactionary. Rather, it allows us to specify more carefully the different dimensions of each element within the historical period being described. By the first criterion, suffragists clearly put moralities of caring to progressive usage: social housekeeping gave women the justification to enter the world of men—an argument that sought, despite its "separate spheres," rhetoric to change the status quo. By the second criterion, suffrage arguments come out as both forward looking and reactionary: a diversity of causes were espoused in connection with social housekeeping, and yet many of the main spokeswomen for suffrage fell into a pattern of political claims that used race and class appeals unabashedly. By our third criterion, exponents of a caring morality could not be considered reactionary. They did not go out searching for antiprogressive allies. In fact, early social housekeeping advocates had looked to Progressive party advocates for support. Unable to find sponsorship of women's emancipation in the major parties, however, suffragists lapsed into an opportunistic political rhetoric that seriously detracted from their otherwise progressive historical role.

The Morality of Caring and the Antipornography Movement

The criteria we have specified above can be of particular use in a discussion of an issue like the antipornography campaigns of the last few years because they help us to avoid the kind of blanket characterizations that come too easily when polemics are intense. And such is surely the case of the present debate around pornography.

The antipornography "cause," which has long had supporters, picked up momentum with the proposal of Catharine MacKinnon and Andrea Dworkin that offered a civic ordinance making pornography a justiciable act of sex discrimination.[9] This movement represents one embodiment of a morality of caring. The symbolic power of this political crusade has appalled many of those who think in terms of abstract rights. The model antipornography ordinances, which are written in the language of rights, sound strained and unconvincing in their constitutional appeals. Without the counterpart moral message, these ordinances would ring hollow. For the moral message is that the unit of responsibility and care—that group with whom one has sexual or sensual relations—must be based on tenderness, not violence; equality, not hierarchy. The social construction of a kin-based network worthy of care and responsibility is the symbolic appeal—it seems to us—to the antipornography movement.

Not only is antipornography a powerful movement among women because it is built on a morality of caring, but it also mobilizes women with its emphasis on the notion of gender difference. As the writing of both Dworkin and MacKinnon suggest, antipornography is a public response warranted by the sexual differences that position women as victims of aggressive male sexuality. "Sexuality," MacKinnon writes, "is that social process which creates, organizes, expresses, and directs desire, creating the social beings we know as women and men as their relations create society" (MacKinnon 1983, 228). Just as work defines the difference for Marxist analysis between those who exploit and those exploited, so for MacKinnon, sex divides classes into "relations in which . . . some fuck and others get fucked." Although this analysis is not part and parcel, by any means, of the much more subdued rhetoric of the civic ordinances Dworkin and MacKinnon have authored, gender difference is indeed embodied in the proposed legislation. According to the ordinance, pornography is not sex-neutral. It means [only] "the graphic, sexually explicit subordination of women." (MacKinnon 1984, p. 501) It is discimination against *women* which MacKinnon and Dworkin seek to bar.[10] Because this movement has been so threatening to many members and allies of the women's movement who see it as nothing more than a bald attack on the First Amendment, it is important to evaluate it on the broader criteria we have developed. It is to this task we now turn.

The suffrage movement served a dynamic function by authorizing women's right to a place in domains from which they had been excluded. But does the antipornography movement help in some analagous fashion to push the boundaries outwards, permitting women greater opportunities in previously inaccessible or restricted realms? The negative response to this question (which we do not share) is that antipornography, at best, concerns the private, nonmaterial dimensions of women's lives and offers to protect women as though they were children. (Friedan 1985) At worst, the movement against pornography is seen as regulating, restricting that which women may choose to view, read, or think and distorting sexual pleasure into an ever present fear of sexual danger. (Vance 1984)

But we find neither of these arguments persuasive, and contend instead that at least on this first dimension—the generation of dynamic social change—antipornography politics must be seen as progressive. Friedan's relegation of pornography to the status of the immaterial rests on her assumption that sex is a private, personal matter and that it is less basic to women's subordination than material (economic) factors. It must be recognized, however, that just as women's opportunities in the nineteenth century depended on their success in establishing a claim to autonomy within the public domain, so women's claims now depend on their ability to evoke public (although not necessarily state) authority in the service of ending women's subordination in the private sphere. Women's sexual subordination in personal relations may be outside the realm of agreed upon issues demanding public action (pay, employment, welfare support of indigent mothers); but it is this very definition of what is properly political that feminist ethics of caring is attempting to address.

That sexuality is immaterial, in the sense of being peripheral to the way people make their living, is also unpersuasive. Leaving aside the fact that producers of pornography make a decent living from their four billion dollar industry (Almquist 1985, p. 42), it is simply undeniable that pornography is part and parcel of a sexual system of power that subordinates women. We need not go as far as MacKinnon and argue that sexuality is at the root of women's oppression.[11] The point is, however, that pornography is one of the significant causes (as well as mirrors) of a system that eroticizes sexual violence and sustains the continued physical and psychological derogation of women.[12]

In two senses, violent, women-degrading pornography is part of the causal chain in the system of women's subordination. First, purely at the level of ideas, violent pornography helps to maintain a normative order based on the making of sexual violence into erotica. Here a distinction between power and violence must be made. There is much that many women and men find erotic in the display of sexual and other manifestations of power. But when that display of sexual power causes harm, as is so much more likely to be the case when violent sexuality is depicted, pornography must be deemed unacceptable. Eva Feder Kittay argues:

> Regardless of how we draw the line between a legitimate and illegitimate sexuality, it appears that there are nonsexual grounds, purely moral considerations which apply to human actions and intentions, that render some sexual acts illegitimate—illegitimate by virtue of the moral impermissibility of harming another person and particularly for the pleasure of obtaining pleasure or other benefit from the harm another incurs. [1983 p. 150]

Second, at the level of behavior, it may be difficult to trace the link between word and deed—to predict as MacKinnon says which man will go out and rape after reading pornography (Blakely 1985, p. 40); but there *is* (laboratory) evidence from the studies of N. Malamuth and C. Donnerstein that pornographic viewing increases male acceptance of violence against women, that attitudes change as a result of exposure to pornography.[13] (MacKinnon 1984, p. 504)

If the antipornography movement helps to curtail these two forms of harm, it has moved women and men to a more elevated plateau of moral behavior. If it has helped to break down one link in the chain of sexual subordination (of which, rape, battering, harassment, incest are all a part), it has also created a dynamic for change in multiple domains of women's lives.

Although some might argue that the link in the chain that must be broken should be the sexual "act" (of prostitution, harassment, rape, battery) rather than the "depiction" of sexual violence, there are indeed good arguments for identifying pornography as a crucial link that can help to unravel the chain. What antipornography proponents have understood is that a campaign around pornography can have far greater mobilizational impact than similar campaigns against other forms of sexual abuse. Prostitution is too easily "ghettoized"—seen as limited to seamy neighborhoods and targeting only "bad girls" as its victims. Even rape (acknowledged to victimize more than just "bad girls" and recognized as widespread in its occurrence) is still often seen as a crime perpetrated by deviant, lawless men, someone else's husband or brother. But even though antipornography critics maintain that antipornography campaigns revitalize the notion of sex perverts committing sex crimes, such a notion is not easy to sustain. Pornography is commonplace—found in your son's bedroom, at the neighborhood drugstore, in the locker, the dormitory room, and now on television. If Jerry Falwell is right, one quarter of all pornography sold is marketed through 7-Eleven stores. (MacNeil-Lehrer Report 1985) If pornography is violence against women, then such violence is more likely to be seen as part of the fabric of society than rape or other forms of sexual abuse.

But if pornography is progressive on the first dimension (broadening the realms within which women can be equal), what about the second dimension we have identified: does the antipornography movement counter diversity? It is interesting that among feminists, the most vehement criticism of antipornography comes from those who share with antipornography proponents a belief that sexuality (albeit socially constructed) is absolutely crucial to the subordination of women. Their argument, however, is that antipornography further subordinates, rather than liberates, women (a) by identifying sex as danger to be feared and avoided, and (b) by its apparent assertion that only egalitarian, nonviolent sex is legitimate. (Vance 1984; Levine 1985)

This argument is real. There are clearly adherents of sado-masochism who mutually desire violent sex and for whom such sex is not harmful.[14] But to the extent that pornography both maintains a normative order that legitimizes the eroticization of violence, and to the extent that it constitutes even a remote cause of violent, nonconsensual, nondesired sex, the "rights" of such adherents to acquire pornographic products deemed important for their sexual gratification must take second place. It is surprising that while pro-sex advocates are ready to state that what is seen as violent by some may be pleasure for others, they are less ready to acknowledge that what is pleasure for some may be violence for others.[15] Racist cartoons abusive of minorities may and do give pleasure to some. But such rights to pleasure must surely be subordinated to the more fundamental right to be free from serious harm. From this point of view, there is a blindness in the pro-sex argument. Pro-sex theorists argue that sexual mores are not natural, but are socially constructed. They are reluctant to acknowledge, however, that sexual violence as a source of sexual pleasure too is socially constructed, and that therefore it can be politically deconstructed. What is the moral difference, they may ask themselves, between the social legitimation of nonheterosexual relations (one of their projects) and the delegitimation of violent sexual relations (the antipornography project)? If pro-sex advocates insisted that pornographic depiction did not cause violent behavior, their position would be more comprehensible.

Our final point here is that while the antipornography movement has made little attempt to mobilize support across socio-economic groups, the issue of pornography is certainly relevant across all strata of society.[16] Given the right linkages, it could well generate working-class as well as middle-class support. In any case, unlike the suffragist case discussed above, there is no outright racism or xenophobia embodied in the antipornography effort.

But the progressive character of the antipornography campaign falters on our third criterion. It is clear that an antipornography movement is found to invite reactionary alliances. Even if antipornography feminists endeavored to disassociate themselves from conservative "anti-smut" moralists as they did in Suffolk County (but did not do in Indianapolis where feminists worked with Beulah Coughenour, a Stop-ERA activist), the right can inevitably be expected to form a common cause even if not an outright alliance with feminist antipornography activists.[17] It is hardly a surprise that no lesser light than Jerry Falwell has spoken in praise of the feminist effort to bar pornography, and that the right has launched a campaign of its own against pornography kings and distributors. (MacNeil-Lehrer Report 1985). This interest from the right was bound to be sparked, whatever form a feminist antipornography campaign was to take.

But the fact that the feminist antipornography movement has pursued civic ordinances that would bar pornography makes the issue of alliances a deeply troubling one and inviting of more reactionary outcomes than if state authority were not to be invoked. By seeking to legitimize the use of state censorship, feminist antipornographers place in the hands of the right a new set of political instruments whose purpose can be put to quite different purposes from those feminists themselves intended.[18]

With the moral majority's interest in resurrecting a moral America, it is worrisome that censorship of pornographic materials could lead easily into censorship of erotica, health education, lesbian and gay literature, and, indeed, to the closing down of many a feminist bookstore. It could be a small step to the censorship of literature depicting homosexual intimacy on grounds that it promotes violence by encouraging sexual practices that cause the proliferation of AIDS.

The reply to these fears by antipornography advocates is that the ordinances are specific enough to bar only women-degrading (or violent and women-degrading) materials. But the distinction between sexually explicit materials that dehumanize women as sexual objects and those that are merely sexually explicit or erotic is not easily specified. Similarly the difference between violently degrading materials and those that are "merely" degrading can be highly contentious. To make these distinctions in clear, legally applicable language requires tools and indeed the motivation to "limit" the ban on pornography strictly to certain categories of sexually explicit material. In a political context in which the state is constituted by few feminists so motivated, it is naive to think that feminist antipornography proponents can keep control of how a ban on sexually explicit literature will be interpreted and used.

By the three criteria we have identified, then, the antipornography mobilization must be seen as incorporating both progressive and reactionary elements. It does offer a radical challenge to a system that helps to subordinate women by making sexual violence erotic; and it subdues diversity only to safeguard women against serious harm. But these progressive or at least acceptably nonreactionary features of the antipornography movement must be seen alongside the problems identified by our third criterion: the existence of unavoidable linkages to repressive alliances that can utilize new sources of state authority.

To label suffrage progressive due to its mobilizational successes, or the antipornography movement reactionary due to its approval by the Reverend Falwell, is to ignore the complex strands woven by any social movement. Clearly there are progressive and reactionary fibers connected with any social movement. In our discussion of suffrage and pornography, we have tried to demonstrate this complexity through a contextualized discussion of the three strands within each movement.

Conclusion

Our perusal of the moral foundation of feminist political discourse confirms Carol Gilligan's central claim—that women reach moral maturity when they "see the actors in (a moral) dilemma arrayed not as opponents in a contest of rights (as do men) but as members of a network of relationships on whose continuation they all depend." (Gilligan 1982, p. 30) We saw in the suffrage movement an exemplification of this point; women felt comfortable making self-interest claims for the vote based on their moral perspective of social housekeeping. We also saw that in the early periods of the feminist revival of the 1960s, there was an attempt to reject a special women's morality. These feminists spoke the (male) language of rules and abstract rights. But the absence of a morality of caring left the women's movement without its own voice. From the left and right, as we saw, feminists quickly brought back the women's moral voice in political discourse. In this sense, women today have reached a new equilibrium—with their own voice—and Gilligan's work has enabled us to see this continuing moral fiber of feminist politics.

But Gilligan wants more than a distinctive women's voice in politics. She is quite explicit in her hopes that the recognition of this "different voice" will "lead to a changed understanding of human development and a more *generative* view of human life." (Gilligan p. 174, emphasis ours) This suggests to us that Gilligan intends that her findings *not* be used to defend the status quo or to bring back some mythical past. Rather, she sees her finding as opening up opportunities for women to use their voice to reform and broaden both public and private domains. Obviously, however, Gilligan's findings can serve as ammunition for reactionary as well as generative purposes. The question we have asked is whether we could state the criteria by which political claims by women based on a moral claim of difference can be judged as helping to create a world of greater vision and opportunity.

Gilligan does not address herself to this question. Her discussion leaves us with just a hope, but not a vision of how her findings could lead to a politics in which an "ethic of care rest[ing] on the premise of non-violence—that no one should be hurt," (Gilligan p. 174) might come about. To be sure, all politics is contextual and the same politics emerging in different settings can often serve very different interests. Nonetheless, it is important to specify criteria by which we can judge feminist political claims so that a work as significant as Gilligan's not be used merely to arrest the advances of women in modern America. We have therefore attempted to state criteria by which to evaluate the political meaning of feminist claims. We have contended that an ethic of responsibility and care is compatible with a more progressive politics when its claims (a) permit a dynamic role for women who employ their voice in an expanding number of public and private domains; (b) permit diversity among all women without ignoring the demands of the poor; and (c) are part of an historic bloc that is sensitive to the constraints faced by other social and cultural groups seeking justice for their causes. With these guidelines, we feel, an ethic of care can be conjoined with a politics of progress.

Notes

1. For a discussion of spiritual feminism, see Spretnak 1982; Ochs 1983.
2. Jean Elshtain's work best exemplifies what we call conservative feminism: a desire to maintain a division between private and public based on a strong family

system built around distinctive male and female roles. (Elshtain 1981a, 1981b) What makes her writing feminist and not simply conservative is the critique she develops of women's historical oppression (including her use of such words as "oppression") and her desire to see the private sphere not limit women as it has done in the past. It is unclear, however, how the division of private and public that she envisions, based as it is on a view of women's and men's biologically-founded separate identities, will, in fact, prove more emancipatory than earlier paradigms. (Cohen and Katzenstein, forthcoming) For a discussion of eco-feminism, see Ynestra King, "Feminism and the Revolt of Nature," *Heresies* 13; for a discussion of the relationship of mothering to pacifism, see Sara Ruddick, 1982; for a discussion of radical or cultural feminism, see Echols, 1984 and her essay in Snitow, 1983.

3. See Zillah Eisenstein (1984) for a distinction between conservative, revisionary feminists.

4. The phrase, "moralities of caring based on gender/sex difference" requires further explication. By this phrase, we refer to the way in which some 20th century suffragists and 1980s antipornography feminists linked the capacity (or incapacity) to practice a morality of caring and responsibility to inequalities of power between men and women. Some suffragists believed that women were endowed with a special moral voice and unless this voice could be heard in public affairs, public life would continue to be degraded by corruption and grievous social ills. Whether this "voice" was part of women's biological makeup or was acquired experientially is left unclear in much of suffragist writing. Antipornography feminists too argue that the realization of a morality of responsibility based on true intimacy and caring is possible only when society is freed of sexual violence. This in turn is possible when men cease to eroticize violence as part of a quest for power. Antipornography feminists walk both sides of the very fine line between arguments of biologically determined and socially learned behavior. Andrea Dworkin for instance discusses the "immutable self of the male" (1979, p. 13) at the same time that she argues that male identity is "chosen" (1979, p. 49).

Hence we wish to make three points about the phrase "moralities of caring based on gender/sex difference." (1) It is the suffragist/antipornography feminist understanding that unless women acquire greater power, a morality of caring and responsibility cannot be realized; (2) The term, gender/sex difference, which we will shorten to "gender difference" in the text, incorporates both the biological and socially learned understanding of that term; (3) Whether suffragists or antipornography feminists ultimately visualize a society based on androgyny rather than difference is not addressed in this chapter, nor is the question of how men might acquire a capacity for caring and responsibility. The focus of the paper, rather, is on the consequences for women of political programs that grow out of a belief in gender-based moralities of caring. The question we ask is how such programs enhance or diminish women's strength as a collectivity and how such programs shape the kind of power women can exercise.

5. The term social housekeeping is used by Mary P. Ryan, 1975, pp. 193–251.

6. We are not suggesting that there is a unicausal (women's activism or any other single factor) explanation for suffrage. What we are suggesting is that women's mobilization has been an important contributant to the passage of suffrage in particular cases of which the United States was one. For a discussion of the circumstances around the passage of suffrage in different countries, see Lovenduski and Hills (1981).

7. That suffrage challenged the separation of spheres by giving constitutional authorization to women's place in the public domain is clear; whether the ballot *then* became instrumental in the challenge to the separation of spheres—whether that is why women used the vote to endorse or defeat candidates supportive of women's concerns is an interesting and researchable issue but not one addressed here.

8. Florence Kelley was called "the ablest legislative general communism had produced" (Rothman 1978, p. 152). Eight years later, the act was overturned, perhaps because by then congressmen knew they did not need to face the repercussions of a women's bloc vote (Lemons, 1973, pp. 153–81). Soon women's positions in public health were overtaken by private male physicians.

9. For sources, see note 13.

10. One clause in the proposed Minneapolis ordinance (sect. 1, 8, 2) states that "The use of men, children or transexuals in the place of women . . ." is pornography but the ordinance is about sex discrimination and is not set out in sex-neutral terminology.

11. See MacKinnon 1983, and MacKinnon June 1984 in which she says "Male domination permeates everything. There are other major issues such as the ones you mentioned. But as segregation was and is central to the second class status of Black people, pornography is central to the second class status of women. It is its embodiment, its way of being practiced, being made socially real." Critics of the antipornography feminists, however, often go to the other extreme. Vanda Burstyn writes, for instance, "sexist pornography is a product of the economic and social conditions of our society—not vice versa" (1985, p. 24). This position that views words and images as mere reflections of society seems uninformed by the rich insights of poststructuralist feminist criticism.

12. Eva Feder Kittay writes: "As symptom, pornography is reflective of certain social and political relations between men and women; although as a mirror, it reflects through hyperbolic distortions. As a cause, pornography is a contributing factor perpetuating a social order in which men dominate. In its casual aspect, pornography is hate literature . . . and is morally wrong for it contributes to a political and moral injustice" (1983 p. 145).

13. See MacKinnon, "Not a Moral Issue," 1984; MacKinnon 1983; MacKinnon, June 1984; Dworkin 1979; Duggan 1984; Blakely 1985; Copp, ed., 1983 and essays therein; *Harvard Law Review* (unsigned), 1984; Hentoff 1984.

14. See Kittay's analysis of the meaning of harm in this context (1983, pp. 153–54).

15. The prosex refusal to entertain seriously the possibility that pornography promotes attitudes conducive to violence is striking. In an attempted refutation of the charge that pornography may promote sexual violence, one prosex essayist writes, "The idea that every time women get a thrill from watching women TV cops Cagney and Lacey shoot a crime suspect, we want to kill . . . runs counter to most women's experience." (Diamond 1985, p. 47). The point is, rather, how would female viewers react if Cagneys and Laceys were regular fare, their victims sexually violated, their exploits the standard entertainment of groups of teenage girls and adult women? Would we really think such viewing matter completely nonformative of the ideas, values, behavior of Cagney/Lacey fans?

16. See Alice Walker's discussion of pornography (MS, February 1980) and Dworkin (1979).

17. In Indiana where the ordinance passed (but has now been declared unconstitutional) Beulah Coughenour, a Stop-ERA activist, introduced the law locally (Duggan, 1984). In Suffolk County, New York, a much broader antiobscenity measure was recently introduced and defeated. Antipornography feminists opposed the law. (Blakely 1985)

18. An antipornography campaign may usefully attempt to change public understanding of violent sexuality and its eroticization as morally repugnant and harmful to women. As Bryden argues (1985, p. 15), feminists have changed the image of the rapist as a victim of an unjust society to one of the woman as a victim of rape, and

have redefined faculty/student sex from a problem of sexual permissiveness to a problem of sexual exploitation. This change in understanding of pornography may have been advanced by the public stir created over the ordinances. But public mobilization that does not involve the state and thus does not invite the "right" to use the tools of censorship would, we argue, be far preferable.

References

Almquist, Heidi. "The Civil Rights Approach to Control of Pornography." B.A. Honors Thesis, Department of Government, Cornell University, April 1985.

Blakely, Mary Kay. "Is One Woman's Sex Another Woman's Pornography: The Question Behind a Major Legal Battle." *MS*, XII, 16 (April 1985).

Blatch, Harriet Stanton and Alma Lutz. *Challenging Years: The Memoirs of Harriet Stanton Blatch*. New York: G.P. Putnam, 1940.

Bridenthal, Renate. "Professional Housewives: Stepsisters of the Women's Movement," in Renate Bridenthal, Atina Grossman, and Marion Kaplan, eds., *When Biology Became Destiny: Women in Weimar and Nazi Germany*. New York: Monthly Review Press, 1984, pp. 153–74.

Bryden, David. "Between Two Constitutions: Feminism and Pornography." *Constitutional Commentary*, vol. 2, no. 1 (Winter 1985).

Burstyn, Varda, ed. *Women Against Censorship*. Vancouver and Toronto: Douglas and McIntyre, 1985.

Catt, Carrie Chapman. "Do You Know," National American Woman Suffrage Association, 507 Fifth Avenue, New York (1913 [brochure, personal library]).

——— and Nettie Rogers Shuler. *Woman Suffrage and Politics: The Inner Story of the Suffrage Movement*. Seattle: University of Washington Press, 1923.

Cohen, Susan and Mary F. Katzenstein. "The War Over the Family Is Not Over the Family," in Sanford Dornbusch and Myra Strober, eds. *Feminism, Children and the New Families*. New York: Guilford Press, forthcoming.

Copp, D. *Censorship and Pornography*.

Costain, Anne N. "Will the Gender Gap Make Women an Electoral Interest in American Politics?" in Carol Mueller, ed. *The Gender Gap*. Beverly Hills, Calif. Sage Publishing Inc., forthcoming.

Cott, Nancy F. *The Bonds of Womanhood: "Women's Sphere" in New England, 1780–1835*. New Haven: Yale University Press, 1977.

———. "The Crisis in Feminism 1910–1930." Paper presented at the Berkshire Conference, Northampton, Mass., June 2, 1984.

Diamond, Sara, "Pornography, Image, and Reality" in Varda Burstyn et. al., *Women Against Censorship*. Toronto: Douglas & McIntyre, 1985.

De Lesseps, Emmanuele, "Female Reality: Biology or Society?" *Feminist Issues*, 1981, pp. 77–100.

Degler, Carl. *At Odds: Women and the Family in America from the Revolution to the Present*. Oxford: Oxford University Press, 1980.

Dubois, Ellen. "Harriot Stanton Blatch and the Progressive Era Women Suffrage Movement." Paper presented at the Berkshire Conference, Northampton, Mass., June 2, 1984.

Duggan, Lisa. "Censorship in the Name of Feminism." *Village Voice*, October 16, 1984.

Dworkin, Andrea. *Pornography: Men Possessing Women*. New York: G.P. Putnam, 1979.

Echols, Alice. "The Taming of the Id: Feminist Sexual Politics, 1968–83," in Carol Vance, ed., *Pleasure and Danger*. Boston: Routledge and Kegan Paul, 1984.

Eisenstein, Hester and Alice Jardine, eds. *The Future of Difference*. New Brunswick, N.J.: Rutgers University Press, 1980.

Eisenstein, Zillah R. *Feminism and Sexual Equality*. New York: Monthly Review Press, 1984.

Elshtain, Jean Bethke. *Public Man, Private Woman: Women in Social and Political Thought*. Princeton: Princeton University Press, 1981a.

———. "Against Androgyny," *Telos* 47 (Spring, 1981b).

Ferguson, Ann; Ilene Philipson, Irene Diamond, Lee Quimby, Carole S. Vance, and Ann Barr Snitow. "Forum: The Feminist Sexuality Debates," *SIGNS*, no. 10 (Autumn, 1984), pp. 106-36.

Freedman, Estelle. "Separatism as Strategy: Female Institution Building and American Feminism, 1870-1930," *Feminist Studies* 5, no. 3 (Fall, 1979), pp. 512-29.

Freidan, Betty. "How to Get the Women's Movement Moving Again," *New York Times Magazine*, November 3, 1985.

Geertz, Clifford. *The Interpretation of Cultures*. New York: Basic Books, 1973.

Gilligan, Carol. *In a Different Voice: Psychological Theory and Women's Development*. Cambridge: Harvard University Press, 1982.

Ginsberg, Benjamin. *The Consequences of Consent: Elections, Citizen Control and Popular Acquiescence*. Menlo Park, Calif. Addison-Wesley Publishing Co., 1982.

Harvard Law Review (note) "Anti-Pornography Laws and First Amendment Values," vol. 98 (1984), pp. 460-81.

Hentoff, Nat. "Is the First Amendment Dangerous to Women?", *Village Voice*, October 16, 1984.

Jagger, Alison M. *Feminist Politics and Human Nature*. Totowa, N.J.: Rowman and Allanheld, 1983.

Jones, Ann Rosalind. "Writing the Body" in Elaine Showalter, ed. *Feminist Criticism*. New York: Pantheon, 1985.

Katzenstein, Mary Fainsod. "Feminism and the Meaning of the Vote." *SIGNS*, vol. 10, no. 1 (Autumn, 1984), pp. 106-36.

Kittay, Eva Feder. "Pornography and the Erotics of Domination," in Carol Gould, ed. *Beyond Domination: Perspectives on Women and Philosophy*. Totowa, N.J.: Rowman and Allanheld, 1983.

Kraditor, Aileen. *The Ideas of the Woman Suffrage Movement, 1890-1920*. New York: W.W. Norton, 1965.

Laitin, David D. "Linguistic Dissociation: A Strategy for Africa," in John Gerard Ruggie, ed. *The Antinomies of Interdependence: National Welfare and the International Division of Labor*. New York: Columbia University Press, 1983, pp. 317-69.

Lemons, J. Stanley. *The Woman Citizen: Social Feminism in the 1920s*. Urbana: University of Illinois Press, 1973.

Levine, Judith. "Sex: Threat or Menace? Perils of Desire." *Village Voice*, Supplement (March 1985).

Lovenduski, Joni and Jill Hills, eds. *The Politics of the Second Electorate: Women and Public Participation*. London and Boston: Routledge and Kegan Paul, 1981.

MacKinnon, Catharine (interview). On Defining Pornography, *Off Our Backs*, June 1984, pp. 14-15.

———. "Not a Moral Issue," *Yale Law and Policy Review*, vol. 2 (1984), pp. 501-25.

———. "Feminism Marxism Method and the State: An Agenda for Theory" in Elizabeth Abel and Emily Abel, eds. *The SIGNS Reader: Women, Gender and Scholarship*. Chicago: University of Chicago Press, 1983.

MacNeil-Lehrer Report, August 12, 1985, special program on pornography.

Malamuth, Neil M. and Edward Donnerstein, eds. *Pornography and Sexual Aggression.* Orlando: Academic Press, 1984.
Ochs, Carol. *Women and Spirituality.* New Jersey: Rowman and Allanheld, 1983.
O'Neill, William L. *Everyone Was Brave: The Rise and Fall of Feminism in America.* New York: Quadrangle Books, 1969.
Pitkin, Hanna Fenichel. *Fortune Is A Woman: Gender and Politics in the Thought of Niccolo Machiavelli.* Berkeley: University of California Press, 1984.
Rabushka, Alvin and Kenneth Shepsle. *Politics in Plural Societies: A Theory of Democratic Instability.* Columbus: Merrill, 1972.
Rich, Adrienne. *Of Woman Born: Motherhood as Experience and Institution.* New York: W.W. Norton, 1976.
Ruddick, Sara. "Preservative Love and Military Destruction: Some Reflections on Mothering and Peace," in Joyce Trebilcot, ed. *Mothering: Essays in Feminist Theory.* New York: Rowman and Allanheld, 1983.
Ryan, Mary P. *Womanhood in America from Colonial Times to the Present.* New York: Franklin Watts, 1975.
Schlafly, Phyllis. *The Power of the Positive Woman.* New York: Harcourt, Brace, Jovanovich, 1977.
Snitow, Ann, Christine Stansell, and Sharon Thompson, eds. *Powers of Desire: The Politics of Sexuality.* New York: Monthly Review Press, 1983.
Spretnak, Charlene. *The Politics of Women's Spirituality: Essays on the Rise of Spiritual Power Within the Feminist Movement.* Garden City: Anchor Books, 1982.
Vance, Carol, ed. *Pleasure and Danger.* Boston: Routledge and Kegan Paul, 1984.
Walkowitz, Judith R. "Male Vice and Female Virtue: Feminism and the Politics of Prostitution in 19th Century Britain," in Snitow, *Powers of Desire,* pp. 419-38.
Willis, Ellen, "Feminism, Moralism and Pornography," in Snitow, *Powers of Desire,* pp. 460-67.
Walker, Alice, "Porn at Home," *MS.* (February, 1980)

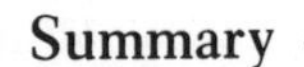

Legalizing Gender-Specific Values

LIZBETH HASSE

Summary

Attorney Lizbeth Hasse discusses, from a legal point of view, the difficulties of implementing a gender-based morality within the existing legal system. Hasse makes no attempt to construct a gender-differentiated ethics, but rather, she points to some practical considerations that should be taken into account by those who formulate moral theory. In her analysis, she focuses on one specific issue: the case of battered wives who murder their abusive husbands. Hasse assesses two defenses of these wives; one that uses the legal vocabulary of excuses, and another that uses the language of justification. Aside from her concerns about the difficulties of instituting change within a criminal law system, which by its very nature is conservative, Hasse enumerates other difficulties. First, she notes the danger for the individual client whose case is tried with some type of unusual defense. Secondly, she worries that the institutionalization of another inequality among the sexes in an already sex-biased legal system could work to women's disadvantage despite the well-intentioned goal of assisting them. S.M.

> Nature has given women so much power that the law has very wisely given them little.
>
> Samuel Johnson, letter to Dr. Taylor, August 18, 1773

This chapter considers some of the possible effects of practically implementing gender-based moral distinctions. Here, I limit my consideration to tentative speculations about some of the consequences of giving legal effect to such a moral theory. This is speculative because, as yet, no particular gender-responsive moral theory has been developed, the implementation of which might be imagined. Thus, I approach my assignment—to discuss the practical consequences of instituting gender-based moral distinctions—without the guidance of a proposed moral theory. The task of exploring just what such a theory would look like is undertaken by others in this volume. This chapter should be considered a discussion of some practical problems that might attend the adoption of a moral theory that explicitly claims that women's morality is, at least in some respects, different from men's, and that the fact of those differences is an essential element of the theory. At this early stage in the development of the moral theory, discussion of possible practical problems, insofar as they must reflect a proposed underlying theory, may be helpful in two general ways: (1) In deciding what kinds of gender-based distinctions raise moral issues, that is, which such distinctions, if any, are properly part of a moral theory; and (2) In considering the question of whether gender-based distinctions in moral theory have any proper and practical place in legal theory.[1]

The example from criminal law taken up here—the implementation of which would have far-reaching structural effects on both criminal and noncriminal law—involves the prosecution of the battered wife who murders her husband. In this case, obviously, the woman is in the position of defendant. The issue for the defense attorney representing the battered wife, as well as for the theoretician, centers on whether or not a gender-based distinction should be drawn as a basis for the legal argument in the battered wife's defense. In contrast, those legal cases most frequently cited in discussion of the legal treatment of women show women on the offensive, taking on the legal system; the woman appears as plaintiff challenging the state because a state action or policy places the woman, because she is a woman, in a disadvantaged position. Still, the structural dissimilarity of the civil and criminal actions, woman as plaintiff in one, defendant in the other, masks the fact that both the civil law challenges and the criminal law situation discussed here arise from conditions of disadvantage and subordination.

In general terms, the example taken up here concerns the dilemma of the lawyer who proposes to expand or transform the law so as to legalize a particular action by women, and to legalize that action specifically and explicitly only in so far as it is an action by women. The lawyer in my example has a choice of two strategies for representing the female defendant. The first is to defend the woman for her illegal or criminal action on the grounds of that particular woman's incapacity, or momentary weakness. The argument here uses the legal vocabulary of excuses. The excuse argument applies to cases in which the defendant is not responsible for her actions; or, the defendant's "diminished capacity," as a result of some considerable provocation, has diminished her responsibility. The defendant's insanity would entitle her to acquittal for any criminal act; if responsible at all, she is only responsible as a sane, willful person. If the act is the result of an uncontrollable or "irresistable impulse," her responsibility may be diminished so that she is partially excused and therefore, subject to less severe punishment than someone who committed the same act with all her wits about her. She did the wrong thing, but she couldn't help it, or at least, she wasn't fully responsible.

The alternative strategy requires systemic revamping of legal doctrine. Here, the nonconforming, hitherto criminal act is defended as a morally acceptable or morally neutral act. The woman's criminal act need not be excused; instead, it is justifiable because it falls within the bounds of acceptable or noncriminal action prescribed by a system that is proposed as an improvement over the present legal system, by a code that is different from the current code. This strategy asks the public to accept a new view of morality—perhaps an "ethics of responsibility,"—to use Carol Gilligan's term,[2] in which the formerly unacceptable act may, with the consideration of new factors, become legally acceptable, in this case, acceptable when performed by a woman. Both these approaches, the excuse and the justification, have troubling consequences where gender-based distinctions are fundamental to the analysis.

I begin with a short quotation from a 1973 U.S. Supreme Court opinion written by Justice Brennan. The case, *Frontiero v. Richardson,* was an early decision in the now slightly more than decade-long history of Supreme Court decisions that attack discrimination on the basis of gender.[3] *Frontiero* found that a particular statute was in violation of the equal protection clause of the Constitution because the statute presumed that spouses of married servicemen were dependents for purposes of medical benefits, but did not extend the same presumptions to spouses of servicewomen.

> Statutory distinctions between the sexes often have the effect of invidiously relegating the entire class of females to inferior legal status without regard to the actual capabilities of its individual members. [Discrimination between sexes, the Court observed,] was rationalized by an attitude of 'romantic paternalism' which in practical effect, put women, not on a pedestal but in a cage.[4]

While this may appear to be a particularly enlightened moment in the history of the Supreme Court's response to discrimination against women, it is not a novel kind of statement for the Court. It is an example of the application of a fundamental legitimating notion of Anglo-American law, that of a rule of law dispensing impartial justice. The rule of law comes into play here to avoid a so-called "invidious distinction," the dissimilar treatment of men and women. This case, which was considered a significant victory for women in 1973, was *procedurally* a typical and not untraditional extension of the American rule of law to correct the inequality built around a classification that the legal system had previously tolerated, indeed had created, by recognizing its legal relevance. Several members of the court decided that the particular distinction between service men and service women was "irrational" and therefore unconstitutional. The plurality, however, formulated a test that held out the promise that *Frontiero* could be a victory for women with far-reaching effects. The plurality generalized its ruling with the statement "classifications based upon sex, like classifications based upon race, or national origin, are inherently suspect."[5] Thus, according to this statement in *Frontiero,* thereafter the government would have to argue for the necessity of all other instances of its disparate treatment of men and women. *Frontiero,* then, is an example of the kind of justice that should issue from a system that purports to draw all its particular rules and decisions in accord with a basic "rule of law" that requires the decision maker to avoid being influenced by the identity (i.e., the gender) of the legal subject, except where the legal relevance of that subject's distinctive features has been demonstrated. *Frontiero* treated the notion of equality between the sexes as requiring identical treatment. The Court would have allowed a rule that, on its face, treated men and women dissimilarly if the Army had argued and established that the rule served administrative efficiency, that it reflected an actual difference, thus effecting identical treatment, and that in those rare instances where that particular difference between the sexes was not present, the nonconforming party would have the opportunity to prove that he or she was an exception to the rule. In *Frontiero,* the Army would have had to argue and show that the rule reflected an actual economic difference between the two categories—the spouses of servicemen and the spouses of servicewomen—that most servicemen were not economically dependent on their spouses and most servicewomen were, and that where the servicewoman could show that she was the chief breadwinner in her family, she, too, could secure benefits for her dependent spouse. The Army did not advance that argument.

In American law, the ideal rule of law implements a morality of basic rights. That morality is grounded largely on an enlightenment notion of natural equality, that men have a potential for equality altered only by environmental influences. According to this view, equality is natural because all individual human beings (and the 17th century philosophers were talking about males) have a natural capacity to reason equal to that of all other human beings and present in the individual regardless of the social setting in which that individual finds himself.

> Good sense is of all things in the world the most equally distributed, for everybody thinks himself so abundantly provided with it that even those most difficult to please in other matters do not commonly desire more of it than they already possess. It is unlikely that this is error on their part; it seems rather to be evidence in support of the view that the power of living a good life and of distinguishing the true from the false, which is properly speaking what is called Good Sense or Reason, is by nature equal in all men.[6]

Thus, the idea of a natural equality is reinforced in legal discourse, and its philosophical underpinnings, by an essentialist theory of human nature. This equality, is a fundamental part of human nature, is an element that is essential to the human subject; possessed by all, it comes to be measured and reflected in the legal theory by a catalogue of basic or essential rights. Perceived diversity, divergence among humans with respect to the substance of those rights, is not an element of human nature, but a contingency dependent upon accidental differences in experience or environment, as a consequence of which different individuals actualize their equal potentials to different degrees.

Kant's version of this is a moral theory that demands that all human beings, all *men* that is, be treated as ends, not merely means, all *legally* capable "legislating members of the kingdom of ends." The Kantian moral position, if translated into America law, supports a rule of law that recognizes a doctrine of fundamental equality between legal subjects and that maximizes personal autonomy by guaranteeing freedom from interference by the state or by others, so that each has an equal opportunity to develop the capacity for reason. The rule of law forbids the imposition of authority or constraint on unwilling or nonparticipating subjects merely on the grounds that the imposition is by law.

In certain legal contexts, application of the rule of law is formulated as egalitarianism. It is a procedural justice. The egalitarian's difficulty is that of agreeing on just what it is that all persons or all men should possess in precisely the same degree so that, whatever differences they have, there is a fundamental sameness which, within a context of virtual equality, would demonstrate that the state is neutral, and that the state has not interfered with or permitted interference with each individual's equal opportunity. The fact of human differences reflects differences in social experiences; the particulars of those differences depend on social context and are consistent with the notion of an equal and universal rational capacity. It is this capacity that the egalitarian recognizes as the essential human quality that is to be protected by social institutions, including, of course, the legal system. Thus, it would be irrational to treat one person any differently from another where each had an equal capacity for reason, the one universal human trait.

In the jurisprudential literature, what this procedural principle boils down to, or is often formulated as, is a principle of equal consideration, equal concern and respect. All persons ought to be treated equally until a rational, justified, or compelling case can be made for a distinction. The simple effect of such a procedure, in a society that protects the individual's capacity for rationality and, therefore, emphasizes noninterference, is to place the "burden of proof" on the one who would impose the different treatment.

In practice, Supreme Court opinion varies on just what counts as reason, justification, or compulsion for making or permitting discrimination by law. The Court's stated requirements range from the loosest—permitting the legalization of distinctions where the government has been "rational," that is, has had some reason for drawing the distinction—to the most restrictive—permitting only those distinctions for which the government can show a necessity or "compelling justification."

The standard applied in individual cases tends to fall somewhere between these two extremes; often the standard imposed is different from the one the Court claims to be following. The result is, quite simply, that in spite of the universal applicability of the procedure, at bottom it rests on and promotes an initial commitment, or an understanding by the decision maker, of just which and whose interests or preferences are to count as the actualizations of the universal human capacity. Application of the principle requires an act of choice whereby an authority decides which differences between human beings are to be ignored and which are to be valued. "So far as the Constitution is concerned," Justice Stewart wrote in one important example, "people of different races are *always* similarly situated."[7] That 1981 statement about racial difference should be compared with Justice Powell's opinion in the *University of California v. Bakke,* a case specifically about racial discrimination, which clearly expressed the attitude that gender discrimination is less repugnant than racial discrimination: "the perception of racial categories as inherently odious stems from a lengthy and tragic history that gender-based classifications do not share. In sum, the court has never viewed such classifications as inherently suspect or as comparable to racial or ethnic classifications for the purpose of equal protection analyses."

In practice, the scope of this equal concern and respect, of the applicability of the universal principle, will be broadened by new sympathies and empathies, by an exercise of imagination by the decision makers. Accordingly, the principle of equality of individuals before the law, which is clearly established *procedurally* by the Constitution forbidding the government to deny any person equal protection of the law, is a rule that has been broadened in scope as the courts take on different categories as relevant or irrelevant human differences and, accordingly, mandate racial, religious, age, gender, and sexual equality, thereby demonstrating ever-expansive American legal imagination.

It was not until 1971 that the Supreme Court expanded its imagination to find that a statutory distinction between the sexes was a violation of the equal protection clause of the 14th Amendment. The case, *Reed v. Reed,* struck down an Idaho statute that automatically preferred male to female administrators of estates where two similarly situated relatives to the deceased were otherwise equally qualified.[8] *Reed* ruled that the Idaho statute was "irrational."[9] Until that recent decision, the Supreme court had not recognized any examples of gender discrimination as violations of equal proteciton. Equal protection requirements were generally satisfied by the rationality of treating the sexes differently on account of the woman's special function within the family and her special "nature." This sentiment had changed very little since Blackstone's 18th century *Commentaries:* "Even the disabilities which the wife lies under are for the most part intended for her protection and benefit. So great a favorite is the female sex of the laws of England."

While its formal analysis may range from a weak "rationality" standard requiring only that the legislature show that it had some reason for its discriminatory rule *(Reed)* to a far stricter test that says that any classification based upon sex is "inherently suspect" *(Frontiero),* the standards for equal protection have not been applied with much rigor or clarity. In practice, what the Supreme Court has done, beginning with *Reed* and including *Frontiero,* is to explicitly adopt the view, in certain particular cases, that a stereotypical view of femininity does not provide justification for government action that denies women access to courts, positions of power, education, or jobs. This trend is reflected primarily in those instances where the law's control over women in explicitly sexual or sexified realms of social life has been recently challenged—divorce, child custody, abortion, rape, conception, statutory rape, marital property, illegitimacy.

Various hurdles to women's participation in society or control over their own bodies have been dismantled primarily on the grounds of a fundamental equality between persons or citizens. That is, the courts explain the results by generalizing them to fit within the terms of gender-neutral categories, e.g., rights to privacy, personal choice, and property. Equality speaks against any argument for easing women's access or for giving more control to women, that takes seriously a fundamental difference between men and women, regardless of whether that difference has biological or historical sources. In the egalitarian analyses, equality or gender-neutrality is rationality. Thus, any decision must employ a category sufficiently generalized such that the result masks the differences between men and women behind a general principle that purports to make those differences insignificant or inessential.

Although most feminists would probably not find the "sex-discrimination" decisions of the past decade and a half to be regressive, the so-called "progress" of the law, in this respect, is not whole heartedly accepted. Critical assessment of the value or the reality of this progress generally takes one of two forms. One critique complains that, despite the Court's rhetoric of equality, the changes are not enough. The Supreme Court has a knack for not seeing some cases in terms of sexual discrimination and, thus, perpetuates the condition. This is the case with decisions involving abortion and pregnancy benefit claims that the court has passed without even considering, in fact, probably deliberately avoiding, issues and facts of sexual difference. This side of the debate would preserve the *equal rights analysis,* the idea that the law must be applied evenly to all, but it would like to stretch the legal imagination to notice or to anticipate formerly unrecognized instances of gender distinction and, thus, to eliminate discrimination along that line.

The more radical critique does not accept the assessment that the legal system has progressed toward ridding disadvantages to women, or even that the system, as it is structured, can do so. Instead, this critique sees the ideology of equality, the principle of nondiscrimination, as a means for perpetuating disadvantages to and domination over women. This objection to the equality regime is that the rule-of-law equal treatment analysis requires men and women to be *similarly situated* before the equal treatment challenge will be triggered. The philosophical tradition on which the equal protection analysis rests recognizes all as similarly situated by virtue of a presocial, individualized capacity for rationality. Any other differences must be attributed to differences in social experiences and are, therefore, irrelevant to the equal treatment analysis. To the extent then that values are generated in social experience, different values need not be recognized by the equal treatment system but must be ignored or erased with an analysis that subsumes small differences under terms of greater generality.

Yet, according to this more radical critique, some differences between the sexes should be recognized as essential, even if not "natural" or biological. The legal analysis, then, would not amplify or extend the "equality" principle, but would apply a principle structured around the essential difference(s). This position insists upon the rationality of recognizing differences rather than equating rationality with that element or attribute that is identical between persons.

This critique complains that formal equality, with its rhetoric of treating likes alike, assumes a much greater sameness than is essentially the case, and only manages to further crystallize a given set of power relations: any subject before the court—statutory rape, for example—presents yet another opportunity for advancement of certain intact and dominant social values. The costs to women of a formal equal treatment procedure are too great.

The government need only show that, in its judgment, men and women are either the same or different with respect to the governmental interest the law advances and the government formulation survives the test. The practical result is the constant resecuring of current power relations in conjunction with the denial of essential differences between women and men; at its best, it is continually and necessarily paternalistic.[11]

The solution proposed by this second critique contemplates an institutionalization of the differences that arise out of fundamental differences, whether or not these reflect differences in life *experiences*. It calls for a reconstruction of the law itself to institutionalize a woman's morality or values and, accurately, to reflect some of the differences, in particular, dissimilarities in moral reasoning, between the sexes. This proposal does not reject the notion of a universal, equal capacity for rationality, but insists that a moral theory must take account of differences in values and moral reasoning regardless of whether those differences arise naturally or historically.

In either case, regardless of whether the theory posits a biological or historical origin for the differences in moral perspectives, very difficult practical and theoretical issues necessarily arise if these differences are taken seriously in a legal context. The problem or accommodation itself may be insurmountable.

To attempt to introduce any transformation into the legal system is an ambitious project indeed. Legal concepts die hard, their longevity guaranteed by the reference to beginnings that is essential to any advancement within a legal system built on adherence to precedent. A decision is legitimate in this system if it constitutes one step in the kind of history that legal decision-making fashions for itself. One consequence of the constraints of such a method is that any legal "reform" that would disrupt the self-determined progression of case history can only be accomplished *judicially* by an aggressively activist court, and then this still is only on a piecemeal, case by case basis. The alternative to this case by case reform is *legislative action*, the formulation of a new rule which, while allowing for a relatively abrupt change or reform in some part of the system, may still fail adequately to address any particular case. I will discuss below one proposal for reform by judicial action where legislative rules and judicial adherence to precedent have failed effectively to counter the phenomenon of wife-beating. My example of legislation is California's felony wife-beating statute, the only such statute in the country.

Originally enacted in 1945, Section 273.5 of the California Penal Code, entitled "Felony to Inflict Corporate Injury on Spouse or Cohabitant," reads in full:

> Any person who willfully inflicts upon his or her spouse, or any person who willfully inflicts upon any person of the opposite sex with whom he or she is cohabiting, corporal injury resulting in a traumatic condition is guilty of a felony, and upon conviction shall be punished by imprisonment in the state prison or in a county jail for not more than one year.

With this statute, drafted in sexually specific (that is, heterosexual) but gender *non*specific (that is, "he" or "she") terms, the California legislature recognized the seriousness of its battered-wife problem. In enacting this law, gender-neutral and, therefore, consistent with the vocabulary of equal protection, the legislative "intent" was to give the battered wife a powerful legal weapon. But does the focus of this provision in fact improve the battered wife's position? Even without the specific wife-beating measure, the battered wife in California might invoke any one of a number of gender-nonspecific criminal statutes, e.g., disturbing the peace, battery, assault, possession of a deadly weapon. It so happens that however well intentioned the legislature's addition of Section 273.5 to the list of charges, statistics show that the wife-beating statute has had little punitive or preventive effect.

In general, we may attribute the ineffectiveness of the statute to a weakness it shares with traditional criminal charges and, in broader terms, with the legal system at large: the husband will not be criminally charged unless the wife (who is often financially dependent upon him, who may fear his later reprisals, who tends to worry about the financial welfare of their family, who may be ashamed of scandal, or of her own responsibility for the disgrace) first turns to the police for help. The police, in turn, are often reluctant to involve themselves in private family disputes. This is just one example of how the private/public distinction, one feature of a system based on noninterference, functions to deny protection to women insofar as they generally inhabit traditionally "private" spheres. The district attorney, too, is equally reluctant to involve the state in such so-called private affairs. Chances of prosecution then are very small. The police, themselves an institutionalization of male force, may be too socialized in traditional patterns of marital abuse to blame the husband for using force to discipline his wife. Or, both wife and police may correctly fear that the husband will become more angry and more violent when the police depart. These are the practical facts. And this is why some lawyers have thought of a new legal measure—a strategy of last resort—for the battered wife who, in fact, is unprotected by the laws, and takes the last resort—protects herself—by killing her husband.

The basis for articulating a legal defense for this woman is to point to the very ineffectiveness of what the law has to offer her and to cite differences between men and women—differences that seem to have a combination of biological and historical sources—as the rational bases for treating men and women differently by law. A battered wife who gets no response from the police must take the law into her own hands. She must resort to "self-help" because she has no alternative but to fight back. The lawyer who presents the "battered-wife murder defense" bases her argument for that gender-based defense on claims about the status of women in a male-dominated legal system: a system, the argument claims, in which the twin doctrines of wife as husband's property and of the privacy of married life as sanctified by law, developed in support of each other to the point where the only rational response for the battered wife is to kill her husband. This defense then must describe the battered wife's murder not only as a systematic product of male-supremacist society, but also as a *legitimate* reaction thereto. The lawyer who argues for a battered-wife defense says that the subjection of women is universal, at least within the relevant context of married life in the United States.

The criminal law system into which this innovative lawyer must fit the proposed battered-wife murder defense divides its exculpatory defense into two categories: excuses and justifications. This is a vocabulary much discussed in the philosophical literature on punishment, particularly in the writings of H.L.A. Hart. In each case, with the use of either an excuse or a justification, the successful defendant is free from criminal responsibility for an act that ordinarily is considered a criminal offense. An excuse, such as mental illness, intoxication, or duress, frees the accused from criminal responsibility because, by reasons of some incapacity *peculiar to her,* she was not sufficiently cognizant or confident to be held morally *blameworthy* for her actions. That is, the act was wrong, immoral, but the action is not blameworthy. Excuses provide exceptions for the frailties of particular individuals. Justifications, on the other hand, address a frailty built into rule-governed systems and acknowledge the strength of human judgment; many acts ordinarily criminalized by the rules are in certain circumstances justified or preferable to the alternative the rules mandate or permit. The law does not anticipate all situations. The accused would have a *justification,* not because she was deluded, or out of control, or somehow incompetent and therefore excusable but, instead, because she knew better than the legal rule. She used her good judgment. In defiance of the letter of the law but in keeping with a higher rule, a moral principle, she chose the action that would be a socially or morally desirable course of behavior.

While California has, as yet, no battered-wife murder defense either in its statutes or case law, the defense, in the form of a justification, has been advanced in that state and in others, and a formal creation of it on analogy with presently available self-defense justifications is not beyond the capacity of the courts or of the legislature. Like most states, California makes self-defense a justification. Homicide is justifiable if the person uses such force as *reasonably* appears to be necessary to resist what he or she *reasonably* fears is a threat imminently to murder or severely to injure any person. The defense rests on proportionality and an analysis of reasonableness. The person entitled to this justification kills, deliberately and reasonably. She or he remains responsible for her or his actions, and these actions are justifiable if, under the circumstances, they were appropriate. Self-defense doctrine insists on proportionality: the immediacy of the danger, hence the immediacy of the response; and the threatened violence, hence the violence of the response. The wife who murders during the course of a violent attack, or when she believes, reasonably, that she is in *immediate* danger of serious bodily harm, is likely to find that her defensive actions fall safely within the region justifiably marked out by self-defense law—the proportionality analysis—as it currently stands.

On the other hand, the battered wife who kills her husband during a long, calm hiatus between beatings was not immediately confronted by a possibly deadly blow. In her defense, she cannot establish the traditional "immediacy of danger" prerequisite. No legal excuse is available to her if she does not fall within the narrowly defined legal categories of insane or intoxicated. Instead, the justification for the rightness of the wife's conduct must appear by some analysis other than proportionality; any reasonable woman should respond to these circumstances in this way. The thrust of the feminist argument is not that the wife was insane, deluded, or intoxicated, as the law defines those conditions for *excusability,* but, rather, that her response was a rational and a correct one, that is a moral and a justifiable one. Her response being an ultimate, extreme one—a capital response—the argument must be that the condition of women is such that she has no other reasonable or moral response.

It follows from this line of reasoning that (even if the court is persuaded that the woman who kills her husband is no less a victim of circumstances than the majority of battered wives who don't), the advocate must show that the exceptional woman's response was right. The advocate must show that if homicide rules were revised to take this kind of case into account, the murdering battered wife would be exonerated by law since her act is the preferred, the least costly, the morally correct response. Here the logic of the defense goes awry, when danger is not *immediately* life-threatening, the interest in protecting life and in eliminating self-help (interests expressed in gender *non*specific terms), especially when the self-help is murder, will override any interest the wife served when she decided to kill.

What the legal situation of the murdering battered wife points up most clearly are the deficiencies of the excuse and justification categories, which may in turn reflect flaws in the way the criminal law system as a whole characterizes criminal intent and responsibility. The excuse/justification distinction is organized around a concept of intent described in terms of the immediacy and degree of the actor's response to a perceived threat. The actor who does not feel forced to act immediately is presumed to have a choice about whether to act and how. The defenses as they stand offer no protection in circumstances where an actor who is not insane or intoxicated is so unable to choose or to take responsibility that the fact there was time to do so is irrelevant in that particular actor's state of mind. Carol Gilligan's *In A Different Voice* is illuminating how life experiences of women, as they differ generally from those of men, have particular effect on women's perceptions of the availability of choice.

> When women feel excluded from direct participation in society, they see themselves as subject to a consensus or judgment made and enforced by the men on whose protection and support they depend and by whose names they are known. A divorced, middle-agd woman, mother of adolescent daughters, resident of a sophisticated university community, tells the story: As a woman, I feel I never understood that I was a person, that I could make decisions and I had a right to make decisions. I always felt that that belonged to my father or my husband in some way, or church, which was always represented by a male clergyman. They were the three men in my life: father, husband, and clergyman, and they had much more to say about what I should or shouldn't do. They were really authority figures which I accepted. It only lately has occurred to me that I never even rebelled against it, and my girls are much more conscious of this, not in the militant sense, but just in the recognizing sense . . . I still let things

> happen to me rather than make them happen, than make choices, although I know all about choices. I know the procedures and the stops and all. (Do you have any clues about why this might be true?) Well, I think in one sense there is less responsibility involved. Because if you make a dumb decision, you have to take the rap. If it happens to you, well, you can complain about it. I think that if you don't grow up feeling that you ever have any choices, you don't have the sense that you have emotional responsibility. With this sense of choice comes this sense of responsibility.
>
> The essence of moral decision is the exercise of choice and the willingness to accept responsibility for that choice. To the extent that women perceive themselves as having no choice, they correspondingly excuse themselves from the responsibility that decision entails.[12]

This gender-specific perception, as Gilligan reports it, if taken into account in the legal analysis would produce a context within which the excuse category could expand to include the murdering battered wife. Either approach, the excuse for or the justification of the battered wife's murder, requires legal recognition of a distinctively female experience.

There are stickier problems with a defense—be it an excuse or a justification—that is sensitive to the position of women in sexist society, a defense that presupposes the inescapability of the woman's condition. That approach also requries the law to recognize that men, no less than women, are trapped in the customary roles their "male-dominated" society fashions for them. If wife beating is one feature of the system, why charge the husband with a felony for committing acts of physical aggression he has been taught and encouraged to pursue? This query may sound sophistic, but it is not idle, for the law has not always been reluctant to recognize and to forgive the response conditioned by social inequality between the sexes: men have been permitted, that is, *justified,* in raping their wives and in killing those who cuckold them. A battered-wife defense would institutionalize another inequality between the sexes by creating a provision that recognizes a universal weakness of women and, as it must also be described, a universal weakness of men: to be woman, the defense claims, is to be helplessly abused by violent men. Thus, the basic and difficult question: is sexification by law, in a system that does not find it easy to take the woman's view, any less likely to work to the disadvantage of women than any sexification by law has in the past? To what extent would the implementation of a theoretical logic of difference, even if the theory accurately reflected "essential" differences, generate social differences beyond those that it has initially recognized? Would differences thus generated prove likely to be oppressive to women? Sexification by law—in the name of chivalry—may indeed be responsible for the history of the law's ineffectiveness in even abating wife beating and for the exclusion of women from the burdens, hazards, and indignities of public office, of jury duty, military service, or serious participation in the labor force. To repeat Blackstone: "so great a favorite is the female sex in the laws of England."

Finally, of course, reform at the level of a defense for murder does nothing to eliminate the violence of husbands against their wives. The justification is an admission that wife beating—universal and unbearable—will continue. Moreover, if male dominance and a male point of view so pervade the legal system, the lawyer's proffer of the battered-wife murder defense may be unconscionable in any particular woman's case. The duty of a lawyer to zealously represent her client within the bounds of the law precludes her use of any particular client's case as a test case to further a social or political cause, or to effect the law-making process. In a criminal trial, where the accused faces the powerful machinery of government prosecution and the possibility of years in jail, zealous representation must require that the lawyer use, to her client's best advantage, the very social and institutional sexism that may have driven the client to do her murderous deed. That is, the lawyer must turn to the woman's advantage the traditional language of absolute judgment, of gender-neutrality, of equality based on rationality, and of an ideology of noninterference in the private domain.

Under the terms of the battered-wife murder defense, the accused would have to assert that she acted rationally and intended the consequences of her violent act—a sure way to frame the prosecution's first-degree murder case against her. To argue a battered-wife murder defense is to expect the judge and jury to understand the wife's acts from a feminist point of view and to understand them as political acts. Should the danger of speaking a language that is foreign to the courts or, to state it another way, should the dangers of arguing the terms of a morality beyond the conceptual limits of an established judiciary, keep the feminist advocate from attempting a construction of the law more in line with a female point of view or a female moral experience?

I have chosen here not to question the proposition that there is a distinctive female morality, an "ethics of responsibility" for example. My focus here is a lawyerly worry about implementation. My concern within the context of the large issues of women and morality is with a danger at the *individual* level, the sacrifice for the test case. This may be only a temporary danger—one that lasts only as long as the testing period. As a lawyer, I can only suggest that, along with a reconstruction of legal rules, there must also be a reinvention of forums for judging moral issues.

Notes

1. I will not discuss here the relationships and distinctions between law and morals or legal theory and moral theory. This topic, important in both jurisprudence and moral theory, must be reconsidered in the context of proposals for and discussions about the form and substance of a workable moral theory that would take serious account of gender differences. My point that consideration of practical legal problems may affect decisions about the content of the moral theory is simply an observation that the process of considering instances of consequences of application often brings to light otherwise hidden assumptions or inconsistencies underlying the theory itself. Unfortunately, the role of application and considerations of the consequences of application as productive critical approaches are often overlooked at the theory-building stage.

2. Carol Gilligan, *In A Different Voice* (1982). Gilligan argues for recognition of

the different moral perspectives of men and women; she suggests that these derive from essentially different life experiences. In arguing for the significant transformative effect that the articulation of women's experience would have on an ethical system, Gilligan argues that women see moral dilemmas distinctively in terms of conflicting responsibilities. In the development of women's moral judgment, "reflective understanding" or "care" emerges as the most useful guide to the resolution of such conflicts. Gilligan describes the maturation of the female's moral sensitivity as an abandonment of absolutes and an awareness of multiple truths leading to an ethic of generosity and care. This ethic represents life, not as "a path," but as "a web where you choose different paths at a particular time, so that it's not like there is just one way;—no factor is absolute." p. 148.

3. 411 U.S. 677 (1973).

4. 411 U.S. at 684.

5. 411 U.S. at 682.

6. Descartes, "Discourse on the Method of Rightly Conducting the Reason and Seeking for the Truth in the Science," part 1 in *Philosophical Works of Descartes*, Haldane and Rose, eds. (1931) p. 81.

7. *Michael M. v. Superior Court of Sonoma County*, 450 U.S. 464, 478 (1981) (concurring opinion).

8. 404 J.S. 71 (1971).

9. Rationality or the rational basis test is one of the easiest tests for a discriminatory rule to satisfy. The legislature need not show either the correctness of its presumptions (i.e. about differences between the sexes) that underlie its rules or that it had compelling reasons or even a substantial justification for treating men and women differently. It need only show that it entertained a reason (for instance, that the greater experience of men in handling estates generally made them better administrators) and had not drafted the rule purely out of caprice. The rationality test then can readily be used to make the status quo a justification and to give a stereotype or any currently existing power structure the force of a legal rule.

10. 450 U.S. 464 (1981).

11. 450 U.S. at 479; this decision upholds the constitutionality of California's gender-specific statutory rape law on the grounds that "young men and women are not similarly situated" with respect to the purpose of the law, which the U.S. Supreme Court, in its own judgment, describes as preventing teenage pregnancy. Punishment of males only is permissible because "a female is surely less likely to report violation of the statutes if she herself would be subject to criminal prosecution."

12. Gilligan, Carol. *In A Different Voice*, p. 67.

The Curious Coincidence of Feminine and African Moralities

Challenges for Feminist Theory

SANDRA HARDING

Summary

Sandra Harding notices that there are many similarities between the theories of feminists such as Carol Gilligan and Africanist theories. Among both feminists and Africanists, there is a tendency to affirm the difference of their respective groups by distinguishing themselves from the dominating class of the white European males. Each group characterizes itself as being less interested in individual autonomy than are white European males, and much more concerned with relations to others and to nature. Both views are characterized by similar ontologies, epistemologies, and moralities, and both theories share certain difficulties that are exacerbated when the correlation between the two theories is noticed.

First, in the implied insistence on the universal usefulness of the dichotomies (masculine v. feminine, European v. African), there is a failure to recognize that both gender and race are social, and therefore, historical categories. Second, there is a tendency to overlook differences within a group when using contrastive schemas. Third, there is the problem of metaphoric explanation, which leads to mistaking correlations for explanations. Harding argues that feminists must face the challenges posed by the comparison of world views and the highlighting of the problems endemic to each. She suggests a "unified field theory" that can account for the embeddedness of gender difference within a larger context of difference, as structured by oppression and exploitation. S.M.

Carol Gilligan has persuasively argued that women and men have distinctive moralities. Men tend to believe that moral problems arise only from competing rights; that moral development requires the increased capacity for fairness; that the resolution of moral problems requires absolute judgments; and that such judgments should be arrived at through the formal, abstract thinking necessary for taking the role of the generalized other. Men worry about people interfering with one another's rights, and they tend to evaluate as immoral only objective unfairness—regardless of whether an act creates subjective hurt. While many women use this rights orientation, women also are concerned with a second set of moral issues that only rarely appear in men's thinking. In this second set, the care orientation, moral problems arise from conflicting responsibilities to particular, dependent others; moral development requires the increased capacity for understanding and care; the resolution of moral problems requires awareness of the possible limitations on any particular problem resolution; and such resolutions should be arrived at through the contextual and inductive thinking characteristic of taking the role of the particular other. Women worry about not helping others when they could, and within this care orientation, subjectively felt hurt appears immoral whether or not it can be justified as fair. Thus, in contrast to standard masculine views of women's morality, expressed through psychological and developmental theories throughout the history of modern Western ethical theory, Gilligan argues that women's morality is not deviant or immature relative to "human morality," but simply different from men's morality. She points out that both sets of concerns are necessary for the moral conduct of human social life.[1]

It should be noted at the start that, as Gilligan argues, these two orientations are not opposites. Justice, the goal of the rights orientation, need not be uncaring; and caring need not be unfair. Rather, they are complementary. However, Gilligan points out that the possibility of violence—or at least of force—stands behind only the rights mode of moral reasoning. Rights are violated at the risk of violence from both individuals and from the state or other authorities. The need for caring is ignored at no such direct risk of violence or force.

Ethical views are not isolated from an individual's total cultural beliefs. Thus, it is not surprising to see reflections of the gendered moralities Gilligan identifies also appearing in forms and processes of knowing. Hilary Rose, Jane Flax, Nancy Hartsock, and Dorothy Smith have all identified the distinctive masculine patterns in Western science, epistemology, and metaphysics.[2] Relatively rigid separations between mind and body, reason and the emotions, the public and the private, self and other, the abstract and the concrete, culture and nature, appear characteristic of (Western) masculine thinking. In each of these dichotomies, men fear that the feminine aspect will dominate and destroy the masculine, so therefore the masculine must dominate. Many of the feminist critics of biology point to this androcentric perspective in the theories and concepts they criticize. Philosopher Sara Ruddick looks at the practices of mothering for a maternal thinking different from the paternal thinking that constitutes what is thought of as Western rationality.[3]

In the course or providing a casual account of gender differences, the feminist, psychoanalytic, object relations theorists perhaps provide the clearest picture of gender-differing ontologies.[4] Gender differences originate, they argue, in infantile developmental processes. As a result of male and female infants' different struggles to separate from their first caretaker, and to establish autonomous, individual identities as social persons, men tend toward an "objectifying" personality and women toward a "relational" one. Conceptions of self, of other people, of nature, and of the appropriate relationship of the self to community and nature are consequently different for men and women. Men tend toward abstract conceptions of their own self. This self is individualistic, separated from others and nature, and threatened by close relationships with others and nature. For men, other people are conceptualized as similarly autonomous individuals, isolated from each other, and threatening to infringe on each other's and the self's projects. Nature, too, is autonomous and separate from humans. It threatens to overwhelm human projects if not carefully controlled. Women tend toward concrete conceptions of the self and others. Their self is experienced as more continuous with women's bodies, with other selfs, and with nature, and threatened by too great separations between the self and these others. For women, other people and nature tend to be conceptualized as dependent parts of relational networks. Humans and nature are continuous with each other. Both Gilligan and many of the epistemologists have pointed to this developmental theory as one possible explanation of the origins of the androcentrism of Western philosophy, ethics, and social thought.

However, whether or not one accepts this psychoanalytic account of the origins of gendered ontologies, ethics, and modes of knowledge seeking, the characteristic division of labor by sex/gender for adults appears to be sufficient to tend to cause gender-differentiated concepts of self, others, and the natural world, and the appropriate relationships between these three. Assigning domestic labor, and especially emotional labor, exclusively to women—in both the household and the workplace—divides human social experience and activity by sex/gender in such a way as to make it likely that women and men will think differently about themselves and their relationships to the world around them.[5] Whatever the origins of gendered concepts, it is clear that we are looking at dichotomized world views. A single set of gendered ontologies emerges within both moral views and cognitive styles.

I do not question that these differences exist between feminine and masculine moralities and between the world views these moralities are part of. Furthermore, far too much of adult social life is spent defensively working out unresolved infantile dilemmas. Different child rearing arrangements that would defuse or even eliminate gendering could help us to develop truly reciprocal selves. We could become persons who could acknowledge and incorporate difference instead of defensively needing to dominate whatever is defined as "other." There is something fundamentally right about the ontological, moral, and cognitive dichotomies and the psychoanalytic theories to which they appeal. Nevertheless, I think that there is also something wrong about these accounts. I am going to question the way we have conceptualized these differences. The problem is that the gender dichotomies appear to be embedded in a larger pattern of difference, one that separates ruling-class men in the West from the rest of us—not just, or perhaps, even, men from women in the West. If this is true, then the casual accounts that appeal to gendering processes are also thrown into doubt. Thus, the focus of my concern here is not Gilligan's work, but the more general characteristics of social relations that tend to produce the contrasting human problematics Gilligan locates in the moral preoccupations of the women and men she studied.

I want to explore some of the implications of the curious coincidence of the gender dichotomies with dichotomies claimed responsible for other forms of domination. It is in terms of similar dichotomies that Russell Means contrasts Native American and Eurocentric attitudes toward nature, and Joseph Needham contrasts Chinese and Western concepts of nature.[6] In particular, one stream of observers of both African and Afro-American social life focuses on the centrality of these kinds of dichotomies to racism, and on an "African World View" that represents the origins of an emancipatory politics, ethics, and epistemology. What these observers call the "African World View" is suspiciously similar to what the feminist literature has identified as a distinctively feminine world view. What they label European or Euro-centric shares significant similarities with what we have been identifying as masculine or androcentric. Thus, on these separate accounts, people (men?) of African descent and (Western?) women appear to have similar ontologies, epistemologies, and ethics, and the world views of their respective rulers also appear to be similar.

It is no surprise to be able to infer that Western men hold a distinctively European world view, though Gilligan and other feminist theorists argue that not all people of European descent hold a masculine world view. And, the Africanist argument, like the European world view it rejects, apparently assumes that the human is identical to the masculine. However, it is startling to be lead to the inference that Africans hold what in the West is characterized as a feminine world view, and that, correlatively, women in the West hold what Africans characterize as an African world view. Furthermore, how are we supposed to think of the world view of women of African descent? As doubly feminine? This particular reasonable inference from the correlation flies in the face of repeated observations that Black women, like women in other subjugated racial, class, and cultural groups, have been denied just the degree of "femininity" insisted upon for women in the dominant races, classes, and cultures.[7] And men in racially dominated groups are consistently denied just the degree of masculinity insisted upon for men in the dominant racial group. In racist societies, womanliness and manliness, femininity and masculinity, are always racial as well as a gender categories. Of course, women of African descent, no less than white women, have presumably gone through distinctively feminine processes of development that bear at least some resemblance to the analagous Western processes (For example, their first caretakers are primarily women; to become a woman is, at least in part, to become a potential mother, to become a potential wife, to become a person devalued relative to men.) The reader can already begin to see the array of conceptual problems generated by looking back and forth between these two literatures.

I must note here at the outset that this overgeneralizing tendency in both the Africanist and feminist literatures, which makes women of African descent disappear from both accounts and their world views incomprehensible when examined from the perspective of the two literatures together, has other unfortunate consequences. White feminists frequently balk at the very idea of an African world view shared by peoples of African descent in the many, very different cultures in which they live. Certainly this literature, produced primarily by Africans and Afro-Americans, draws our attention away from important cultural differences and may create fictitious commonalities. But certainly no more so than feminist accounts that attribute unitary world views to women and men respectively, ignoring differences created by the social contexts of being black or white, rural or industrialized, Western or non-Western, past or present. And there may well be very general commonalities in each case that can be found across all these cultural differences. After all, we are not uncomfortable speaking of a medieval world view or a modern world view, despite the cultural differences in the peoples to whom we attribute these very general conceptual schemes. I shall discuss these issues in somewhat greater detail later.[8]

Here, I will present the African world view and then draw attention to some problematic consequences of its correlation for feminist theorizing. Finally I will suggest some alternative ways in which we might conceptualize the nature and causes of these overlapping world views.

The African World View

A paradigm of the African vs. European dichotomy can be found in a paper entitled "World Views and Research Methodology," by the Black American economist, Vernon Dixon.[9] (I will quote extensively from Dixon's writings lest the reader think either Dixon or I use sexual metaphors to describe the phenomenon he examines.) Dixon outlines these world views in order to explain why it is that the economic behavior of Afro-Americans is persistently perceived as deviant when viewed in the context of neoclassical economic theory. Thus, his argument is that the "rational economic man" of this European theory is, in fact, only European. Aspects of Afro-American economic behavior that appear irrational from the perspective of neoclassical economic theory appear perfectly rational when understood from the perspective of an African world view.

Dixon locates the major difference between the two world views in the European "Man-to-Object" vs. the African "Man-to-Person" relationship, where this relationship is "between the "I" or self (man) and everything that differs from that "I" or self. This latter term means other men, things, nature, invisible beings, gods, wills, powers, etc., i.e., the phenomenal world."[10]

> In the Euro-American world view, there is a separation between the self and the nonself (phenomenal world). Through this process of separation, the phenomenal world becomes an Object, an 'it.' By Object, I mean the totality of phenomena conceived as constituting the nonself, that is, all the phenomena that are the antithesis of subject, ego, or self-consciousness. The phenomenal world becomes an entity considered as totally independent of the self. Events or phenomena are treated as external to the self rather than as affected by one's feelings or reflections. Reality

> becomes that which is set before the mind to be apprehended, whether it be things external in space or conceptions formed by the mind itself.[11]

Dixon cites empirical studies such as one that found in Euro-American students "a systematic ' . . . perception of conceptual distance between the observer and the observed; an objective attitude, a belief that everything takes place out there in the stimulus'. This distance is sufficiently great so that the observer can study and manipulate the observed without being affected by it."[12]

This fundamental Euro-American separation of the self from nature and other people results in a characteristic "objectifying" of both. The presence of "empty perceptual space"[13] surrounding the self and separating it from everything else extracts the self from its natural and social surroundings and locates all the forces in the universe concerned with furthering the self's interests inside the circle of empty perceptual space—that is, in the self itself. Outside the self are only objects that can be acted upon or measured—i.e., known. Nature is an "external, impersonal system" which, since it "does not have his interest at heart, man should and can subordinate . . . to his own goals."[14] "The individual becomes the center of social space," and so "there is no conception of the group as a whole except as a collection of individuals."[15] Thus, "the responsibility of the individual to the total society and his place in it are defined in terms of goals and roles which are structured as autonomous."[16] "One's rise up the ladder of success is limited only by one's individual talents. Individual effort determines one's position."[17] This conception of the self, as fundamentally an individual, also limits ones obligations and responsibilities.

> One retains the right to refuse to act in any capacity. It is not expected that a man, in pursuing his own goals of money-making and prestige will remain dedicated to the goals of a given firm, college, or government agency if he receives an offer from another institution which will increase his salary or status. The individual only participates *in* a group; he does not feel *of* the group. In decision making, therefore, voting rather than unanimous consensus prevails.[18]

In the African world view, there is no gap between the self and the phenomenal world. "One is simply an extension of the other."[19] For people with this kind of ontology, there is

> a narrowing of perceived conceptual distance between the observer and the observed. The observed is perceived to be placed so close to the individual that it obscures what lies beyond it, and so that the observer cannot escape responding to it. The individual also appears to view the "field" as itself responding to him; i.e., although it may be completely objective and inanimate to others, because it demands response it is accorded a kind of life of its own.[20]

Given this conception of the self and its relationship to the phenomenal world, Africans

> experience man in harmony with nature. Their aim is to maintain balance or harmony among the various aspects of the universe. Disequilibrium

> may result in troubles such as human illness, drought, or social disruption. . . . According to this orientation, magic, voodoo, mysticism are not efforts to overcome a separation of man and nature, but rather the use of forces in nature to restore a more harmonious relationship between man and the universe. The universe is not static, inanimate or "dead"; it is a dynamic, animate, living and powerful universe.[21]

Furthermore, "the individual's position in social space is relative to others. . . . The individual is not a human being except as he is part of a social order."[22] "Whatever happens to the individual happens to the whole group, and whatever happens to the whole group happens to the individual."[23] In this communal rather than individualistic orientation, "an individual cannot refuse to act in any critical capacity when called upon to so so."[24] Thus Afro-Americans will often "unquestioningly go against their own personal welfare for other Blacks . . . even though the former know that the latter are wrong. They will co-sign loans for friends while aware that their friends will default and that their own finances will suffer."[25] An orientation toward interpersonal relationships has predominance over an orientation to the welfare of the self.

For Europeans, knowledge seeking is a process of first separating the observer (the self) from what is to be known, and then categorizing and measuring it in an impartial, disinterested, dispassionate manner. In contrast, Africans "know reality predominantly through the interaction of affect and symbolic imagery."[26] The interaction of affect and symbolic imagery, in contrast to intuition, requires "inference from or reasoning about evidence."[27] But in contrast to European modes of gaining knowledge, it refuses to regard as value-free what is known, or as impartial, disinterested, and dispassionate either the knower or the process of coming to know. The self's feelings, emotions, and values are a necessary and positive part of his coming to know.

In summary, Dixon argues that the African world view is grounded in a conception of the self as intrinsically connected with, a part of, both the community and nature. The community is not a collection of fundamentally isolated individuals, but is ontologically primary. The individual develops his sense of self through his relationships within his community. His personal welfare depends fundamentally upon the welfare of the community, rather than the community's welfare depending upon the welfare of the individuals who constitute it. Because the self is continuous with nature rather than apart from and against it, the need to dominate nature as an impersonal object is replaced by the need to cooperate in nature's own projects. Coming to know is a process that involves concrete interactions that acknowledge the role that emotions, feelings, and values play in gaining knowledge, and that recognizes the world-to-be-known as having its own values and projects.

There are differences between the two dichotomies—not so much in what is attributed to Europeans and men as in the world views attributed to Africans and women. The feminist and Africanist accounts of our own realities are simply different. This should not be surprising since there are important differences between the life worlds of Africans and Afro-Americans on the one hand, and women of European descent on the other. I return to this point later. But the similarities are nevertheless striking. Europeans and men are thought to conceptualize the self as autonomous, individualistic, self-interested, fundamentally isolated from other people and from nature, and threatened by these "others" unless the "others" are dominated by the self. For both groups, the community is perceived as being merely a collection of similarly autonomous, isolated, self-interested individuals, with which one has no intrinsic relations. For both groups, nature replicates the image of the community. Nature too, is an autonomous system from which the self is fundamentally separated and that must be dominated to alleviate the threat of the self's being controlled by it. To Africans and women are attributed a concept of the self as dependent on others, as defined through relationships to others, as perceiving self-interest to lie in the welfare of the relational complex. Communities are relational complexes that are ontologically and morally more fundamental than the individuals defined through the relations to each other that constitute the community. Nature and culture are inseparable, continuous with each other.

From these contrasting ontologies "follow" constrasting ethics and epistemologies. To Europeans and men are attributed ethics that emphasize rule-governed adjudication of competing rights between self-interested, autonomous others, and epistemologies that conceptualize the knower as fundamentally separated from the known, and the known as an autonomous "object" that can be controlled through dispassionate, impersonal, "hand and brain" manipulations and measures. To Africans and women are attributed ethics that emphasize responsibilities to increasing the welfare of social complexes through contextual, inductive, and tentative decision processes, and epistemologies that conceptualize the knower as a part of the known, the known as affected by the process of coming to know, and that process as one that unites manual, mental, and emotional activity.

Obviously, there are many problems with taking the claims in these literatures at face value and in the form in which they have been presented. But I think these claims can be reconstructed to reveal some important theoretical and political truths.

Problems

Feminists and Africanists clearly have located differences in what we respectively call feminine vs. masculine, and African vs. European world views. However, before we noticed the correlation between the two dichotomies, there were already severe conceptual problems within each literature. Recognition of the correlation intensifies these problems.

As feminists, we need to apply the kind of criticism to our own theories that we have so effectively aimed at androcentric thinking. There, we have argued that what men define as a problem in need of explanation, and how that problem is conceptualized, are the major sources of the inadequate explanations of nature and social life that constitute what is counted as knowledge. For instance, as Gilligan has argued, it is not women's "deviant" morality that uniquely stands in need of explanation, but, more importantly, men's preoccupation with such limited moral focuses. How should the conceptual framework within which we feminists define our own problematics shift when we try to take account of this curious coincidence between African and feminine world views? Might we be led toward different kinds of casual explanations than those we have often favored?

In the interests of brevity, I shall simply identify three of these problems for the gender dichotomy that are exacerbated by recognition of the curious coincidence of this dichotomy with the racial one. The first is the ahistoricity of all such dichotomies. The second is a problem inherent to contrast schemas. The third is the problem of metaphoric explanation—what the anthropologist Judith Shapiro has happily called gender totemism.[28] These three problems all appear in similar form in the African/European dichotomy, and I leave it to the reader to identify those analagous problems.[29] Significantly, all the problems with these dichotomies originate, not in the emancipatory discourses of feminism and African liberation, but in the sexist and racist discourses that precede and accompany them. However, I suggest that rethinking these criticisms in this particular context—that of trying to account for the correlation between the dichotomized sets of world views—provides us with a constructive focus for our theorizing that has been missing from many earlier formulations of these criticisms.

AHISTORICITY

A number of feminist critics have pointed out that generalizing from the gender-differing traits or behaviors observed in any particular culture or subculture to what is universally masculine and feminine ignores the effects of history and culture on human belief and behavior. Should we expect to find the ontological, epistemological, and moral configurations we can observe in women more or less like ourselves also in female gatherers, peasants, slaves, 19th century industrial workers, heads of state, or members of aristocracies? Are the presumed commonalities of women's social experiences as female, and as daughters, wives, and mothers, strong enough to create shared world views in spite of the differences in the character and meanings of these experiences created by race, class, and culture? (I cannot remind the reader often enough that a similar problem appears in the Africanist literature.)

The apparent similarities between the world views of women and people of African descent escalate the force of this criticism. Given the usual androcentrism of both the Western anthropologists and the "native informants" who are reporting the Afro-American and African world view, we can be fairly confident that what we are hearing about in this literature is primarily African men's world view. (However, it is also possible that differences between the genders are not quite so marked in peoples who have been subjected to domestic and international imperialism. After all, as noted earlier, the dominant racial group tries to decrease the self-esteem of the dominated group by forbidding to it the forms of masculinity and femininity extolled for the dominant group. As Angela Davis has remarked about Black men and women subjected to the American slave experience, racism enforced a certain miserable form of gender equality.) At any rate, since the masculine and Euro-centric world views are not so surprisingly a relatively clear reflection of the assumptions underlying Western political, psychological, and philosophic thought, and especially since the Enlightenment, should we not seek their origins in historically narrower, more specific, social experiences than those common across gender difference or across racial difference? Perhaps the dichotomy we need is one between modern, Western men, and the rest of us.

PROBLEMS WITH CONTRAST SCHEMAS

Feminine vs. masculine and African vs. European are contrast schemas.[30] These particular ones originated primarily in men's and Europeans' attempts to define as "other" and subhuman, groups they intended to and did subjugate. (It is an interesting and important question to what extent Africans and women, respectively, also participated as acts of rebellion in the conscious or unconscious construction of these contrast schemas.) While the original social process of creating the genders is lost to our view in the distant mists of human history,[31] the social process of creating races is entirely visible in relatively recent history. The concept of Europe and the distinctiveness of its peoples only began to appear during Charlemagne's unification of the Holy Roman Empire. The concept of Africa first appeared in European writings during the advent of Imperialism.[32] Plato and Aristotle did not think of themselves as Europeans, nor did they think of the "wooly headed Nubians" living on the southern shores of the Mediterranean as African. We can see differences between the races in the United States created and legitimated by slavery, the genocide of Native Americans, 19th and early 20th century immigration, labor, and reproductive policies, institutionalized anti-Semitism, and other forms of racism. Historians describe similar political proceses that have simultaneously legitimated and created modern forms of observable gender differences.

There are several points to be made here. Racial and gender contrast schemas originate within projects of social domination. Therefore, we should look to the history of those projects to locate the primary causes of subsequent differences between the races and genders. I suggest that when we look at these racial and gender domination projects together, we will notice that it is the same group of white, European, bourgeois men who have legitimated and brought into being for the rest of us life worlds different from theirs. In this sense, it is one contrast schema we have before us, not two. And it is not one primarily of our making, either ideologically or in actual experience. Moreover, any contrast schema distorts particular differences at the expense of other commonalities. Is it observable differences between men and women we want to emphasize in feminist theory, or differences between the social projects and fantasy lands of white, bourgeois males and the projects and hopes of the rest of us? Furthermore, such schemas also exalt commonalities at the expense of differences. The masculine and Euro-centric world view(s) appears more coherent than do the collective world views of those it defines as "other." It is different subjugations to which we are assigned by our single set of rulers, and these differences occur within women's history and African history as well as between the two histories. Finally, while there is no denying that men and women in our culture live in different experiential worlds, there is something at least faintly anachronistic about our emphasis on these differences during a period when they are presumably disappearing for many of us. Imagine how much greater these differences were for the sex-segregated lives of the 19th century bourgeoisie. As the divisions of human activity and social experience that created the "men" and "women" in the bourgeois 19th century sense disappear, should we not expect feminine and masculine world views in these groups to begin to merge? As a woman doing "men's work" as well as traditional "women's work," I notice that my ethical concerns are more often rights oriented than are those of women who are still immersed fulltime in family and childrearing. Furthermore, was not the Counterculture of the 60s objecting, much as do Gilligan's women, to the limited moral and political choices offered them? Does anyone really want to say that the 60s expressed a feminine revolution?[33] Could anyone do so without falling into the problem of gender totemism I take up next?

The contrast schema is valuable for identifying the far less than human aspects of the Western world view within which we are all supposed to want to live out our lives. Focusing on women's and Africans' different realities clarifies how much less than human that world view is. My cautions here are about tendencies to exalt women's different reality when it is less than fully human, not the only alternative reality, and is disappearing.

THE PROBLEM OF METAPHORIC EXPLANATION

Race and gender metaphors have often been used to explain other phenomena. The behavior of Africans, Afro-Americans, native Americans, and other racially dominated groups; male homosexual behavior; and the reproductive behavior of females (and sometimes even of males) among apes, sheep, bees, and other non-humans have all been characterized as "feminized" (and by scientists!). Women's subjugation or the condition of the proletariat is described as slavery where the rhetorical appeal is to the image of African slavery.

That is not happening in either of the literatures we are considering. But a more subtle kind of metaphoric explanation may be occurring. Namely, differences that correlate with sex difference are conceptualized as gender differences; those that correlate with race difference are conceptualized as racial differences. As we all know, correlation is not the most reliable form of explanation. For instance, because women in our culture tend to have an ethic of caring rather than of rights, this is conceptualized as feminine. If men of African descent also tend toward an ethnic of caring rather than rights, we need to look beyond Western women's distinctive social experiences to identify the social conditions tending to produce this kind of ethics. Our gender totemism obscures for us the origins of the gender dichotomies we observe. What is interesting about the totemism anthropologists describe is not the relationship between the signifier and the thing signified, but between the signifiers. It is not the relationship between one tribe and wolves, and another tribe and snakes that anthropologists have found revealing, but between the meanings of wolves vs. snakes for both tribes.[34] Similarly, attention to gender totemism in our characterization of world views leads us to examine the meanings of masculinity and femininity for both men and women rather than the fit between these meanings and observable beliefs and behaviors. Why is it important for women and men to be culturally assigned different moralities? What social arrangements do such designations legitimate?

Towards a "Unified Field Theory"

Thinking about this curious coincidence directs us to seek different kinds of explanations of observable gender differences than those we have favored. What we need is something akin to a "unified field theory"; that is, one that can account for the gender differences, but also for the dichotomized Africanist/Euro-centric world views. If we had such a theory we would certainly have an intellectual structure quite as impressive as that provided by Newton's laws of mechanics, for it would be able to chart the "laws of tendency of patriarchy" and also the "laws of tendency of racism," their independent and conjoined consequences for social life and social thought. I make no pretenses to be able to formulate such a useful conceptual apparatus. However, I can point to three analytical notions that illuminate different casual aspects of the correlated dichotomies, and out of which might be constructed the framework for such a powerful social theory.

However, before I turn to these three notions, I want to eliminate one popular idea from this collection of fruitful analytical instruments. The biological explanations that some feminists and Africanists (not to mention, of course, sexists and racists) have favored lose their last vestiges of plausibility once we acknowledge the coincidence.[35] Now, it cannot be denied that our sex-differing embodiments do and should tend to give us different kinds of life experiences. Feminism should not want to replicate Cartesian denial of the importance of our sexed embodiment. Menstruation, female orgasm, pregnancy, birthing, lactation, and menopause are distinctive to females, and it would be odd if these distinctive life experiences had no effect at all on our beliefs and behaviors.[36] But African men do not have these life experiences, and yet their world view apparently resembles European women's more than it does European men's. In the creation of world views, the effects of biologically differing experiences evidently are outweighed by other differences in life experiences. Perhaps these considerations will not convince those feminist and African emancipationists interested in exploring further possible casual relations between biological difference and mental life, but it should at least alert them to the need for more complex and empirically reliable explanatory accounts than any produced so far.

"THE FEMININE" AND "THE AFRICAN" AS CATEGORIES OF CHALLENGE

Historians have suggested that "the feminine" functioned as a "category of challenge" in eighteenth century French thought.[37] Perhaps this notion can be used more generally to conceptualize the similarities in the world views of women and peoples of African descent. We can think of both "the feminine" and "the African" as having important functions as categories of challenge. The categories were, in the first place, but mirror images of the culturally-created categories, "men" and "European." They had no substantive referents independent of the social relations created by, and self-images of, men and Europeans. Women were "not men"—they were what men reject in themselves. Africans were "not European"—they were what Europeans rejected in their own lives. (And, perhaps, these categories also express what women and Africans, respectively, claimed for themselves as unappropriatable by the increasing hegemony of a masculinized and Euro-centric world view). As categories of challenge, the feminine and African world views name what is absent in the thinking and social activities of men and Europeans, what is relegated to "others" to think, feel, and do. In their calls for science and epistemologies, ethics and politics that are not loyal to gender or race dominance projects, we can see in Africanism and feminism "the return of the repressed."[38]

While this notion illuminates ideological aspects of the world views characteristic of Western men and the various groups making up "the rest," it needs to be supplemented by more concrete accounts of the differences in social activity and experience that make the dichotomized views appropriate for different peoples. The next two notions are useful for this task.

CONCEPTUALIZERS VS. EXECUTORS

Marxists point out that it is the separation of the conception and execution of labor within capitalist economic production that permits the bourgeoisie to gain control of workers' labor.[39] Where craft laborers are the ones who know how to make a pair of shoes or a loaf of bread, in industrialized economies, this knowledge of the labor process is transferred to bosses and machines. Capitalist industrialization has increasingly infused all human labor processes. Now, industrial processes are responsible not only for the things made in factories, but also for such products of human labor as the results of scientific inquiry, social services, and encultured children.

This analysis of the increasing division of labor between conceptualizers and executors illuminates additional aspects of the shared relationship between European and African labor, on the one hand, and men's and women's labor, on the other. Imperialism can be understood as enforcing the transfer to Europeans and Americans of the conceptualization and control of the daily labor of Africans. The construction of an ideology that attributed different natures and world views to Europeans and Africans occurred as an attempt by Europeans and Americans to justify this imperialism. This ideology justified the exploitation underway. With the coming of imperialism to Africa, Americans and Europeans seized the power to decide what labor Africans would perform and who would benefit from this labor. Henceforth, Africans would labor to benefit Euro-American societies, whether as diamond miners, as domestic servants, as the most menial of industrial wage laborers, or as wage or salve labor on plantations in Africa or America. But the practices of imperialism made the ideological distinctions between Europeans and Africans come true to some extent. Only Europeans were permitted to perform the conceptualizing, administrative labor that requires the kind of world view attributed to Europeans. Prior to the arrival of Europeans in Africa, vast trade networks had been organized by Africans; influential centers of African Islamic scholarship existed—Africans had conceptualized and administered a variety of pan-African activities. The conceptualization and administration of complex human activities by peoples of African descent was appropriated by imperialistic nations.[40] Thus, the African vs. the European world views are simultaneously ideological constructs of the imperialists, and also true reflections of the dichotomized social experience imperialism went on to create. (We have here, incidentally, a richer understanding of the nature of ideologies than various popular uses of the term suggest.)

Similarly, the emergence of male domination among our distant ancestors can be understood as the transfer of the conceptualization and control of women's sexuality, reproduction, and production labor to men—a process intensified and systematized in new ways during the last three centuries in the West. Engels referred to this original moment as "the world historic defeat of the female sex."[41] Here, too, the attribution of different natures and world views to women and men originally occurs, presumably, as an ideological construct by the dominators (we can certainly see this process in the last three centuries even if its origins in human history are only dimly graspable), but subsequently becomes true as the control of women's labor is shifted from women to men.

But now, peoples engaged in struggles against imperialism and male dominance are conceptualizing their own labor and experience counter to their rulers conceptions. It is precisely the fact that Blacks and women increasingly conceptualize their own activities that permits the emergence of Africanism and feminism. Furthermore, this charge has economic, political, and social origins that lie outside Africanism and feminism. For women, the revolution in birth control, the increased need for women in public employment and the consequent double-day of work are key conditions that permit women to conceptualize their own labor and experience in new ways. For Africans, the "internal logic" of capitalism, which requires more consumers, higher-skilled labor, and legitimations of both by local, state, and international economic, political, and educational policies, is among the conditions that permit Africans to conceptualize their own labor and experience in new ways. The political dynamics that created "Africans" and "women" in the first place are disappearing, as are the Africans and women defined originally by the appropriation of the conceptualization of their activity and experience. (I am not arguing that racism and sexism are disappearing, but that they are taking new forms.) Those still caught in the economic, political, and intellectual confines of the "feminine" and the "African" are precisely not the movers and shakers of these movements for emancipation. Those who participate in Africanist and feminist political struggles have far more ambiguous race and gender options, respectively, than the Africans and women whose emancipation they would advance. At least among women, it is precisely those whose economic and political options remain only sex specific, only traditional, who are most resistant—and for good concrete reasons—to the feminist political agenda.[42]

Thus, we should expect differences in cognitive styles and world views from peoples engaged in different kinds of social activities. And we should expect similarities from peoples engaged in similar kinds of social activities. The kind of account I am suggesting here finds precedents in tendencies within the sociology of knowledge. Examinations of social structure reveal why adversarial modes of reasoning are prevalent in one culture and not in another; why instrumental calculation infuses one culture's content and style of thought but not another's. Why is it that the free will vs. determinism dispute does not surface in ancient Greek philosophy, but is so central in European thought from the 17th century on? Why is it that we hear nothing about individual rights in ancient Greek thought—a model of misogyny and appeals to the naturalness of many kinds of domination. Something happened to European, bourgeois men's life expectations during the 15th to 17th centuries to insure that a focus on individuals, their rights, the effect of the "value-neutral," impersonal "laws" to which men discovered their bodies were subject, and the power of men's wills would have to become crucial problematics if these men were to understand themselves and the new world they found themselves in. Was there anything in European women's social experience during this period (15th to 17th century) to lead them to focus on such issues? Probably yes and no, if one freely reads the disputes in history. What about women in the purportedly traditional nuclear families in the West today? Why should they be expected to hold a world view organized around distinctions among forces within and outside their control, or on problems of adjudicating between the conflicting rights of autonomous individuals? What about the social experience of the peoples in the cultures Europe has colonized? We should not expect there to be much reason for salves to find interest in the free will vs. determinism dispute, or issues of individual rights. For reasons originating in an analysis of social relations, we should expect white, bourgeois, European men to have cognitive styles and a world view that is different from the cognitive styles and world views of those whose daily activities permit the direction of social life by those men.

DEVELOPMENTAL PROCESSES

In the form in which they have been presented, the developmental explanations for the gender-differing world views cited as possible support for Gilligan's discoveries, and elaborated by the feminist object relations theorists, are thrown into doubt by this correlation. No doubt there are similar processes of producing gender in individuals cross culturally. Gender-differing patterns of separation from the first caretaker, of being inserted in one's gender-proper place in the world of the father, and of gaining an individual and gendered identity are presumably common to all young humans in cultures structured by male-dominance. But these commonalities do not appear powerful enough to produce distinctively cross-cultural masculine and feminine world views—at least not the world views generalized from modern, Western gender differences.

Nevertheless, it is possible that object relations theory can be historicized in illuminating ways. One hint about how to do so is provided by Isaac Balbus.[43] He argues that if we take the intensity of the infant's initial identity with its caretaker (mother) as one cultural variable, and the severity of the infant's separation from that caretaker as another cultural variable, object relations theory can account for the growth of different forms of the state, and for different cultural attitudes toward nature. He points out that there are thoroughly misogynous cultures that are loath to dominate other cultural groups and/or nature, and less misogynous cultures that regularly engage in the domination of other groups and of nature. Balbus is not concerned with issues of racism, and he only begins to explore the anthropological and historical evidence that reveals cultural variations in the intensity of infant identity with the caretaker and the subsequent severity of separation that occurs.

Obviously, a great deal of theoretical and empirical work must be done for this intriguing theory to explain how Western men's infantile experience leads to one set of ontologies, ethics, and modes of knowledge seeking, while the infantile experience of the rest of us tends to produce a different set. The core of the self we keep for life appears to be highly influenced by our prerational experiences as infants—by the opportunities child-rearing patterns offer us to identify with paternal authority, both as a reaction to and a refuge from initial maternal authority. Thus, it would be foolish to overlook the contributions a theory of infantile enculturation could make to the unified field theory that we need.

Conclusion

This essay appears to have travelled far afield of considerations of women's morality. However, I think such a trip is necessary in order to bring to this topic an enlarged vision of the social constraints within which moral concerns are formulated by women and men in different cultures. I am affirming the tendency in the most radical feminist and Africanist thought to identify and legitimate the distinctive cognitive styles and ethical concerns of women and people of African descent. Though the emancipation efforts of our foremothers and forefathers were brave and well-designed attacks on the biological determinist thinking and politics of the male-domination and racism that respectively they faced, we can see the problems with asserting that women's emancipation lies in wanting to be just like men, or that Black emancipation will occur when people of African descent become just like their oppressors. We are different, not primarily by nature's design, but as a result of the social subjugations we have lived through and continue to experience. And yet, those histories of social subjugation offer a hope for the future. From those small differences that we can now observe between the genders and among the races in different cultures can emerge a vast difference between the defensively gendered and raced cultures we are, and the reciprocity-seeking, difference-appreciating, raceless and genderless cultures we could become. We could have cultural difference without the cultural domination endemic to so much of the history of gender and race. (I take race, like gender, to be a social construct and, thus, to have a history.) But to move in that direction, we need a more adequate definition of the forces investing in sexism and racism.

The "women's morality" Gilligan has so astutely drawn to our attention is, most likely, the kind of morality appropriate for everyone in the daily interactions with those dependent upon us, and upon whom we depend, where we should be unwilling to use "rights" and force to obtain our moral goals. The pity is that Western men are not produced in such a way that they can recognize the inappropriateness of a rights orientation in many aspects of social life, and that Western women and non-Western peoples have such limited access to the rights available to Western men.[44]

Notes

1. Carol Gilligan, "Women's Place in Man's Life Cycle," *Harvard Educational Review* 49:4 (1979); *In a Different Voice: Psychological Theory and Women's Development*, (Cambridge: Harvard University Press, 1982). Gilligan is careful to point out that girls and women appeal equally to the "rights orientation" and the "care orientation" in justifying their moral decisions. However, boys and men far less often reason through the "care orientation," and the incidence of their appeal to these concerns decreases as they age. In the talk she gave at the Stony Brook conference, she suggested that there is something about achieving adult masculine identity in our culture that appears to require the suppression of that concern for caring that is more evident in boys' youthful reasoning. Thus, in referring to these contrasting moral orientations as "feminine" and "masculine," I am not implying that they are "natural" or even universally correlated with the actual moral reasoning exhibited by women and men, but only that the "care orientation" is less often and the "rights orientation" more often to be found in men's moral thinking. These two moral orientations appear to be associated with femininity and masculinity.

2. Hilary Rose, "Hand, Brain and Heart: A Feminist Epistemology for the Natural Sciences," *Signs* 9:1 (1983); Jane Flax, "Political Philosophy and the Patriarchal Unconscious: A Psychoanalytic Perspective on Epistemology and Metaphysics," in S. Harding and M. Hintikka, *Discovering Reality: Feminist Perspectives on Epistemology, Metaphysics, Methodology and Philosophy of Science*, (Dordrecht: D. Reidel, 1983); Nancy Hartsock, "The Feminist Standpoint: Developing the Ground for a Specifically Feminist Historical Materialism," in Harding and Hintikka; Dorothy Smith, "Women's Perspective as a Radical Critique of Sociology," *Sociological Inquiry* 44 (1974); "Some Implications of a Sociology for Women," in N. Glazer and H. Waehrer, eds., *Woman in a Man-Made World* (Chicago: Rand-McNally, 1977); "A Sociology for Women," in J. Sherman and E. Beck, eds., *The Prism of Sex: Essays in the Sociology of Knowledge* (Madison: University of Wisconsin Press, 1979). See also, Sandra Harding, "Is Gender a Variable in Conceptions of Rationality? A Survey of Issues," *Dialectica* 36:2-3 (1982); reprinted in Carol Gould, ed., *Beyond*

Domination: New Perspectives on Women and Philosophy, (Totowa, N.J.: Rowman and Allenheld, 1983); and *The Science Question in Feminism,* (Ithaca: Cornell University Press, 1986).

3. Sara Ruddick, "Maternal Thinking," *Feminist Studies* 6:2 (1980).

4. See Flax (cited above); Nancy Chodorow, *The Reproduction of Mothering,* (Berkeley: University of California Press, 1978); Dorothy Dinnerstein, *The Mermaid and the Minotaur: Sexual Arrangements and Human Malaise* (New York: Harper and Row, 1976). See also the uses of which Dinnerstein's version of this theory is put in the last two chapters of Isaac Balbus, *Marxism and Domination,* (Princeton: University Press, 1982). we shall raise questions about the ability of this account to provide a causal explanation of such general characteristics of human thought as these ontologies.

5. See the Hartsock and Smith papers cited above.

6. Russell Means, "The Future of the Earth," *Mother Jones;* Joseph Needham, "History and Human Values: A Chinese Perspective for World Science and Technology," in Hilary Rose and Steven Rose, eds., *Ideology of/in the Natural Sciences,* (Cambridge: Schenkman, 1979).

7. See Bettina Aptheker, *Woman's Legacy* (Amherst: University of Massachusetts Press, 1982; Angela Davis, "The Black Woman's Role in the Community of Slaves," *The Black Scholar,* December 1971; Gisela Bock, "Racism and Sexism in Nazi Germany: Motherhood, Compulsory Sterilization, and the State," *Signs* 8:3, (1983); Bell Hooks, *Ain't I a Woman* (Boston: South End Press, 1981), and *Feminist Theory From Margin to Center* (Boston: South End Press, 1984). In racially stratified cultures, androcentrism and sexism always prescribe different restrictions for women in the subjugated and dominant races; in gender stratified societies, racism takes different forms for men and women. In the Stony Brook lecture, Gilligan reported that the only group of women she had studied in which the "care orientation" did not figure in their moral reasoning was a (small) group of Black women medical students. See the novels of Buchi Emecheta, especially *The Slave Girl* (New York: George Braziller, 1977), and *The Joys of Motherhood,* (London: Heineman, 1980) for one vision of growing up female in Nigeria. The novels and poetry of Alice Walker, Tony Morrison, Audre Lorde, Paule Marshall, Ntozake Shange, and many other Black American writers present this experience on this side of the Atlantic.

8. The issues of this paper are developed from a much longer argument that appears as Chapter 7 in *The Science Question in Feminism.* A number of the conceptual problems I can only point to here are explored more fully in this longer essay.

9. Vernon Dixon, "World Views and Research Methodology," in L.M. King, V. Dixon, W.W. Nobles, eds., *African Philosophy: Assumptions and Paradigms for Research on Black Persons,* (Los Angeles: Fanon Center Publication, Charles R. Drew Postgraduate Medical School, 1976). See also the sources Dixon cites, and Gerald G. Jackson, "The African Genesis of the Black Perspective in Helping," in R.L. Jones, ed. *Black Psychology* (2nd ed.), (New York: Harper & Row, 1980), p. 314-31.

10. Dixon, p. 54-55.

11. Dixon, p. 55.

12. *Ibid.*, quoting Rosalie Cohen, "The Influence of Conceptual Rule-sets on Measures of Learning Ability," George Gamble and James Bond, *Race and Intelligence,* American Anthropologist (1971), p. 47.

13. Dixon, p. 58.

14. *Ibid.*

15. *Ibid.*
16. *Ibid.*
17. *Ibid.*
18. Dixon, p. 58-59.
19. Dixon, p. 61.
20. *Ibid.*, quoting Rosalie Cohen (see note 12).
21. Dixon, p. 62-63.
22. Dixon, p. 63.
23. *Ibid.*, quoting John S. Mbiti, *African Religions and Philosophy*, (London: Heinemann, 1969), p. 108.
24. Dixon, p. 64.
25. *Ibid.*
26. Dixon, p. 69-70.
27. Dixon, p. 70.
28. Judith Sharpiro, "Gender Totemism and Feminist Thought," paper presented to the University of Pennsylvania Mid-Atlantic Seminar for the Study of Women and Society, October 17, 1984.
29. As indicated earlier, I can only briefly point to these problems here. See Chapter 7 of *The Science Question in Feminism* for a more comprehensive discussion.
30. For a discussion by an anthropologist of the problems with contrast schemas, see Robert Horton, "Levy-Bruhl, Durkheim and the Scientific Revolution," in R. Horton and R. Finnegan, eds., *Modes of Thought: Essays on Thinking in Western and Non-Western Societies*, (London: Faber and Faber, 1973). See also Paulin Hountondji, *African Philosophy: Myth and Reality* (Bloomington: University of Indiana Press, 1983), and Lanciany Keita, "African Philosophical Systems: A Rational Reconstruction," *The Philosophical Forum* 9:2-3 (1977-78) for (African) philosophers' criticisms of the African vs. European schema.
31. For an attempt to peer through those distant mists, see Salvatore Cucchiari, "The Gender Revolution and the Transition from Bisexual Horde to Patrilocal Band: The Origins of Gender Hierarchy," in Sherry B. Ortner and Harriet Whitehead, eds., *Sexual Meanings: The Cultural Construction of Gender and Sexuality*, (New York: Cambridge University Press, 1981).
32. See Keita (cited above).
33. Some observers come pretty close to such a claim. See, e.g., David Riesman's characterization of the "other directed" young emerging in urban centers in the 1950s, in Chapter 1 of *The Lonely Crowd* (New Haven: Yale University Press, 1973): Christopher Lasch's bewailing of *The Culture of Narcissism* (New York: Warner Books, 1979). See Balbus's discussion of the 60s for a more sensitive analysis of the emergence of a cultural mentality that was in different respects both less masculinist and more intensely misogynous (cited above). See, also, Dennis Altman, *The Homosexualization of America* (Boston: Beacon Press, 1983) for clues to the continuation of these tendencies into the 1970s and 80s.
34. See Shapiro (cited above).
35. Examples of biological determinist accounts by African emancipationists can be found in Dubois Phillip McGee, "Psychology: Melanin, The Physiological Basis for Psychological Oneness," in L.M. King, V.J. Dixon, W.W. Nobles, eds., *op. cit.* With respect to gender differences, the Lacanian followers of Freud appear to be arguing against their object relations colleagues that no variety of "alternative parenting"—by fathers, homosexual co-parents, etc.—can overcome the effects of the mother-child bond or the father's phallic presence. However, even the object relations theorists soemetimes intimate that biology is to blame for "sexual arrangements and human malaise". Dinnerstein (cited above) discusses the legacy the "obstetrical dilemma" at the dawn of human history left for human gender relations.

Again, while Mary O'Brien insists that biology is not destiny, her account of differences in the consciousnesses we have of our reproductive systems suggests a biological basis for gender ideology in *The Politics of Reproduction* (New York: Routledge and Kegan Paul, 1981). Whether or not they are in fact writing within the assumptions of feminist theory as they assume, Jean Elshtain and Carol MacMillan think feminism would be advanced by a better understanding of the significances of biological difference; see Jean Elshtain, "Feminists Against the Family," *The Nation,* Nov. 17, 1979; *Public Man, Private Woman: Women in Social and Political Thought* (Princeton: University Press, 1981); "Antigone's Daughters," *Democracy* 2:2 (1982); Carol MacMillan, *Woman, Reason and Nature,* (Princeton: University Press, 1982).

36. And, at any rate, public policy needs to recognize these biological differences: pregnancy does not "contingently" happen to occur in female bodies, as the Supreme Court has recently held; occupational hazards have different effects on male and female reproductive systems.

37. See Maurice Bloch and Jean Bloch, "Women and the Dialectics of Nature in Eighteenth Century French Thought," in Carol MacCormack and Marilyn Strathern, eds., *Nature, Culture and Gender* (Cambridge: University Press, 1980).

38. The phrase is Jane Flax's (cited above).

39. See Harry Braverman, *Labor and Monopoly Capital,* (New York: Monthly Review Press, 1974.)

40. See Keita (cited above).

41. Friedrich Engels, *The Origin of the Family, Private Property and the State,* (New York: International Publishers, 1942).

42. See e.g., Kristin Luker, *Abortion and the Politics of Motherhood,* (Berkeley: University of California Press, 1984).

43. See Chapter 9 in earlier citation.

44. I thank Eva Kittay and Diana Meyers for their helpful questions that enabled me to strengthen this paper.

Index

Contributors

KATHRYN PYNE ADDELSON is a member of the philosophy department and the program in the history of the sciences at Smith College. She has worked with a community organizing group in Chicago and with the Society for Women in Philosophy. Her paper is taken from a book-length manuscript in progress. Relevant to the method and thesis of her article is the evolution of her career. She reports that she grew up in a blue-collar, Irish Catholic home in Providence, Rhode Island, and was a high school truant. After high school, she had her first daughter, Catherine Casey Pyne, and five years later, her second daughter, Shawn Pyne. She then attended Indiana University and Stanford University where she received her Ph.D.

JONATHAN E. ADLER is an associate professor of philosophy at Brooklyn College, CUNY. He received his Ph.D. from Brandeis University and his D.Phil. from Oxford University. He has published articles in epistemology, philosophy of science, philosophy of psychology, and philosophy of education.

ANNETTE C. BAIER is a professor of philosophy at the University of Pittsburgh. She has previously taught at Carnegie-Mellon University, The University of Sydney, The University of Auckland, and The University of Aberdeen. She studied at The University of Otago and Oxford University. She has published many articles in the philosophy of mind, ethics, and the history of philosophy, some of which are collected in her recent book *Postures of the Mind* (University of Minnesota Press 1985 and Methuen Press 1986). She is also working on a book about David Hume.

SEYLA BENHABIB is an associate professor of political theory at Harvard University. She has also taught at Yale and at Boston University. She has published articles on nineteenth and twentieth century social and political theory; she is the author of *Critique, Norm, and Utopia: A Study of the Foundations of Critical Theory* (Columbia University Press 1986); the translator of Herbert Marcuse's *Hegel's Ontology and the Theory of Historicity* (forthcoming MIT Press); and the co-editor of a special issue of *Praxis International* on *Feminism as Critique* (January 1986, forthcoming in book form from Polity Press).

MARILYN FRIEDMAN is an assistant professor of philosophy and the Director of Women's Studies at Bowling Green State University. She is editor of the Newsletter for the Society for Women in Philosophy. She received her doctorate from the University of Western Ontario in London, Canada, and has published articles in the areas of feminist theory, ethics, and social philosophy. A feminist conception of justice is the theme of her current research.

CAROL GILLIGAN is an associate professor in the area of developmental psychology at the Harvard Graduate School of Education. She is the author of *In a Different Voice: Psychological Theory and Women's Development* (Harvard University Press 1982), and she has published numerous articles on adolescence and on moral development.

SANDRA HARDING is a professor of philosophy and Director of Women's Studies at the University of Delaware. She is the author of *The Science Question in Feminism* (Cornell University Press 1986); the editor of *Can Theories Be Refuted? Essays on the Duhem-Quine Thesis* (Reidel 1976); and, with Merrill Hintikka, of *Discovering Reality: Feminist Perspectives on Epistemology, Metaphysics, Methodology and Philosophy of Science* (Reidel 1983).

LIZBETH HASSE practices law in San Francisco and Berkeley. She is a graduate of University of California, Berkeley's Boalt Hall School of Law and the Graduate Program in Jurisprudence and Social Policy at that campus. She has taught constitutional and contract law, as well as legal theory in the Rhetoric and Legal Studies departments at U.C. Berkeley and at the Université de Paris V—René Descartes in Paris. She is currently working on a manuscript concerning juridical notions of meaning in First Amendment freedom of speech jurisprudence.

VIRGINIA HELD is a professor of philosophy at Hunter College and the Graduate School of the City University of New York. She has also taught at Barnard, Dartmouth, UCLA, and Yale and is author or editor of seven books, the most recent of which is *Rights and Goods: Justifying Social Action* (Free Press/Macmillan 1984). She has written a number of articles in feminist theory and is currently working on a book in this area.

THOMAS E. HILL, JR. is a professor of philosophy at the University of North Carolina at Chapel Hill. He has previously taught at UCLA, Pomona College, and Johns Hopkins University. He has published numerous articles on Kant's ethics and on a variety of issues in moral philosophy, including "Servility and Self-respect" (*The Monist* 1973) and "Autonomy and Benevolent Lies" (*Journal of Value Inquiry* 1984).

MARY FAINSOD KATZENSTEIN is an associate professor of government and women's studies at Cornell University. She has written two books on India, *Ethnicity and Equality: The Shiv Sena Party and Preferential Policies in Bombay* (Cornell 1979) and *Migrants, Preferential Policies and the Middle Class* (Chicago 1981) with Myron Weiner. She is presently co-editing a book on the Women's Movement in the United States and Western Europe with Carol Mueller.

EVA FEDER KITTAY is an associate professor of philosophy at the State University of New York at Stony Brook. She received her B.A. from Sarah Lawrence College and her Ph.D. in philosophy from the Graduate School of the City University of New York. She has taught, lectured, and published articles on feminist and ethical issues, as well as on the philosophy of language. Her book, *Metaphor: Its Cognitive Force and Its Linguistic Structure* is forthcoming in the Clarendon Library of Logic and Philosophy Series, Oxford University Press.

DAVID D. LAITIN is a professor of political science at the University of California, San Diego. He is the author of *Politics, Language, and Thought: The Somali Experience* (Chicago, 1977) and *Hegemony and Culture: Politics and Religious Change Among the Yoruba* (Chicago, 1986). Under the auspices of the Howard Foundation and the German Marshall Fund, he has recently completed a year of field research in Barcelona, studying the politics of language normalization in Catalonia.

DIANA T. MEYERS is an associate professor of philosophy at the University of Connecticut. She is the author of *Inalienable Rights: A Defense* (Columbia University Press 1985) and of *Self, Society, and Personal Choice* (Columbia University Press, 1989). With Kenneth Kipnis, she has edited *Economic Justice: Private Rights and Public Responsibilities* (Rowman and Allanheld 1985), *Political Realism and International Morality: Ethics in the Nuclear Age* (Westview Press 1987, and *Philosophical Dimensions of the Constitution* (Westview Press 1988).

SARA RUDDICK teaches philosophy and literature at the Eugene Lang College of the New School for Social Research. She is co-editor of *Working It Out: 23 Women Writers, Artists, Scientists and Scholars Write About Their Life and Work* and of *Between Women: Biographers, Novelists, Critics, Teachers and Artists Write About Their Work on Women.* She has written on Virginia Woolf, ethics, political theory, and feminist theory. She is completing a book entitled *Preservative Love and Military Destruction: Making Feminist Connections Between Mothering and Peace.*

GEORGE SHER is a professor of philosophy at the University of Vermont. He has published numerous articles in ethics and social and political philosophy.

CHRISTINA HOFF SOMMERS is an associate professor of philosophy at Clark University. She has edited two ethics collections, *Vice and Virtue in Everyday Life* (Harcourt, Brace, Jovanovich 1984) and *Right and Wrong* (Harcourt, Brace, Jovanovich 1985). She is the author of several articles in the area of moral philosophy.

MICHAEL STOCKER is a reader in Philosophy at La Trobe University. He received his B.A. from Columbia College and his Ph.D. from Harvard University. He is the author of numerous articles in ethics and moral psychology.